Great Women OF THE BIBLE

OLD TESTAMENT

Great Women OF THE BIBLE

OLD TESTAMENT

JIMMY SWAGGART

Jimmy Swaggart Ministries
P.O. Box 262550 • Baton Rouge, Louisiana 70826-2550
www.jsm.org

ISBN 978-1-934655-93-1
09-120 • COPYRIGHT © 2013 World Evangelism Press®
20 21 22 23 24 25 26 27 28 29 / Sheridan / 12 11 10 9 8 7 6 5 4 3

TABLE OF CONTENTS

FOREWORD

I take great joy in dedicating this Book, *"GREAT WOMEN OF THE BIBLE,"* to my wife, Frances. When the Lord gave her to me many, many years ago, He did so with the Call of God on my life in view, and that Call was to be world Evangelism.

Outside of the Moving and Operation of the Holy Spirit in this effort, I basically owe everything to Frances. I have watched her face dark days but never with a lack of Faith. In fact, I have never seen her lose Faith but always, and without reservation, keep the end result in view, in other words, what God has called us to do. The reason is simple: when the Lord called me, even as a child, He, as well, called her. That's the way it ought to be, and that's the way it is.

Frances was not raised in a Pentecostal home, but rather a Methodist home. However, when the Lord Saved her and baptized her with the Holy Spirit, she instantly became that which I have been almost all of my life. I speak of the great Pentecostal experience.

She has been my greatest booster from the very beginning. Many years ago when I started to make records, she saw something in my music that I really did not see. I can remember, time and time again, her standing in the control room of some of the greatest recording studios in the world, with some of the greatest engineers in the world sitting at the console, and she would say to them, *"That's not right,"* or, *"That's exactly what I want."* She was almost always right.

She has an uncanny ability to read people—far beyond my personal capacity to do so. To be sure, if anyone fits the description of the last Chapter of Proverbs, she does!

Her program, *"FRANCES AND FRIENDS,"* which is aired over the *"SONLIFE BROADCASTING NETWORK,"* actually has the largest audience of any program on the network, whether television, radio, or the Internet. She did do and has done all of that by the Leading and Operation of the Holy Spirit. In fact, I personally have given almost no advice whatsoever.

One day, when I have the privilege of standing before the

Lord, and measurement is done as it regards the Work that He has called us to do, whatever that measurement turns out to be, of the two of us, Frances will get the major part of the credit, and she very well deserves that.

When we first began evangelistic work, for that's what the Lord called us to do, Donnie was in school. For some five years, she taught him the Calvert School Course, and during all of that time, never missed a single Service in Church. To be sure, it wasn't easy at all trying to make a home for us on the field. It meant that, in those days, we changed locations every three to four weeks. In fact, Donnie attended some 32 schools. I'm trying to let you know how committed she is to the Work of God.

She is the one who encouraged me to make records. Without that encouragement, I doubt very seriously if I would have ever recorded anything. She is the one who strongly encouraged me to go on radio back in 1969. I'm speaking of the *"Campmeeting Hour,"* which aired then Monday through Friday. She was the one who encouraged me to go on television and, please believe me, making the jump from radio to television was not simple, quick, or easy. However, her attitude was and always so, *"God has called us to do it, and we can do it."* By the Grace of God, we did it.

So, I will close this statement respecting Frances with the words of Solomon as it regarded his mother, Bath-sheba. The Holy Spirit through him said:

"Give her of the fruit of her hands; and let her own works praise her in the gates" (Prov. 31:31).

"How firm a foundation, you Saints of the Lord,
"Is laid for your Faith in His Excellent Word!
"What more can He say than to you He has said,
"To you, who for refuge to Jesus have fled?"

"Fear not, I am with you, O be not dismayed,
"For I am your God, I will still give you aid;

"I will strengthen you, help you, and cause you to stand,
"Upheld by My Gracious, Omnipotent Hand."

"When through the deep waters I call you to go,
"The rivers of sorrow shall not overflow;
"For I will be with you your trials to bless,
"And sanctify to you your deepest distress."

"When through fiery trials your pathway shall lie,
"My Grace, all sufficient, shall be your supply;
"The flame shall not hurt you, I only design,
"Your dross to consume, and your gold to refine."

INTRODUCTION

As we span the pages of the Word of God, it quickly becomes obvious as to the tremendous contribution made by women to the Work of God. Many read the stories of these women, at least, what little the Bible says about them, and mostly never see the drama that transpired. For instance, Jochebed, the mother of Moses, was the one used by God to literally save the Israelites and the great Plan of God. In other words, it all hinged on her. No, we are not speaking of the birth of Moses but of her being led by the Spirit and, thereby, following the Directions of the Lord. It took great Faith to build a little tiny Ark in which to lay the baby Moses, and then to push it out from the bank of the Nile, close by to where the daughter of Pharaoh was. At that moment, the entirety of the fate of Israel hung in the balance, but this woman's Faith saved the day.

We sometimes fail to remember that under the Ministry of the great Apostle Paul, the very first Convert on European soil was, in the Words of Scripture, *"A certain woman named Lydia, a seller of purple, of the city of Thyatira, which worshipped God, heard us: whose heart the Lord opened, that she attended unto the things which were spoken of Paul."*

The Scripture then says, *"And when she was baptized, and her household, she besought us, saying, If you have judged me to be faithful to the Lord, come into my house, and abide there. And she constrained us"* (Acts 16:14-15).

As stated, she was the first Convert in Europe, and, as well, her house was, no doubt, the first Church in Europe. Of course, the city where all of this took place was Philippi.

Then there is Mary Magdalene. She was the very first one to herald the Resurrection of our Lord, a privilege, one might say, unparalleled (Jn. 20:17-18). This is to but name only a few. As we go through the Word of God looking at some of these women, stalwarts of Faith, and we note the tremendous contributions they made to the Work of God, it quickly becomes obvious as to their worth and their value, to say the least.

THE FALL

Because of the Fall and due to the fact that Eve was the first to lose her way, women were somewhat placed into a secondary position. It was not this way with the Lord, even as we shall see, as God used, even mightily so, those who are sometimes referred to as the weaker gender.

It would not be proper, as would be obvious, to place Eve in the category of great women of the Bible, but yet, due to the fact that, in a sense, she is the mother of all the living, she should be addressed, which we will attempt to do.

THE HELPMATE FOR ADAM

"And Adam gave names to all cattle, and to the fowl of the air, and to every beast of the field; but for Adam there was not found a helpmate for him" (Gen. 2:20).

All of this was meant to show the first man that the animal kingdom, as beautiful and helpful as some of them were, would be of no help to Adam, at least, the help he needed.

To be sure, the Lord already knew all of this, but He wanted Adam to know this as well. Ellicott said:

"But while he could tame many, and make them share his dwelling, he found among them (the animals) no counterpart of himself, capable of answering his thoughts and of holding with him rational discourse."[1]

The Lord knew all the time what He would do, for, in fact, it had been planned from before the foundation of the world (I Pet. 1:18-20).

I think one can say without any fear of contradiction that the Lord always creates a desire in our hearts for something which He proposes to give, although we may understand little about it to begin with.

Adam had no way of knowing what the Lord would do, but he did know there was a deep longing within his heart for companionship—a type of companionship which would be completely compatible with himself, but yet, would not be exactly the same as himself. That's the reason he inspected the animal kingdom very closely.

PROPER COMPANIONSHIP

Other than his personal relationship with the Lord, there is nothing more important for a man than a proper helpmate. In fact, he can never really know all that the helpmate can be until he fully knows the Lord as he should.

I thank God every day of my life that He was gracious enough to give me Frances. Truly, she has filled this role, and continues to fill this role, to its utmost. In other words, as far as I'm concerned, it would not be possible for the Lord to have given me anything better.

When the Lord said, *"Helpmate,"* He meant exactly that. A woman has intuition that a man just doesn't have. She has greater sensitivity to things than he has and, thereby, is able to discern, I think, to a greater extent.

In view of this, the Holy Spirit through Paul said, *"Wives, submit yourselves unto your own husbands, as unto the Lord"* (Eph. 5:22).

This means that the husband is to act and conduct himself as the Lord; consequently, it would not be hard for any woman to submit herself to a man of that particular character and kindness.

He then said, *"Husbands, love your wives, even as Christ also loved the Church, and gave Himself for it"* (Eph. 5:25).

Christ loved the Church enough to die for it. The husband is to love his wife accordingly.

AN IDEAL MARRIAGE

One of the great problems in marriage, and perhaps the greatest problem, is for the husband, wife, or both to demand of their partner what only Christ can provide. I am persuaded that this is the cause of most marriage problems, even with Christians.

The human being can only be properly satisfied and fulfilled in Christ. However, if the husband tries to make the wife meet this spiritual need, or vice versa, there will be burnout. Regrettably, that's the problem with many, if not most.

Addressing Christians, one cannot really know Christ fully unless one knows and understands the Cross. Otherwise, he is serving and trusting *"another Jesus"* (II Cor. 11:4), which means that Christ cannot truly and properly be to that person what He wants to be because his faith is misplaced. Let's say it in a stronger way:

No Believer can know Christ exactly as he should unless he knows him in relationship to the Cross. Only there can he find *"more Abundant Life"* (Jn. 10:10). In truth, every single Christian in the world has *"more Abundant Life."* One cannot be Saved without having this particular *"Life"*; however, most Christians never enjoy this *"Life"* because they do not understand the Cross (Col. 2:10-15). Then, not really enjoying this Life because they don't understand the Cross, they look to their mates to meet the need in their hearts, which no human being can possibly do.

THE CREATION OF THE WOMAN

"And the LORD God caused a deep sleep to fall upon Adam, and he slept: and He took one of his ribs, and closed up the flesh instead thereof" (Gen. 2:21).

This records the first anesthesia.

Quite obviously, the Lord explained all of this to Adam after it was done. To be sure, He, no doubt, explained every facet of His Creation to the first man exactly as it is recorded here.

This information, even word for word, was passed down from generation to generation. However, it was not until Moses, some 2,500 years after Adam, that a complete record was made, in that which we now know as the Book of Genesis in your Bible.

Incidentally, in the Hebrew, the term, *"Lord God,"* is actually, *"Yahweh God."*

THE RIB

The phrase, *"And He took one of his ribs, and closed up the flesh instead thereof,"* indicates in the Hebrew far more than a rib. It speaks of the rib with the accompanying flesh, which included the blood, the nerves, etc. This means that woman is one side of man. Though he may have several sides to his nature and character, yet, without woman, one integral portion of him is wanting.

In a sense, in this procedure, Adam was a figure of Him Who was to come. Out of the Side of Christ, the Last Adam, the Second Man, His Spouse, the Church, was formed when He slept the sleep, the deep sleep of death upon the Cross. His Side was opened, and there came out Blood and Water, Blood to purchase His Church and Water to purify it to Himself (I Jn. 5:6).

BUILT A WOMAN

The short phrase, *"Made He a woman,"* in the Hebrew actually says, *"Built He a woman."*

Horton says, *"When God created the man the Word 'form' was used, which is the same word used of a potter forming a clay jar. But the word 'build' here seems to mean God paid even more attention to the creation of the woman."*[2]

THE WEDDING

The phrase, *"And brought her unto the man,"* implies a formal presentation.

When Adam awakened from his *"deep sleep,"* the Lord, as the Attending Physician, was standing over him. He had placed Eve, for that's what her name would be, a distance away, perhaps hidden from view.

And then, possibly without further explanation but with Adam knowing that something wonderful had transpired, He *"presented"* the woman unto the man. This was the first marriage.

All of this implies the solemn bestowment of her in the bonds of the marriage covenant, which is hence called the *"Covenant of God"* (Prov. 2:17); indicating that God is the Author of this sacred institution.

As God was present at this *"wedding,"* He desires to be present at all weddings. The reason that over half of the marriages in this nation conclude in divorce is because God is not present at the wedding and is, therefore, little present, if at all, in the union.

If the young man and young lady will earnestly seek the Lord as it regards their mate, earnestly desiring His Will, to be sure, the Lord will answer this all-important prayer. Sadly, most marriages aren't in the Will of God, so they little hold together. Then, after marriage, if Christ is one's Lord, such a marriage will be blessed and, therefore, fruitful.

SHE SHALL BE CALLED WOMAN

"And Adam said, This is now bone of my bones, and flesh of my flesh: she shall be called woman, because she was taken out of man" (Gen. 2:23).

The phrase, *"And Adam said, This is now bone of my bones, and flesh of my flesh,"* refers to the fact that this one is proper. None of the animal kingdom would suffice simply because they were different. However, this beautiful woman standing before Adam *"was bone of his bones, and flesh of his flesh."* He was meaning that Eve was man's counterpart, not merely in feeling and sense—his flesh—but, also, in his solid qualities.

In several of the Semitic dialects, *"bone"* is used for *"self."* So, in essence, he was saying, *"This is now self of my self, and flesh of my flesh."*

Martin Luther said concerning this moment, *"The little word 'now' is very meaningful. It expresses the love of Adam, who longed for communion with a woman so full of affection and holiness. Today the bridegroom still longs for his bride, but his love is no longer pure because of sin. Adam's love for Eve was most pure, cordial, and pleasing to God."*

WOMAN

The phrase, *"She shall be called woman, because she was taken out of man,"* presents a beautiful description of marriage. Everything the man has, the woman has also. Both are of the same mind and goodwill toward each other so that the man differs in no way from the woman except by the dissimilarity of sex.

As someone has beautifully said, *"God did not take the woman out of man's feet to be stepped on as an inferior; nor out of his head to be put on a pedestal as a superior; but from his side close to his heart as an equal."* She was to take her share of responsibility and to love him and be loved by him.

HIS WIFE

"Therefore shall a man leave his father and his mother, and shall cleave unto his wife: and they shall be one flesh" (Gen. 2:24).

This proclaims the Plan and Sanction of God regarding marriage. Let it be unequivocally understood that this in no way places a seal of approval upon same-sex marriages, which, in effect, are an abomination in the Eyes of God. Homosexuality is a grievous sin and cannot be condoned under any circumstances. As stated, it is abominable in God's Eyes.

In fact, it is so bad that the word translated *"dogs"* in Revelation 22:15 refers to homosexuals. The passage says:

"For without are dogs, and sorcerers, and whoremongers, and murderers, and idolaters, and whosoever loves and makes a lie."

Concerning the sin of homosexuality, Paul said:

"For this cause God gave them up unto vile affections: for even their women did change their natural use into that which is

against nature:

"And likewise also the men, leaving the natural use of the woman, burned in their lust one toward another; men with men working that which is unseemly, and receiving in themselves that recompense of their error which was meet" (Rom. 1:26-27).

Whenever legislators legalize same-sex marriages, they are, in effect, blaspheming God. They are making a mockery out of Creation, which will ultimately bring upon their heads the Judgment of God. Making sin *"legal"* doesn't make it right; it only exacerbates the problem.

The hope for the homosexual, and any other sinner, for that matter, is to come to Christ, Who will deliver such a person from the terrible bondages of darkness, cleanse them, and set them free. It can only be done, however, in Christ.

Coming back to the original thought of the Text, unless God unites the man and the woman, there is no real marriage but only an unhallowed connection, legitimized by man's laws, but not sanctioned by God's.

ONE FLESH

The phrase, *"And they shall be one flesh,"* pertains to one in unity and essence. In effect, this phrase also explains the Trinity. While there are Three Persons in the Godhead, *"God the Father, God the Son, and God the Holy Spirit,"* They are One in Unity and Essence.

The *"one flesh"* is at least one of the reasons that premarital sex or extramarital activity is so wrong. Sex is never to be looked at as merely a physical pleasure. While it is that, it definitely is not merely that. It is the joining together physically of what has already been joined together spiritually between a husband and wife who truly love each other, and who truly love God. In that sense, this presents a holy thing.

As stated, in a broad sense, the sex act between a loving husband and wife, who truly love the Lord, is typical of one's union with Christ. As marriage is not merely a psychological or philosophical union but something far deeper, likewise, one's union with Christ is actually likened by the Holy Spirit as marriage.

Paul said concerning this very thing:

"Wherefore, my brethren, you also are become dead to the Law by the Body of Christ; that you should be married to another, even to Him Who is raised from the dead, that we should bring forth fruit unto God" (Rom. 7:4).

As well, Believers, in a sense, are referred to by John as *"the Bride, the Lamb's Wife"* (Rev. 21:9).

While the union of husband and wife is *"one flesh,"* the union of Christ and the Believer is, in essence, *"one spirit."*

NAKED?

"And they were both naked, the man and his wife, and were not ashamed" (Gen. 2:25).

As it regards the word, *"Naked,"* concerning God, the Scripture says:

"Who only has immortality, dwelling in the Light which no man can approach unto . . ." (I Tim. 6:16).

This Passage tells us that God is enswathed in Light.

Inasmuch as Adam and Eve are made in the Image of God and in His Likeness, it stands to reason that their original covering was the same as that of God's, which was Light. In fact, this will probably be the covering of the Glorified Body at the First Resurrection of Life.

Sadly, the covering of Light was lost at the Fall.

ASHAMED

"And were not ashamed," is said simply because there was nothing to be ashamed about.

When we stand one day in the celestial Eden, where they neither marry nor are given in marriage, will garments of such incomparable splendor be ours. In the meantime, let us say with Isaiah:

"I will greatly rejoice in the LORD, My Soul shall be joyful in My God; for He has clothed Me with the garments of Salvation, He has covered Me with the robe of Righteousness, as a bridegroom decks himself with ornaments, and as a bride adorns herself with her jewels" (Isa. 61:10).

THE SERPENT

"Now the serpent was more subtle than any beast of the field which the LORD God had made. And he said unto the woman, Yes, has God said, You shall not eat of every tree of the Garden?" (Gen. 3:1)

This Scripture draws attention to the animal, which Satan used to carry out his perfidious intentions.

Due to the fact that this was before the Fall, and everything God had created was good, we know that the word, *"Subtle,"* used here is not negative, but rather positive. It describes qualities which, in themselves, were good, such as quickness of sight, swiftness of motion, activity of the self-preserving instinct, and seemingly intelligent adaptation to its surroundings.

As well, there is every evidence that it moved upright at that time, consigned to its belly only after the Fall, as a part of the curse leveled upon it. Some argue that this is unlikely due to the skeletal makeup of the serpent; however, this could very well have changed at the Fall, which it, no doubt, did.

Satan is not mentioned here, but it is obvious that he is the one using the serpent as a tool.

EVIL SPIRITS

Of course, the question must be asked as to whether Satan was there personally or, in fact, was using a demon spirit. Actually, it seems as if he was using an evil spirit. Satan is a fallen Angel and, as such, cannot literally inhabit the physical body of anyone or anything; however, demon spirits definitely can function in this capacity and do so commonly. So, the manner of this temptation probably was that Satan was using a demon spirit to function through this animal, which evidently gave permission in some way for its body and faculties to be used. I don't think an evil spirit could have entered the body of this serpent otherwise. As well, it seems from all of this that the serpent had a limited power of choice, which means that he had a limited intelligence. If he could speak, and every evidence is that he could, then he must have had at least some intelligence.

If, in fact, the serpent was an unwitting tool in the hand of Satan, then I think that the Lord would not have placed a curse upon this animal, using the words, *"Because you have done this, you are cursed . . ."* (Gen. 3:14).

SATAN

We wonder why Satan and demon spirits were even allowed in the Garden or, in fact, on the Earth at all.

There would seem to be two reasons, which have to do with cause and effect:

1. The rebellion of Lucifer evidently took place before the world was brought back to a habitable state and before Adam and Eve were created. The reason God allowed Lucifer to continue in a state of freedom after his rebellion has to come under the term, *"the Mystery of God"* (Rev. 10:7). We do not know why the Lord allowed this, and He, as well, hasn't seen fit to reveal His Reasons.

2. We do know that God uses Satan constantly. Of course, Satan's effort is to *"steal, kill and destroy,"* but, naturally, God always has something else in mind (Jn. 10:10).

As an example, man had to be tested. Even though there were no doubt other ways and means that God could have used, He carried out the testing by allowing Satan certain latitude in the Garden. As we all know, this testing didn't turn out too well, resulting in the Fall.

Our knowledge, as is obvious, is very, very limited in all of this for the simple reason that the Story of the Bible is not the story of the creation and the fall of Lucifer, but rather the story of the Creation, the Fall, and the Redemption of mankind, which proclaims Jesus Christ and Him Crucified. Even though the Evil One plays heavily into this, as would be overly obvious, he is, in fact, secondary.

The principle player in the entirety of the Bible is the *"Lord Jesus Christ."* The principle purpose is *"Redemption,"* and the principle Object of this Redemption, of course, is *"man,"* who is God's Greatest Creation. The principle means by which Redemption is carried out is the *"Cross."*

THE FIRST TEMPTATION

The question, *"And he said unto the woman, Yes, has God said, You shall not eat of every tree of the Garden?"* presents the beginning of the first temptation.

It begins with Satan twisting the Word of God, trying to make it say something that it did not really say. He did the same with Christ in the wilderness of temptation (Mat. 4:6). In fact, every single going astray of a human being is because he ignores the Word of God, as all unredeemed do, or else, he misinterprets the Word of God, as do Christians. Admittedly, while it's not misinterpreted intentionally, the end result is the same.

An individual who is lost doesn't take the wrong road intentionally, but irrespective of good intentions, he is still lost, and with negative results.

That's the reason it's absolutely imperative for the Believer to know and understand the Word of God. Knowing the Bible, which certainly can be done, if the person will apply himself, should be a lifelong project. Unfortunately, most Christians presently little know the Word of God; consequently, they take the word of whatever preacher strikes them in a positive sense. In other words, they look on the outward, which is a poor way to judge the situation. In effect, they have placed their lives and, possibly, even their souls, in the hands of this individual, taking his word for whatever is done.

Untold millions are in Hell right now because of this very thing. They didn't know the Word of God and took the word of somebody else, which proved to be wrong, and caused them to be eternally lost. Nothing could be worse than that!

Remember this: Satan does not so much deny the Word as he does pervert the Word (Gal., Chpt. 1).

THE WOMAN

"And the woman said unto the serpent, We may eat of the fruit of the trees of the Garden:

"But of the fruit of the tree which is in the middle of the Garden, God has said, You shall not eat of it, neither shall you touch it, lest you die" (Gen. 3:2-3).

Verse 2 begins by stating, *"And the woman said unto the serpent,"* which proclaims Satan leveling his attack against Eve instead of Adam. To be sure, his use of Eve was only a means to get to Adam.

Had the Fall stopped with Eve, which means that it would not have included Adam, the damage would have been confined to Eve. Due to the fact that it is the man who contains the seed of procreation, his partaking of the forbidden fruit meant that not only would he fall, but the entirety of the human race which would follow after him would be fallen as well! In effect, all of humanity which would ever be born, with the exception of Jesus Christ, was in the loins of our first parent.

Evidently, Satan thought that Eve was the more susceptible to his suggestions. Paul said concerning this incident:

"And Adam was not deceived, but the woman being deceived was in the transgression" (I Tim. 2:14).

Whatever Satan's reasons for using Eve to get to Adam, we learn from this, or, at least, we should, that the Evil One plays very, very dirty. Honesty and integrity are foreign to this fallen Angel. That's the reason that if we attempt to match wits with him, even as Eve did, we, as well, will do the same as Eve.

In the matter of temptation, we are told to have no dialogue whatsoever with the Evil One, but rather, *"Submit yourselves therefore to God. Resist the Devil, and he will flee from you"* (James 4:7).

Peter also said:

"Be sober, be vigilant; because your adversary the Devil, as a roaring lion, walks about, seeking whom he may devour:

"Whom resist steadfast in the Faith, knowing that the same afflictions are accomplished in your brethren who are in the world" (I Pet. 5:8-9).

FORBIDDEN FRUIT

From Verses 2 and 3, we know that Eve very well knew the prohibition leveled by God.

In fact, the trial of our first parents was ordained by God because probation was essential to their spiritual development and self-determination. However, as He did not desire that they should be tempted to their fall, He would not suffer Satan to tempt them in a way that should surpass their human capacity. The tempted might, therefore, have resisted the tempter. In other words, they did not have to fail.

THE STRANGE WAYS OF TEMPTATION

Many scoff at the temptation of Eve simply because they do not understand the Creation. A serpent who speaks seems to them but idle tales, so they discount it as fable:

• The Bible is the Word of God, which means that every single word between the covers is true. As well, the Bible doesn't merely contain truth, it is Truth. Inspiration guarantees the veracity not only of the thought, but even down to the very word. In other words, the Holy Spirit literally searched through the vocabulary of Moses, as He did every writer of the Sacred Text, until the right word was found, and then it was used as the Law-Giver wrote the Text.

• Before the Fall, the Creation was totally different than it is now. The idea that the serpent could speak seemed to pose no surprise for Eve; consequently, even as previously stated, it evidently had at least a limited ability to speak.

At any rate, Satan used the most unusual means by which to get the attention of Eve and, ultimately, Adam, which he did. Maybe we can say that in the case of every temptation, it comes in a most unusual manner, designed to carry forth its intended purpose. What is that purpose?

Satan wants you to believe a lie!

THE SERPENT SAID

"And the serpent said unto the woman, You shall not surely die" (Gen. 3:4).

This presents a position which has now gone terribly wrong. Eve should not have answered Satan when he spoke to her the first time. That was her first mistake.

I have to believe that Eve was of vast intelligence along with her husband, Adam. They had God as their Teacher. However long that was, which could have been 40 days and 40 nights, God's Probationary Number, it was of monumental consequence. Despite all of that, she was now on the way to total deception.

This shows us that vast intelligence is not the answer. It does show us that obedience to the Word of God in every respect is the answer. Deception can only come about whenever we leave the Word. The sad thing about the modern church is that it little knows the Word.

DENIAL OF THE WORD

The phrase, *"You shall not surely die,"* proclaims an outright denial of the Word of God but with a subtle twist, as we shall see in the next Verse. Among other things, this is probably what Jesus was referring to when He said to the Pharisees concerning Satan:

*"You are of your father the Devil, and the lusts of your father
you will do. He was a murderer from the beginning, and abode
not in the truth, because there is no truth in him. When he speaks
a lie, he speaks of his own: for he is a liar, and the father of it"*
(Jn. 8:44).

What does he lie about? The answer is simple, *"Everything!"*

So, in Eve's case, the moment she took herself out of the
Hands of God—out of the position of absolute dependence upon
and subjection to His Word—she abandoned herself to the government of sense, as used of Satan for her entire overthrow.

THE ENTRANCE OF DEATH

God never intended for Adam and Eve to die, or any who
would come after them. Even though man was made of the dust
of the Earth, still, he was meant to live forever by virtue of the
Tree of Life.

It was sin, i.e., *"the Fall,"* which brought on death. It is
referred to as *"original sin."* The first type of death which occurred was separation from God. This was spiritual death and
was that which the Lord meant.

With spiritual death having set in, the physical body was
ultimately affected. Due to the fact that man was driven out
of the Garden, therefore, unable to partake of the Tree of Life,
physical death would ultimately occur. Even then, the physical
body was so wondrously made that it took nearly 1,000 years
for our first two or three generations to die.

All life comes from God. With man cut off from God because
of sin, man finds himself cut off from life.

It seems as if God did not explain all of this to Adam and Eve,
rather just telling them not to eat of the Tree of the Knowledge
of Good and Evil. They were to obey without question. The
tragedy is, they did not obey and in their disobedience, they
would then find out the terrible truth, which I have just briefly
explained. This was the *"knowledge"* of which they sought but
to their chagrin, it was not to be what they thought.

EYES OPENED?

"For God does know that in the day you eat thereof, then your eyes shall be opened, and you shall be as gods, knowing good and evil" (Gen. 3:5).

The lie proposed by Satan presents the promise of the impartation of power to perceive physically, mentally, and spiritually objects not otherwise discernable. It suggested the attainment of higher wisdom, which, in effect, claims a higher wisdom than God. Unfortunately, Satan has not stopped peddling that lie from then until now. Worse yet, untold hundreds of millions, even billions, of souls have bought it.

Paul addressed this by saying, *"Professing themselves to be wise, they became fools"* (Rom. 1:22).

As one small example, on September 11, 2001, the world was stunned and shocked by the senseless suicide bombing of the World Trade Center in New York City, and the Pentagon in Washington, D.C. Thousands lost their lives, and the sorrow of tens of thousands will be felt until they die. As shocking and horrible as that was, however, the world is full of such activity, even on a daily basis, although on a smaller scale. It's all the result of the *"higher wisdom"* promised by Satan. That's why Jesus said:

"The thief comes not, but for to steal, and to kill, and to destroy: I am come that they might have life, and that they might have it more abundantly" (Jn. 10:10). The truth is, all eyes have been blinded as a result of the Fall. That is the reason our leaders cannot see the danger of the religion of Islam, foolishly claiming that it is a great and wonderful religion, with a few fanatics that's causing the problem. Nothing could be further from the truth. While all Muslims aren't murderers, virtually all Muslims are definitely in sympathy with the murderers. We refuse to see that because we are blinded.

In fact, one's eyes are opened only, and I mean only, as one accepts Christ as one's personal Saviour. This is what Jesus was talking about when He said:

". . . Except a man be born again, he cannot see the Kingdom of God" (Jn. 3:3).

KNOWING GOOD AND EVIL

The phrase, *"And you shall be as gods, knowing good and evil,"* in effect, says, *"You shall be as Elohim."* It was a promise of Divinity.

God is Omniscient, meaning that He is all-knowing; however, His Knowledge of evil, and that knowledge is thorough, we might quickly add, is not through Personal experience. By His Very Nature, He is totally separate from all that is evil, and He hates it. The knowledge of evil that Eve would learn would be by moral degradation, which, of course, God never experienced, and, in fact, could not experience. It would not be by intellectual insight that her ambitions would be fulfilled.

THE LUST OF THE EYES

"And when the woman saw that the tree was good for food, and that it was pleasant to the eyes, and a tree to be desired to make one wise, she took of the fruit thereof, and did eat, and gave also unto her husband with her; and he did eat" (Gen. 3:6).

Verse 6 presents to us the first step of the three steps which lead ever downward. The Apostle John mentioned this:

"For all that is in the world, the lust of the flesh, and the lust of the eyes, and the pride of life, is not of the Father, but is of the world" (I Jn. 2:16).

If we are to notice, the *"lust of the eyes"* came first with Eve while the *"lust of the flesh"* was presented first by John. Why the disparity?

Eve had no lust of the flesh at this stage. She was pure and innocent. So, the first assault to her at this time had to be the *"lust of the eyes,"* which would then be followed by the other two.

Once man had fallen, the *"lust of the flesh"* is always first, followed by the *"lust of the eyes"* and the *"pride of life."*

This is the pattern! More or less, it sets the stage for all spiritual failure.

David's problem is a perfect example, even as recorded in II Samuel, Chapter 11.

The *"lust of the flesh"* was already prevalent in David because of a lax spiritual condition.

He then *". . . saw a woman washing herself; and the woman was very beautiful to look upon"* (II Sam. 11:2), which constitutes the *"lust of the eyes."* The *"lust of the flesh"* is already prevalent, so the *"lust of the eyes"* comes easy.

The Scripture then says, *"And David sent messengers, and took her; and she came in unto him, and he lay with her. . . ,"* which constitutes the *"pride of life"* (II Sam. 11:4). This *"pride of life"* says, *"I am king,"* and it makes no difference that she is married to another man; if I want her, I will take her.

As stated, in one way or the other, more or less, this is the pattern of all sin.

Eve, at this time, having no *"lust of the flesh,"* came to failure by the *"lust of the eyes"* when she *"saw that the tree was good for food."*

She had no business even being around the tree. There were other types of trees in the Garden, bearing all manner of fruit, which were available to her at any time. However, at the bidding of the Evil One, she succumbed to his suggestions, and now she minutely inspects this Tree of the Knowledge of Good and Evil.

THE LUST OF THE FLESH

The phrase, *"And that it was pleasant to the eyes,"* constitutes the *"lust of the flesh."* However, let us state that the entirety of this ungodly trio, the *"lust of the eyes,"* the *"lust of the flesh,"* and the *"pride of life,"* were all outward at this stage as it regards Eve, whereas they are all inward following the Fall. Nevertheless, even from an outward position, they were lethal. If they were lethal even from an outward position, how much deadlier are they inwardly! Then her eyes saw the fruit, and her flesh wanted it. As stated, at the present time, it is a little different:

Since the Fall, the flesh wants it, and when the eyes see it, the victim is pretty much helpless because of the *"pride of life."*

THE PRIDE OF LIFE

The phrase, *"And a tree to be desired to make one wise,"* presents the *"pride of life."*

"Pride" is, no doubt, the foundation sin of all sins. It is the bottom line regarding what caused the Fall. In reality, Eve had no *"pride of life"* before she fell, but she did see the potential of such. It was the potential that dragged her down, i.e., *"to be like God,"* but to be like Him in an unlawful way.

Pride is the reason the sinner refuses to come to Christ or even admit his need for Christ. Pride is also the reason the Christian doesn't walk in victory. This pride makes him think that he can live this life without subscribing to God's Order, which is the Cross of Christ.

THE FRUIT

The phrase, *"She took of the fruit thereof, and did eat,"* constitutes the Fall. It was not that there was some type of chemical in the fruit which caused the problem, but rather disobedience to God. In effect, she was saying, as all who sin say, that she was smarter than God.

From that moment, billions have continued to *"take of the fruit thereof, and eat."* They have found, exactly as Eve found, that it didn't bring, and it doesn't bring, that which is supposed.

HER HUSBAND

"And gave also unto her husband with her; and he did eat," refers to the fact that evidently Adam was an observer to all

these proceedings. That being the case, he lifted no hand or voice to stop Eve from this terrible thing. Some claim that he ate of the forbidden fruit, which she offered him, out of love for her. Let me answer that in this way:

No one ever sins out of love, so the reason he did this thing is even worse than her reason. She was deceived, but the Scripture plainly says, *"Adam was not deceived . . ."* (I Tim. 2:14).

While he yielded to the temptation, he did not do so out of deception. So, the only reason we can give as to why he did this thing is that he then entered into unbelief. He did not exactly, at that time, believe what God had said about the situation. So, he took of the fruit and did eat, and when he did, he died instantly. We refer to spiritual death, which means separation from God. As stated, physical death would ultimately follow.

OPEN EYES

"And the eyes of them both were opened, and they knew that they were naked; and they sewed fig leaves together, and made themselves aprons" (Gen. 3:7).

Their eyes being opened refers to the consciousness of guilt as a result of their sin.

Sin makes the most excellent and glorious of all God's Creatures vile and shameful. It defaces the Image of God. It separates man from God. It disorders all the faculties of the soul.

Once this thing was done, the promised results came, but it was not what they thought it would be. Instead of it making them *"like gods,"* it showed them that they were like beasts and brought the first sense of shame.

The first thing that their opened eyes saw was themselves, and the immediate result of the sight was the first blush of shame.

NAKED

"And they knew that they were naked," refers to the fact that they had lost the enswathing light of purity, which previously

had clothed their bodies. They were shamed before God and Angels; disgraced in the highest degree; and laid open to the contempt and reproach of Heaven and Earth and their own consciousness. Sin is a reproach to any people!

THE JUDGMENT OF GOD

The word, *"Naked,"* as presented here, has more to do with them being naked to the Judgment of God than it does an absence of clothing. God cannot abide sin, and sin must be judged.

Of course, we know, as we shall see, God provided for this Judgment by the giving of His Only Son, Who took the Judgment for us. However, if Christ is refused, there remains no more sacrifice for sin, and Judgment must inevitably fall (Heb. 10:12, 26).

FIG LEAVES

"And they sewed fig leaves together, and made themselves aprons," presents the clothing Adam and Eve provided for themselves, which did very well until God appeared but was then to be found worthless. Sinners clothe themselves with morality, sacraments, and religious ceremonies; they are as worthless as Adam's apron of fig leaves.

In this, we see true Christianity and mere religion. The former is founded upon the fact of a person being clothed, of course, with the Robe of Righteousness; the latter, upon the fact of him being naked. The former has this as its starting ground while the latter has it as its goal. All that a true Christian does is because he is clothed with the Robe of Righteousness. This is made possible by Christ and what Christ did at the Cross. It is imputed to believing sinners upon Faith in the Finished Work of Christ. All that religion does is in order that he may be clothed. In other words, he is working for his Salvation while the former is working because of his Salvation.

The more we examine man's religion and all its phases, the

more we shall see its thorough insufficiency to remedy his state.

MAN'S CONDITION

We're looking here at man's condition and how this condition can be rectified.

Man knows that he is *"naked."* He may not like to admit it, and many may even deny it, but he knows! The question is, *"How is his condition remedied?"*

Man has a choice, and it's not really a very complex choice to make. The only way his situation can be remedied is by his acceptance of Christ and, more particularly, what Christ did for him at the Cross. If he does that, he will find that a perfect, pure, spotless Righteousness, the Righteousness of God, will be imputed unto him, and done so instantly. The situation is then resolved.

However, if he refuses God's Remedy and resorts to fig leaves, which, regrettably and sadly, characterizes much of the world for all time, he will find himself continuing to be *"naked."*

If man has a problem, and this problem seems to affect all, it's the problem of the *"fig leaves."*

THE VOICE OF THE LORD GOD

"And they heard the Voice of the LORD God walking in the Garden in the cool of the day: and Adam and his wife hid themselves from the Presence of the LORD God amongst the trees of the Garden" (Gen. 3:8).

The Voice of the Lord God had heretofore been a pleasant sound. Now, it is the very opposite. Whereas the sound of His Voice had once been a sound of delight, it is now a sound of dread, fear, and even stark terror.

It is not that the Voice of the Lord had changed, for it hadn't. It was the same Voice that they had heard since Creation. He hadn't changed, but they had.

Paul wrote, quoting David, *". . . Today if you will hear His Voice, harden not your hearts"* (Heb. 4:7; Ps. 95:7-8).

We find in this that the Lord seeks the sinner. Actually, He seeks the sinner to a far greater degree than we could begin to imagine. That's why He came down to this Earth, took upon Himself human flesh, and did so in order that He might die on a Cross that the debt could be paid—a debt, incidentally, that we could not pay. He is still saying:

"Come unto Me, all you who labor and are heavy laden, and I will give you rest.

"Take My Yoke upon you, and learn of Me; for I am Meek and Lowly in heart: and you shall find rest unto your souls.

"For My Yoke is easy, and My Burden is light" (Mat. 11:28-30).

He's still saying, *"Come unto Me!"*

GUILT

The phrase, *"And Adam and his wife hid themselves from the Presence of the LORD God among the trees of the Garden,"* presents our first parents doing so not in humility, as unworthy to come into God's Presence, or through modesty, but rather from a sense of guilt.

Expositor's say:

"Here is the dawn of a new era in the history of humanity. The eye of a guilty conscience is now opened for the first time, and God and the Universe appeared in new and terrible forms."[3]

It played out to an alarming dread of God. But yet, there is no way to flee from God because God is everywhere, i.e., *"Omnipresent."* So, we find that guilt blinds the reason of men.

Christ Alone can remove the guilt, which is done instantly upon acceptance of Him as one's Lord and Saviour. Paul said:

"There is therefore now no condemnation to them who are in Christ Jesus, who walk not after the flesh, but after the Spirit" (Rom. 8:1).

The Greek scholars say that this Verse can be translated, *"There is therefore now no guilt to them who are in Christ Jesus...."*

The unredeemed don't know what it is to be without guilt;

consequently, they cannot imagine living without this terrible malady.

Guilt plays a tremendous part in all suicides, nervous breakdowns, and emotional disturbances and, actually, is a factor in every adverse thing that happens to a human being. However, not ever having experienced a time without guilt, the unredeemed have no idea as to what a guilt-free life actually is. It is the most wonderful, the most glorious, the most fulfilling lifestyle that one could ever begin to enjoy, but the unredeemed have no conception as to what that means. It's what Jesus was speaking of when He said:

". . . I am come that they might have life, and that they might have it more abundantly" (Jn. 10:10).

With the fall of our first parents, guilt came into the physical, mental, and spiritual makeup of the individual. As stated, it is not possible for it to be removed except by the acceptance of Jesus Christ as one's Lord and Saviour. We must never forget that what Christ does for us was all made possible by the Cross (Gal. 2:20-21; 6:14; Eph. 2:6-18; Col. 2:14-15).

THE CALL

"And the LORD God called unto Adam, and said unto him, Where are you?" (Gen. 3:9).

This Passage presents God seeking the first man. He has been doing so ever since.

Matthew Henry said:

"This inquiry after Adam may be looked upon as a gracious pursuit, in kindness to him, and in order to his recovery. If God had not called to Him, to reclaim Him, His condition had been as desperate as that of fallen angels."

He went on to say:

"This lost sheep had wandered endlessly, if the Good Shepherd had not sought after him, to bring him back, and in order to that, reminded him where he was not, where he should not be, and where he could not be either happy or easy."[4]

WHERE ARE YOU?

The question, *"And said unto him, Where are you?"* presents the question of all questions. To be sure, the Lord knew exactly where Adam was, but He wanted Adam to know where He was.

Williams says:

"Adam hides from God, not because of any change in God, but because of the change in himself, wrought by the entrance of sin. The covering he provided for himself did very well until God appeared and was then found to be worthless."[5]

Adam's absence was clear proof that something was wrong. Before this, he had welcomed the Divine approach, but now, there is dread and fear. Every Believer should take this question to heart, asked by our Heavenly Father so long ago, *"Where are you?"*

As we've already stated, God knows where each of us is. Being Omniscient (all-knowing), He knows everything about us, but, oftentimes, we don't know ourselves exactly where we are. It takes that Clarion Call to bring us to our senses!

FEAR

"And he said, I heard Your Voice in the Garden, and I was afraid, because I was naked; and I hid myself" (Gen. 3:10).

Verse 10 presents the first words which came out of the mouth of our first parent after the Fall. He said, *"I was afraid."* Why was he afraid?

Concerning this moment, Calvin said:

"His consciousness of the effects of sin was keener than his sense of the sin itself."

Lange said:

"This is the first instance of that mingling and confusion of sin and punishment which is the peculiar characteristic of our Redemption-needing humanity."[6]

Luther said:

"The words, 'Where are you?' are words of Divine Law, directed by God to Adam's conscience. God wanted Adam to know that he who hides himself from Him is never hidden from Him, and that he who runs away from Him can never escape Him."

The type of fear which characterizes Adam is fear brought on by guilt. That's why guilt is such a hazard; it carries with it a tremendous amount of negative baggage.

This type of fear sees God in a completely erroneous way. It sees Him as someone to be dreaded; someone to be avoided. Let the reader understand this:

Sin is a horrible business, actually, the cause of all sorrow, heartache, and destruction in this world and, as well, always brings heavy guilt. However, sin should be taken to the Lord, as distasteful and shameful as it might be. There's no one else who can do anything about one's sin except the Lord of Glory. His Answer for sin is the Cross, and only the Cross, which is the greatest example of love that humanity has ever known.

God forbid that we should fail the Lord in any capacity; however, regrettably and sadly, the sin problem plagues the whole of the human race, even the godliest at times. But, as bad as it might be, and as shameful as it might be, as the great song says:

"Take it to Jesus, take it to Jesus,

"He is a Friend that's well-known."

The great mistake made by the human race, even by the church, is that we take the sin elsewhere. We take it to the psychologist, which, to be blunt, and I mean to be blunt, can do nothing! We take it to fellow human beings but no matter how godly they may be, still, they can, as well, do nothing. Beautifully and wondrously, John the Beloved told us what to do:

"If we confess our sins, He is Faithful and Just to forgive us our sins, and to cleanse us from all unrighteousness" (I Jn. 1:9).

HIDING FROM GOD

The phrase, *"Because I was naked; and I hid myself,"* presents a foolish effort.

Luther said:

"From this we learn how great is the evil of sin. Unless God helps and calls the sinner, he will forever flee God, try to excuse his sin by lies, and add one wrong to another until he ends in blasphemy and despair."

How foolish it is to seek to hide from God. God knows all things, so, to hide from Him is impossible. He had heard the Voice of God in the Garden and said that it made him afraid. Had he not heard God's Voice when He had commanded him not to eat of the forbidden tree? Why was he not afraid of God then, and why did he not hide himself at that time?

Believe it or not, men are still seeking to hide themselves from God; however, they do it in strange ways.

Many will not go to church at all because they surmise that God is in church and that He will then apprehend them. They don't seem to realize that God is everywhere.

Then again, some try to hide themselves from God in church. They try to do so behind a cloak of religion.

THE FIRST QUESTION

"And He said, Who told you that you were naked? Have you eaten of the tree, whereof I commanded you that you should not eat?" (Gen. 3:11).

The question, *"And He said, Who told you that you were naked?"* carries Adam's mind from the effect to the sin that had caused it. As long as a man feels sorrow only for the results of his action, there is no real repentance and no wish to return to the Divine Parent.

What he had described as a want or imperfection, which was his being naked, was really the result of his own act.

Man is afraid because he is naked; not only unarmed, therefore, afraid to contend with God, but unclothed, therefore, afraid even to appear before Him. We have reason to be afraid of approaching God if we are not clothed and fenced with the

Righteousness of God. Nothing else will cover the shame of our nakedness.

However, the sin has grown worse, as all sin grows worse. While Adam did admit that he was naked, untold millions presently deny being naked even though they are obviously so. Adam did hide from God, or rather tried to do so, but man presently doesn't even actually try to hide. He brazenly confronts God, of which we see the type in Genesis, Chapter 4, as it regards the actions of Cain.

THE SECOND QUESTION

"Have you eaten of the tree, whereof I commanded you that you should not eat?" carries the answer with a question. That is exactly what Adam and Eve had done! They had eaten of the tree whereof the Lord commanded that they should not partake.

It is not so much the occasion of the sin of which the Lord enquires but of the consciousness of nakedness that is addressed here. The Lord then asks the question that points to the true cause of man's nakedness, which, of course, proclaimed the Divine Knowledge of the transgression.

The way the question is framed removes the pretext of ignorance and also points to the fact that the sin had been carried out in direct violation of the Divine prohibition.

ADAM SAID

"And the man said, The woman whom You gave to be with me, she gave me of the tree, and I did eat" (Gen. 3:12).

The phrase, *"And the man said,"* proclaims the course of action that will be taken. Adam then and there could have confessed his sin but chose another route. Consequently, there is no record in the Word of God that he ever fully made things right with the Lord. He is not listed in Hebrews, Chapter 11, along with the great Faith worthies, and, more than likely, he died lost.

There are some who claim that his tomb is in Jerusalem. There is another rumor which claims that his body was placed in the Ark, along with Noah and his family at the time of the Flood. Actually, the rumor claims that his coffin is still in the Ark, where it is ensconced on Mt. Ararat.

We can get an idea of what God intended for this man, our first parent, to be by the Holy Spirit through Paul referring to Jesus as the *"Last Adam"* (I Cor. 15:45).

THE EXCUSE

"The woman whom You gave to be with me, she gave me of the tree, and I did eat," portrays the immediate effects of the Fall:

• Adam now has, it seems, little sense of responsibility and no feeling that he had a duty toward Eve and ought to have watched over her and helped her when tempted.

• In effect, he blames God for his predicament. He, in fact, insinuates that God was accessory to his sin! God gave him the woman, and she gave him the fruit. So, in a secondary way, he blames Eve also!

It is strange that man wants to be like God but, as stated, in an unlawful way, and then when things go wrong, as they will, he wants to blame God. He seems to forget that if he is like God, he will have to take responsibility for his actions.

THE WOMAN

"And the LORD God said unto the woman, What is this that you have done? And the woman said, The serpent beguiled me, and I did eat" (Gen. 3:13).

With the Lord now turning to Eve, it presents Him, at least, at the moment, not responding to Adam. He rather turns to Eve, and we will find that her answer is far nobler than that of Adam. But yet, she still does not properly repent, actually casting aspersions on the serpent.

THE QUESTION

The question, *"What is this that you have done?"* places the emphasis on the pronoun *"you."*

Of course, God readily knew what Eve had done, why she did it, how she did it, and all about what had happened. In fact, that was not the point of the question.

Two questions:

1. *"Where are you?"*
2. *"What is this that you have done?"*

These two questions really comprise the human problem.

The Lord continues to ask the human race, *"Where are you?"* This implies, as previously stated, a place of trouble, difficulties, guilt, and bondage. However, that place and position was not arrived at without culpability on our part. It is because we have done something wrong! In effect, we have sinned against God, the failure of which has put us in this place of distress.

THE SERPENT

The phrase, *"And the woman said, The serpent beguiled me, and I did eat,"* presents Eve blaming the serpent.

In a sense, she was blaming God, as well, simply because God had made the serpent. So, in effect, she was saying, *"Lord, if You hadn't made the serpent, I wouldn't be in this predicament!"*

Did Satan beguile and deceive Eve through the serpent? Yes, he did! In fact, Satan is still the great deceiver (II Cor. 4:4). However, we should realize that God did not accept this excuse, as Verse 16 shows.

When she said, *"And I did eat,"* she was in actuality saying, *"It's true, I did eat, but it was not my fault."*

THE LORD GOD

"And the LORD God said unto the serpent, Because you have done this, you are cursed above all cattle, and above every beast

of the field; upon your belly shall you go, and dust shall you eat all the days of your life" (Gen. 3:14).

The phrase, *"And the LORD God said unto the serpent,"* presents no question or interrogation being posed toward the serpent at all. God judges him, and it is in listening to this Judgment that the guilty pair hears the first great Promise respecting Christ.

THE CURSE

The curse leveled on this animal reduced him from possibly the highest place and position in the animal kingdom to the lowest.

The very fact that the Lord leveled a curse at this creature lets us know that the animal must have had some intelligence, a limited power of choice, and even the power of limited speech.

The reptile, not being a moral creature, could not be cursed in the sense of being made susceptible of misery. However, it might be cursed in the sense of being deteriorated in its nature and, as it were, consigned to a lower position in the scale of being, which it was.

THE EXTENT OF THE CURSE

The Lord pronouncing the sentence that the serpent would from now on crawl on its belly evidently means that it had previously gone erect. That being the case, it would have possessed a backbone, which would have given it the capability of standing upright, etc. The curse changed its skeletal framework. The serpent would now be crawling on its belly. The eating of dust is not meant to be taken literally, but means that its mouth is where the dust is. All of this refers to its inferior position.

ENMITY

"And I will put enmity between you and the woman, and between your seed and her Seed; it shall bruise your head, and

you shall bruise His Heel" (Gen. 3:15).

The phrase, *"And I will put enmity between you and the woman,"* refers to the fact that Satan used the woman to bring sin into the world, and the Lord will use the woman to bring the Redeemer into the world, Who will save from sin.

However, in all of this, we are not to think that the Virgin Mary crushed the power of the Devil by giving birth to Christ. While she definitely was greatly honored by the Lord in being able to serve in this capacity, the truth is, Mary only provided a house, so to speak, for the Birth of the Redeemer into this world. It is the Lord Jesus Christ, and the Lord Jesus Christ Alone, Who has redeemed us. He did so by the giving of Himself on the Cross, in the pouring out of His Precious Blood (Eph. 2:13-18).

In fact, Jesus had no similarities to His Brothers and Sisters simply because Joseph was not actually His Father, and Mary only provided for Him a house, so to speak, for some nine months.

While we certainly hold Mary in high regard, it is, in fact, an abomination that the Catholic church has attempted to make her a co-redemptress. Such thinking and Mary-worship can be construed as none other than blasphemy.

HER SEED

The phrase, *"And between your seed and her Seed,"* refers to those who follow Satan (your seed) and those who follow Christ (her Seed).

In fact, this *"enmity,"* which refers to hatred, is played out in graphic detail in Chapter 4 of the Book of Genesis, referring to Cain and his brother Abel, whom Cain murdered.

This *"enmity"* or animosity is prevalent between the unredeemed and the Redeemed. It shows in the religions of the world which oppose Christ, and the more wicked these religions, the more opposition to Christ. In fact, the religion of Islam is the greatest example of all. It is, without a doubt, the most wicked religion in the world; consequently, it hates Christ with a venom, one might quickly add.

Islam hates Israel simply because the Bible proclaims the Truth that Isaac is the one through whom the Redeemer would come (Gen. 21:12). As well, the land of Israel was promised to Abraham's seed, who is Isaac and not Ishmael (Gen. 28:13). The Muslims claim that Ishmael is Abraham's seed and that the land of Israel belongs to them. Muhammad, as are all Arabs, is a descendant of Ishmael. This conflict is the reason for the constant war of the Muslim world against Israel and their hatred for the United States. They hate Israel, and they hate the Lord Jesus Christ. Inasmuch as the Muslims look at America as the great citadel of Christianity, we are referred to by them as the *"great Satan."*

Some have tried to claim that Islam is a religion of love and a religion of peace. Nothing could be further from the truth. It is a religion of hate and a religion of war, violence, and murder. In fact, if Islam had its way, in other words, if it had the power to do so, there would be no United States of America. They would blot it off the face of the Earth. That they don't do so is not for a lack of the will, but rather a lack of the way.

THE WOMAN

"Unto the woman He said, I will greatly multiply your sorrow and your conception; in sorrow you shall bring forth children; and your desire shall be to your husband, and he shall rule over you" (Gen. 3:16).

The phrase, *"Unto the woman He said,"* presents Judgment that was bitter, to say the least, which, as well, had to do with the Fall. In other words, it had far-reaching effects.

And yet, even though the Lord placed a curse upon the serpent, He did not do so as it regarded Adam and Eve, at least, as it regarded them personally. This referred to the fact that human beings are candidates for Restoration.

CONCEPTION

The phrase, *"I will greatly multiply your sorrow and your conception,"* carries forth the idea that with the fall of Adam, all of humanity, in essence, fell because all were in his loins (I Cor. 15:21-22). Adam was the fountainhead of the human race. What he did, all would do. That's the reason that in order for man to be redeemed, there would need to be another Adam sent into the world, Whom Paul referred to as the *"Last Adam,"* Who was the Lord Jesus Christ (I Cor. 15:45).

The word, *"Conception,"* and the, *"Multiplying of sorrow,"* is used here simply because children were originally intended by God to be brought into the world literally as *"sons of God"* (Lk. 3:38). Instead, due to the Fall, all children would be conceived in sorrow, referring to the fact that they would be brought into the world in the *"likeness of Adam"* with his fallen nature (Gen. 5:3). As a result of this fallen nature, i.e., *"the sin nature,"* man's every bent and direction would be toward sin, hence, all the pain, suffering, privation, poverty, want, sickness, dying, death, war, etc.

CHILDREN

The phrase, *"In sorrow you shall bring forth children,"* refers to that which we have just said. How many mothers have wept bitter tears because their sons and daughters have turned out to be murderers, thieves, etc.? How many have had their hearts broken by the actions of their children? While Christ has made it possible for all of this to be ameliorated, without Him, to be sure, the *"sorrow"* definitely prevails.

RULE

The phrase, *"And your desire shall be to your husband, and he shall rule over you,"* refers to the fact that because of Eve being the prime actor in sin, henceforward, she was to live in subjection to Adam.

Among the heathen, the punishment was made very bitter by the degradation to which a woman was reduced. In fact, this continues unto this hour in the ranks of Islam.

As Paul teaches, thankfully, in Christ, the whole penalty has been abrogated (Gal. 3:28), and the Christian woman is no more inferior to the man than is the Gentile to the Jew or the bondman to the free. This was made possible by what Jesus did at the Cross. There He totally and completely liberated mankind, which, of course, included all women. So, every iota of freedom which a woman presently possesses, which should be totally and completely equal to that of the man, is owed completely to Christ and what He did at the Cross.

Prior to the Fall, woman was the helpmate of her husband and his equal. After the Fall, she was no longer his equal. However, now, in Christ, she has been restored to that previous position of equality.

In the marriage relationship, the husband is to love the wife as Christ loved the Church and gave Himself for it (Eph. 5:25), and the wife is to respect the leadership of the husband.

ADAM

"And unto Adam He said, Because you have hearkened unto the voice of your wife, and have eaten of the tree, of which I commanded you, saying, You shall not eat of it: cursed is the ground for your sake; in sorrow shall you eat of it all the days of your life" (Gen. 3:17).

Verse 17 proclaims the fact that Adam didn't listen to God, but rather his wife.

Eve is representative here of people who tend to be used by Satan to draw others away from the Word of God. Man can listen to man, or man can listen to God. He cannot listen to both! The tragedy is, most in the world are listening to men instead of God. In fact, the Holy Spirit in I Timothy 2:14 teaches that Adam sinned more deeply than his wife. She is condemned in Verse 16 to subjection to him. Prior to that condemnation, she was his helpmate and equal.

THE TREE

The tree of which the Lord speaks is the Tree of the Knowledge of Good and Evil, as portrayed in Genesis 2:17.

As we have previously stated, the problem with the tree in question was not evil properties in the fruit, but rather disobedience to the Word of God.

THE CURSE

The phrase, *"Cursed is the ground for your sake; in sorrow shall you eat of it all the days of your life,"* presents the cursing of the habitation. What the Earth would have been, in fact, was intended to be, which was a paradise, has now been altered, and altered severely.

As well, the phrase, *"All the days of your life,"* proclaims the death sentence, which means that life is now terminal, all as a result of *"spiritual death,"* which was and is separation from God.

As well, as *"sorrow"* was to be the end result of the children conceived and brought forth, likewise, *"sorrow"* would be the result of one's labor.

Matthew Henry said, *"Man's business shall from henceforth become a toil to Him. Observe here that labor is our duty, which we must faithfully perform; not as creatures only, but as criminals, we are bound to work; it is a part of our sentence, which idleness daringly defies. Uneasiness and weariness with labor are our just punishment, which we must patiently submit to, and not complain of, since they are less than our iniquity deserves."*

Henry went on to say:

"Let us not by inordinate care and labor make our punishment heavier than God has made it; but study to lighten our burden, by regarding providence in all, and expecting rest shortly, but only if we live for God."[7]

The Righteousness of God is to be acknowledged in all the sad consequences of sin. Yet, in God's Sentence, there is Mercy. Man is not sentenced to eat dust as the serpent but only to eat the herb of the field.

THORNS AND THISTLES

"Thorns also and thistles shall it bring forth to you; and you

shall eat the herb of the field" (Gen. 3:18).

Verse 18 proclaims the fact that left to itself, the ground will no longer bring forth choice trees laden with generous fruit, such as Adam found in the Garden, but will now rather bring forth *"thorns"* and *"thistles."*

The tendency of the Earth is now toward decay and degeneration, again, all because of the curse. In the renewed Earth, the Golden Age of Paradise, and we speak of the coming Millennial Reign, will return, meaning that the curse will then be lifted.

HERB OF THE FIELD

The next Verse tells us how the herb is to be brought forth.

Even with modern equipment, the produce of the Earth is brought forth only with great care and diligence. Even then, it is prone to destruction regarding the elements, insects, etc. We can thank original sin for that.

If it is to be noticed, I think one could also say without fear of contradiction that it's the nations of the world which embrace Christianity, or, at least, a modicum of Christianity, which serve as the breadbaskets of the world. Nations which do not recognize Jesus as Lord can little feed their people, much less help feed others. One might say the following:

- Much Bible, much food
- Little Bible, little food
- No Bible, no food.

SWEAT

"In the sweat of your face shall you eat bread, until you return unto the ground; for out of it were you taken: for dust you are, and unto dust shall you return" (Gen. 3:19).

The phrase, *"In the sweat of your face shall you eat bread,"* proclaims the fact not only of hard labor, as it regards the producing of food, but, as well, presents itself as proof, and we continue to speak of sweat, that man is returning to the Earth.

It tells of exhaustion and waste.

Toil is the lot of the human race, as stated, that which God never originally intended.

DUST

"For dust you are, and unto dust shall you return," perhaps can be explained in the following manner:

To prove the immortality of the soul equally proves the mortality of the body.

Bishop Butler said, *"Death is the division of a compound substance in its component parts; but as the soul is a simple substance, and incapable of division, it is per se incapable of death. The body of Adam, composed of particles of earth, was capable of division, and our first parents in Paradise were ensured of an unending existence by a special gift, typified by the Tree of Life. But now this gift was withdrawn, and henceforward the sweat of man's brow was in itself proof that he was returning to the Earth."*[8]

ADAM AND CHRIST

In one way or the other, men constantly claim that the sentence passed upon Adam was too harsh and too severe. As is usual, man continues to blame God for his dilemma. Even after some 6,000 years of recorded history, he refuses to acknowledge the blame as being his own.

To be sure, the situation is made worse by man ignoring the fact that sin demanded such a sentence. Above all that, Jesus answered that sentence by becoming the Last Adam, which wrought Redemption for man. Note the following:

• Travailing pain came with sin. We read of the travail of Christ's Soul, even though He had no sin (Isa. 53:11), and the pains of death which He suffered (Acts 2:24).

• Subjection came with sin. In answer to this, Christ was made under the Law (Gal. 4:4).

• The curse came with sin. In answer to that horror,

Christ was made a curse for us and, in effect, died a cursed death (Gal. 3:13).

 • The thorns came in with sin. In answer to that, Jesus was crowned with thorns for us.

 • Sweat, as well, came in with sin. The Scripture says of Him that His Sweat for us was as it had been great drops of blood.

 • Sorrow came with sin. He was a Man of sorrows, acquainted with grief.

 • Death came with sin. He became obedient unto death. Thus is the cure as wide as the cause.

Concerning the Fall, Matthew Henry said:

"Man's soul was ruined by the Fall; the image of God was defaced; man's nature was corrupted, and he became dead in sin. The design of God was to restore the soul of man; to restore life, and the image of God, in conversion; and to carry on this work in Sanctification, until He should perfect it in Glory."[9]

One must also say that man's body was ruined; by the Fall, it became subject to death. The design of God was to restore it from this ruin, and not only to deliver it from death by what He did at the Cross through His Son, the Lord Jesus Christ, but to deliver it, as well, from mortality itself in making it like unto Christ's Glorious Body.

EVE

"And Adam called his wife's name Eve; because she was the mother of all living" (Gen. 3:20).

The name *"Eve"* means *"Life"* or the *"mother of all living."* The idea is, through Eve alone could human life be continued and the *"woman's Seed"* be obtained, Who was to raise up man from his fall. While woman's punishment consists in the multiplication of her *"sorrow and conception,"* she becomes, thereby, only more precious to man.

And yet, Eve did not fully understand what the Lord had said concerning the *"Seed of the woman."* In fact, it would not be fully brought out until the Prophet Isaiah gave clarity to the Promise by saying, *". . . Behold, a virgin shall conceive . . . "* (Isa. 7:14). This Prophecy made it clear that the Saviour was not to be the offspring of the union of a man and wife. In the New Testament, this fact was revealed still more clearly by the Angel (Lk. 1:26-38). Since then, there was promised man, through the Seed of the woman, Deliverance from the Law, sin, and death. There was given to him a clear and sure hope of the Resurrection and renewal in the future life. It is clear that man could not remove sin and its punishment by his own power, nor could he escape death and make amends for his disobedience by his own power. Therefore, the Son of God had to sacrifice Himself and secure all this for mankind. He had to remove sin, overcome death, and restore what Adam had lost by his disobedience.

MOTHER OF ALL LIVING

The last phrase of Verse 20 proclaims the power of procreation. But yet, some believe that by Adam giving the name Eve to his wife, it pertains to the proclamation of his Faith. That is possible, but I think not!

Faith in the *"Promised Seed"* was the requirement for Salvation. There is some evidence that Adam and Eve may have made a start toward God. In other words, they may have initially expressed Faith; however, every evidence is that they soon abandoned their Faith.

The Scripture tells us of the Faith of Enoch, who was contemporary with Adam, at least, for a period of time. However, it says nothing about the Faith of Adam (Heb. 11:5-6).

COATS OF SKINS

"Unto Adam also and to his wife did the LORD God make coats of skins, and clothed them" (Gen. 3:21).

The coats of skins present the fact that the first thing that died was a sacrifice, or Christ in a figure, Who is, therefore, said to be the Lamb slain from the foundation of the world (I Pet. 1:18-20).

Let it be known that it is the *"LORD God"* Who furnished these coats, and not man himself. This tells us that Salvation is altogether of God and not at all of man. All Adam and Eve could do was to fashion a garment out of fig leaves, which, regrettably, man has been attempting to do ever since.

Sin is not a cheap affair and cannot be satisfied by a cheap solution. Sin is devastating and can only be addressed by the Sacrifice of Christ, which was, incidentally, the ultimate Sacrifice.

FROM THE VERY BEGINNING, THE CROSS!

The manner in which the Lord would redeem the human race has never been in question. In fact, that was decided by the Godhead even before the foundation of the world (I Pet. 1:18-20).

Someone asked me once, *"Was it Who Christ was or What He did that effected our Salvation?"*

Up front, it had to be both, *"Who He was and What He did."*

While Who He was, namely Deity, was absolutely necessary, still, Jesus Christ, in fact, had always been God. As God, He had no beginning, which means that He was unformed, unmade, uncreated, has always been, always is, and always shall be. However, all of that, as wonderful and glorious as it was and is, did not redeem anybody. In fact, His Virgin Birth did not redeem anyone, nor did His Miracles or Healings! The fact that He spoke as no man ever spoke did not effect any Redemption even though all of these things were of extreme significance.

It is what He did on the Cross which effected Redemption. That's why Paul said:

"For Christ sent me not to baptize, but to preach the Gospel: not with wisdom of words, lest the Cross of Christ should be made of none effect" (I Cor. 1:17).

As well, when we're given a vision of Heaven through the eyes of John the Beloved, and I speak of his great Vision on the Isle of Patmos, we see there the central theme being *"Jesus Christ and Him Crucified,"* all signified by the constant use of the Apostle of the term *"Lamb"* (Rev. 5:6, 8, 12-13).

So, it begins with the Cross, and it ends with the Cross. John used the term, *"Lamb,"* signifying Christ and what He did at the Cross, some 28 times in the Book of Revelation, seven times in the last two Chapters alone.

In fact, the last time in the Bible the term, *"Lamb,"* is used, and we continue to speak of the Son of God, it is used in relationship to the fact that there is *"no more curse."* In other words, the terrible curse that was leveled at the dawn of time, as it regards Adam's fall, was eliminated by the Lord Jesus Christ at great price, which was the shedding of His Life's Blood on the Cross (Rev. 22:3).

COVERING

The short phrase, *"And clothed them,"* proclaims the fact that such a covering came at a price, the death of the animals in question; consequently, these coats of skin had a significance. The beasts, whose skins they were, had to be slain, slain before the eyes of Adam and Eve, to show them what death is that they might see that they themselves were mortal and dying (Eccl. 3:18). As well, this sacrifice would also show them the terrible awfulness of sin. As repeatedly stated, it would typify the coming Redeemer.

Jesus said to the church at Laodicea:

"I counsel you to buy of Me gold tried in the fire, that you may be rich; and white raiment, that you may be clothed, and that the shame of your nakedness do not appear" (Rev. 3:18).

The Laodiceans had abandoned the Cross. They were trusting in other things; consequently, the shame of their nakedness was obvious.

All of this becomes even more striking when we realize that the Laodicean church typifies the church at this present time. It is referred to as the apostatized church. Let the reader

understand that the apostasy addressed here is the abandonment of the Cross.

In the last several decades, all types of things have been suggested as the proper *"covering."* Many think of their denomi-
nation as their covering; others think of particular preachers,
while others think of their own good works.

Irrespective as to what it might be and how good it might
seem to be on the surface, if the *"covering"* is not the Blood of
the Lamb, and that exclusively, then it is nothing but fig leaves.
It is something that God will not honor, in fact, cannot honor.
This is the sin of the modern church.

TO KNOW GOOD AND EVIL

*"And the LORD God said, Behold, the man is become as one of
Us, to know good and evil: and now, lest he put forth his hand, and
take also of the Tree of Life, and eat, and live forever"* (Gen. 3:22).

The statement of Verse 22 refers to the Lord knowing *"evil"*
by the Power of Omniscience, which knows all things, but never
by personal experience. The Scripture says, *". . . for God cannot
be tempted with evil . . ."* (James 1:13).

This means that He cannot have anything to do with evil in
any regard. He is Perfectly Righteous, actually, the thrice-Holy
God (Rev. 4:8).

As well, the pronoun, *"Us,"* proclaims the Trinity. No, when
the Lord used the pronoun, *"Us,"* He wasn't speaking of Himself
and Angels, as suggested by some. As well, fallen Angels know what
evil is by personal experience but not by omniscience because
they do not have that attribute. Such pertains only to Deity.

THE TREE OF LIFE

The phrase, *"Lest he put forth his hand, and take also of
the Tree of Life, and eat, and live forever,"* proclaims the fact
that the fruit of this particular tree evidently contained certain
properties designed by God, which would cause the human body
to remain forever young, thereby, living forever. And yet, at

the same time, we must be quick to say that this tree had such power not because of its peculiar nature, but because of the Divine Word attached to it, which made it a life-giving tree.

At the dawn of time, man was denied access to *"the Tree of Life,"* while at the conclusion of the Dispensations, due to what Christ has done at the Cross, the *"Tree of Life"* will once again be opened to man (Rev. 22:1-2).

EXPELLED FROM THE GARDEN OF EDEN

"Therefore the LORD God sent him forth from the Garden of Eden, to till the ground from whence he was taken" (Gen. 3:23).

Man being expelled from the Garden of Eden was actually an act of Mercy. Man was expelled from the Garden lest by eating of the Tree of Life he should perpetuate his misery.

To bring this up to modern times, think of an Adolf Hitler or a Joseph Stalin living forever! Also, think of the Muslims, who murdered several thousands of people by their acts of atrocity in New York City and Washington, D.C., plus their actions in Libya and, in fact, atrocities that really never end with these people. While being driven from the Garden of Eden and access to the Tree of Life was definitely a punishment, in the long run, because of their state, it was definitely a blessing.

Ellicott says:

"Adam had exercised the power of marring God's Work, and if an unending physical life were added to the gift of freewill now in revolt against God, his position in that of mankind would become most miserable. Man is still able to attain to immortality, but it must now be through struggle, sorrow, penitence, faith, and death. Hence a paradise is no fit home for him. The Divine Mercy, therefore, commands Adam to quit it, in order that he may live under conditions better suited for his moral and spiritual good."[10]

TILL THE GROUND

The phrase, *"To till the ground from where he was taken,"* refers to a place of toil, not to a place of torment. Matthew

Henry said:

"Our first parents were excluded from the privileges of their state of innocency, yet they were not abandoned to despair."[11]

The word, *"Till,"* as used here, is the same Hebrew word rendered *"dress"* in Genesis 2:15. Adam's task is the same, but the conditions are now altered. In other words, it will now be far more difficult than was previously intended.

EXPULSION

"So He drove out the man; and He placed at the east of the Garden of Eden Cherubims, and a flaming sword which turned every way, to keep the way of the Tree of Life" (Gen. 3:24).

The phrase, *"So He drove out the man,"* combined with the word, *"Sent,"* in the previous Verse, implies that Adam and Eve definitely didn't want to depart Paradise. Consequently, the two words, *"Sent,"* and, *"Drove,"* convey the ideas of force and displeasure. In other words, God had to force Adam and Eve to leave.

However, there is one thing that all men must learn. Whatever God does with us is always and without exception for our best. In other words, if we did what we wanted to do, whatever that might be, to be sure, it would turn out to be destructive not only to others but, also, to ourselves. To Adam and Eve, it seemed harsh to be driven out of the Garden and not allowed access anymore. However, the Plan of God was for their everlasting good, as well as all of humanity, because, in essence, what God did to our first parents was done to the entirety of the human race.

The idea was that they would look to the coming *"Promised Seed"* of Genesis 3:15. Had they partaken of the Tree of Life in their fallen state, such would have consigned them to an eternal life of torment, which would grow worse by the millennia. Only the *"Promised Seed"* could alleviate the dilemma!

CHERUBIM

The phrase, *"And He placed at the east of the Garden of Eden*

Cherubims, " evidently refers to the entrance to the Garden.

Incidentally, it is believed by some Bible scholars that the Garden of Eden was situated at the very site where Babylon would later be built.

There is some evidence, as we shall see, that a sanctuary was built there, and we continue to speak of the entrance to the Garden.

Who and What are these Cherubims?

There are all types of opinions. Some say they are the fullness of the Deity. Some say they are symbolic of earthly life. Others, say they speak of the angelic nature. Still others claim they represent the Divine Manhood of Jesus Christ.

Wordsworth says, and I think he is right:

"The Cherubims are symbolic of redeemed and glorified humanity."

He went on to say:

"Combining with the intelligence of human nature the highest qualities of the animal world, as exhibited in the lion, the ox, and the eagle (Rev. 4:7), they were emblematic of creature life in its most absolute perfect form. As such they were caused to dwell at the gate of Eden to intimate that only when perfected and purified could fallen human nature return to Paradise. "[12]

Carrying forth the same principle, the Veil, which hung between the Holy of Holies, where resided the Ark of the Covenant, and the Holy Place, had Cherubims embroidered on it (Ex. 26:31-32). In effect, the Cherubims on the Veil said the same thing as the Cherubims at the entrance of the Garden of Eden. Man was not allowed entrance. In fact, only the High Priest of Israel could go into the Holy of Holies in the Tabernacle and the Temple, and then, only once a year, which was on the Great Day of Atonement, and then, not without blood. In other words, he had to offer up the blood of the sacrifice on the Mercy Seat, which covered the Ark of the Covenant. This, as well, carried two Cherubim, one on either end, facing each other, and looking down upon the Mercy Seat. This High Priest was a Type of Christ, Who would one day offer up His Own Blood on the Cross of Calvary, which He did! That alone opened up the way to God, making it possible for man to come into the very Presence of God. However, let it ever be known that this can be done only by our Faith in the Finished Work of Christ. The writer of Hebrews tells us:

"Let us (Believers) *therefore come boldly into the Throne of Grace, that we may obtain Mercy, and find Grace to help in time of need"* (Heb. 4:16).

Let us say it again that the way into Paradise has now been opened by the Lord Jesus Christ, which He accomplished by the shedding of His Own Precious Blood, which was effected at the Cross of Calvary. That's the reason that Paul said:

"For Christ sent me not to baptize, but to preach the Gospel: not with wisdom of words, lest the Cross of Christ should be made of none effect" (I Cor. 1:17).

THE FLAMING SWORD

The phrase, *"And a flaming sword which turned every way, to keep the way of the Tree of Life,"* served as an emblem of the Divine Glory in its attitude toward sin.

"To keep the way of the Tree of Life," presents itself as an interesting statement. While it pertains to the way being kept shut, it also, at the same time, states that the way is to be kept open. In other words, the idea is, even as we've already stated, while God did drive Adam and Eve from the Garden, He went with them with a Promise of bringing them (mankind) back. This was done by the *"Promised Seed,"* Who is the Lord Jesus Christ, and Who effected the open way by what He did at the Cross.

When Adam and Eve were driven out of the Garden, they went into a world which exhibited everywhere the lamentable results of the Fall. The Cherubim with the flaming sword did forbid fallen man to pluck the fruit of the Tree of Life, but God's Revelation would point him to the Death and Resurrection of the Seed of the woman as that wherein life would be found beyond the pallor of death, and so it was.

As a consequence, Adam was a safer man outside the bounds

of Paradise than he would have been within in his fallen state, and for this reason: within, his life depended on himself, whereas, outside, it depended on another, even a Promised Christ.

If the Cherubim and flaming sword closed up the way to Paradise, which they were forced to do, the Lord Jesus Christ has opened *"a new and living way"* into the Holiest of all. *"I am the Way, the Truth, and the Life: no man comes unto the Father, but by Me"* (Jn. 14:6; Heb. 10:20).

FAITH

In the knowledge of all of this, the Believer now moves onward through a world, which is under the curse—where the traces of sin are visible on all hands. He has found his way, by Faith, and we speak of Faith in Christ and Him Crucified, to the bosom of the Father. While he can secretly repose there, he is cheered by the Blessed Assurance that the One Who has conducted him thither is gone to prepare a place in the many mansions of the Father's House. As well, He will soon come again and receive him unto Himself amid the Glory of the Father's Kingdom.

Great Women OF THE BIBLE

OLD TESTAMENT

Chapter One

SARAH

The Wife Of Abraham

SARAH
The Wife Of Abraham

ABRAHAM AND SARAH

"Now these are the generations of Terah (Abraham's father)*: Terah begat Abram, Nahor, and Haran; and Haran begat Lot.*

"And Haran died before his father Terah in the land of his nativity, in Ur of the Chaldees.

"And Abram and Nahor took them wives: the name of Abram's wife was Sarai; and the name of Nahor's wife, Milcah, the daughter of Haran, the father of Milcah, and the father of Iscah.

"But Sarai was barren; she had no child" (Gen. 11:27-30).

As Abraham is referred to, in a sense, as the *"father of the faithful,"* I think, likewise, that it could be said that Sarah could be looked at as the *"mother of the faithful."*

Of course, in telling the story of Sarah, Abraham will have to be included to a certain extent, as should be obvious. But yet, I wish to do my best to limit the account to Sarah because she is the subject of this Chapter.

BARREN

Even at the beginning of this narrative, the Holy Spirit is quick to tell us that *"Sarai was barren; she had no child."* Satan knew that it would be absolutely imperative for a male child to be born to this couple, that is, if the Seed of the woman was to be born into this world. Consequently, he would make her barren, and God would allow him to do so. In this, we see one of the greatest tests of Faith, which brought about many failures on Abraham's part, but, ultimately, great victory.

SOME HISTORY REGARDING ABRAHAM AND SARAH

"And Terah took Abram his son, and Lot the son of Haran his son's son, and Sarai his daughter-in-law, his son Abram's

wife; and they went forth with them from Ur of the Chaldees, to go into the land of Canaan; and they came unto Haran, and dwelt there.

"And the days of Terah (Abraham's father) *were two hundred and five years: and Terah died in Haran"* (Gen. 11:31-32).

It is said that Ur of the Chaldees, located a little north of what is now referred to as the Persian Gulf, was one of the most modern cities in the world of that time. So, because of a Revelation from God, Abraham and his family would have left these modern conveniences—modern for that time—to go to a land to which they had never been and to live a nomadic existence for the rest of their lives. How many would be willing to do that?

In a sense, when God called Abraham, He also called Sarah.

JEWISH HISTORICAL COMMENTARIES

The Jewish Targums (historical commentaries of sorts) say that Abraham's family was idol-makers. In other words, they made the idol which represented the moon god, *"Ur,"* for which the city was named.

Whether this is correct or not, we know that Abraham and his family were idol-worshippers, and so we have to venture the thought that whatever Revelation it was that God gave to Abraham, it was so powerful, so obvious, and left such a mark upon the Patriarch that he would never be the same again. To be sure, this is a Conversion that so changed a man that he would now forsake all that he has known all his life to reach out by Faith to something that he really could not see—except by Faith.

We know that Abraham had this Revelation when he was in Ur of the Chaldees, but how long he stayed there before he left for Canaan, with the stop in Haran, we aren't told. I suspect it would not have been very long because as the First Verse of the next Chapter proclaims, the Command of the Lord was explicit.

Abraham left Haran when he was about 75 years old. Whether Terah, Abraham's father, accepted the Lord is not clear. There is some small evidence that he did because he, as well, left Ur of the Chaldees and got as far as Haran, where he died.

THE REVELATION

"Now the LORD had said unto Abram, Get out of your country, and from your kindred, and from your father's house, unto a land that I will show you" (Gen. 12:1).

Even though Sarah is only mentioned in passing as it regards Abraham leaving his comfortable home in Ur of the Chaldees, still, she was very much a part of what was taking place. The Call of God to Abraham had to be powerful indeed for him to uproot his family in order to go to a place of which they knew nothing.

I should think that a move of this nature is much harder on the wife than it would be the husband. As we have stated, Ur of the Chaldees was a very modern city for its day. Sarah was accustomed to the finer things of life. She, no doubt, enjoyed her home in Ur, but now, her husband tells her that the Lord has spoken to him, and that he was to leave and go to a place of which they knew nothing, which was over 1,000 miles away. So, Sarah had to at least share somewhat in the Call of her husband.

If it is to be noticed, the phrase, *"Now the LORD had said unto Abram,"* refers to instructions that had been given to the Patriarch sometime previously.

This Chapter is very important, for it records the first steps of this great Believer in the path of Faith. There were Believers before him (a few), but the Scripture speaks of him as the father of all Believers who would come after him (Rom. 4:16).

While Abraham obeyed, it seems that family ties at first held him back. Though called to Canaan, he, nevertheless, tarried at Haran till nature's tie was snapped by death and then, with unimpeded step, he made his way to the place to which *"the God of Glory"* had called him.

All of this is very full of meaning. The flesh is ever a hindrance to the full Power of the Call of God. We tend to settle for less than that which God intends.

We are slow to learn that everything we need, and I mean everything, is found totally and completely in Christ. While we are quick to say, *"Amen,"* to the words I have just dictated, we are slow to actually come to the place of full surrender. *"Self-will"* hinders! The *"flesh"* hinders! However, we make excuses for all of this by loading the flesh and self-will with religious phraseology.

THE CALL OF GOD

Whatever it is that God calls us to do, that which He called Abraham and Sarah to do, it is always beyond what we would at first see or think. Embodied in the Call is not only a work to be done but, as well, the ingredients for Spiritual growth. With the Holy Spirit, it is always growth. To be frank, the growth must be brought about, or the work cannot be done. Here, I would dwell for a moment on the Cross of Christ. There is only one Way all of this can be achieved, and that's by and through the Cross. If we do not understand the Cross, then we cannot really understand the Way of God. In fact, if the Cross is removed from Christianity, Christianity then loses its Power (I Cor. 1:18), and, for all practical purposes, becomes little more than the religions of the world. While it might have a better ethic, it's an ethic that really cannot be reached without the Cross.

SEPARATION

The phrase, *"Get out of your country, and from your kindred, and from your father's house,"* proclaims the reason that many cannot be used of God. They refuse to separate themselves from certain things in this world and, therefore, unto God.

This which the Lord demanded of Abraham, He, in effect, demands of all. It is:

- *"Our country"*: the true Believer *"seeks a country"* simply because that which the world offers can never satisfy and, therefore, simply will not do (Heb. 11:14). The things of this world lose their attraction. Money is a means to an end. The old song, *"This World is not my Home, I'm Just a Passing Through,"* becomes the song of the Redeemed. If one lays up treasures here, one's heart will be here simply because one's heart is where one's treasure is.

I'm positive, as previously stated, that this was not a pleasant thing for Sarah. She would be leaving everything she knew, not to speak of the comforts which her present life then afforded. In fact, she would live in a tent the rest of her life. However, this I can guarantee, were you to speak to her now, she would say, *"Ten thousand times over am I glad that I obeyed the Lord alongside my husband, Abraham."*

- *"Separate from your kindred"*: now we belong to Christ. We are bought with a price, and a great price at that. Even though we continue to love our family, even love them very deeply, Christ and what He wants and desires takes precedence over our family and everyone else, for that matter. Regrettably, many aren't willing to do that.

- *"From your father's house"*: this demand about leaving all of their kindred, of course, was not only for Abraham but Sarah as well. In fact, she would never see them again.

TO CANAAN

"And Abram took Sarai his wife, and Lot his brother's son, and all their substance that they had gathered, and the souls that they had gotten in Haran; and they went forth to go into the land of Canaan; and into the land of Canaan they came" (Gen. 12:5).

From Haran to Canaan was approximately 350 miles. Abraham had 318 trained men with him (Gen. 14:14), meaning that they were trained to fight as soldiers. They were totally loyal to Abraham and, actually, in a sense, a part of his household. In fact, there may have been as many as a 1,000 people in this entourage.

As well, Abraham, at that time, was extremely rich in silver and gold, as well as flocks and herds. In other words, he was a mighty man!

EGYPT

"And it came to pass, when he was come near to enter into Egypt, that he said unto Sarai his wife, Behold now, I know that you are a fair woman to look upon" (Gen. 12:11).

Abraham and Sarah, now in Canaan, meet with hostility in the form of a famine. So, Abraham, without approval from the Lord, for there is no record that he sought the Lord about this matter, went down into Egypt. It would prove to be a very unfortunate decision. I might quickly add, anything we do that's not in the Will of God will always lead to trouble.

Concerning this wrong direction, Mackintosh says:

"Nothing can ever make up for the loss of our communion with God. Exemption from temporary pressure, and the accession of even the greatest wealth, are but poor equivalents for what one loses by diverging a hair's breadth from the straight path of obedience."

He then went on to say:

"Let us, instead of turning aside into Egypt, wait on God; and thus the trial, instead of proving an occasion of stumbling, will prove an opportunity for obedience."

And then:

"Shall we deny Him by plunging again into what from which His Cross has forever delivered us? May God Almighty forbid! May He keep us in the hollow of His Hand, and under the shadow of His Wings, until we see Jesus as He is, and be like Him, and with Him forever, and yes with Him forever."[1]

PARTAKING OF EGYPT

It is not possible to go into Egypt, spiritually speaking,

without partaking of Egypt. The Christian who thinks that he can beat this game is only fooling himself. If we go into Egypt, we ultimately become like Egypt.

Much is at stake here, even the great Plan of Redemption. At this time, Sarah is about 65 years old, but yet, a very beautiful woman. She would live to be 127 (Gen. 23:1).

Satan's plan was formidable. The entirety of Faith on the Earth at this time, at least, as far as we know, was wrapped up in Abraham. To be frank, in a sense, it is the same presently.

All Faith must be anchored in the Word of God, which, in reality, is the Story of the Cross. To be particular, our Faith must ever have as its Object the Cross of Christ. We aren't speaking of the wooden beam on which Jesus died, but rather what He there did (Rom. 6:3-11; I Cor. 1:17-18, 21, 23; 2:2, 5; Gal. 2:20-21; 6:14; Col. 2:10-15; I Pet. 1:18-20).

Satan's plan with Abraham was that he would leave Canaan as a result of the famine, which he did, and go to Egypt. There, the plan would then be set in motion for Pharaoh to impregnate Sarah, which was meant by the Evil One to thwart the coming of the Redeemer.

However, how could this be since Sarah was barren?

Irrespective, even though, at this time, she could not be impregnated, still, because of her beauty, Pharaoh would have kept her in his harem. Thus, he would have foiled the Plan of God for Sarah to bring forth Isaac, which she ultimately did, who would be in the lineage of the coming Redeemer. So, now we begin to see just how important all of this really is.

THE EGYPTIANS

"Therefore it shall come to pass, when the Egyptians shall see you, that they shall say, This is his wife: and they will kill me, but they will save you alive" (Gen. 12:12).

• God had a plan: that plan was for Abraham and Sarah to bring a son into the world through whom, ultimately, the Messiah, the Redeemer of the world, would come.

• Satan had a plan: that plan was to foil the Plan of God and to do so through the weakness of Abraham.

• Abraham had a plan: Abraham's plan is not now the Plan of God, but is rather a plan of deception, which God can never honor.

DECEPTION

"Say, I pray you, you are my sister: that it may be well with me for your sake; and my soul shall live because of you" (Gen. 12:13).

Concerning this, Matthew Henry said:

"Observe a great fault which Abraham was guilty of in denying his wife, and pretending that she was his sister. The Scripture is impartial in relating the miscarriages of the most celebrated Saints, which are recorded, not for our imitation, but for our admonition; that he who thinks he stands, may take heed lest he fall. His fault was, dissembling his relation to Sarah, equivocating concerning it, and teaching his wife, and probably all his attendants, to do so too, what he said about her being his sister, was in a sense true (Gen. 20:12), but with a purpose to deceive. He concealed a truth, so as in effect to deny it, and to expose thereby both his wife and the Egyptians to sin."[2]

By this deception, Abraham greatly placed in danger the entirety of the Plan of God. He seemed to think that the great Promise of God concerning *"his seed"* (Gen. 12:7) concerned him alone. In other words, as it regarded his thinking, Sarah didn't matter that much respecting the carrying out of this great conviction. He would merely obtain another woman, which showed up in his sinning regarding Hagar. In fact, the Lord would bluntly tell the Patriarch at a later time, *". . . As for Sarai your wife . . . I will bless her, and give you a son also of her . . . and she shall be a mother of nations; kings of people shall be of her"* (Gen. 17:15-16). In other words, this was a grievous sin committed by Abraham, in fact, on more than one count. When one goes down into Egypt, one no longer trusts God.

PRESUMPTION

Abraham erroneously thinks that by offering his wife to the harem of Pharaoh, he will save himself. He didn't seem to realize, at least, at this time, that the Plan of God included Sarah as much as it included him. Perhaps her being barren, not able to bear children, caused him to dismiss her in this capacity. However, he was wrong, dead wrong!

All of this was presumption. The Patriarch merely presumed certain things because of an imperfect faith.

True Faith will never sell God short, and true Faith will never resort to the deceptive machinations of mere man. True Faith always reaches for the impossible and will settle for nothing less than God's Best. In fact, as it regards true Faith, it is either all or nothing! God could not condone any of the efforts of Abraham. It must be totally of God, or else, it is not of Faith. For it to truly be Faith, it must be Faith in Christ and what He has done for us at the Cross.

Any time we mix our plans into the Plans of God, His Plan is instantly nullified. True Faith is always all God and none of man. While man is the instrument, it is God Who does the doing, and with man intended to be obedient.

SARAH'S BEAUTY

"And it came to pass, that, when Abram was come into Egypt, the Egyptians beheld the woman that she was very fair" (Gen. 12:14).

It is said by some that at this time, Egyptian custom demanded that any foreign Prince coming into Egypt would have to give into the harem of Pharaoh a daughter or a sister. This being done, it was supposed to guarantee the good behavior of such a one while in Egypt. Refusal to do such was considered to be an act of war.

So, Abraham would claim that Sarah was his sister, which would make her acceptable for the harem of Pharaoh.

PHARAOH'S HOUSE

"The princes also of Pharaoh saw her, and commended her before Pharaoh: and the woman was taken into Pharaoh's house" (Gen. 12:15).

Whatever was the custom of those particular times regarding the question at hand, the Text seems to indicate that there was much more to the situation regarding Sarah than for her to merely become the member of a harem, which means that she was just one of many women.

The Text strongly implies that Pharaoh was looking for a particular woman, one whom he imagined to be of particular quality, who would be the mother of his child and, therefore, the heir to the throne of Egypt. This, evidently, was Satan's plan, devised to defeat the Promise of God, which would ultimately stop the coming of the Messiah into the world. Consequently, we can see how fully Abraham fell into the trap, which was laid for him. Even though he was a man of Faith, in fact, one of the greatest men of Faith who has ever lived, still, his present position, strangely enough, is because of unbelief. Despite the famine, he should have remained in Canaan and trusted the Lord for Deliverance. Resorting to Egypt is never without its compromise and attendant result.

RICHES

"And he (Pharaoh) entreated Abram well for her sake: and he had sheep, and oxen, and he asses, and menservants, and maidservants, and she asses, and camels" (Gen. 12:16).

We find from this Passage that Pharaoh valued Sarah very highly. Even though she was approximately 65 years old, she, evidently, was beautiful, to say the least. It is not unlikely at all that the Lord had a hand in this regarding her beauty but, most definitely, it did not pertain to Pharaoh.

PLAGUE

"And the LORD plagued Pharaoh and his house with great

plagues because of Sarai Abram's wife" (Gen. 12:17).

Concerning this, Matthew Henry said:

"Let us notice the danger Sarah was in, and her deliverance from this danger. If God did not deliver us, many a time, out of those straits and distresses which we bring ourselves into, by our own sin and folly, and which therefore we could not expect any deliverance, we should soon be ruined; nay, we had been ruined long before this. He deals not with us, thank God, according to our deserts."[3]

In what manner Pharaoh came to know that the plagues falling on his house were because of Sarah, we aren't told.

Sarah was blameless in this, the fault being that of Abraham. From this Passage, we learn that the Believer can be a blessing or a curse; it all depends upon his Faith. At this time, Abraham was faithless, or he wouldn't have been there to begin with.

The cause of all problems is the Believer leaving the Cross, and the solution to all problems is the Believer coming back to the Cross. When Abraham left Canaan to go to Egypt, he left the Altar, i.e., the Cross (Gen. 12:8). When he went back to Canaan, where God had directed him to begin with, he went back to the Altar (Gen. 13:4). It is always the Cross, of which the Altar is but a Type.

WHAT HAVE YOU DONE UNTO ME?

"And Pharaoh called Abram, and said, What is this that you have done unto me? why did you not tell me that she was your wife?" (Gen. 12:18).

Abraham had told those who were representing Pharaoh that Sarah was his sister. In fact, this was a half-truth. She was the daughter of his father but not the daughter of his mother (Gen. 20:12). However, because he intended to deceive, God looked at this episode as a *"lie."*

As a Child of God, even a man of Faith, despite his present situation, it lay within the Power of Abraham to be a blessing or a curse. However, the curse comes only because of wrongdoing on the part of the Believer. It is not possible for a Believer to knowingly and willingly put a curse on anyone. Such activity is always of Satan; however, the Believer will definitely be a curse if his faith is in the wrong place, even as Abraham.

As we've already stated, in the path of Faith, the Christian is a blessing to the world, but in the path of self-will, a curse.

QUESTIONS

"Why did you say, She is my sister? so I might have taken her to me to wife: now therefore behold your wife, take her, and go your way" (Gen. 12:19).

Pharaoh had three questions for Abraham:

1. What is this that you have done to me?
2. Why did you not tell me that she was your wife?
3. Why did you say, *"She is my sister?"*

At this time, Egypt was at least one of the most powerful nations in the world, which means that Pharaoh was one of the most powerful men in the world. Little did he realize the magnitude of these questions.

As he speaks this day to Abraham, little does he know, despite Abraham's present problems, that this is the man the Holy Spirit would refer to as *"the father of us all"* (Rom. 4:16). And yet, the picture that he would get of the Patriarch would be one of subterfuge, chicanery, and deception.

However, before we criticize Abraham, we best look at ourselves. Are we in the path of Faith or that of self-will? According to that answer, we will be a blessing or a curse!

DEPARTURE

"And Pharaoh commanded his men concerning him: and they sent him away, and his wife, and all that he had" (Gen. 12:20).

Because of Abraham, Pharaoh and his family are plagued with great plagues, and this heathen prince hurries this Man of God out of his land as he would chase away a pestilence.

Even though the monarch was very unhappy concerning the turn of events, the implication here is that he knew within his spirit that this man Abraham was more than meets the eye. With anyone else, he would, no doubt, have taken off his head. However, with Abraham, the implication is that he was careful not to do anything to him or even retrieve the animals which he had given to the Patriarch.

From the Scripture, we're given the bare bones of what actually took place. The mighty Pharaoh saw the Power of God, even though it was in a negative way. What effect it had on him, other than this which we see in the Scripture, we aren't told.

HAGAR

"Now Sarai Abram's wife bore him no children: and she had an handmaid, an Egyptian, whose name was Hagar" (Gen. 16:1).

For the Promise of God to be fulfilled, a child would have to be born through whom, ultimately, the Messiah, the Redeemer of the world, would come. The idea is, God would have to become Man in order to redeem man.

Paul said, *"For if by one man's offence* (the fall of Adam) *death reigned by one; much more they which receive abundance of Grace and of the Gift of Righteousness shall reign in life by One, Jesus Christ"* (Rom. 5:17).

He then said:

"And so it is written, The first man Adam was made a living soul; the Last Adam (the Lord Jesus Christ) *was made a quickening spirit* (one who makes alive)*"* (I Cor. 15:45).

The child that Abraham and Sarah must have had to do with the Incarnation, God becoming Man. In fact, this is what all of this is about.

Concerning this dark episode in the history of Abraham, Williams says:

"Chapter 15 sets out the Faithfulness of God, Chapter 16 the faithlessness of Abraham. The Covenant that secured to Abraham

riches far exceeding the wealth of Sodom was the more amazing because it necessitated the death of Him (Christ) Who made it! Such was the faithful love to which Abraham responded with unbelief and impatience. The Apostle says you have need of patience that you may inherit the Promises. The 'flesh' can neither believe nor wait for a Divine Promise."

Williams continues, *"The path of Faith is full of dignity, the path of unbelief full of degradation. Abraham, finding that God has failed to give him a son, and tired of waiting, no longer sets his hope upon God, but upon an Egyptian slave girl. The natural heart will trust anything rather than God. Abraham thinks that he can, by his clever plan, hasten and bring to pass the Divine Promise. The result is misery. He succeeds in his plan, Ishmael is born; but better were it for Abraham and the world had he never been born! It is disastrous when the self-willed plans of the Christian succeed."*[4]

THE VOICE OF SARAH

"And Sarai said unto Abram, Behold now, the LORD has restrained me from bearing: I pray you, go in unto my maid; it may be that I may obtain children by her. And Abram hearkened to the voice of Sarai" (Gen. 16:2).

Sarah saying, *"The LORD has restrained me from bearing,"* proclaims the usual impatience of unbelief. Abraham should have treated it accordingly and waited patiently on the Lord for the accomplishment of His Gracious Promise. However, we have a problem here, and the problem is the flesh.

The poor heart prefers anything to the attitude of waiting. Concerning this, Mackintosh said:

"It will turn to any expedient, any scheme, any resource, rather than be kept in that posture. It is one thing to believe a promise at the first, and quite another trying to wait quietly for the accomplishment thereof."[5]

How different it would have been had Sarah said, *"Nature has failed me, but God is my resource."*

GOD'S INSTRUMENT

Though we may receive the Revelation, most of the time, the Lord gives very little information concerning His Leading. He expects us to ardently seek His Face as it regards direction. To be sure, He has planned everything, even down to the minute detail, but, most of the time, we don't know the details.

All of this is meant to teach us trust and Faith. It, as well, is meant to teach us patience.

Hagar was not God's Instrument for the accomplishment of His Promise to Abraham. God had promised a son, but He had not said that the son would be Hagar's. To be sure, their foray into that direction would only seek to multiply their sorrow. In fact, Abraham never asked the Lord about that which Sarah suggested. Surely, Abraham's mission was of such magnitude that we are still suffering the results of that ill-fated direction. In fact, the horror of September 11, 2001, is a direct result of Abraham's lack of faith, i.e., *"sin."*

TEN YEARS IN THE LAND OF CANAAN

"And Sarai Abram's wife took Hagar her maid the Egyptian, after Abram had dwelt ten years in the land of Canaan, and gave her to her husband Abram to be his wife" (Gen. 16:3).

Let the reader understand, as it regards the morality of this act, we find that marriage with one wife was the original Law of God (Gen. 2:24), and that when polygamy was introduced, it was coupled by the inspired narrator with violence and license (Gen. 4:19). Monogamy was the rule, as we see in the households of Noah, Terah, Isaac, and others; but many, like Esau and Jacob, allowed themselves a greater latitude. In so doing, their conduct falls below the level of Biblical morality, but everyone's actions are strongly influenced by the general views of the people among whom we live. In Abraham's case, it must be said in his defense that with so much depending on his having offspring, he took no steps to obtain another wife but remained content with the barren Sarah. When he did take Hagar, it was at his wife's request and for a reason, which seemed to them adequate, and even sacred.

Abraham and Sarah had now been some 10 years in Canaan. Even as we have previously stated, 10 being the number of completion, is it possible that, at this time, God had planned to bring forth Isaac? Perhaps it would be better to ask the question in another way:

"How much do our failures of Faith hinder in our lives that which God desires to do?" Or worse still, *"How much does it delay us with what He desires to do?"*

Of course, only God can answer that; however, I think we must come to the conclusion that failure certainly doesn't help. If it doesn't help, then, in some way, it definitely must hurt, and that is despite the fact that God is Gracious and Merciful!

And yet, we must always understand, God doesn't work from what might have been, from what should have been, or from what ought to have been, but rather from what is.

DESPISED!

"And he went in unto Hagar, and she conceived: and when she saw that she had conceived, her mistress was despised in her eyes" (Gen. 16:4).

Hagar now becomes pregnant. Noting, no doubt, the accolades which came her way, she begins to treat Sarah in a haughty manner. Having no grace of faith, she, as well, has no regard for Sarah and, thereby, oversteps her position. She looks down on Sarah with contempt because Sarah is barren and she wasn't.

IT IS YOUR FAULT . . .

"And Sarai said unto Abram, My wrong be upon you: I have given my maid unto your bosom; and when she saw that she had conceived, I was despised in her eyes: the LORD judge between

me and you" (Gen. 16:5).

Concerning all of this, Williams says:

"The Epistle to the Galatians declares that Sarah and Hagar represent the two principles of Law and Grace. Hagar represents Salvation by works; Sarah, Salvation by Faith. These principles are opposed to one another. Ishmael is born as the result of man's planning and energy. Isaac is born as the result of God's planning and energy. In the birth of Ishmael, God had nothing to do with him, and as regards the birth of Isaac man was dead. So it is today, Salvation by works entirely depends on man's capacity to produce them; Salvation by Faith upon God's ability to perform them.

"Under a Covenant of works, God stands still in order to see what man can do. Under the Covenant of Grace, man stands still to see what God has done. The two Covenants are opposed; it must be either Hagar or Sarah. If Hagar, God has nothing to do with it; if Sarah, man has nothing to do with it."[6]

SARAH AND HAGAR

"But Abram said unto Sarai, Behold, your maid is in your hand; do to her as it pleases you. And when Sarai dealt hardly with her, she fled from her face" (Gen. 16:6).

While the Scripture doesn't say exactly what Sarah did, whatever it was, it must have been severe. It is believed by some expositors that she actually had one of the servants to administer corporal punishment to her in the form of a whipping. Whatever it was, it was so severe that Hagar fled the premises.

THE ANGEL OF THE LORD

"And the Angel of the LORD found her by a fountain of water in the wilderness, by the fountain in the way to Shur" (Gen. 16:7).

Every evidence is that the *"Angel of the LORD"* mentioned here is none other than a preincarnate appearance of the Lord Jesus Christ.

Upon meeting Hagar, the Lord promises to bless her, tells her He has heard her affliction, and comforts her.

Regrettably, later on, she despised this Grace and sought to murder the divinely given child, which would later come, who would be Isaac.

She calls the name of the well where she met Jesus, the Lord, *"The well of living after seeing,"* for she said, *"Do I live after seeing God?"* She did live, but not as the other woman whom Jesus met at Jacob's well. These wells and these women are contrasted here.

QUESTIONS

"And He said, Hagar, Sarai's maid, from where did you come? and where will you go? And she said, I flee from the face of my mistress Sarai" (Gen. 16:8).

As we shall see, the Lord will not recognize her marriage to the Patriarch. He will remind her of her original position as a bondwoman, from which liberty was not to be obtained by running away, but rather by submission.

As we found with Lot, we find here, as well, that even with a servant girl, even one who did not necessarily believe the Covenant, inasmuch as she was in the household of Abraham, she would receive special attention by the Lord. In fact, He would save her life because had she continued on her journey, she would, no doubt, have perished in the wilderness.

SUBMISSION

"And the Angel of the LORD said unto her, Return to your mistress, and submit yourself under her hands" (Gen. 16:9).

In the case before us in this Chapter, it is evident that Hagar was not God's Instrument for the accomplishment of His Promise to Abraham. He had promised a son, no doubt, but He had not said that this son should be Hagar's. In point of fact, we find from the narrative that both Abraham and

Sarah *"multiplied their sorrow"* by having used Hagar to bear them a son as a recourse. Sarah's dignity was trampled down by an Egyptian bondwoman, and she found herself in the place of weakness and contempt.

The only true place of dignity and power is the place of felt weakness and dependence. There is no one so entirely independent of all around as the man who is really walking by Faith and waiting only on God. However, the moment a Child of God makes himself a debtor to nature or to the world, he loses his dignity and will speedily be made to feel his loss. It is no easy task to estimate the loss sustained by diverging, in the smallest measure, from the path of Faith. And now, Sarah feels that loss.

THE BONDWOMAN

However, *"the bondwoman"* cannot be eliminated by hard treatment. When we make mistakes, as Sarah did, and find ourselves called upon to encounter the results thereof, we cannot counteract those results by carrying ourselves with a high hand. We frequently try this method, but we're sure to make matters worse thereby.

If we have done wrong, we should humble ourselves, confess the wrong, and wait on God for Deliverance, but Sarah didn't do that. So, far from waiting on God for Deliverance, she seeks to deliver herself in her own way. However, it will always be found that every effort which we make to rectify our errors, previous to the full confession thereof, only tends to render our paths more difficult. Thus, Hagar had to return and give birth to her son, the son which proved to be not the Child of Promise at all, but a very great trial to Abraham and his house, even as we shall see.

Grace forgives the sin and restores the soul, but that which is sown must be reaped. Abraham and Sarah had to endure the presence of the bondwoman and her son for a number of years and then see the separation brought about in God's Way.

There is a peculiar blessedness in leaving ourselves in God's Hands. Had Abraham and Sarah done so on the present occasion, they would never have been troubled with the presence of the bondwoman and her son. However, having made themselves debtors to nature, they had to endure the consequences, and so do we!

DID HAGAR TRULY SUBMIT?

The Lord told Hagar to go back and to submit herself totally and fully to Sarah. While she did this somewhat, she did not fully obey. As we shall see, she submitted outwardly but never really submitted from her heart.

THE SEED

"And the Angel of the LORD said unto her, I will multiply your seed exceedingly, that it shall not be numbered for multitude" (Gen. 16:10).

Looking at Hagar, she is like so many in the modern church. She is in the Church, i.e., *"the Covenant,"* but actually never really a part of it. She never recognized Isaac as the Promised Seed and, in fact, actually plotted the murder of Isaac (Gal. 4:29). So, she represents all who will seek to obtain the Promise *"after the flesh,"* which refers to doing so other than by the Cross (Gal. 4:23-25).

In the natural, the Arab people of this particular time (2012) number well over 100 million. In the spiritual sense, the church is filled with these *"workers of the flesh,"* so much so that it cannot be *"numbered for multitude."*

Isaac represents the Cross while Ishmael represents the flesh. These two directions are ever before the Church. One or the other must be chosen. Whichever one is chosen, the other one must be cast out. Regrettably and sadly, the far greater majority of the modern church has cast out the *"Cross"* in favor of the *"flesh."* The true way is to cast out the bondwoman and her son. In fact, if the *"Promise"* is to be obtained (all that Jesus did for us at the Cross), they must be cast out (Gal. 4:30).

ISHMAEL

"And the Angel of the LORD said unto her, Behold, you are with child, and shall bear a son, and shall call his name Ishmael; because the LORD has heard your affliction" (Gen. 16:11).

The fault of her situation did not belong with Hagar, but rather with Abraham and Sarah. However, she ultimately forfeited what the Lord would have done for her by opposing His Plan, which was Isaac.

The Lord does not condone mistreatment, irrespective as to who does it or to whom it is done. While Hagar definitely had not treated Sarah right after it was found that she had conceived, still, this gave Sarah no right to mistreat this servant girl. As Believers, we do not return kind for kind regarding evil.

The Lord tells Hagar to name the son that will be born to her *"Ishmael."* The name means, *"God hears,"* but it has nothing to do with Ishmael, but rather the plight of Hagar.

PERSONALITY

"And he will be a wild man; his hand will be against every man, and every man's hand against him; and he shall dwell in the presence of all his brethren" (Gen. 16:12).

These predictions describe the Arab people perfectly. They cannot get along with anyone in the world, and they cannot even get along among themselves.

At the present time, they have tried to unite regarding the destruction of Israel. However, despite the fact that they are about 25 or 30 times larger than Israel regarding population, they have failed to make any inroads in regards to this effort. It is mostly because they cannot agree among themselves. Ishmael opposed the Cross in his efforts to kill Isaac, and his descendants have continued in the same vein. So, he dwells in the presence of all his brethren (Israel) but does not subdue them and, in fact, never will subdue them.

SARAH

"And God said unto Abraham, As for Sarai your wife, you shall not call her name Sarai, but Sarah shall her name be" (Gen. 17:15).

The name *"Sarai"* means, *"My princess,"* referring to the fact that she was Abraham's princess alone.

"Sarah" simply means, *"Princess."* The idea is, whereas she was formerly Abraham's princess only, she will now be recognized as a princess generally and, in fact, as the *"mother of the Church."* Actually, she is now to be a *"Princess to the Lord."*

If it is to be noticed, the letter *"H"* is taken from the name *"JeHovaH,"* as in the change of Abram into Abraham, with the name Sarai being changed to Sarah.

The very fact of the changing of the name of Sarah spoke volumes to Abraham or, at least, certainly should have. Formerly, she belonged only to him, but now, in essence, she will belong to the entirety of the world. The very change of her name proclaimed the fact that she was now to be a great part of the Covenant.

As well, the change to a Hebrew form of the name, which the new name *"Sarah"* proclaims, shows a complete break with the past. She would never return to her birthplace, for she was to focus her life on the Promise of God.

As well, the change of her name proclaims a giant step taken toward the fulfillment of the *"Seed of the woman"* bruising the head of Satan. As we previously stated regarding the prediction given by God in Genesis 3:15, the Lord, in essence, was saying to Satan, *"You have used the woman to pull down My Choice Creation, and I will use a woman to lift that Creation back to its original status."* All of this portrays the fact that God has so much more for us than our own pitiful efforts can provide. That's the reason that Salvation must be all of God and none at all of man.

THE COVENANT

"And I will bless her, and give you a son also of her: yes, I will bless her, and she will be a mother of nations; kings of people shall be of her" (Gen. 17:16).

This is the first time in all of God's Dealings with Abraham that He had mentioned the fact that the promised son would be of Sarah and, one might say, *"Sarah's own son."* In effect, the Promise regarding Sarah was very similar to that regarding Abraham, at least, as it pertains to entire nations proceeding from her.

The word *"bless"* refers to all the things that God can do, which means that He can do all things, but, more particularly, it refers to the culmination of all Blessing, Who is the Lord Jesus Christ.

The Covenant of Circumcision was to be in force until the Messiah would come. Inasmuch as this rite was carried out on the male member and not on women, for they were exempt, it shows us several things.

It shows us that man was responsible for the Fall inasmuch as the seed of procreation is in him. As well, the foreskin of the male member being removed by circumcision was to be a reminder to the people of Israel of original sin, which is hereditary, one might say, and remains in us till we die. Even though Eve was tempted and actually fell first, due to the fact that the seed was alone in the man and not in the woman, we find that women were exempted by God from circumcision. Thus, God foreshadowed in the Circumcision rite the whole theology of Redemption, namely, both sin and Grace.

It reminded the Jews of the fact that all men by nature are children of wrath on account of hereditary sin (Eph. 2:1-3). It also reminded them of Grace, for it indicated the Birth of Christ from a virgin. He was to abrogate Circumcision and save all men from sin and death, and do so by His Own Death.

LAUGHTER

"Then Abraham fell upon his face, and laughed, and said in his heart, Shall a child be born unto him who is an hundred years old? and shall Sarah, who is ninety years old, bear?" (Gen. 17:17).

Concerning that which is recorded in this Verse, Ellicott says, *"The Jewish interpreters regarded Abraham's laugh as one of joy, and Sarah's as one of unbelief (Gen. 18:12). Actually, that seems to be the case, and our Lord confirmed the view that joy was uppermost in Abraham's heart, as it regards these things (Jn. 8:56)."*[7]

These questions asked by Abraham were not questions of unbelief or derision. They were really an exclamation of holy wonder. What reason declared impossible was possible to Faith. Paul said of him:

"He considered not the deadness of Sarah's womb" (Rom. 4:19).

When we read these illustrations, it should make us ashamed of ourselves. If Abraham felt such joy and expressed it accordingly as it regarded a Promise, for that's all he had then, how much more should we rejoice presently when, in fact, that Promise has totally and completely been realized in the Lord Jesus Christ?

This Salvation is that which can be felt. It is that which is experienced not only in conduct, but also in joy, which fills the soul to overflowing, and in doing so, invigorates the spirit. I am persuaded that most stress, worry, anxiety, fear, and all of their attendant woes can be throttled completely by Believers exhibiting expressions of Faith, for this is exactly what Abraham did. So, what am I saying?

FAITH REJOICES

I'm saying that Faith rejoiced and that Faith always rejoices. When we realize what Jesus has done for us at the Cross, that His Work is not merely a Promised Work but a Finished

Work, then we must shout for joy. How can we do less, considering this great Salvation that fills our hearts? If Abraham laughed in wonder and exclamation, which, in essence, was a laugh of victory, how can we as Believers presently do less!

I feel that these Passages completely abrogate a cold, lifeless, even one might say, a cold storage faith. A faith that never rejoices, never marvels, and never exclaims with joy, I seriously doubt to actually be Faith. If it's true Faith, which refers to Christ and what Christ has done for us at the Cross, then there must be a joy which accompanies such Faith. It must be that which occasions us to marvel constantly, even as did Abraham.

Again, I emphasize the fact that he had only the Promise while we now have the possession.

THE COVENANT

"And God said, Sarah your wife shall bear you a son indeed; and you shall call his name Isaac: and I will establish My Covenant with him for an Everlasting Covenant, and with his seed after him" (Gen. 17:19).

Concerning this *"Everlasting Covenant,"* Williams says:

"The great subject of this Chapter is the expansion of the Covenant already revealed in Chapters 12 and 15. The new features introduced are the purposes of God as it regards Israel and the Gentiles, pertaining to Salvation. Both of the countless multitudes of redeemed men spring from Abraham as the first vessel of promise and the root of all who should after him believe unto life everlasting.

"At the same time this Chapter sets out the two principles upon which these Divine purposes are founded. These principles are 'death' and 'Grace.' The sign of Circumcision expressed the one, the Divine Promise the other.

"Man must ever have a sentence of death written upon his death, which Circumcision did, and Grace brings to this dead man life and ever-enduring riches. The sign of Circumcision, therefore, declared man to be absolutely without moral value,

and justly, as a sinner, sentenced to death. Grace which comes in the Covenant, takes up Abraham who was by nature an idolater, declares him to be a righteous man because he believed the Testimony of God, and makes him the root out of which Israel and the redeemed nations shall proceed."[8]

So, we have Circumcision, which points to man's sin, and the Covenant, which points to Christ, Who will lift man out of his sin, and will do so by the Cross. The Covenant must of necessity include the Cross, even as Genesis 3:15 proclaims.

THE EVERLASTING COVENANT

As we have previously stated, this Covenant, which God established with Abraham, pointed to Christ and what Christ would do to redeem humanity; therefore, it could be called an *"Everlasting Covenant"* (Heb. 13:20).

This *"Everlasting Covenant"* is to be established with Isaac and not with Ishmael.

The world of Islam claims the very opposite, that Ishmael was the promised seed and, therefore, the heir of the Covenant. As well, they claim that Christ is not the fulfillment of the Covenant, but rather Muhammad.

Of course, only a cursory examination of the Koran will prove the fallacy of such claims. In attempting to relate Bible illustrations, Muhammad puts people in the wrong generations, which are glaring mistakes. This also is glaring evidence that what he proposed to be Divine is, in fact, not inspired at all, but rather the prattle of an unregenerate man. The Holy Spirit doesn't make mistakes, and Muhammad's futile attempts to rewrite history proclaimed the utter foolishness of the claims of inspiration.

At the present time (2012), in America's so-called fight against terrorism, our diplomats are demanding that Israel come to an agreement with the Palestinians.

The irony of all of this is, it doesn't take a seasoned diplomat to instantly recognize the futility of such an effort. How can agreements be made with people who respect agreements not at all? As well, how can agreements be made with those who have sworn your destruction? To be sure, the Palestinians aren't attempting to have a *"piece"* of Israel, which they may call their homeland, but rather they want every Jew dead and the entirety of the land of Israel to be claimed as their own. So, again I ask the question, *"How can agreements be made with a mindset of that nature?"*

No, even as the Word of God broadly proclaims, the Covenant is with Isaac and not with Ishmael. This means that the land of Israel belongs to the Jews and to no one else. In fact, it belongs to God. This means that even Israel doesn't have the right to give great portions of it to the Palestinians or anyone else, for that matter.

To be frank, the Country of Jordan, which is several times larger than Israel, has plenty of room for the Palestinians. In fact, the Country of Jordan was originally carved out by the British to be a homeland for the Palestinians. However, the problem is spiritual and not material, which means that it's not really the land area in question here, but rather the Word of God.

THE BLESSING OF ISHMAEL

"And as for Ishmael, I have heard you: Behold, I have blessed him, and will make him fruitful, and will multiply him exceedingly; twelve princes shall he beget, and I will make him a great nation" (Gen. 17:20).

The Lord, of course, kept this Promise as it regards Ishmael (Gen. 25:13-16). He has multiplied exceedingly, and the Blessing comes down even unto this hour.

However, the Blessing pronounced here is certainly not because of Ishmael, but rather because of Abraham, and Abraham alone. The Blessing should have caused the Arabs to serve God as it regards the Bible; however, most of them have completely gone astray, following the Koran. It is a web of deceit and will lead all of its followers to eternal perdition.

THE COVENANT AND ISAAC

"But My Covenant will I establish with Isaac, which Sarah shall bear unto you at this set time in the next year" (Gen. 17:21).

In this one Verse, the Lord says several things:

• For the third time in this dialogue with Abraham, the Lord promised that Sarah would bear a son, and that, despite her age.

• Furthermore, this child would be born within the next year.

• Even though He would bless Ishmael, it was with Isaac that the Covenant would be established.

COMMUNION

"And He (God) *left off talking with him, and God went up from Abraham"* (Gen. 17:22).

Communion with God is the most profitable exercise there is. Paul taught us this in his Epistle to the Ephesians. He said:

"Now unto Him Who is able to do exceeding abundantly above all that we ask or think, according to the power that works in us,

"Unto Him be Glory in the Church by Christ Jesus throughout all ages, world without end. Amen" (Eph. 3:20-21).

It has been said that God's Proper Name is the *"Hearer of Prayers,"* but the problem is, most of the time, we do not know what we ask (Mat. 20:22).

Martin Luther said concerning this:

"Our hearts are too weak to understand the great things which God desires to give us. We worry about the time, place, and means for God to help us. We make our goals too narrow and small, for we must always wrestle with unbelief in our hearts."

He went on to say, *"We poor weak persons can never really understand the exceeding Grace and Mercy of God. We*

have a God Who wants to give us far more than we ask or think.
Therefore since we do not know how and what to ask, the Holy
Spirit intercedes for us with groanings which cannot be uttered
(Rom. 8:26)."

And then he said, *"I write this in order that no one may de-*
spair on account of his unworthiness, or also on account of the
high majesty of God Whom we address in our prayers. Nothing
is too great for Him for which we pray, even if we ourselves do
not understand the things for which we ask. Abraham received
far more than he requested, and in this he left us an example
that we should not discontinue our pleadings before the Lord,
but surely believe that they will never be without fruit or ben-
efit. God regards the heart and knows the groanings in us which
we cannot utter, indeed, which even we ourselves cannot un-
derstand, for we are like the little children who stammer their
prayers before going to sleep."

SARAH

"And Abraham hastened into the tent unto Sarah, and said,
Make ready quickly three measures of fine meal, knead it, and
make cakes upon the hearth" (Gen. 18:6).

The *"fine meal"* mentioned here should have been translated, *"Fine flour,"* for that's actually what it says in the
Hebrew.

Flour was used in the Thank Offering (Meat Offering),
and was meant to represent the Perfection of our Incarnate
Lord (Lev. 2:1). So, even though Abraham little recognized
the situation, it was all planned by the Holy Spirit.

While we can certainly pass off this incident as merely an
action of hospitality, I think to do so would belittle the Action
of the Holy Spirit. Of course, the true reason for the Visit of
our Lord and the two Holy Visitors was to announce the conception that Sarah would experience and, as well, the destruction of Sodom and Gomorrah, which also would affect Lot, all
of which are obvious. At the same time, we must come to the

conclusion that everything done by the Lord is never without Spiritual significance. There is a lesson in every action, move, and word.

While we must not take flights of fancy with that which is done, at the same time, we must not discount that which is done, but rather do our very best to ascertain what the Holy Spirit is saying to us and learn thereby.

WHERE IS SARAH?

"And They said unto him, Where is Sarah your wife? And he said, Behold, in the tent" (Gen. 18:9).

The question, *"Where is Sarah your wife?"* proclaims the Omniscience of the Lord. As there is no evidence that she had previously revealed herself, the Lord could have known her name only by the fact that He knows all things.

It would seem from the following conversation that Abraham had not revealed to Sarah this which the Lord had told him some days, or perhaps, some weeks earlier about her having a son (Gen. 17:16). If, in fact, he didn't tell her, which it seems he didn't, why not?

While there is no evidence that Abraham doubted the Lord, there is evidence that possibly he doubted himself. Had he heard correctly? Did the Lord really tell him this, or did he fabricate it in his own mind?

Sometimes we can want something so badly that we can imagine God telling us all types of things when, in reality, He hasn't.

As well, of all people, Abraham knew the impossibility of Sarah having a child, especially considering that she was now 90 years of age, and he was 100 (Gen. 17:17).

Irrespective as to what Abraham thought, the Lord, it seems, desired at this time that Sarah would also know, and that the information would not be withheld from her. He knew she was listening, so He then tells Abraham what is shortly to come to pass.

A SON

"And He said, I will certainly return unto you according to the time of life; and, lo, Sarah your wife shall have a son. And Sarah heard it in the tent door, which was behind him" (Gen. 18:10).

It is evident that this statement concerning *"returning . . . according to the time of life,"* denotes some fixed period. Jewish tradition says that it means, *"According to this time next year."*

The statement is emphatic, *"Sarah your wife shall have a son."* As we've already stated, Sarah is now 90 years old and Abraham 100. Why did God wait this long?

God's Timing is just as important as His Actions. Among other things, and probably the most important, all hope of the flesh had to die before this Miracle could be brought about. This should be a great lesson for all of us.

What do we mean by *"all hope of the flesh"* dying?

When Abraham and Sarah finally came to the place that they knew and understood that they could not bring about this great Promise of God by their own machinations, despite how hard they might try, then all hope of the flesh was gone. In other words, they could not within themselves do this thing. So, when they finally ceased from their own actions, God then would perform a Work of the Spirit; then and only then would Sarah conceive.

IMPOSSIBLE!

"Now Abraham and Sarah were old and well stricken in age; and it ceased to be with Sarah after the manner of women" (Gen. 18:11).

At this particular juncture, the Holy Spirit is quick to emphasize the point that, in the natural, it was impossible for Sarah to conceive. As well, Abraham was also *"well stricken in age."*

As Believers, we must not look at the impossibilities, at least, things which are impossible to us. We must look to God, with Whom nothing is impossible. Jesus plainly said concerning so-called impossibilities:

". . . with God all things are possible" (Mat. 19:26).

As well, we should understand that God is no respecter of persons, and that He is the Same yesterday, today, and forever.

Now, that doesn't mean that God will give children to women who are 90 years old and their husbands who are 100. If it's God's Will for such to be, then it will be; however, God never functions against His Will and Wisdom.

The Will of God for our lives is of extreme importance, as all of us should understand. True Faith will never circumvent that will, nor will it even desire anything that's not according to God's Will. People, who think they can bring anything into being by using some little formula of Faith, are in for a rude awakening. God will never allow His Word to be used against Himself. In fact, if man could do that, he would make himself God, and do so in short order. That's been the great problem with mankind from the beginning and continues to be the great problem in the church. Men twist and pervert the Word of God, attempting to make it their servant, when God will never allow such things. In fact, the Word of God and the Will of God go hand in hand, and all of it is tied to the Finished Work of Christ on the Cross.

UNBELIEF

"Therefore Sarah laughed within herself, saying, After I am waxed old shall I have pleasure, my lord being old also?" (Gen. 18:12)

Upon the announcement that Sarah would have a son, even at her advanced age, the Scripture says that Abraham laughed (Gen. 17:17). However, his laugh was the laughter of Faith, while the laughter of Sarah is the laughter of unbelief. It is incredulous to her that she could have a child, being 90 years old, or that Abraham could father a child, being 100 years old. While her unbelief did not stop the process, it did solicit a mild rebuke from the Lord, even as we shall see.

There are always two ways of receiving God's Promises; the one of which secures but the other of which imperils their fulfillment (Mk. 9:23; 11:23).

As we shall see, the Lord will seek to pull Sarah from unbelief to Faith, and He will do so in three different ways:

1. He will proclaim the fact that the thing promised is not beyond the Resources of Jehovah to accomplish.

2. He will do so, as well, by a further certification of the event.

3. He will also do so by an impressive display of Miraculous Power, first, in searching Sarah's heart, and second, in arresting Sarah's conscience.

RESPONSE

"And the LORD said unto Abraham, Wherefore did Sarah laugh, saying, Shall I for sure bear a child, which am old?" (Gen. 18:13)

We should note several things from this particular Passage.

As should be obvious, God knows all things. He knows the reaction of our spirit, and He knows the things which we say. So, we should be very careful what we say and what we do as it regards the Lord and His Work.

MIRACLES

"Is anything too hard for the LORD? At the time appointed I will return unto you, according to the time of life, and Sarah shall have a son" (Gen. 18:14).

In Verse 13, one of the Divine Visitors announces himself as *"Lord,"* which, in effect, proclaims this as a Preincarnate Appearance of Christ. He now remonstrates in Verse 14 that nothing is too hard for the Lord. The actual Hebrew rendering is, *"Is anything too wonderful for Jehovah?"*

I think the way the phrase is translated, as it regards *"too hard,"* leaves a wrong impression. The truth is, as it regards Miracles, there is nothing even hard for the Lord, much less too hard! The idea, as presented here in the English version, seems to be that while God can do such a thing, it would be difficult. The actual rendering is that not only can He do whatever is necessary, but, as well, it's not even hard for Him to accomplish the task. In other words, He does whatever is needed with ease.

TIME APPOINTED

The words, *"Time appointed,"* tell us that God had long since appointed a time for Sarah to have a child. It had been appointed, to be frank, even before Sarah was born (I Pet. 1:18-20).

We are not teaching predestination here as it regards the wills of individuals; we are rather teaching the Foreknowledge of God. God being Omniscient, that is, all-knowing, has the capacity and, in fact, does know the past, the present, and the future. This doesn't mean that He predestines people to act in certain ways, but that, as stated, through foreknowledge, He can know what they will do.

For instance, He knew that Abraham and Sarah would accept Him as Lord and Saviour. He also knew that even though they would stumble in their efforts, they wouldn't stumble according to their Faith. In other words, despite the lapses as recorded here, they would always respond favorably to the Lord with Faith renewed. Therefore, all along, it had been appointed that Sarah would ultimately have a son, irrespective of circumstances, events, her advanced age, or Abraham's advanced age. What had been appointed, God was able to carry it through.

Let me quickly say to the reader that the Lord has appointed certain things for you also. You must continue to believe and not allow yourself to be pulled aside by circumstances and hindrances. Despite the occasional setback, you must continue to believe. Remember, *"It is appointed,"* which means it's going to happen.

REBUKE

"Then Sarah denied, saying, I did not laugh; for she was afraid. And He said, No; but you did laugh" (Gen. 18:15).

Unbelief will never stop at skepticism but will always degenerate into works of the flesh, such as *"lying."*

When confronted, Sarah denied that she had laughed. She now stands in the Presence of Jehovah, and the Scripture says, *"She was afraid."*

Unbelief always tenders fear. We need never fear God in a negative way when we are functioning in Faith. It is always when we are functioning in unbelief that such fear is brought about.

The Lord gently rebuked her by simply saying, *"But you did laugh."*

The narrative ends there, at least, as it regards Sarah; however, it is positive that the rebuke had its intended result. She was smitten in her conscience, knowing that she had doubted God, and was now brought back to a place of Faith.

How many times does the Lord gently rebuke us? Our sin, even as that of Sarah, is far more serious than we realize; but, in Grace, the Lord gently sets us straight and doesn't bring Judgment on us. When we look at Sarah and evaluate her actions here, we should do so with the thought in mind that we ourselves have been in the same position, possibly many times. However, as with Sarah, the Lord only gently rebuked us and, thereby, did not bring upon us the Judgment which we deserved.

DECEPTION

"And Abraham journeyed from thence toward the south country, and dwelled between Kadesh and Shur, and sojourned in Gerar.

"And Abraham said of Sarah his wife, She is my sister: and Abimelech king of Gerar sent, and took Sarah" (Gen. 20:1-2).

This is the same sin that Abraham had committed in Egypt. Exactly as Lot, he left the path of Faith, thereby, trusting in his own ingenuity, which always gets us into trouble. Because it's so important, please allow me to say again what we've said many paragraphs back.

Every sin is always a departure from Faith. Faith in Christ and Him Crucified is the only answer to the sin problem, as it is to every problem. The trouble is, as it regards sin, the church too often deals with symptoms instead of the cause. In fact, the church little knows the cause, so it manufactures its own causes.

One of the primary examples is, *"If we sin,"* so the church says, *"we do so because that's what we want to do."* While sin definitely is a matter of choice, it is not a choice as one thinks.

The real choice is, do we follow the Ways of the Lord, which is the Cross of Christ, or do we follow other ways?

INTERVENTION

"But God came to Abimelech in a dream by night, and said to him, Behold, you are but a dead man, for the woman which you have taken; for she is a man's wife" (Gen. 20:3).

Three things are said here:

1. God revealed Himself to Abimelech in a dream.

2. What the Lord said to Abimelech greatly scared him. In essence, He said, *"If you touch Sarah, you can consider yourself a dead man."*

3. If God had not intervened, Abraham's sin would have been disastrous. If it is to be noticed, Sarah is again referred to by the Holy Spirit as Abraham's wife. The *"sister"* thing was mentioned only by Abraham and not by the Lord. The truth is, Sarah was Abraham's half-sister, both of them having the same father but not the same mother.

It had been some 20 years since the episode in Egypt, but an old sin is an easy sin.

ABIMELECH

"But Abimelech had not come near her: and he said, LORD,

will You slay also a righteous nation?" (Gen. 20:4).

The Lord had intervened with a dream before Abimelech had a chance to come near Sarah.

The Philistine prince, already knowing of the destruction of Sodom and Gomorrah, fears that he and his people are in for the same destruction unless the Lord is pacified quickly.

He refers to God as, *"LORD,"* in effect, referring to Him as Deity. The question begs to be asked, *"Why then would he not serve God?"* considering the Power that the Lord had just unleashed as it regards the destruction of the cities of the plain. They were close to Philistine territory, to say the least, and God appeared, in a sense, to this Philistine prince in a dream. Surely that was enough evidence to prove to this man that Jehovah was the True God.

The same question can be asked presently of the untold millions in this world who know about God, but yet, refuse to serve Him. However, the major problem with most who live in a so-called Christian nation is that they actually think they are serving Him when, in reality, they've never been Born-Again. Deception is an awful thing, and it has many ways in which to plague the human race. Once again, we come back to Faith.

Millions have Faith in God, but it's in the wrong kind of way. True Faith is always anchored in Jesus Christ and Him Crucified. Otherwise, while it may be very religious, it is not acceptable to God. Regrettably, Faith in Christ and His Cross is not acceptable to much of the world, and even not much of the church.

CLEAN HANDS

"Said he not unto me, She is my sister? and she, even she herself said, He is my brother: in the integrity of my heart and innocency of my hands have I done this" (Gen. 20:5).

This heathen prince pleads his innocence before God, at least, as far as the matter of Sarah is concerned. Abraham claimed that Sarah was his sister, and Sarah backed up what he had said by claiming that Abraham was her brother. So, on this basis, Abimelech took her into his harem.

In this matter, the man was innocent. It was Abraham, and Sarah, as well, who had done wrong.

Forgetting God's Ability to protect his life, Abraham had resorted to the same stratagem which he had adopted in Egypt years before. Here we have the father of the faithful carried away by taking his eye off God. He is no longer a man of Faith, but rather of craftiness and deception.

How true it is that we are only strong as we cling to God in the sense of our perfect weakness. So long as we are in the path of His Appointment, nothing can harm us. Had Abraham simply leaned on God, the men of Gerar would not have meddled with him; and it was his privilege to have vindicated God's Faithfulness in the midst of the most appalling difficulties. Thus, too, he would have maintained his own dignity as a man of Faith.

DISHONORING GOD

Concerning this, Mackintosh said:

"It is often a source of sorrow to the heart to mark how the Children of God dishonor Him, and, as a consequence, lower ourselves before the world by losing the sense of His sufficiency for every emergency. So long as we live in the realization of the Truth that all our hope is in God, so long shall we be above the world in every shape and form. There is nothing so elevating to the whole moral being as Faith: it carries one entirely beyond the reach of this world's thoughts; for how can those of the world, or even worldly-minded Christians, understand the life of Faith? Impossible! The springs on which it draws lie far away beyond their comprehension. They live on the surface of present things. So long as they can see what they deem a proper foundation of hope and confidence, so long they are hopeful and confident; but the idea of resting solely on the promise of an unseen God, they understand not.

"But the man of Faith is calm in the midst of scenes in which nature can do nothing. In fact, none but those who know God can ever reprove the actings of Faith; for none but they really understand the solid and truly reasonable ground of such actions."

PROTECTION

"And God said unto him in a dream, Yes, I know that you did this in the integrity of your heart; for I also withheld you from sinning against Me: therefore suffered I you not to touch her" (Gen. 20:6).

Not only does Abimelech assert his position, but the Lord admits the plea. And yet, this Philistine king indulges in polygamy and claims the right of taking the female relatives of anyone passing through his territory to add them to his harem exactly as Egypt.

However, his words mean no more than that he was not consciously violating any of his own rules of morality and, thus, illustrate the Gospel principle that men will be punished not by an absolute decree, but equitably, according to their knowledge (Lk. 12:47-48).

Abimelech was doing wrong and was suffering punishment, but the punishment was remedial for his advancement in right-knowing and right-doing. It is thus by means of Revelation that men have attained to a proper understanding of the moral Law. Though often called, *"the Law of Nature,"* yet, nature does not give it but only acknowledges it when given.

The inner Light, in fact, is but a faint and inconstant glimmering, for Christ Alone is the True Light; for only by Him does the Law of Nature become a clear rule for human guidance (Mat. 6:23; Jn. 1:9; Rom. 2:14-15).

A PROPHET

"Now therefore restore the man his wife; for he is a Prophet, and he shall pray for you, and you shall live: and if you restore

her not, know that you shall surely die, you, and all who are yours" (Gen. 20:7).

It should be noticed in this Text that even though Abraham has done wrong, very wrong, his position as a Prophet had not been diminished or, in fact, any part of his Calling.

In the history of God's People, whether we look at them as a whole or as individuals, we are often struck with the amazing difference between what we are in God's View and what we are in the view of the world. God sees His People in Christ. He looks at us through Christ hence, He sees us *"without spot or wrinkle or any such thing."* We are as Christ is before God. We are perfected forever, as to our *"standing"* in Christ.

However, the truth is, in ourselves, we are poor, feeble, imperfect, stumbling, and inconsistent creatures. It is what we are in ourselves, and that alone, that the world takes knowledge of; therefore, that is the reason the difference seems so great between the Divine and the human estimate. Thus, when Balak seeks to curse the seed of Abraham, Jehovah's word is, *"I have not beheld iniquity in Jacob, neither have I seen perverseness in Israel."*

He then said, *"How goodly are your tents, O Jacob, and your tabernacles, O Israel"* (Num. 23:21; 24:5).

The outward observance was very obvious that, in the natural, Israel did not measure up to these things. However, that's the way God saw them simply because He looked at them through Christ. He does the same with all Believers, again, because of Christ.

WHEN WE CEASE TO BE BIBLICAL . . .

According to many modern Pentecostal denominations, due to his failure, Abraham would have had to cease all ministry for two years, etc. Now, while such foolishness may sound satisfactory to the carnal ear, such thinking and action are actually an abomination with God. It belittles the Sacrifice of Christ, actually saying that what Jesus did at the Cross is not enough.

When we cease to be Biblical, we become foolish, very foolish!

At the same time, it should be understood that this in no way means that God condones sin in any fashion. It's just that sin and wrongdoing are so evil and so bad that only Christ and what He did at the Cross can cleanse the stain. Man's foolish efforts at punishment, or his own ways and means of atonement, are woefully insufficient. Again, I emphasize the fact that when we try to add something to the shed Blood of Christ, we greatly insult the Lord and His Finished Work.

Abraham was a Prophet before the problem, he was a Prophet during the problem, and he was a Prophet after the problem. No, this does not condone the problem, and, in fact, great hurt always accompanies sin, as should be obvious. However, as we've already stated, sin is so awful, so terrible, and so destructive that it took the Cross to address this thing. If we try to use other means or methods to address sin other than the Cross, we sin greatly.

ABIMELECH AND ABRAHAM

"Then Abimelech called Abraham, and said unto him, What have you done unto us? and what have I offended you, that you have brought on me and on my kingdom a great sin? you have done deeds unto me that ought not to be done" (Gen. 20:9).

We find here that the questions which Abimelech posed to Abraham were very similar to those posed by Pharaoh concerning the same sin (Gen. 12:18).

As Abimelech spoke to Abraham, his words were unquestionably designed to convey a severe reproach, which it did.

It seems that Abimelech's conversation stems more so from fear and frustration than anything else.

It is interesting that this heathen king understood the word *"sin,"* which means that he had some knowledge of God, which was greatly increased after the dream he had.

As well, it is interesting that he really did not accuse

Abraham of sin, but rather of Abraham putting him in a position to where he might have sinned, and sinned greatly. This would have affected the entirety of his kingdom. This is what he gathered from what the Lord told him in the dream, and he was right about the matter. When he spoke about what Abraham had done, he merely said, *"You have done deeds unto me that ought not to be done."*

All of this shows that he was greatly afraid of Abraham. To be frank, he conducted himself exactly as he should have. God rewarded him by healing him and all of his household of the plague, which had caused them great problems.

FEAR

"And Abraham said, Because I thought, Surely the fear of God is not in this place; and they will kill me for my wife's sake" (Gen. 20:11).

Abraham speaks of the fear of God, but the truth is, he was operating in human fear and not in faith. So, in his mind, he projected a scenario, which, in fact, would never have happened.

How so often we modern Believers operate in the same capacity. We operate from the spirit of fear, rather than the Power of Faith. Even at our highest, too often, we make our plans and then ask God to bless those plans. Such a position is that which God will not take. He blesses only the Plans which He Alone has instituted.

WIFE

"And yet indeed she is my sister; she is the daughter of my father, but not the daughter of my mother, and she became my wife" (Gen. 20:12).

If it is to be noticed, Abraham dwells on the fact that Sarah is indeed his half-sister while the Holy Spirit emphasizes the fact of the lady being his wife (Vss. 2-3, 7).

As stated, Sarah was apparently Abraham's half-sister,

being Terah's daughter by another wife. We gather from her calling her child Sarai—that is, princess—that Sarah's mother was not a concubine as Hagar, but belonged to the same noble race.

Many Christians, I'm afraid, think little of this which Abraham did in referring to Sarah as his sister; however, the motive was deception. Placing Sarah in this very compromising position was what Satan desired. If he could have impregnated her by Pharaoh or Abimelech, the Plan of God would have been seriously hindered, and may have delayed it for a long period of time. In fact, only the Intervention of God stopped this effort by the Evil One.

While we expect Satan to do everything within his power to hurt and hinder, he can only bring his plans to fruition if he can get a Saint of God, as Abraham, to cooperate with him. While Abraham did so unwittingly, still, the danger was the same. The real sin was Abraham leaving the path of Faith, as that is always the real sin with us presently.

SARAH

"And it came to pass, when God caused me to wander from my father's house, that I said unto her, This is your kindness which you shall show unto me; at every place where we shall come, say of me, He is my brother" (Gen. 20:13).

This deception, it seems, was formulated by Abraham at the very beginning of his sojourn, which, of course, was many years earlier. It is somewhat understandable at Abraham doing such a thing in his earliest days, even though it was wrong at that time, as well. It is harder to understand these many years later.

Abraham had seen God do great and mighty things for him. He and his small band, as the Lord led and guided them, had defeated powerful armies some years earlier, and did so without the loss of a single person, and, as well, recovered all that had been stolen and taken. This was a Miracle of unprecedented proportions.

Also, the Lord had appeared to him several times, even

had visited him, which was the time before the destruction of Sodom and Gomorrah. At this particular time, Abraham had been given almost the entirety of the Revelation concerning the birth of his Miracle child. He now knew that it would not be Ishmael, but rather the one who would be born to Sarah, even though she had not been able to conceive in all of these years.

So, why did he need to lie to Abimelech, especially, this late in the day, so to speak?

The answer to this is probably not as complicated as it first seems.

Faith is a daily exercise. In other words, we cannot live off of yesterday's Faith. This means that we must take up the Cross on a daily basis (Lk. 9:23). That being done, our Faith will continue to grow, otherwise, we can cause ourselves some problems, as did Abraham.

THE GIFTS

"And Abimelech took sheep, and oxen, and menservants, and womenservants, and gave them unto Abraham, and restored him Sarah his wife" (Gen. 20:14).

Once again, the Holy Spirit calls attention to the fact that Sarah was Abraham's wife.

Abimelech gave these things to Abraham simply because he recognized the Power of God. In other words, he didn't want to offend the Lord, so he would give His Prophet these gifts, which Abraham took.

His taking the gifts meant that he accepted the apology of Abimelech, and, at the same time, he was saying, *"I am sorry for my actions."* The giving of gifts and the receiving of gifts were very special in those days and held high meaning.

THE REPROOF

"And unto Sarah he said, Behold, I have given your brother a thousand pieces of silver: behold, he is to you a covering of the

eyes, unto all who are with you, and with all other: thus she was reproved" (Gen. 20:16).

Abimelech reproved Sarah by referring to Abraham as her *"brother,"* when, in reality, all knew that he was her husband. In effect, this heathen prince is telling her, *"Don't do that again. It doesn't become you."*

And then, by using the phrase, *"Behold, he* (Abraham) *is to you a covering of the eyes* (and), *unto all who are with you, and with all others,"* he is saying, *"If you openly claim Abraham as your husband, this, to be sure, will be protection enough for you."*

In other words, he was saying to her that God would protect the both of them. What a rebuke, and coming from a heathen, at that!

HEALING

"So Abraham prayed unto God: and God healed Abimelech, and his wife, and his maidservants; and they bore children" (Gen. 20:17).

Evidently, Abimelech related to Abraham the physical problem which had beset them. It seems to have affected himself and his wife, as well as all who were of his household, however many that may have been. It seems the women could not conceive, and we know from the next Verse that the Lord had instigated this.

We learn from these two Verses that not only can the Lord heal, but, as well, He can cause physical problems if, in fact, it serves His Purpose.

THE MALADY

"For the LORD had fast closed up all the wombs of the house of Abimelech, because of Sarah Abraham's wife" (Gen. 20:18).

The advent of sickness came about as a result of sin, which caused the Fall. In fact, Satan is the primary author of sickness and disease. In the beginning, God never intended for man to be so afflicted. In fact, had there not been the Fall, there would be no such thing as sickness or disease, or dying, for that matter. Man was originally created to live forever and would have done so by partaking of the Tree of Life if the Fall had not occurred.

Horton says that in the midst of all of this, *"God was faithfully watching over Sarah as the mother of the promised son, the one who would carry on the Blessings of God's Covenant."*[10]

THE MIRACLE

"And the LORD visited Sarah as He had said, and the LORD did unto Sarah as He had spoken" (Gen. 21:1).

This Chapter presents a new Creation. The Divine Title *"Elohim,"* and not *"Jehovah,"* appears throughout it, with the exception of Verses 1 and 33. In these Verses, God is *"Jehovah"* because it touches His Covenant Relationship as a Saviour.

The birth of Isaac had to do with the Incarnation of the Lord Jesus Christ. The first Adam had failed and failed miserably, which plunged the human race into an abyss of wickedness and evil, resulting in death. In fact, sin gave Satan a legal right to hold the entirety of humanity in captivity, which he did. The only hope for the human race, the fallen sons of the first Adam, was for God to become Man and, thereby, die on the Cross. He would be referred to as the *"Last Adam,"* because there would never be a need for another one, and the *"Second Man"* (I Cor. 15:45, 47).

Even though Jesus Christ was God and, in fact, had always been God and would always be God, still, as God, He could not redeem humanity, that is, if He was to be true to His Character. The simple reason was, for man to be redeemed, that is, if it was to be done lawfully, there would have to be a death, and God cannot die. So, God would become Man.

However, to become Man, a line would have to be established, actually beginning with Abraham. As a Prophet, Abraham was a Type of Christ. It would go through the lineage of David, who was king, and who would be a Type of Christ in his kingly posture. Hence, the genealogy of Christ opens in Matthew with the words, *"The Book of the generation of Jesus Christ, the Son of David, the Son of Abraham"* (Mat. 1:1).

So, this lineage had to begin in the Lord, and in the Lord only. That's the reason that all hope of the flesh had to die before Isaac could be born. When that hope, or the efforts of Abraham and Sarah, totally and completely died, the Lord would then miraculously give life to Sarah's dead womb, even though she was 90 years of age, and would empower Abraham, even though he was 100 years of age.

Here we have the accomplished Promise—the blessed fruit of patient waiting upon God. Let it be understood that none ever waited in vain.

"For Sarah conceived, and bore Abraham a son in his old age, at the set time of which God had spoken to him" (Gen. 21:2).

God's Word gave Abraham strength to beget, Sarah to conceive, and Isaac to be born. Three times repeated in two Verses, the clause points to the supernatural character of Isaac's birth.

The *"set time"* tells us that God's Timing is a part of His Will and is just as important as what is done. As we've already stated, the hope of the flesh had to totally and completely die in both Abraham and Sarah before this great Miracle could be brought about. It is the same with us presently.

The work that is carried out in our hearts and lives by the Lord must be totally of the Lord. The biggest problem that He has with Believers, believe it or not, is unbelief. We keep trying to do for ourselves, exactly as did Abraham and Sarah, what only God can do. In this Chapter, we will see exactly why it cannot be done by our own ingenuity and ability.

ISAAC

"And Abraham called the name of his son who was born unto him, whom Sarah bore to him, Isaac" (Gen. 21:3).

A year before, the Lord had told Abraham that Sarah

would bear a son and that his name should be called *"Isaac"* (Gen. 17:19). Isaac means *"laughter,"* and he was named this for a purpose and a reason.

As stated, Isaac was to be the progenitor and Type of the Messiah, Who would one day come. As such, He would bring Salvation to this hurting world, which would be the occasion of unspeakable joy.

"Laughter" speaks of blessing, increase, healing, life, well-being, and good things, hence, Jesus saying, *". . . I am come that they might have life, and that they might have it more abundantly"* (Jn. 10:10). As Isaac was a Type of Christ, it would not be wrong to say that one of the Names of Christ is *"Laughter."*

SARAH

"And Sarah said, God has made me to laugh, so that all who hear will laugh with me" (Gen. 21:6).

The birth of Isaac, as would be obvious, was an occasion of great joy. However, the joy expressed here was of far greater degree, to which we have already alluded, than the mere fact of what had happened, as wonderful as that was. All of this leads to Christ, and Christ brings an unparalleled joy to all who accept Him and, thereby, know Him.

Sarah had once laughed in unbelief. She now laughs in Faith, a laughter, incidentally, expressing joy which will never end.

THE MIRACLE OF FAITH

"And she said, Who would have said unto Abraham, that Sarah should have given children suck? for I have born him a son in his old age" (Gen. 21:7).

This is a poem and could very well have been a song.

The question that Sarah asks in her poem or song refers to the fact that what had happened was beyond human reasoning and most definitely beyond human ability. Who would have thought that Sarah, barren all of her life, at 90 years of age, would give birth to a baby boy? But that's exactly what happened because it was a Work of the Lord.

"And Sarah saw the son of Hagar the Egyptian, which she had born unto Abraham, mocking" (Gen. 21:9).

According to the time that Isaac was weaned, Ishmael would now be anywhere from 17 to 20 years old.

The *"mocking"* by Ishmael of Isaac is mentioned by Paul in Galatians 4:29. He uses the word, *"Persecuted,"* which carries the meaning in the Greek of a desire to murder. So, Ishmael, spurred by Hagar, wanted to murder Isaac.

The Jewish Targums say that Ishmael had planned Isaac's murder by stealth. He would feign that he was playing a game with the young child, would shoot arrows in the distance, and then have Isaac run and fetch them. The plan was for one of the arrows to hit Isaac and kill him, with it then being claimed it was an accident. However, Sarah saw what was happening, whatever it might have been at that time, and demanded the expulsion of the bondwoman and her son.

Paul used this in Galatians, Chapter 4, as an allegory. The word *"allegory"* simply means, *"A symbolic representation."*

We have in this example, even as Paul used it, Isaac symbolizing the new nature, i.e., *"the Divine Nature,"* which comes into the Believer at Conversion, and Ishmael, who represents the old nature. The birth of the new nature demands the expulsion of the old. It is impossible to improve the old nature. In other words, Ishmael must go.

A NEW LIFE

Paul said in Romans 8:7 that the old nature is *"enmity against God, that it is not subject to the Law of God, neither indeed can be."* George Williams said, *"If therefore it cannot be subject to the Law of God, how can it be improved? How foolish therefore appears the doctrine of moral evolution!"*[11]

Regeneration is not a change of the old nature but the

introduction of a new. It is the implantation of the nature of life of the Last Adam, by the Operation of the Holy Spirit, founded upon the accomplished Redemption of Christ. The moment the sinner believes in his heart and confesses with his mouth the Lord Jesus, he immediately becomes the possessor of a new life, and that Life is Christ. He is born of God, now is a Child of God, and, as Paul put it, is a son of the free woman (Rom. 10:9; Gal. 3:26; 4:31; Col. 3:4; I Jn. 3:1-2).

Mackintosh said:

"Nor does the introduction of this new nature alter, in the slightest degree, the true, essential character of the old."[12]

Concerning this, the Scripture says:

"The flesh lusts against the Spirit, and the Spirit against the flesh: and these are contrary the one to the other . . ." (Gal. 5:17).

IN ISAAC SHALL YOUR SEED BE CALLED

"And God said unto Abraham, Let it not be grievous in your sight because of the lad, and because of your bondwoman; in all that Sarah has said unto you, hearken unto her voice; for in Isaac shall your seed be called" (Gen. 21:12).

The birth of Isaac did not improve Ishmael but only brought out his real opposition to the child of Promise. He might have gone on very quickly and orderly till Isaac made his appearance; but then, he showed what he was by persecuting and mocking the child of Promise.

What then was the remedy? Was it to make Ishmael better? It was by no means to make him better, but, *"cast out this bondwoman and her son; for the son of this bondwoman shall not be heir with my son, even with Isaac."* Here was the only remedy. That which is crooked cannot be made straight. Therefore, you have to get rid of the crooked thing altogether and occupy yourself with that which is divinely straight. It is labor lost to seek to make a crooked thing straight. Hence, all efforts after the improvement of the old nature are utterly futile so far as God is concerned.

SARAH

"And Sarah was an hundred and twenty-seven years old: these were the years of the life of Sarah.

"And Sarah died in Kirjath-Arba; the same is Hebron in the land of Canaan: and Abraham came to mourn for Sarah, and to weep for her" (Gen. 23:1-2).

This means that Isaac was 37 years old when his mother Sarah died, and Abraham, at that time, was 137.

"Arba" is the old name of *"Hebron."* Abraham must have moved here from Beer-sheba temporarily.

Perhaps the phrase, *"In the land of Canaan,"* is given regarding the place of Sarah's death in order that we might know that she did not die in the country of the Philistines, but rather in the *"Promised Land."* Upon coming into the Promised Land, which took place about 400 years later, Caleb took *"Kirjath-Arba"* as his possession (Josh. 15:13-14). The sadness of Abraham in losing Sarah was, I think, to a greater degree than normal. She had fought this good fight of Faith with him every step of the way. Consequently, in a sense, as he was the *"father of us all"* (Rom. 4:16), Sarah was the *"mother of us all"* (I Pet. 3:6).

FAITH

"And Abraham stood up from before his dead, and spoke unto the sons of Heth, saying,

"I am a stranger and a sojourner with you: give me a possession of a buryingplace with you, that I may bury my dead out of my sight.

"And the children of Heth answered Abraham, saying unto him,

"Hear us, my lord: you are a mighty prince among us: in the choice of our sepulchers bury your dead; none of us shall withhold from you his sepulcher, but that you may bury your dead" (Gen. 23:3-6).

As we have stated, love weeps for Sarah, but Faith *"stood up from before his dead."*

Abraham's statement to the sons of Heth that he was *"a stranger and a sojourner among you"* was a confession that he sought, as his real inheritance, a better country, even a heavenly (Heb. 11:13).

The request for a *"buryingplace"* for Sarah is the first mention of a grave in Scripture.

The Patriarch's request of the sons of Heth that he might purchase a gravesite for Sarah was a sign of his right and title to the land of Canaan, which the sons of Heth would not have understood.

They offer to give him a buryingplace without cost, but the Patriarch, for reasons these individuals would never have understood, could not accept their largess. With perfect courtesy, therefore, though, likewise, with respectful firmness, he declines their offer.

THE POSSESSION

"And the field of Ephron, which was in Machpelah, which was before Mamre, the field, and the cave which was therein, and all the trees that were in the field, that were in all the borders round about, were made sure.

"Unto Abraham for a possession in the presence of the children of Heth, before all who went in at the gate of his city.

"And after this, Abraham buried Sarah his wife in the cave of the field of Machpelah before Mamre: the same is Hebron in the land of Canaan.

"And the field, and the cave that is therein, were made sure unto Abraham for a possession of a buryingplace by the sons of Heth" (Gen. 23:17-20).

Thus, we may view this beautiful Chapter in a twofold light:

1. As setting before us a plain, practical principle, as to our dealings with the world, that such dealings must always be aboveboard, forthright, and honest.

2. We should do everything with the idea in mind that the Blessed Hope is ever before us and should ever animate the man of Faith.

Putting both these points together, we have an example of what the Child of God should ever be. The hope set before us in the Gospel is a glorious immortality. This, while it lifts the heart above every influence of nature and the world, furnishes a high and holy principle with which to govern all our dealings with those who are without. *". . . we know that, when He shall appear, we shall be like Him; for we shall see Him as He is"* (I Jn. 3:2).

What is the Scriptural effect of this?

"Every man who has this hope in him purifies himself, even as He is pure" (I Jn. 3:3).

In the cave of Machpelah, the remains of Abraham and those of Isaac, Rebekah, Jacob, and Leah were deposited. Of the great patriarchal family, Rachel alone was not buried here.

"As I journey through the land singing as I go,
"Pointing souls to Calvary to the crimson flow,
"Many arrows pierce my soul from without, within;
"But my Lord leads me on, through Him I must win."

"When in service for my Lord dark may be the night,
"But I'll cling more close to Him, He will give me Light;
"Satan's snares may vex my soul, turn my thoughts aside;
"But my Lord goes ahead, leads whatever betide."

"When in valleys low I look toward the mountain height,
"And behold my Saviour there, leading in the fight,
"With a tender hand outstretched toward the valley low,
"Guiding me, I can see, as I onward go."

"When before me billows rise from the mighty deep,
"Then my Lord directs my bark; He does safely keep,
"And He leads me gently on through this world below;
"He's a Real Friend to me, O I love Him so."

Great Women OF THE BIBLE

OLD TESTAMENT

Chapter Two

REBEKAH

The Wife Of Isaac

REBEKAH
The Wife Of Isaac

ABRAHAM

"And Abraham was old, and well stricken in age: and the LORD had blessed Abraham in all things" (Gen. 24:1).

In fact, the Patriarch was now about 140 years old and would actually live to the age of 175 (Gen. 25:7). He lived some 35 years after Isaac was married and lived to see Esau and Jacob nearly grown up.

Chapters 22 through 24 present a startling picture.

• In Chapter 22, the son is offered up.

• In Chapter 23, Sarah is laid aside, which is typical of Israel. Because of rebellion and the Crucifixion of Christ, Israel was laid aside as a Nation.

• In Chapter 24, the servant is sent forth to procure a bride for Isaac, with this bride being typical of the Church, who would take the place of Israel, at least, throughout the Dispensation of Grace.

When we turn to the New Testament, we see a remarkable similarity:

• The Rejection and Death of Christ, typified by the offering up of Isaac.

• The setting aside of Israel after the flesh because of their rejection of Christ.

• The calling out the Church to occupy the high position of the Bride of the Lamb.

So, in this Chapter, we shall see a portrayal of that just mentioned.

Some may ask if we are, in fact, to view this particular Chapter as a *"type"* of the calling out of the Church by the Holy Spirit. Perhaps, as Mackintosh says, it would be better to look at it as an illustration of that glorious work. He went on to say:

"We cannot suppose that the Spirit of God would occupy an unusually long Chapter with the mere detail of a family

compact, were that compact not typical or illustrative of some great truth."[1]

I personally believe that this Chapter, the obtaining of a bride for Isaac, furnishes us with a beautiful illustration or foreshadowing of the great mystery of the Church. It is important to see that while there is no direct Revelation of this mystery in the Old Testament, there are, nevertheless, scenes and circumstances which, in a very remarkable manner, shadow it forth, which are portrayed in this Chapter.

ISAAC

"And Abraham said unto his eldest servant of his house, who ruled over all that he had, Put, I pray you, your hand under my thigh:

"And I will make you swear by the LORD, the God of Heaven, and the God of the Earth, that you shall not take a wife unto my son of the daughters of the Canaanites, among whom I dwell:

"But you shall go unto my country, and to my kindred, and take a wife unto my son Isaac" (Gen. 24:2-4).

THE ELDEST SERVANT

The *"eldest servant"* mentioned here is referred to in that manner throughout the entirety of this Chapter. It is done so for a particular reason if, in fact, this Chapter is also meant to portray the Holy Spirit seeking a bride for Christ, which is the Church, which I believe it is. If this is true, then this servant must be none other than Eliezer of Damascus.

The business of the Holy Spirit is not to glorify Himself, even though He is God, but rather to glorify Christ (Jn. 16:13-14).

Before Eliezer went on this all-important journey, he had to swear by the Lord, the God of Heaven, that he would not choose one of the daughters of the Canaanites as a wife for Isaac. He was instructed to go to Abraham's country from whence the Patriarch had come, and we speak, in this case, of Nahor, which was near the city of Haran. It was about a 700 mile journey from Beer-sheba.

THE THIGH

The placing of the hand of the servant under the thigh of the Patriarch seems to be an origination of Abraham inasmuch as nothing similar can be found elsewhere in the Bible.

The thigh, as the source of posterity, has been regarded as pointing to Abraham's future descendants, in particular, to Christ, the Promised Seed. So, the oath was the equivalent to a swearing by Him Who was to come, namely Christ.

Abraham knew that his Calling and purpose in life were to bring about the promised son, which had now been done. Through this son, the great Nation of Israel would come forth, all for the intended purpose of bringing the Son of God into the world. So, not only was Isaac of extreme importance as a person, as would be obvious, but the young lady to whom he would be married would figure prominently in that importance as well. She must not be a daughter of the Canaanites, but rather of his own people.

CANAANITES!

What was the difference between the Canaanite women and those of his own family back in Haran?

There were at least three reasons that Abraham demanded that Eliezer not choose a woman of the Canaanites:

1. It is undoubtedly correct that the Lord moved upon Abraham to do what he did. Abraham's entire family were descendants of Shem, of whom the Prophecy declared that the Blessing (Christ) would come (Gen. 9:26).

2. There is a good possibility that the Canaanite races or people were already being infiltrated by fallen Angels, bringing forth the race of giants, with the entirety of some tribes totally contaminated in some way. Genesis 6:4 says, *"There*

were giants in the Earth in those days (before the Flood); *and also after that* (after the Flood), *when the sons of God came in unto the daughters of men, and they bore children to them. . . ."* As well, the Canaanites were descendants of Ham, who had been cursed (Gen. 9:25).

3. Due to the Revelation given to Abraham by God, the entirety of his family, whomever they might have been, knew God in some fashion, whereas the Canaanites knew Him not at all.

THE COMMAND OF THE LORD

"And the servant said unto him, Peradventure the woman will not be willing to follow me unto this land: must I needs bring your son again unto the land from where you came?

"And Abraham said unto him, You beware that you bring not my son thither again.

"The LORD God of Heaven, Which took me from my father's house, and from the land of my kindred, and Who spoke unto me, and Who swore unto me, saying, Unto your seed will I give this land; He shall send His Angel before you, and you shall take a wife unto my son from thence" (Gen. 24:5-7).

Several things are said here:

• Eliezer, not being the one to whom the Word from the Lord was given concerning this thing, foresees potential problems. But yet, he would totally submit to Abraham's Faith despite these potential difficulties. Blessed is the Pastor who has men like this in his church, who can recognize Faith.

• By no means was Isaac to be taken to the particular land where his wife was to be found. The Promised Land was his home, and opportunity for temptation must not be put in his way. His Calling is Canaan even though he, as his father, Abraham, will not live to see the Promise brought to pass.

• According to Verse 7, every indication is that the Lord had given Abraham instructions as to what to do.

• The Lord would send an Angel, who would precede Eliezer, and, thereby, prepare the way.

FAITH

"And if the woman will not be willing to follow you, then you shall be clear from this my oath: only bring not my son thither again.

"And the servant put his hand under the thigh of Abraham his master, and swore to him concerning that matter" (Gen. 24:8-9).

Even though Abraham mentions the possibility of the particular woman chosen by the Holy Spirit not being willing to follow, this is said only to placate Eliezer. Abraham knows that the woman chosen by the Lord will, in fact, be willing to follow Eliezer back to the land of Canaan in order to be the wife of Isaac. However, under no circumstances was the idea to be entertained that Isaac himself was to go to Haran, even if the woman demanded she meet him before such a journey be undertaken. The instructions were specific: Isaac was to remain in Canaan, and the woman was to come to Canaan to be with him.

Eliezer realized that such was a tall order. He wondered in his mind if he could get a woman to do such a thing, considering that she had never met Isaac, didn't know what he was like, but yet, she would be committing her entire life to this unseen man. However, Eliezer had Faith.

Regarding these conditions, Eliezer did as Abraham commanded him as it regarded him putting his hand under the thigh of the Patriarch and, in effect, swearing to an oath.

Far more here was at stake than meets the eye. I think that Eliezer completely understood what was at stake, at least, as much as one could at that particular time. In fact, the entirety of the Plan of God hung on this being carried out, and being carried out exactly as the Lord had told Abraham that it must be carried out.

ALL THE GOODS

"And the servant took ten camels of the camels of his master, and departed; for all the goods of his master were in his hand:

and he arose, and went to Mesopotamia, unto the city of Nahor" (Gen. 24:10).

Camels were the largest beasts of burden, at least, in that particular area. *"Ten"* in the Bible is the number of completion. So, a little bit of everything that Abraham had was placed on those camels. No doubt, Eliezer had many other servants with him in order to help him on this long journey.

If we follow the narrative through, believing that this portrays Abraham as a Type of God the Father, Isaac as a Type of Christ, and Eliezer as a Type of the Holy Spirit, with Rebekah being a type of the Church, i.e., *"the bride of Christ,"* then we must come to the conclusion that all that the Father has actually belongs to Christ, but that it has been placed into the Hands of the Holy Spirit, Who will dispense it as He sees fit. The reader must remember that Isaac, in a figure, has already been offered up in Sacrifice and resurrected, hence, a Type of the Exalted Christ. He, according to the Heavenly Father, has sent the Holy Spirit into the world to seek a bride for the Son of God.

While Eliezer was under strict orders from Abraham, still, he could dispense these goods as he saw fit. To be sure, the goods would be dispensed only to the right people.

THE CAMELS

"And he made his camels to kneel down without the city by a well of water at the time of the evening, even the time that women go out to draw water" (Gen. 24:11).

The long journey of some 700 miles, which probably took several weeks, has now been completed. He has arrived at the city of Nahor, which is very near Haran.

Inasmuch as he has now arrived, he will immediately begin his quest for a bride for Isaac.

Where Eliezer would begin his quest should provide us food for thought. He didn't go to a place of amusement, but rather to a *"well"* where the women drew water, which, needless to say, was a laborious task. In other words, he was looking for a young lady who was industrious, zealous, not afraid of hard work, and who was responsible. He could only find her at such a place as this.

PRAYER

"And he said, O LORD God of my master Abraham, I pray You, send me good speed this day, and show kindness unto my master Abraham.

"Behold, I stand here by the well of water; and the daughters of the men of the city come out to draw water:

"And let it come to pass, that the damsel to whom I shall say, Let down your pitcher, I pray you, that I may drink; and she shall say, Drink, and I will give your camels drink also: let the same be she who You have appointed for Your Servant Isaac; and thereby shall I know that You have showed kindness unto my master" (Gen. 24:12-14).

Let's look at what is done here:

• Eliezer is looking to the Lord to lead him and guide him. He does not at all trust his own instincts or personal wisdom. He needs Leading from the Lord, so he will seek the Lord. How much this should be a lesson to all of us as well.

• Also, we should understand as Believers that due to the fact that Abraham is the *"father of us all"* (Rom. 4:16), everything that happened to him in some way applies to us. Naturally, we are speaking in the spiritual sense.

• If it is to be noticed, he does not for a moment forget that the mission on which he has embarked is for Abraham.

• He is specific in his prayer, asking for a certain thing; consequently, it is obvious that he believes that God hears and answers prayer.

• Camels drink a lot of water; therefore, anyone who would slake their thirst, much less, 10 of these animals, would have to draw a lot of water. This, within itself, is a huge task. So, he put the following before the Lord:

• He would approach the young lady and ask her for a

drink of water, which she would graciously give to him. Then, as well, she would offer to give the camels water. If the young lady did all of this, then she was to be the one *"appointed for Your Servant Isaac."*

• As is obvious, Eliezer certainly didn't make it easy. Asking that the Lord would impress upon her to water the camels, as well, narrowed down the field considerably. What young lady would want to draw that much water, especially for a stranger?

REBEKAH

"And it came to pass, before he had done speaking, that, behold, Rebekah came out, who was born to Bethuel, son of Milcah, the wife of Nahor, Abraham's brother, with her pitcher upon her shoulder" (Gen. 24:15).

BEAUTIFUL

"And the damsel was very fair to look upon, a virgin, neither had any man known her: and she went down to the well, and filled her pitcher, and came up" (Gen. 24:16).

The girl was beautiful, and, as well, she was a virgin. Also, she was industrious, as is obvious here.

This is a picture of what the Lord expects the Church to be. In His Eyes, the Church is beautiful. As well, the Lord expects the Church to follow Him exclusively and not depend on self or other people, which He will always look at as *"spiritual adultery"* (Rom. 7:1-4). If, in fact, Rebekah is a type of the Church, then it is plain to see that the Lord expects the Church to be industrious, i.e., *"busy in the Work of the Lord."* Even though this young girl was beautiful, she did not think herself too good to perform this task of drawing water at the well, which was not easy, to say the least.

Most of the wells in those days were fed by a spring, with a series of steps that led down to the well. Consequently, to walk up those steps carrying one or two goatskins full of water was no easy task, especially, to do it over and over again.

THE SIGN

"And the servant ran to meet her, and said, Let me, I pray you, drink a little water of your pitcher" (Gen. 24:17).

Evidently, Rebekah was the first girl to show up at the well and apparently came up at the very time Eliezer was arriving. He will now put the first part of his plan into operation. Upon seeing the girl but still not knowing who she was, he would ask her for a drink of water from her pitcher.

I would say the request was unusual, especially considering that a man was asking such of a woman. She could easily have told him to go draw his own water, but she didn't. She responded exactly as he hoped she would.

DRINK

"And she said, Drink, my lord: and she hastened, and let down her pitcher upon her hand, and gave him drink" (Gen. 24:18).

She not only acquiesced to his request, but she did so gleefully and promptly.

As she gave him to drink, we, as members of the Body of Christ, are to give the Water of Life to a hurting, dying world. As she drew from the well, we are to draw from the Well, i.e., *"Christ."* Jesus said, *". . . If any man thirst, let him come unto Me, and drink"* (Jn. 7:37).

THE SECOND PART OF THE SIGN

"And when she had done giving him drink, she said, I will draw water for your camels also, until they have done drinking" (Gen. 24:19).

Without him asking her to do so, she immediately volunteered to draw water for the camels exactly as he had asked the Lord that the chosen girl would do.

As stated, camels drink a lot of water. So, the girl had to make quite a few trips down the stairs to the well and then bring back those heavy goatskins full of water.

HER CONDUCT

"And she hasted, and emptied her pitcher into the trough, and ran again unto the well to draw water, and drew for all his camels" (Gen. 24:20).

Eliezer had servants who might have spared Rebekah of her labor; but he interfered not that he might observe her conduct and await the answer to his prayer.

Her conduct, in itself, so amiable and so exactly in unison with his wishes, struck him with a kind of amazement. It was accompanied with a momentary hesitation as to whether all of this could be true.

Recovering from his astonishment and being satisfied that the Lord had indeed heard his prayer, as we shall see, he now will present her with gifts, which must have been a surprise to her.

THE LORD

"And the man wondering at her held his peace, to witness whether the LORD had made his journey prosperous or not" (Gen. 24:21).

"Wondering at her," means that he *"eagerly or carefully watched her."*

Eliezer keenly observed all that Rebekah said and did and then carefully came to the conclusion that this beautiful and kind maiden was the destined bride of the son of his master. The Lord had answered his prayer.

It should be noticed here the degree that Eliezer sought the Lord, looked to the Lord, and depended on the Lord. I cannot overemphasize the fact that this should be a great lesson to us as Believers. Presently, due to what Christ has done at the

Cross, the Holy Spirit gives us this help constantly, or, at least, He desires to do so, whereas such help afforded in Abraham's day was sporadic at best. Presently, the Holy Spirit abides permanently (Jn. 14:16-17).

Modern Christians are constantly proclaiming that they wish that the Lord would give them the type of help that He gave Eliezer. The truth is, He will do even more now because He now has greater latitude due to the Cross. The problem is not with the Holy Spirit, as the problem is never with the Holy Spirit. The problem is us! Most Christians have very little prayer life, but it is obvious that Eliezer had a very personal relationship with the Lord. He had allowed Abraham's Faith to become his Faith. Likewise, Abraham's consecration was also his consecration.

The modern Believer can get as close to the Lord as he so desires. It's never up to the Lord; He is always ready. The slackness is always on our part.

GIFTS

"And it came to pass, as the camels had done drinking, that the man took a golden earring of half a shekel weight, and two bracelets for her hands of ten shekels weight of gold" (Gen. 24:22).

In 2012 dollars, the *"golden earring of half a shekel weight"* would be worth presently about $300. Incidentally, it was a nose ring instead of an earring.

Whether the two bracelets weighed *"ten shekels"* each or both weighed *"ten shekels,"* we aren't told. At any rate, *"ten shekels weight of gold"* would be worth, in today's money, about $6,000.

In the spiritual sense, these gifts, which came from Eliezer, are types of Gifts of the Spirit and, in fact, represent all good things which the Lord does for us. The fact that these were items of *"gold"* proclaims the fact that they were all of God.

I suspect that Rebekah was somewhat taken aback when she was given these very expensive gifts.

Whenever the believing sinner comes to Christ, the Holy

Spirit immediately begins to give good, beautiful, and wonderful things to us, which, in fact, never ends all the days of our lives. To be sure, what He gives us is of far greater value than the symbolism of gold suggested here. While He takes care of us financially and materially, as well, His Greater Blessings are in the spiritual sense. The mature Christian soon finds that out.

As well, the gifts presented to Rebekah by Eliezer were in no way meant to pay her for the work she had done. In fact, Eliezer could have asked someone to water these camels for a small fraction of what he gave Rebekah. No! These were gifts because Eliezer suspected that this was the one whom God had chosen. He was right!

A TREASURE HOUSE

We soon learn in living for God that we really cannot earn anything from Him. In fact, the Lord has nothing for sale. If He did, we certainly would never be able to afford such wonders. His Gifts are free and freely given. As well, they are lavishly given because He is Rich in the things we desperately need, whatever that might be.

Oh, how I sense His Presence even as I attempt to elaborate on this gesture of Eliezer, which took place so long, long ago. How much the Lord wants to give us good things! How much He longs to lavish His Largess on us! Then again, how so very valuable are His Gifts, and they just keep on coming. It is like we are admitted into a treasure house. We go into one room, which is filled with all types of riches. Then, we see a door, which leads to another room with even more riches. It seems that the rooms never end, and the riches just keep getting greater and greater.

Rebekah now only has these token gifts. She will soon be wed to Isaac, which means that all He has that is bountiful, to be sure, will then become hers in totality.

When we come to Christ, we become *"... heirs of God, and joint-heirs with Christ ... "* (Rom. 8:17).

QUESTIONS

"And said, Whose daughter are you? tell me, I pray you: is there room in your father's house for us to lodge in?" (Gen. 24:23)

Two questions are asked here:

1. *"Whose daughter are you?"* Considering that the signs requested of the Lord by Eliezer have now been granted, he must know who the young lady is. The question will tender a positive response, even as we shall see, and, at the same time, as it follows the *"Type,"* is meant to point to identification with Christ. Rebekah will soon belong to Isaac, who is a Type of Christ, even as the believing sinner is soon to belong to Christ.

2. *"Is there room in your father's house for us to lodge in?"* presents the question that the Holy Spirit asks of every believing sinner. We must make room for Christ. In fact, the Holy Spirit is constantly asking untold millions around the world, *"Is there room for Me?"*

"And she said unto him, I am the daughter of Bethuel the son of Milcah, which she bore unto Nahor" (Gen. 24:24).

Rebekah mentions her father's mother to show that she was descended from a highborn wife and not from a concubine. However, Eliezer would welcome the information as proving that, not only on the father's side but, also, on the mother's, she was Isaac's cousin, Milcah being the daughter of Haran, Abraham's brother.

This is probably the time that he gave her the jewels which he was holding in his hand.

ROOM TO LODGE IN

"She said moreover unto him, We have both straw and provender enough, and room to lodge in" (Gen. 24:25).

Her answer was in the positive exactly that for which Eliezer had hoped. In essence, she was saying that they would give Eliezer and those with him everything that they had regarding hospitality, and, as well, would make room for them as it regarded their lodging.

Little did she know or understand how important and how significant were the words she was saying. Little did she realize where this invitation would lead or that individuals would be talking about her thousands of years into the future because of her saying, *"Yes,"* to the Lord Jesus Christ, for, in a sense, that's exactly what she was doing.

When the great invitation comes to us, in whatever capacity, may our answer be as open and as broad as that of Rebekah.

WORSHIP

"And the man bowed down his head, and worshipped the LORD" (Gen. 24:26).

It is obvious that Eliezer had a close walk with the Lord. It is obvious that the Faith of Abraham was his Faith as well! It is obvious that he was accustomed to being led by the Lord. His demeanor, his attitude, and his response all point to total consecration.

Abraham had entrusted to his hand the future of the entirety of the Plan of God. What a responsibility he had, and how so much with dignity, responsibility, and forthrightness did he carry out this which he was assigned to do. May we do as well!

In the Hebrew language, the word, *"Bowed down,"* expresses reverent inclination of the head. The second verb, *"Worshipped,"* proclaims a complete prostration of the body, which means that Eliezer fell prostrate on the ground, worshipping the Lord in thankfulness to Him for the Guidance and the Leading which had been given at this time.

A PRAYER OF THANKSGIVING

"And he said, Blessed be the LORD God of my master Abraham, Who has not left destitute my master of His Mercy and His Truth: I being in the way, the LORD led me to the house of my master's brethren" (Gen. 24:27).

This prayer of Eliezer proclaims the fact that this man knew and understood the Grace of God, which he exclaims by mentioning the Mercy of the Lord and, as well, *"His Truth."* Mercy being a product of Grace proclaims the fact that Eliezer understood this great Doctrine. To be sure, if Grace is properly understood, *"Truth,"* as well, will be properly understood.

The short phrase, *"I being in the way,"* refers to him being in the way of Mercy and Truth, which is the place that every Believer ought to be and, in fact, can be.

As well, if Grace and Truth are properly understood and entertained, there will, at the same time, be Leading and Guidance by the Lord, which refers to a place of deep consecration.

THE WITNESS

"And the damsel ran, and told them of her mother's house these things.

"And Rebekah had a brother, and his name was Laban: and Laban ran out unto the man, unto the well" (Gen. 24:28-29).

How far Rebekah lived from the well, we aren't told. However, it must have been only a short distance, possibly, several hundreds of yards.

The indication is that she first went and told her family what had just transpired. Even though this is the logical narration of the story, still, it is that which every Believer should do. We should witness first to our families and then to all others as well. A story so wonderful, so grand, and so glorious begs to be told. To be sure, the Gospel Message is the Grandest Story ever told. How right was the songwriter:

"What a wonderful Light in my life has been shone,
"Since Jesus came into my heart!"

OBSERVATION

"And it came to pass, when he saw the earring and the

bracelets upon his sister's hands, and when he heard the words of Rebekah his sister, saying, Thus spoke the man unto me; that he came unto the man; and, behold, he stood by the camels at the well" (Gen. 24:30).

Every true Christian has gifts given to him by the Lord, which should be an obvious sign to the world. The Bible said that Laban *"saw"* and *"heard."* He saw the gifts, and he heard the words which his sister said.

As it regards our lives, the world should *"see"* what the Lord has done for us, and then they will *"hear"* what we have to say concerning the tremendous Miracle which has transpired.

Laban then went to Eliezer.

PREPARATION

"And he said, Come in, you blessed of the LORD; why do you stand without? for I have prepared the house, and room for the camels.

"And the man came into the house: and he ungirded his camels, and gave straw and provender for the camels, and water to wash his feet, and the men's feet who were with him" (Gen. 24:31-32).

Laban was an idolater (Gen. 31:30); however, by him referring to Eliezer as *"blessed of the LORD,"* we know that he had some knowledge of the Lord. In fact, the original Revelation given by God to Abraham had, no doubt, instituted the worship of Jehovah in the household. But yet, they were still clinging to their idols, which, regrettably, is indicative of many modern Christians.

Many presently serve God, but, at the same time, the things of the world prove to be an allurement. In fact, Israel had the same problem, hence, the Prophet Samuel saying to them, *". . . prepare your hearts unto the LORD, and serve Him Only . . ."* (I Sam. 7:3).

The idea was, they were serving the Lord and Baal at the same time. Regrettably, that problem didn't die with Israel.

THE MESSAGE

"And there was set meat before him to eat: but he said, I will not eat, until I have told my errand. And he said, Speak on" (Gen. 24:33).

We are witnessing here a perfect example of proper responsibility. That which was uppermost on his mind was not his own wants and needs, but rather the very purpose for which he came, which was to relay the message that Abraham had given him to relay.

All of this has to do with the protocol of that day, which was rigidly observed at that particular time.

Continuing to stand on protocol, Eliezer will request that he be given permission to speak even before the hospitality of food is enjoyed. If Laban had not conceded, he would not have entered his house, but Laban did concede.

Incidentally, we will hear more of Laban, and I speak of the time of Jacob. He was a man of greed and through greed, he lost Jacob. As well, as we shall see, it seems to be greed that forces his attention at this present time with his sister Rebekah and with Eliezer.

THE BLESSING

"And he said, I am Abraham's servant.

"And the LORD has blessed my master greatly; and he is become great: and He has given him flocks, and herds, and silver, and gold, and menservants, and maidservants, and camels, and asses" (Gen. 24:34-35).

Eliezer identifies himself but does so by promoting Abraham, which the Holy Spirit always does as it regards God the Father and God the Son. In fact, it is said of the Spirit:

"Howbeit when He, the Spirit of Truth, is come, He will guide you into all Truth: for He shall not speak of Himself; but whatsoever He shall hear, that shall He speak: and He will show you things to come.

"He shall glorify Me: for He shall receive of Mine, and shall show it unto you" (Jn. 16:13-14).

This is exactly what Eliezer is now doing! He gives praise and glory to the Lord for all the good things which have happened. He credits the Lord with blessing Abraham with material things, which Laban would have readily understood.

GOD WILL!

Let the reader know and understand that the Lord will do the same thing presently as He did then. He is no respecter of persons and what He has previously done, He definitely will continue to do.

So, every Believer ought to believe the Lord for the Blessings of God regarding all things as well as financial and material things. Our problem is, *"We have not because we ask not."* And then, far too often, *"We ask, and receive not, because we ask amiss, that we may consume it upon our lusts"* (James 4:2-3).

However, should the Lord place material things into our hands, if we genuinely desire to bless the Work of the Lord, to be sure, the Lord will definitely bless. In fact, He desires to bless! He wants to bless! If we will ardently seek His Face, consecrate ourselves fully to Him, and look to the Cross for all things, understanding that it was there that the price was paid, to be sure, God will bless us spiritually, physically, domestically, and financially.

I can sense the Presence of the Lord even as I dictate these words. I believe that you the reader can sense the Lord as well. He loves you! He wants to bless you! He will do so in all things because He has all things. God is good and as the song says, *"He's not good just some of the time, but God is good all the time."*

ISAAC WAS GIVEN ALL

"And Sarah my master's wife bore a son to my master when she was old: and unto him has he given all that he has" (Gen. 24:36).

In this short sentence, so much is said.

Isaac was the Miracle child born to Sarah when she was 90 years old and Abraham was 100. This proclaims the Miracle-working Power of Almighty God.

Even though Eliezer did not mention this here, this *"son"* was to be the seed who would bring the *"Seed of the woman"* into the world, which had been predicted immediately after the Fall in the Garden of Eden (Gen. 3:15).

Isaac is now a grown man, and Abraham has given to him all of his riches, which means that he was a very wealthy man.

Laban would have been little impressed by the great spiritual riches, which, in fact, had made all the other things possible, so they were not mentioned. However, he was greatly impressed by the material riches, so this is what Eliezer addressed. As a point of information, this is what he should have addressed because Laban could little have understood spiritual things.

Likewise, the Heavenly Father has given all things unto the *"Son,"* and the Son has given all things to us exactly as everything that belonged to Isaac would be given to Rebekah, who was a type of the Church.

Some would claim that she was a type of Israel, in fact, being the mother of Israel, so to speak. While the latter is true, we must go to Romans 4:16 where the Holy Spirit through Paul proclaims the fact that Abraham is the *"father of us all."* He is speaking of Israel and the Church. So, I think the ground referring typology is safe regarding my conclusions respecting the symbolism.

A WIFE

"And my master made me swear, saying, You shall not take a wife to my son of the daughters of the Canaanites, in whose land I dwell" (Gen. 24:37).

As everything was to be a certain way regarding Isaac, likewise, it is the same for the Christian presently. The Lord has a Will for all things, and it's our business to find what that

Will is and then wholeheartedly obey that Will.

THE ANGEL

"But you shall go unto my father's house, and to my kindred, and take a wife unto my son.
"And I said unto my master, Peradventure the woman will not follow me?
"And he said unto me, The LORD, before Whom I walk, will send His Angel with you, and prosper your way; and you shall take a wife for my son of my kindred, and of my father's house" (Gen. 24:38-40).

As we have stated, the Lord had already informed Abraham that He would prepare the way before Eliezer, even by sending an Angel to protect him and to prepare for his arrival. It is obvious that this is exactly what was done, and in short order. When the Lord is in a thing, it works well. When man does it without the help of the Lord, it is one problem after the other.

THE OATH

"Then shall you be clear from this my oath, when you come to my kindred; and if they give not you one, you shall be clear from my oath" (Gen. 24:41).

The Lord, as is obvious, had so ingrained into Abraham the necessity of what was to be done that he is fearful lest it not be carried out exactly as the Lord wanted. He even made his trusted servant, Eliezer, take an oath that he would strictly follow all directions.

The reason Abraham was adamant in this is because it was the Word of the Lord. Even though they didn't have a Bible in those days, with the first Books yet to be written by Moses some 400 years later, still, what the Lord told the Patriarch was very exact and, in fact, would be written by Moses at the later time mentioned.

We should be so zealous presently to follow the Word of the

Lord exactly as it is given. The first question that should be asked about anything and everything is, *"Is it Scriptural?"*

PROSPERITY

"And I came this day unto the well, and said, O LORD God of my master Abraham, if now You do prosper my way which I go" (Gen. 24:42).

The prosperity of which Eliezer speaks refers to the petition he will lay before the Lord, and he prays that God will answer his prayer.

The account here given is one of the greatest examples in the entirety of the Word of God of a man's relationship with the Lord as the man seeks for Guidance and Leading, as did Eliezer. This is available for every Believer. At the present time, the Holy Spirit abides within the hearts and lives of every Believer, which was not the case during the time of Eliezer. If Eliezer could have this type of relationship with the Lord during these days, we surely can now as well!

THE PETITION

"Behold, I stand by the well of water; and it shall come to pass, that when the virgin comes forth to draw water, and I say to her, Give me, I pray you, a little water of your pitcher to drink;

"And she say to me, Both you drink, and I will also draw water for your camels: let the same be the woman whom the LORD has appointed out for my master's son" (Gen. 24:43-44).

Eliezer had reason that he would stand by the well inasmuch as women came during the day to draw water. As men generally did not perform this task, he felt this would be the best place to begin.

However, as it concerned this girl, she first had to be a virgin and, second, she had to be a part of Abraham's family. He could not tell by looking at her as it regarded these things. So, his petition was this:

He would ask of her a drink of water and if she willingly gave him the water and, at the same time, offered to draw water for his camels, this would be the woman.

Considering that he had men with him who could have easily drawn the water and, as well, that this was a very hard task, it would have to be the Lord for this young lady to offer her kindness in this regard. However, that was the petition he put before the Lord. Anyone would have to agree that if it was met, it would have to be the Lord. No young lady out of the blue, so to speak, would volunteer to make many trips down the steps to the well, thereby, carrying the heavy load back in order to water the camels.

THE ANSWER

"And before I had done speaking in my heart, behold, Rebekah came forth with her pitcher on her shoulder; and she went down into the well, and drew water: and I said unto her, Let me drink, I pray you.

"And she made haste, and let down her pitcher from her shoulder, and said, Drink, and I will give your camels a drink also: so I drank, and she made the camels drink also" (Gen. 24:45-46).

Before Eliezer had even finished silently praying, Rebekah appeared on the scene. He asked her for a drink of water, and she immediately acquiesced to his request. She also instantly volunteered to water the camels as well.

However, he had one more hurdle to cross.

FAMILY

"And I asked her, and said, Whose daughter are you? And she said, The daughter of Bethuel, Nahor's son, whom Milcah bore unto him: and I put the earring upon her face, and the bracelets upon her hands" (Gen. 24:47).

Lo and behold, when asked about her family, she was a member of the family of Abraham. It is beautiful as to how the Lord put all of these pieces together in such short order. What a wonderful thing to have the Lord working for you!

What a glorious thing to be able to ask His Help, Leading, and Guidance and for Him to instantly give it.

WORSHIP

"And I bowed down my head, and worshipped the LORD, and blessed the LORD God of my master Abraham, which had led me in the right way to take my master's brother's daughter unto his son" (Gen. 24:48).

If it is to be noticed, Eliezer is not at all ashamed to confess before these men his dependence on the Lord. We should presently, as well, be so forward.

FROM THE LORD

"And now if you will deal kindly and truly with my master, tell me: and if not, tell me; that I may turn to the right hand, or to the left.

"Then Laban and Bethuel answered and said, The thing proceeds from the LORD: we cannot speak unto you bad or good.

"Behold, Rebekah is before you, take her, and go, and let her be your master's son's wife, as the LORD has spoken" (Gen. 24:49-51).

After Eliezer relates these things to these men, they are quickly made to see that all of this is entirely beyond their scope of comprehension. They do not attempt to elaborate on the subject or, it seems, to even ask any questions. Their statement, *"The thing proceeds from the LORD,"* in effect, said it all. They immediately gave their consent for Rebekah to go back with this man to the home of Isaac, some 700 miles distance.

This was a very long journey in those days, and they would probably never see Rebekah again.

THANKS TO THE LORD

"And it came to pass, that, when Abraham's servant heard their words, he worshipped the LORD, bowing himself to the

earth" (Gen. 24:52).

For every victory, Eliezer worshipped the Lord, which speaks volumes of this man. His worship was not merely a silent *"thank you,"* but he was very physical, even prostrating himself on the ground.

When we understand how important all of this was, which I think Eliezer realized its vast significance, at least, as far as it was possible then, we can understand his reaction.

I think we are safe in saying that the Lord through Abraham had entrusted this man with the future of the great Salvation Plan. I think that Eliezer felt this. I seriously doubt that he understood it all, but, to be sure, I believe he understood enough to know of the great significance of what was happening.

THE GIFTS

"And the servant brought forth jewels of silver, and jewels of gold, and raiment, and gave them to Rebekah: he gave also to her brother and to her mother precious things.

"And they did eat and drink, he and the men who were with him, and tarried all night; and they rose up in the morning, and he said, Send me away unto my master" (Gen. 24:53-54).

The gifts now were lavish. Considering how rich Abraham was and how important this event, the worth of all this was undoubtedly staggering.

There is a possibility that Abraham was one of the richest men in the world. In fact, he could very well have been the richest. God had blessed him exceedingly and abundantly so.

TARRY NOT

"And her brother and her mother said, Let the damsel abide with us a few days, at the least ten; after that she shall go.

"And he said unto them, Hinder me not, seeing the LORD has prospered my way; send me away that I may go to my master.

"And they said, We will call the damsel, and inquire at her mouth" (Gen. 24:55-57).

Perhaps a little different than the custom, Eliezer wanted to depart immediately. His mission was all-important, and he could not rest until the young lady was safe by Isaac's side.

There is no doubt that the Holy Spirit was working as it regarded the situation, not only as it pertained to Eliezer but, as well, as it pertained to Rebekah and her family.

THE GREAT QUESTION

"And they called Rebekah, and said unto her, Will you go with this man? And she said, I will go" (Gen. 24:58).

One can certainly understand the feelings of this family, taking into consideration that they would probably never see Rebekah again. This could not be easy for her mother and father, as well as her brother. So, they asked for 10 days in order to say their goodbyes, which would include all of the relatives.

However, Eliezer felt in his spirit that he must leave immediately, so Rebekah was given the choice as to what she wanted to do.

She was asked the great question, *"Will you go with this man?"* Her answer seems to be without hesitation. She said, *"I will go."*

Whenever we come to Christ, we, in effect, must give up our families, our friends, and everything, for that matter. That certainly doesn't mean that we cease to love them; not at all. In fact, we love them even more, but Christ comes first.

To be sure, when the Holy Spirit poses the question to each of us, *"Will you go with this man?,"* speaking of Christ, our answer must be quick, as was the answer of Rebekah, *"I will go!"* It is a journey that, in fact, will never end.

THE BLESSING

"And they sent away Rebekah their sister, and her nurse, and Abraham's servant, and his men.

"And they blessed Rebekah, and said unto her, You are our sister, be thou the mother of thousands of millions, and let your seed possess the gate of those who hate them" (Gen. 24:59-60).

No doubt, the blessing they posed upon Rebekah was standard; however, little did they realize that the staggering numbers they presented would, in fact, come to pass. Every single person who has ever come to Christ is a part of these *"thousands of millions."*

As well, through Jesus Christ, victory in every capacity has been won, and victory in every capacity will continue to be won.

FOLLOW THE MAN

"And Rebekah arose, and her damsels, and they rode upon the camels, and followed the man: and the servant took Rebekah, and went his way" (Gen. 24:61).

Not only did Rebekah's nurse go with her but other young ladies, as well, as represented by the word, *"Damsels."* This showed that her family was quite wealthy also.

The Scripture says that they *"followed the man,"* speaking of Eliezer.

We are to follow the Holy Spirit in all of His Leading, and always, without exception, He will lead us to Christ.

PRAYER

"And Isaac came from the way of the well Lahai-roi; for he dwelt in the south country.

"And Isaac went out to meditate in the field at the eventide: and he lifted up his eyes, and saw, and, behold, the camels were coming" (Gen. 24:62-63).

It is beautiful that Isaac first laid his eyes on his bride-to-be while in prayer.

Evidently, he had gone out to a place of solitude to seek the Face of the Lord, possibly, about the mission of Eliezer concerning the obtaining for him a wife.

It is doubtful that he expected Eliezer back so soon. He knew the long distance to where his father Abraham had sent Eliezer and about how long it would take to get there and to get back. However, he had no idea as to how long Eliezer would be once he arrived there. So, I doubt very seriously that he was expecting the servant back this soon.

Thoughts, no doubt, filled his mind. Would Eliezer be successful? If so, what would she look like?

He was not to be disappointed. The Lord would arrange this match, and that which the Lord does is always beautiful and glorious. While in prayer, he happened to look up, and, behold, the camel train was coming.

REBEKAH

"And Rebekah lifted up her eyes, and when she saw Isaac, she lighted off the camel.

"For she had said unto the servant, What man is this who walks in the field to meet us? And the servant had said, It is my master: therefore she took a veil, and covered herself" (Gen. 24:64-65).

All the thoughts that Isaac had, no doubt, were present in the mind of Rebekah as well. What would he be like?

In a sense, her commitment was even greater than that of Isaac. While he would be able to remain with his family to the end of his days, she had left her family back in Haran and actually would never see them again. She had left all for this man, whom she had never seen, but, to be sure, she definitely was not to be disappointed.

Again, the Lord has arranged all things, and His Arrangements are always perfect.

We aren't told what the thoughts of Isaac were or those of Rebekah at the moment of their meeting. Perhaps it was too personal for the Holy Spirit to divulge this meeting, but this one thing is certain: both were very pleased at what the Lord had chosen.

ELIEZER

"And the servant told Isaac all things that he had done" (Gen. 24:66).

After Isaac had met Rebekah, Eliezer then related to him the

Blessings of God upon his journey. God had moved wondrously, and the mother of Israel, for that's exactly what Rebekah would be, would be everything that Isaac would ever want. To be sure, Isaac would be everything that Rebekah would ever want or desire.

HIS WIFE

"And Isaac brought her into his mother Sarah's tent, and took Rebekah, and she became his wife; and he loved her; and Isaac was comforted after his mother's death" (Gen. 24:67).

Incidentally, in those days, the primitive marriage ceremony consisted solely of the taking of a bride before witnesses.

If it is to be noticed, the word, *"Death,"* is added here by the translators. It was not in the original Text. It is as if the Holy Spirit would not conclude this beautiful narrative with a note of sorrow.

Isaac being comforted by Rebekah after his mother's death shows that he did not make comparisons between his mother and Rebekah, which allowed his wife to be the queen of the home, even as she should have been. In other words, she didn't have to compete with Sarah, meaning that Isaac did not constantly compare the two. And so is told this beautiful love story, which symbolizes Christ and the Church, represented by Isaac and Rebekah. However, the emphasis seems to be on Eliezer, who symbolized the Holy Spirit, as he secured the bride for Isaac. Likewise, the Holy Spirit is making up the Church at present as a bride for Christ.

ISAAC AND REBEKAH

"And Isaac was forty years old when he took Rebekah to wife, the daughter of Bethuel the Syrian of Padan-aram, the sister to Laban the Syrian" (Gen. 25:20).

"Laban the Syrian" is mentioned here simply because he will figure very prominently as it regards Jacob, Rebekah's

son, who we will study momentarily.

Under Abraham's guidance, the Lord will choose the wife of Isaac. That which the Lord chooses is always right. That which we choose is almost always wrong and probably one could say without fear of contradiction, that which we choose is always wrong.

As an aside, the Lord will, as well, choose a wife or a husband for every young man and young lady who looks to Him for Leading and Guidance. In fact, if we will only ask the Lord to lead us and guide us in all things, He will definitely do such. The problem with most modern Believers is that they very seldom seek the Lord as it regards anything. Such is so foolish, considering Who the Lord is and what he can do, and then compare that with our own pitiful fallibility.

I need the Leading of the Lord in every single thing which I attempt. Be it little or large, I want His Leading, His Guidance, etc.

BARREN

"And Isaac entreated the LORD for his wife, because she was barren: and the LORD was entreated of him, and Rebekah his wife conceived" (Gen. 25:21).

As stated, we find that Satan hindered the birth of Jacob, through whom the Lord would work, and did so for some 20 years. The Lord allowed him to do such.

Why?

Anything and everything that Satan does, he does only by permission from the Lord. To be sure, he is subject to the Lord in every capacity (Job, Chpts. 1-2).

So, as it regards Believers, this means that the Lord uses Satan in order to strengthen the Faith and trust of Believers. How does He do that?

As mentioned, He allows Satan a modicum of latitude. Of course, Satan means to hurt us and even destroy us. However, the Lord's Reasons are altogether different, as should be overly obvious.

He wants us to do exactly what Isaac did.

ENTREATED THE LORD

Twenty years is a long time, but Isaac didn't give up. During this time, he kept entreating the Lord and pleading with the Lord to heal Rebekah that she might be able to conceive and to bear children.

As well, even though he and his wife naturally wanted children, and wanted them very much, the real reason was far more important. The birth of a son to this union was just as important as his Miracle birth had been as it regarded his father and mother, Abraham and Sarah. For the Plan of God to be brought forth, which pertains to the Redemption of all of mankind, Isaac and Rebekah would have to have a son.

As far as Rebekah was concerned, nature was dead. In other words, she could not have a child. However, God is able to overrule all of these things. He wanted Isaac to continue to believe Him, to not give up, and to not lose heart. In other words, this was a test of Faith, as all things, as it pertains to Believers, are tests of Faith.

The answer ultimately came because the Lord was entreated of him, and Rebekah conceived.

What was the Lord's Reasoning behind all of this, and we speak of the barrenness of both Sarah and Rebekah?

Among other things, it was to show that the children of Promise were to be not simply the fruit of nature, but the Gift of Grace.

THE STRUGGLE

"And the children struggled together within her; and she said, If it be so, why am I thus? And she went to inquire of the LORD" (Gen. 25:22).

The phrase, *"And the children struggled together within*

her," pertains to the fact that there were twins in her womb. However, the *"struggle"* carries with it a tremendous spiritual meaning.

Two energies, the one believing and the other unbelieving, struggled within her and was present even before they were born. It is like the two natures, sin nature and Divine nature, within the Believer.

So, as we had in the union of Abraham and Sarah the beginning of the Divine Plan, we have with Isaac and Rebekah the opposition to that Divine Plan, which, strangely enough, centers up in the same family.

Jacob and Esau, as we shall see, represent the two natures struggling within the Believer. There is only one way that victory can be achieved over the sin nature, and that is by subscribing to God's Prescribed Order, which is the Cross.

The question, *"If it be so, why am I thus?"* probably means, *"If I have thus conceived in answer to my husband's prayers, why do I suffer in this strange manner?"*

In answer to this question which plagued her heart, she took it to the Lord.

THE ANSWER TO PRAYER

"And the LORD said unto her, Two nations are in your womb, and two manner of people shall be separated from your bowels; and the one people shall be stronger than the other people; and the elder shall serve the younger" (Gen. 25:23).

The two nations God told her about were the Edomites and Israelites. From her womb, that is, from the time of their birth, Jacob and Esau would be separated, divided, and even hostile, for they would have nothing in common. Exactly as the Lord said would happen, the elder people descended from Esau, who was born first, who served the people descended from the younger son, Jacob.

This was fulfilled when the Edomites were made subject to King David (II Sam. 8:13-14).

However, the greater fulfillment will have to do with the coming Millennial Reign. Then Israel will be the supreme Nation on Earth, and all other nations will look to her, with Jesus Christ at her head.

As well, the descendants of Esau would also fall in with the descendants of Ishmael, both being the Arab people, with the animosity between these people and Israel continuing unto this very hour.

THE SIN NATURE AND
THE DIVINE NATURE

As well, the two boys represent the two natures in the Christian. We speak of the sin nature and the Divine nature (Rom., Chpt. 6; II Pet. 1:4). In one sense, that was the reason for the struggle between the two unborn babies while they were yet in their mother's womb.

Esau was born first and represents the sin nature with which, due to Adam's fall, every person is born. This simply means that the nature of the person is bent totally and completely toward sin, disobedience, and rebellion to God.

When the believing sinner is Born-Again, he now has the Divine nature, which is stronger than the sin nature. So, when the human being is born as a little baby, he is born with a sin nature, inherited, one might say, from Adam. When he is Born-Again, that is, if he is, he now has the Divine nature.

However, the sin nature doesn't leave once the believing sinner is Born-Again. To be sure, it is made ineffective, but it is still there. If the Believer doesn't understand God's Prescribed Order of Victory, which speaks of the sanctified life, the sin nature will once again have a revival, so to speak, and will begin to dominate the person exactly as it did before Conversion. This is sad but true! In fact, at this very moment, untold millions of Christians are being dominated by *"Esau,"* i.e., *"the sin nature,"* even though they love the Lord very much.

WHY ISN'T THE SIN NATURE
REMOVED AT CONVERSION?

It is allowed by the Lord to remain for disciplinary reasons. In other words, it helps to discipline us. When we realize that the sin nature can be resurrected quickly and can once again dominate us, which makes life miserable, to say the least, such causes us to cling to the Lord even more so, realizing that this is a constant danger.

One day, when the Trump of God sounds, the sin nature will be no more. Paul said:

> "In a moment, in the twinkling of an eye *(proclaims how long it will take for this change to take place)*, at the last trump *(does not denote by the use of the word 'last' that there will be successive trumpet blasts, but rather denotes that this is the close of things, referring to the Church Age)*: for the trumpet shall sound *(it is the 'Trump of God' [I Thess. 4:16])*, and the dead shall be raised incorruptible *(the Sainted dead, with no sin nature)*, and we shall be changed *(put on the Glorified Body)*.
>
> "For this corruptible *(sin nature)* must put on incorruption *(a Glorified Body with no sin nature)*, and this mortal *(subject to death)* must put on immortality *(will never die)*" (I Cor. 15:52-53).

WHAT EXACTLY IS THE SIN NATURE?

It's the nature that we inherited from our first parent, Adam. Before Adam fell, he was ruled by the Divine nature, which meant that his thoughts were constantly on God and proclaimed every Blessing that one could think. However, when he disobeyed the Lord, he instantly fell, meaning that he instantly died spiritually, which means that sin overtook him in every capacity. In other words, his nature became sin and disobedience 24 hours a day, 7 days a week, one might say.

And now, every human being in the world that's ever been born, with the exception of Christ, is born with this sin nature, typified by Esau and Jacob.

As stated, when the believing sinner comes to Christ, the sin nature is unplugged, so to speak, even though allowed to remain. It will remain totally ineffective in our lives if we follow God's Prescribed Order. Let me say it again, God's Prescribed Order is the only way one can live a victorious life. The Lord doesn't have several ways, only one.

In a very abbreviated form, please allow me to give this order:

GOD'S PRESCRIBED ORDER
OF LIFE AND LIVING

• Jesus Christ is the Source of all things we receive from God (Jn. 1:1-3, 14, 29; Col. 2:10-15).

• While Jesus Christ is the Source, the Cross of Christ is the Means, and the only Means, by which all of these wonderful things are given to us (Rom. 6:1-14; Col. 2:10-15).

• With our Lord as the Source and the Cross as the Means, our Faith must ever be in Christ and the Cross. In other words, the Object of our Faith must be Christ and the Cross in every capacity (I Cor. 1:17, 18, 21, 23; 2:2).

• With Christ as our Source and the Cross as our Means, and our Faith anchored squarely in Christ and the Cross, and maintained in Christ and the Cross, the Holy Spirit, Who works exclusively within the parameters, so to speak, of the Finished Work of Christ, will help us to live this life of victory perpetually. While the Bible does not teach sinless perfection, it most definitely does teach that sin is not to have dominion over us (Rom. 6:14; 8:1-11; Eph. 2:13-18).

That which you have just read in very abbreviated form is God's Prescribed Order of Victory. It is the only way that the Believer can have victory over the sin nature and live the life that he ought to live.

ESAU

"And when her days to be delivered were fulfilled, behold, there were twins in her womb.

"And the first came out red, all over like an hairy garment; and they called his name Esau" (Gen. 25:24-25).

As stated, Esau is a type of the sin nature which is *". . . enmity against God: for it is not subject to the Law of God, neither indeed can be"* (Rom. 8:7).

His name Esau means, *"the hairy one,"* which speaks of sensuality. In other words, he was a man of the world and cared not at all, as we shall see, for the Things of God, although he was of the godly family. How can one be so close to the things of God, and yet, be so devoid of spiritual things?

JACOB

"And after that came his brother out, and his hand took hold on Esau's heel; and his name was called Jacob: and Isaac was threescore years old when she bore them" (Gen. 25:26).

Isaac was 40 years old when he and Rebekah married. He was 60 years old when the two boys were born, showing that they had been some 20 years trying to have children but succeeded only when the Lord intervened.

Usually there is a considerable interval—an hour or more—between the birth of twins; but here, Jacob appears without delay, following immediately after his brother. This means there was absolutely no interval between them. Though very rare, yet similar cases have been chronicled from time to time.

That being the physical explanation, there is a spiritual sense greatly involved here, as well.

In later years, because of Jacob's own unworthy conduct, Esau would refer to this phenomenon of birth (Gen. 27:36).

These boys were named by their mother. She was, no doubt, led by the Holy Spirit, especially considering that their names so very much characterized their dispositions once they were grown.

To be at a person's heel is to be his determined pursuer, and one, who, on overtaking, throws him down. This, in a sense, at least, in the spiritual, characterizes Jacob. He wanted the birthright mostly for spiritual reasons but went about to get it in all the wrong ways.

To Abraham was given the great Doctrine of *"Justification by Faith."* About thirteen and one-half Chapters are devoted to the Patriarch.

Jacob, instead, signifies Sanctification, with about twenty-five and one-half Chapters devoted to this Patriarch. This shows us that *"living the life"* is far more complicated than *"receiving the life."*

Perhaps in Jacob as no other personality of the Bible, we find the greatest illustration of the great quest for victory. We plainly see ourselves in Jacob, even as intended by the Holy Spirit. If not, then you're not looking at yourself properly.

We find the motive of Jacob as being very good, but his actions at times being very deplorable.

ISAAC'S LOVE FOR ESAU

"And the boys grew: and Esau was a cunning hunter, a man of the field; and Jacob was a plain man, dwelling in tents.

"And Isaac loved Esau, because he did eat of his venison: but Rebekah loved Jacob" (Gen. 25:27-28).

The original language proclaims the fact that Esau was a wild, undisciplined man who lived a wild life, seeking sport and adventure. In contrast to him, Jacob was a quiet, mature individual. The Hebrew *"tam"* also means that he was sensible, diligent, dutiful, and peaceful. He could be counted on to carry out the duties of life. He was orderly and paid attention to business.

But yet, Isaac loved Esau while Rebekah loved Jacob.

While Isaac certainly should have loved Esau, the type of love he manifested toward him was against the Word of God. He was determined to give the blessing of the birthright to Esau even though his oldest son cared not at all for spiritual things.

At this stage, Isaac seems to have forgotten his very purpose and reason for living.

Regrettably and sadly, Isaac is a symbol of the church. If left to its own devices, it will give the birthright to Esau every time. What was Isaac thinking? What is the modern church thinking? What do I mean by the modern church?

I mean that the modern church all too often places its hand of approval upon an Esau while altogether ignoring or even opposing Jacob. In other words, it will place its seal of approval on one not chosen by God. When I say the church, I am primarily speaking of organized religion.

And yet, if one is not led exclusively by the Spirit, this is what one is liable to do. Even the mighty Samuel would have chosen one of the other brothers in place of David simply because he looked on the outward appearance, as do most (I Sam. 16:6-7).

THE BIRTHRIGHT

"And Jacob sod pottage: and Esau came from the field, and he was faint:

"And Esau said to Jacob, Feed me, I pray you, with that same red pottage; for I am faint: therefore was his name called Edom.

"And Jacob said, Sell me this day your birthright" (Gen. 25:29-31).

Even though Esau was hungry, this had little, if anything, to do with his trading the birthright for a bowl of stew.

The first emphasis is on Jacob wanting the birthright.

Exactly what was the birthright? It was:

• Succession to the earthly inheritance of Canaan.

• Possession of the Covenant Blessing, which included his seed being as the stars of the sky and all the families of the Earth being blessed in him.

• Progenitorship of the Promised Seed, which was the greatest Blessing of all, and spoke of Christ.

The firstborn was to receive the birthright, and Esau, by a

few minutes, was the firstborn.

As it can be seen, the birthright then dealt primarily with spiritual things, of which Esau had no regard or concern.

Under the Mosaic Law, which would come about 400 years later, the privileges of the firstborn were clearly defined:

- The official authority of the father.
- A double portion of the father's property.
- The functions of the domestic priesthood.
- More than likely, the birthright in Isaac's time included these same privileges.

Deplorable as was his character, still, Jacob valued Divine and Eternal Blessings. Had he placed himself in God's Hands, the Prophecy made to his mother before he was born would have been fulfilled to include him. As well, it would have been without the degradation and suffering, which his own scheming brought upon him.

The domestic priesthood meant that the eldest son acted as Priest for the family and offered the sacrifices, which God had commanded Adam and his sons to offer.

PROPHET?

"And Esau said, Behold, I am at the point to die: and what profit shall this birthright do to me?

"And Jacob said, Swear to me this day; and he swore unto him: and he sold his birthright unto Jacob.

"Then Jacob gave Esau bread and pottage of lentiles; and he did eat and drink, and rose up, and went his way: thus Esau despised his birthright" (Gen. 25:32-34).

The natural heart places no value on the things of God, as we see evidenced in the choices made by Esau. To the natural heart, God's Promises are a vague, valueless, powerless thing simply because God is not known; hence, it is that present things carry such weight and influence in man's estimation. Anything that man can *"see,"* he values because he is governed by sight and not by Faith. To him, the present is everything; the future is a mere uninfluentual thing—a matter of the merest uncertainty. Thus it was with Esau.

His question, *"What profit shall this birthright do to me?"* characterizes the majority of the human race. The *"present"* is everything while the *"future"* is nothing. As a result, they abandon all interest in eternity! The things of God did not interest the eldest son of Isaac, so he despised his birthright: thus, Israel despised the present land (Ps. 106:24); thus, they despise Christ (Zech. 11:13); and thus, those who were bidden to the marriage despised the invitation (Mat. 22:5).

Think about it! To Esau, a mess of pottage was better than a title to the land of Canaan.

GERAR

"And Isaac dwelt in Gerar" (Gen. 26:6).

There is no indication that the Lord told Isaac to go to Gerar. The indication is that he went there according to his own leading and direction. It was not the Lord! Events proved that. Anything toward Egypt, and Gerar was toward Egypt, always proves to be disastrous. That being the case, it is also very dangerous to go to Gerar because, as stated, that is toward Egypt. We are to shun the very appearance of evil.

DECEPTION

"And the men of the place asked him of his wife; and he said, She is my sister: for he feared to say, She is my wife; lest, said he, the men of the place should kill me for Rebekah; because she was fair to look upon" (Gen. 26:7).

Evidently, Rebekah, as Sarah, was very attractive. Possibly the ones who inquired about Rebekah were emissaries from Abimelech. At any rate, Isaac lied to them, telling them that Rebekah was his sister.

It is positive that Isaac knew in detail of his father's episode in Egypt and the wrongness of the act. So, why did he follow the same course?

FAITHLESSNESS

"And it came to pass, when he had been there a long time, that Abimelech king of the Philistines looked out at a window, and saw, and, behold, Isaac was sporting with Rebekah his wife.

"And Abimelech called Isaac, and said, Behold, of a surety she is your wife; and why did you say, she is my sister? And Isaac said unto him, Because I said, Lest I die for her" (Gen. 26:8-9).

Deception can succeed only for a short period of time. Isaac forgets himself and kisses his wife in a place where he can be seen and, in fact, was seen. So, Abimelech calls him on the carpet, so to speak. Then the truth comes out.

Once again, God's Primary Emissary on Earth is humiliated. Now, let it be known and understood that sin always humiliates, irrespective of who commits it. In fact, as should be obvious, the humiliation is even worse according to the position of the individual in question.

ABIMELECH

"And Abimelech said, What is this you have done unto us? one of the people might lightly have lain with your wife, and you should have brought guiltiness upon us.

"And Abimelech charged all his people, saying, He who touches this man or his wife shall surely be put to death" (Gen. 26:10-11).

Basically the same questions are put to Isaac by Abimelech as were put to his father by Pharaoh.

Concerning this, Matthew Henry said:

"There is nothing in Isaac's denial of his wife to be imitated, nor even excused. The impartiality of the sacred historian records it for our warning, and to show that Righteousness comes not by the Law, but by Faith in Christ."[2]

The sin of Isaac was greater than the sin of his father

Abraham. While no sin is to be excused, Isaac had this unsavory example before him, so there was no excuse for what he did.

ESAU

"And Esau was forty years old when he took to wife Judith the daughter of Beeri the Hittite, and Bashemath the daughter of Elon the Hittite:

"Which were a grief of mind unto Isaac and to Rebekah" (Gen. 26:34-35).

At 40 years of age, Esau was the same age as Isaac his father when some 60 years before, he had married Esau's mother, Rebekah.

The names of these two women who married Esau are remarkable, showing that the Hittites spoke a Semitic tongue. *"Judith,"* as the feminine form of Judah, means, *"Praise."* *"Bashemath"* means, *"Fragrant,"* and was the name also of a daughter of Solomon (I Ki. 4:15).

No doubt, Esau reasoned in his mind that these girls were little different, if at all, than the family of Abraham back in Haran. However, there was a great difference; the greatest being that God had commanded that wives be taken from the family of Abraham and not from the Canaanites. Whatever the other reasons, that is enough! The family of Abraham was in the line of Shem, Noah's son, from whom the Messiah would come. Also, Canaan and his line were cursed (Gen. 9:25-26).

THE BIRTHRIGHT

"And it came to pass, that when Isaac was old, and his eyes were dim, so that he could not see, he called Esau his oldest son, and said unto him, My son: and he said unto him, Behold, here am I.

"And he said, Behold now, I am old, I know not the day of my death:

"Now therefore take, I pray you, your weapons, your quiver and your bow, and go out to the field, and take me some venison;

"And make me savory meat, such as I love, and bring it to me, that I may eat; that my soul may bless you before I die.

"And Rebekah heard when Isaac spoke to Esau his son. And Esau went to the field to hunt for venison, and to bring it" (Gen. 27:1-5).

As the record will show, if Esau was ready to sell the birthright for a mess of pottage, his father was prepared to sell it for a dish of venison! Concerning this, Williams said:

"Humbling picture of a man of God under the power of his lower sensual nature, i.e., 'the sin nature'!"[3]

Isaac had been told by God at the time of Jacob's birth that he (Jacob) was to possess the birthright. But yet, he ignores this Word from the Lord and proceeds in his determination to give this birthright to Esau, despite the fact that Esau knew the Lord not at all!

PERFECT MEN AND WOMEN?

So, Rebekah overhears the intention of Isaac and proceeds to manage the affairs herself; therefore, she steps outside the path of Faith.

We may wonder about all of this, considering that these people were the Church of that particular time; however, the Lord definitely had and has a Purpose in setting before us all the traits of man's flawed character. We will find that it serves two means.

1. It is to magnify God's Grace.

2. It is meant to serve as a warning for you and me.

The truth is, all of this is done, not at all to perpetuate the memory of sins, which are forever blotted out from God's Sight. In fact, all the flaws, sins, and wrong directions of Abraham, Isaac, and Jacob, plus every other Believer who has ever lived, have been perfectly washed away, with each of these individuals taking their place amid *"the spirits of just men made perfect."*

In all of this, we see that God has not been dealing with perfect men and women, but with those of *"like passions as we are,"* and that He has been working and bearing with the same failures, the same infirmities, and the same errors as those over which we mourn everyday.

REBEKAH

"And Rebekah spoke unto Jacob her son, saying, Behold, I heard your father speak unto Esau your brother, saying,

"Bring me venison, and make me savory meat, that I may eat, and bless you before the LORD before my death.

"Now therefore, my son, obey my voice according to that which I command you" (Gen. 27:6-8).

Here we have the aged Patriarch, Isaac, standing, as it were, at the very portal of eternity, the Earth and nature fast fading away from his view. Yet, he was occupied about *"savory meat"* and was about to act in direct opposition to the Divine Council by blessing the elder instead of the younger.

Thus, Rebekah reasons that if Isaac will do this thing, which is against God, she is justified in her actions of deception. However, wrongdoing is never justified! It always reaps a bitter result exactly as it did here.

DECEPTION

"Go now to the flock, and fetch me from thence two good kids of the goats; and I will make them savory meat for your father, such as he loves:

"And you shall bring it to your father, that he may eat, and that he may bless you before his death.

"And Jacob said to Rebekah his mother, Behold, Esau my brother is a hairy man, and I am a smooth man:

"My father peradventure will feel me, and I will seem to him as a deceiver; and I shall bring a curse upon me, and not a blessing" (Gen. 27:9-12).

Rebekah's plan is one of deception and is not pleasing at all to the Lord. However, such is the path of the flesh; it always seems right to the natural heart and mind.

We may look at this and think that such chicanery died with Jacob and his mother; however, regrettably, that is not the case.

My following statements will be strong, but I feel them to be absolutely correct.

Having lived for the Lord almost all of my life, and as the writer of Amazing Grace said, *"Through many dangers, toils, and snares, I have already come,"* in this, I've learned a few things:

From experience and, above all, my study of the Word of God and the Revelations given to me by the Lord concerning the Word, I personally believe, if one doesn't walk the path of Faith, one will practice the life of spiritual deception. There are only two paths, *"Faith"* and *"flesh."*

To walk the path of Faith, one must ever understand what Faith actually is. The Holy Spirit through Paul defined it very ably. He said:

"I am crucified with Christ: nevertheless I live; yet not I, but Christ lives in me: and the life which I now live in the flesh (our natural walk) *I live by the Faith of the Son of God, Who loved me, and gave Himself for me"* (Gal. 2:20).

Notice the way that Paul used the term *"the Faith of the Son of God."*

This refers to what Jesus did for us at the Cross, which was the great Sacrifice of Himself. In fact, Christianity is often referred to as *"the Faith,"* with that latter term always referring to what Christ did at the Cross.

So, it's the Cross, or it's deception!

THE CURSE

"And his mother said unto him, Upon me be your curse, my son: only obey my voice, and go fetch me them.

"And he went, and fetched, and brought them to his mother:

and his mother made savory meat, such as his father loved.

"And Rebekah took goodly raiment of her eldest son Esau, which were with her in the house, and put them upon Jacob her younger son:

"And she put the skins of the kids of the goats upon his hands, and upon the smooth of his neck:

"And she gave the savory meat and the bread, which she had prepared, into the hand of her son Jacob" (Gen. 27:13-17).

It should be understood that Rebekah wanted the Blessing for Jacob, not just because he was her favorite son, but because she knew this was the Will of the Lord. However, her means of obtaining this showed a lack of trust and, thereby, constituted a work of the flesh. In essence, by resorting to trickery, she was doing the same thing that Sarah did as it regarded a son being born to Abraham by Hagar. Both women would seek to *"help"* God, but the Lord, irrespective as to whom the people might be, can never accept such help.

We are observing here the greatest hindrance to the Christian experience. We do not trust the Lord, or else, we do not know how to trust the Lord, which is more often the case than many would realize.

If the Believer doesn't understand the Cross of Christ, he will invariably seek to do exactly what Rebekah here sought to do. He will resort to the flesh because, as stated, if the path of Faith is not properly trod, there is nowhere else to go but the way of the flesh.

THE DECEPTION

"And he came unto his father, and said, My father: and he said, Here am I; who are you, my son?

"And Jacob said unto his father, I am Esau your firstborn; I have done according as you bade me: arise, I pray you, sit and eat of my venison, that your soul may bless me.

"And Isaac said unto his son, How is it that you have found it so quickly, my son? And he said, Because the LORD your God

brought it to me" (Gen. 27:18-20).

Jacob brings the Lord into his perfidiousness. So it is with all Believers who fail God. It is bad enough to do wrong, but to attempt to make the Lord a part of our wrong makes it infinitely worse.

Inasmuch as our very bodies are temples of the Holy Spirit (I Cor. 3:16), then the Third Person of the Triune Godhead must observe all we do, whether good or bad. In a sense, even though never touched by sin Himself, it never fails to grieve Him, and to do so to a degree perhaps we will never understand. Of course, I speak of the Holy Spirit (Eph. 4:30).

THE DEED

"And Isaac said unto Jacob, Come near, I pray you, that I may feel you, my son, whether you be my very son Esau or not.

"And Jacob went near unto Isaac his father; and he felt him, and said, The voice is Jacob's voice, but the hands are the hands of Esau.

"And he discerned him not, because his hands were hairy, as his brother Esau's hands: so he blessed him.

"And he said, Are you my very son Esau? And he said, I am.

"And he said, Bring it near to me, and I will eat of my son's venison, that my soul may bless you. And he brought it near to him, and he did eat: and he brought him wine and he drank" (Gen. 27:21-25).

The depth of Rebekah's sin carried out by her son Jacob is labeled very correctly, I think, by Matthew Henry.

He said:

"Rebekah wronged Isaac by practicing an imposition upon him; she wronged Jacob by using her authority and persuasion to tempt him to wickedness; she sinned against the Lord, and dishonored His Power and Faithfulness, by supposing He needed such means of effecting His Purpose, and fulfilling His Promise.

"She put a stumblingblock in Esau's way, and furnished him with a pretext for enmity, both against Jacob and against

the Salvation of the Lord, by putting Jacob upon acting such a treacherous part.

"It was one of those crooked measures which have too often been adopted to accomplish the Divine Promises; as if the end would justify, or at least excuse the means."[4]

The entirety of the transaction speaks of fraud. All these parties are to be blamed:

- Isaac for endeavoring to set aside the Divine Will.
- Esau for wishing to deprive his brother of the Blessing he had himself relinquished to him.
- Rebekah and Jacob for wishing to secure it by fraudulent means, not trusting wholly in the Lord.

As an aside, how remarkable it is in this amazing Creation of God that of all the billions of people in this world, every voice is different.

THE BLESSING

"And his father Isaac said unto him, Come near now, and kiss me, my son.

"And he came near, and kissed him: and he smelled the smell of his raiment, and blessed him, and said, See, the smell of my son is as the smell of a field which the LORD has blessed:

"Therefore God give you of the dew of Heaven, and the fatness of the Earth, and plenty of corn and wine:

"Let people serve you, and nations bow down to you: be lord over your brethren, and let your mother's sons bow down to you: cursed be everyone who curses you, and blessed be he who blesses you" (Gen. 27:26-29).

It is observed by Matthew Henry that *"the Blessing given by Isaac is expressed in very general terms."* He went on to say that *"no mention is made of those distinguishing mercies included in the Covenant with Abraham."*[5]

The first part of the Blessing is a generalization. It speaks of the Blessings of the Earth belonging to the recipient.

However, in Verse 29, it becomes much more particular,

with even the entirety of the Earth bowing down to him. The idea pertains to Christ.

The Incarnation would bring the Son of God into the world. So, this Blessing would only pass through Jacob and many others, and be realized only in Christ. Even yet, it hasn't been fulfilled in totality but most definitely shall be at the Second Coming. It is ironic; the Blesser is Christ, and the Blessing is also Christ!

ESAU

"And it came to pass, as soon as Isaac had made an end of blessing Jacob, and Jacob was yet scarce gone out from the presence of Isaac his father, that Esau his brother came in from his hunting.

"And he also had made savory meat, and brought it unto his father, and said unto his father, Let my father arise, and eat of his son's venison, that your soul may bless me.

"And Isaac his father said unto him, Who are you? And he said, I am your son, your firstborn Esau" (Gen. 27:30-32).

Does not Jacob realize that Esau will soon come upon the scene? Perhaps he thought that Esau cared so little for the birthright that he would raise no objection. However, if he thought all of this, why did he not say such to his father without trying to deceive the old man?

The truth is, Esau did want the Blessing but not for the right purpose and reason. As well, he would treat the transaction made between him and his brother, as it regards the birthright, as no more than a joke. However, he finds to his dismay that he has been out-tricked!

• Esau represents those in the church who would walk the path of self-will.

• Jacob represents those who know the path of Faith but would leave that path and suffer greatly.

• Isaac represents those who are in positions of leadership and know so little of the Mind of God that they would give the birthright to the Devil instead of Christ.

What an ignominious mess! I wonder how much the church has really changed, if any at all?

A JUST FEAR

"And Isaac trembled very exceedingly, and said, Who? where is he who has taken venison, and brought it to me, and I have eaten of all before you came, and have blessed him? yes, and he shall be blessed.

"And when Esau heard the words of his father, he cried with a great and exceeding bitter cry, and said unto his father, Bless me, even me also, O my father.

"And he said, Your brother came with subtilty, and has taken away your blessing" (Gen. 27:33-35).

Concerning this, Ellicott says, *"The trembling of Isaac was not from mere vexation at having been so deceived, and made to give the blessing contrary to his wishes. What Isaac felt was that he had been resisting God. Despite the Prophecy given to Rebekah, and Esau's own unspiritual character and heathen marriages, he had determined to bestow on him the birthright by an act of his own will; and he had failed. But he persists no longer in his sin,"* although he does acknowledge the subtlety of Jacob.

Isaac trembles at what he had almost done, which would have given the Blessing of Abraham to this ungodly, unspiritual son, whom the Holy Spirit refers to as a *"fornicator"* (Heb. 12:16).

"The will of the flesh" made Isaac wish to bless Esau, but Faith in the end conquered (Heb. 11:20), and he cries respecting Jacob, *"I have blessed him, and he shall be blessed."*

Hebrews 12:17 recalls Esau's bitter weeping when he found that he had lost the birthright, and now he failed with his tears to cause his father to change his mind. He found no place of repentance in his father's will.

REPENTANCE?

As Paul describes this *"repentance"* (Heb. 12:17), he is not speaking of true Repentance, for Esau manifested no such thing. He is referring to Esau attempting to change the mind of his father, Isaac. Esau wanted the material part, but he had no interest whatsoever in the spiritual part, which was, in reality, the substance of the birthright. In fact, Esau little desired the birthright, if at all, but wanted the Blessing. How so similar to many in the modern church!

JACOB

"And he said, Is not he rightly named Jacob? for he has supplanted me these two times: he took away my birthright; and, behold, now he has taken away my blessing. And he said, Have you not reserved a blessing for me?

"And Isaac answered and said unto Esau, Behold, I have made him your lord, and all his brethren have I given to him for servants; and with corn and wine have I sustained him: and what shall I do now unto you, my son?

"And Esau said unto his father, Have you but one blessing, my father? bless me, even me also, O my father. And Esau lifted up his voice, and wept.

"And Isaac his father answered and said unto him, Behold, your dwelling shall be the fatness of the Earth, and of the dew of Heaven from above.

"And by your sword shall you live, and you shall serve your brother; and it shall come to pass when you shall have the dominion, that you shall break his yoke from off your neck" (Gen. 27:36-40).

Only one son could inherit the spiritual prerogatives of the birthright and the temporal lordship which accompanied it.

Concerning Verse 39, the actual Hebrew reads, *"Your dwelling shall be of the fat places of the Earth."* However, most expositors consider that the preposition, *"Of,"* should be translated, *"From."* Thus, it would read, *"Behold your dwelling shall be away from the fat places of the Earth, and away from the dew of Heaven from above, and by your sword you shall live."*

EDOMITES

This is closer to the original intent of the Hebrew language and, as well, more aptly describes the descendants of Esau, the Arabs. For the most part, their domicile or dwelling has been the desert and not otherwise. As well, they have been and are a violent people, thereby, fulfilling Verse 40, *"And by your sword you shall live."*

The Edomites were the descendants of Esau. The Prophecy was fulfilled in that they were in subjection to Israel for many, many years. However, in the first days of Joram, and then of Ahaz, Edom revolted and recovered its freedom exactly as Isaac had prophesied in Verse 40.

So, in reality, there was no blessing for Esau as there can never be a blessing for those who would demean the Ways of God, thereby, setting their own course.

As we have stated, the Blesser is the Lord Jesus Christ, and the Blessing is the Lord Jesus Christ. In fact, Christ being born into this world and, thereby, redeeming lost humanity by going to the Cross is what all of this is all about. God had to have a lineage of Faith through whom He could come as a Man, and the lineage of Abraham produced these people. It is Jesus Christ, or it is nothing!

He said of Himself, *"I am the Way, the Truth, and the Life: no man comes unto the Father, but by Me"* (Jn. 14:6).

JESUS CHRIST

In essence, Jesus Christ is the coin of this spiritual realm. It is not the Church, not good works, and not good deeds, but Faith in Christ and what Christ has done for us at the Cross.

Jesus Christ Alone was and is the Son of God, and Jesus Christ Alone went to the Cross and paid the price for man's Redemption (Jn. 3:16; Gal. 1:4). So, everyone in this world who places their Faith and trust in Muhammad, Buddha, the Pope, the Church, denominations, or good works will be eternally lost. Let no one think that Faith in the Church, or whatever, equates with Faith in Jesus Christ. It must be Christ and Christ Alone. And more so, it must be *"Christ and Him Crucified"* (I Cor. 1:23; 2:2).

REBEKAH

"And Esau hated Jacob because of the Blessing wherewith his father blessed him: and Esau said in his heart, The days of mourning for my father are at hand; then will I kill my brother Jacob.

"And these words of Esau her elder son were told to Rebekah: and she sent and called Jacob, her younger son, and said unto him, Behold, your brother Esau, as touching you, does comfort himself, purposing to kill you.

"Now therefore, my son, obey my voice; and arise, flee thou to Laban my brother to Haran;

"And tarry with him a few days, until your brother's fury turn away;

"Until your brother's anger turn away from you, and he forget that which you have done to him: then I will send, and fetch you from thence: why should I be deprived also of you both in one day?" (Gen. 27:41-45)

Esau had no cause to hate Jacob. He knew that the Prophecy had given the birthright to Jacob. As well, he knew that his profligate lifestyle did not warrant such. He had no desire to be the Priest of the family, in fact, no desire for the Things of God whatsoever. So, his hatred was fueled by ungodliness and not for any imagined wrong.

It must be remembered that Esau was in the Covenant but, actually, not part of the Covenant. Although he was in the sacred family, he was not really a spiritual part of the sacred family. As previously stated, so are millions of modern church members. They are in the Church, but not really of the Church.

They claim the Lord, but they aren't really of the Lord.

JACOB

As we have stated, Jacob himself was a sad illustration of the destructive power of fallen human nature, but yet, he truly loved the Lord and truly wanted the things of the Lord. In fact, Jacob is a type of the consecrated Child of God, who tries by self-will to attain from the Lord what can only be attained through and by the Holy Spirit. As Jacob, we have to learn that lesson the hard way also.

How so much his life mirrors my own and yours! However, even though it will take some time and he will pass through many dangers, toils, and snares, ultimately, Jacob, the deceiver, the supplanter, the heel-catcher, will become *"Israel"* the *"soldier of God."*

MORE DECEPTION

"And Rebekah said to Isaac, I am weary of my life because of the daughters of Heth: if Jacob take a wife of the daughters of Heth, such as these which are of the daughters of the land, what good shall my life do me?" (Gen. 27:46)

There is no doubt that Rebekah was concerned about *"the daughters of the land"* and none of them being a suitable wife for Jacob. She, of course, is the very recipient of this which Abraham demanded concerning a wife for his son, Isaac. However, her real reason, at this time, for sending Jacob away was not that which she told Isaac, but rather because she feared for his life as it regarded the anger of Esau.

So, we cannot exonerate Rebekah altogether from a charge of duplicity in this. This is what she wanted Isaac to believe, but it is not the real reason.

The *"few days"* of Verse 44 would turn into some 20 years, and she, in fact, would never again see Jacob. She would die before his return to the Land of Promise.

Such is the path of self-will. How it must have broken her

heart a thousand times over that she never saw her son again.

I think there is no doubt that Rebekah ultimately made all of this right with God, but there is no way she could undo the results of her act. This would haunt her for the rest of her life.

THE HAND OF GOD

How different it would have been had she left the matter entirely in the Hands of God! This is the way in which Faith manages instead of us trying to do it ourselves. Jesus said concerning these very things, *"Which of you by taking thought can add to his statue one cubit?"* We gain nothing by our anxiety and planning; we only shut out God, and that is no gain.

It is always a just Judgment from the Hand of God to be left to reap the fruits of our own devices. I know of few things sadder than to see a Child of God so entirely forgetting his proper place and privilege as to take the management of his affairs into his own hands. The birds of the air and the lilies of the field may well be our teachers when we so far forget our position of unqualified dependence upon God.

Out of this Text, we also learn what a profane person actually is, even as the Holy Spirit described Esau (Heb. 12:16). It is one who would like to hold both worlds, one who would like to enjoy the present without forfeiting his title to the future. It is the person who attempts to use God instead of God using him. Please understand, we're not speaking here of those of the world but those in the Church, those who claim Divine privilege.

REBEKAH

So ends the narrative concerning Rebekah, the wife of Isaac and the mother of Esau and Jacob.

Jacob himself closed out his life in Egypt but was buried in the field of Machpelah.

Jacob said, *"There they buried Abraham and Sarah his wife; there they buried Isaac and Rebekah his wife; and there I buried Leah"* (Gen. 49:31).

Great Women of the Bible

OF THE

BIBLE

OLD TESTAMENT

Chapter Three

RACHEL AND LEAH

RACHEL AND LEAH

To do justice to both Rachel and Leah, who were sisters, incidentally, and both wives of Jacob, it is imperative that we do them together. If we try to do them separately, I personally feel that it would be somewhat confusing.

As we shall see, these two played a tremendously important part in the great Plan of God. Leah and Rachel would bring forth seven sons who would head up seven Tribes of Israel. The concubines brought forth four sons, making 11 in all. The complement of 13 sons, who would make up the entirety of the Tribes of Israel, was completed with the two sons of Joseph, Manasseh and Ephraim. From this lineage, even as we shall see, would come the great Tribes of Israel, who would be used by God, despite their imperfections, to bring the knowledge of Jehovah into the world. In fact, Israel alone was the only monotheistic people on the face of the Earth, meaning they worshipped one God, Jehovah. Every other nation in the world was polytheistic, meaning they worshipped many gods, actually, demon spirits. That's part of the reason the Lord would not allow or, at least, seriously warned Israel not to fraternize with surrounding nations. It was because of the influence of demon spirits. Sadly, Israel would not listen!

THE JOURNEY

"Then Jacob went on his journey, and came into the land of the people of the east" (Gen. 29:1).

This *"journey,"* even as we shall see, was to last for some 20 years. In it, Jacob would learn much but would still need another Revelation before the total change would come. More than anything else, these 20 years were to make him see the need for change.

God will not really begin to reveal Himself until the end of flesh is seen. If, therefore, I have not reached the end of my flesh in the deep and positive experience of my soul, it is morally impossible that I can have anything like a just apprehension of God's Character. Regrettably, it takes a long time to come to the end of self-will.

This is what this *"journey"* is all about!

We will find in the coming scenario that the problem of deception is still with Jacob. An old sin is an easy sin!

Jacob was now in Mesopotamia, about 450 miles from Beer-sheba.

THE WELL

"And he looked, and behold a well in the field, and, lo, there were three flocks of sheep lying by it; for out of that well they watered the flocks: and a great stone was upon the well's mouth" (Gen. 29:2).

As we shall see, it is obvious that this well could only be used at fixed times. A great stone covered its mouth, which probably required two or three men to remove it.

From the way the scenario unfolds, more than likely, Laban, the father of Rachel, owned this well. I say this because immediately upon her arrival with the sheep, the stone is rolled away, and her sheep are watered first. The rest, though they had been there long before her, had to bide their time until her sheep were watered.

Considering the value of wells of that particular time, this is probably the truth of the matter.

Jacob comes upon this well and sees sheep and shepherds gathered by it. They are evidently waiting for the stone to be rolled away so their sheep can be watered.

WATER

"And there were all the flocks gathered: and they rolled the stone from the well's mouth, and watered the sheep, and put the stone again upon the well's mouth in his place" (Gen. 29:3).

This Verse mainly tells us how the sheep were watered at

this particular well. As stated, it probably belonged to Laban and was only opened at certain times.

HARAN

"And Jacob said unto them, My brethren, from where do you come? And they said, Of Haran are we" (Gen. 29:4).

In those days, signs were not on every corner giving directions, etc. As well, one did not ask just anyone concerning distances or directions. Robbers were lying in wait for those who were lost or disoriented.

So, when Jacob asked these shepherds where they were from, with their reply being, *"Haran,"* which was actually his destination, he knew he was close. This, no doubt, reminded him of God's Promise to guide him on his journey.

For the Lord to be with one, to guide one, to lead one, to give direction, and to help in that which at first seems to be but small things, but which quickly leads to large things, is the greatest Blessing that one could ever know. As wonderful as it was, this which the Lord promised to do for Jacob is available to every single Believer, irrespective as to whom he might be. Paul quotes the Master when he said:

". . . I will never leave you, nor forsake you.

"So that we may boldly say, The Lord is my Helper, and I will not fear what man shall do unto me" (Heb. 13:5-6).

However, such relationship is not automatic with the Believer. The Believer must actively want and desire such relationship and must ask the Lord to provide such. It is a prayer that the Lord will definitely answer; however, He will not push His Way in, always waiting for the initiative to be taken by the Believer.

LABAN

"And he said unto them, Do you know Laban the son of Nahor? And they said, We know him" (Gen. 29:5).

Laban, it is remembered, is Rebekah's brother. He is the

one who primarily dealt with Eliezer, the servant of Abraham, who had come to find a bride for Isaac (Gen., Chpt. 24).

The language spoken then by the shepherds was probably Chaldean. Jacob, who spoke Hebrew, was evidently able to converse with them either because he had learned Chaldee from his mother or, as is more probable, because the dialects were not then greatly dissimilar.

He called Laban the son of Nahor though he was the grandson. In both Hebrew and Aramaic, there is no separate word for grandson. *"Son"* means any descendant down the line.

RACHEL

"And he said unto them, Is he well? And they said, He is well: and, behold, Rachel his daughter comes with the sheep" (Gen. 29:6).

This is the first mention of Rachel in the Bible. She will figure very prominently in the great Plan of God, being the mother of Joseph and Benjamin. She was the ancestress of three of the great Tribes of Israel, Benjamin, Ephraim, and Manasseh, the latter two being the sons of Joseph. She and her sister, Leah, were honored by later generations as those *"who together built up the house of Israel"* (Ruth 4:11).

The evidence is that Laban was not so well to do financially. His daughter is serving as a shepherdess. She was evidently raised to do her part in the family and, thereby, was taught responsibility and industry. From such, the Lord drew the mothers of Israel.

In all of this, we see the Hand of the Lord working, which is a pleasure to behold. Jacob, who must have a wife in order for the great Plan of God to be brought forth, is led to this particular well, even at the exact time that Rachel appears.

THE SHEEP

"And he said, Lo, it is yet high day, neither is it time that the

cattle should be gathered together: you water the sheep, and go and feed them.

"And they said, We cannot, until all the flocks be gathered together, and till they roll the stone from the well's mouth; then we water the sheep" (Gen. 29:7-8).

Knowing that the shepherds have brought the sheep for water, Jacob wonders as to why they are not attending to the task but seemingly waiting.

More than likely, the reason was that Laban owned the well, and the flocks could not be watered until Rachel had watered her flock first.

Wells were very valuable in those days, especially in the places of hot, dry climates, which this was. So, a system for watering undoubtedly was worked out with the various different flocks in the area.

The stone at the well's mouth, which is so often mentioned here, was to secure the water; for water was scarce—it was not there for everyone's use.

RACHEL, THE SHEPHERDESS

"And while he yet spoke with them, Rachel came with her father's sheep: for she kept them" (Gen. 29:9).

At this point Laban had no sons, although later he would have. As the younger daughter, Rachel was assigned to the task of keeping the sheep, which she did. How old Rachel was at this time, we have no way of knowing, but she was probably only about 15 or 16 years old.

LOVE AT FIRST SIGHT

"And it came to pass, when Jacob saw Rachel the daughter of Laban his mother's brother, and the sheep of Laban his mother's brother, that Jacob went near, and rolled the stone from the well's mouth, and watered the flock of Laban his mother's brother" (Gen. 29:10).

Three times the Holy Spirit has Moses to repeat the term, *"His mother's brother."* It is not done unintentionally. The idea is, Jacob has met with his own relations, with *"his bone and his flesh."*

This is some proof that Laban owned this well in that Rachel waters her sheep first, or, at least, Jacob waters them for her at this time.

It is highly unlikely that Jacob would have acted here as he did had he not learned from Rachel or, possibly, even the waiting shepherds, that the well belonged to Laban, and that no sheep were to be watered until Rachel had first watered hers.

The Scripture says, *"When Jacob saw Rachel. . . ."* Every evidence is that it was love at first sight.

RACHEL

"And Jacob kissed Rachel, and lifted up his voice, and wept" (Gen. 29:11).

The Patriarch is overcome with emotion, and I think mostly at the joy of seeing the Hand of God working in his life. Truly the Lord was with him. While he was very happy to have met his relatives, which meant that his long journey was now over, I think the greatest joy of all was that of a spiritual note. As well, he may have known at that very note, and informed by the Spirit of God, that Rachel was to be his wife. He, of course, would not, at that moment, have told her that, but, more than likely, the Spirit of the Lord definitely informed him of such.

RELATIONS

"And Jacob told Rachel that he was her father's brother, and that he was Rebekah's son: and she ran and told her father" (Gen. 29:12).

Jacob was actually the nephew of Laban. Terms of relationship were used in a very indefinite way among the Hebrews.

We will find that Jacob's love for Rachel is one of the Bible's outstanding examples of human love—seven years *"seemed to him but a few days because of the love he had for her"* (Gen. 29:20).

When she told her father, Laban, about Jacob, I wonder if he did not recall when his sister Rebekah, those many years before, had come to him when Eliezer had come on behalf of Abraham, as it regarded a bride for Isaac.

LABAN

"And it came to pass, when Laban heard the tidings of Jacob his sister's son, that he ran to meet him, and embraced him, and kissed him, and brought him to his house. And he told Laban all these things" (Gen. 29:13).

Laban now did almost exactly what he had done those many years before when he was told by Rebekah of Eliezer. As he ran then to meet Abraham's servant, he now runs to meet Jacob.

The Patriarch now relates to Laban all the things which had happened between him and Esau. No doubt, He especially gave all the information which Laban required about his mother Rebekah, who was Laban's sister.

Laban would most likely have been well over 100 years of age at this time, possibly, even as much as 120.

THE BARGAIN

"And Laban had two daughters: the name of the elder was Leah, and the name of the younger was Rachel.

"Leah was tender eyed; but Rachel was beautiful and well favored.

"And Jacob loved Rachel; and said, I will serve you seven years for Rachel your younger daughter.

"And Laban said, It is better that I give her to you, than that I should give her to another man: abide with me.

"And Jacob served seven years for Rachel; and they seemed to him but a few days, for the love he had to her" (Gen. 29:16-20).

Would the deception that Laban was now planning to carry out on Jacob have been carried out if, in fact, Jacob had not tried to practice deception on his father, Isaac?

I think not! The Scripture emphatically states, *"that we reap what we sow"* (Gal. 6:7-8). Even though the Passage in Galatians is speaking of sowing to the flesh or sowing to the Spirit, still, the principle is the same.

So, Jacob loved Rachel and agreed to serve Laban some seven years for her hand, so to speak.

It would seem from these statements that Jacob served Laban for seven years before Rachel became his wife; however, the terminology employed rather refers to a contract or agreement. Jacob married both Leah and Rachel immediately, the first in which he was deceived into doing so, and the second by intention. Now, he must serve 14 years, which he did.

THE AGREEMENT IS MADE

"And Jacob said unto Laban, Give me my wife, for my days are fulfilled, that I may go in unto her" (Gen. 29:21).

His *"days being fulfilled"* simply means that the contract had been agreed upon that he was to serve Laban seven years for Rachel. This is proven by Verse 30.

THE BARGAIN SEALED

"And Laban gathered together all the men of the place, and made a feast" (Gen. 29:22).

After everything had been agreed upon as it regarded Jacob serving Laban for seven years, Laban would now make a great feast and invite all the notables of the area to the wedding. However, Laban, as we shall see, has something else in mind altogether.

LEAH

"And it came to pass in the evening, that he took Leah his daughter, and brought her to him; and he went in unto her.

"And Laban gave unto his daughter Leah Zilpah his maid for an handmaid.

"And it came to pass, that in the morning, behold, it was Leah: and he said to Laban, What is this you have done unto me? did I not serve with you for Rachel? wherefore then have you beguiled me?" (Gen. 29:23-25).

When Leah went into Jacob, she, no doubt, was wearing a veil, and, as well, the room was probably dark.

She evidently said nothing that night, but the next morning, to Jacob's surprise, it was not Rachel who had been given to him, but rather Leah.

The question, *"Did not I serve with you for Rachel?"* could have been translated, *"Did not I agree to serve with you for Rachel?"*

SEVEN OTHER YEARS

"And Laban said, It must not be done in our country, to give the younger before the firstborn.

"Fulfill her week, and we will give you this also for the service which you shall serve with me yet seven other years.

"And Jacob did so, and fulfilled her week: and he gave him Rachel his daughter to wife also.

"And Laban gave to Rachel his daughter Bilhah his handmaid to be her maid.

"And he went in also unto Rachel, and he loved also Rachel more than Leah, and served with him yet seven other years" (Gen. 29:26-30).

Concerning Laban's contention that the custom in his country was that the younger must not be married before the firstborn, of that, there is no proof. It seems to be something that Laban concocted on his own. There was some evidence of such in India but not in his part of the world.

Laban now offers Rachel to Jacob for seven more years, making 14 total; however, Jacob did not complain about the situation, perhaps seeing that he had little choice in the matter.

His actions seem to suggest that he knew that he was now paying for his deception regarding Isaac and his brother. Consequently, he accepts the situation.

CHASTISEMENT

The Lord actually doesn't punish His Children, but He definitely does chastise His Children.

What is the difference?

Chastisement is designed to teach us something while punishment contains no instruction, only hurt. Jacob seems to recognize this and accepts it.

This in no way meant that Laban was right in what he did, and, to be sure, the Lord would deal with him, as the Lord deals with all. However, Jacob suffered such with there being no evidence that he sought to take matters into his own hands.

WHAT THE LORD SAW

"And when the LORD saw that Leah was hated, He opened her womb: but Rachel was barren" (Gen. 29:31).

The word, *"Hated,"* here means *"loved less."*

There is no indication that Jacob mistreated Leah, but there is indication that Rachel did. The Lord saw all of this, and, as a result, He made Leah fruitful. At the same time, He made Rachel barren.

In fact, Leah was the ancestress of both David and Jesus. There could have been no greater honor than that!

We learn from all of this the minute involvement of the Lord in all things. He knows all, sees all, and involves Himself in all!

All of this shows that whatever Laban did, Leah was not a party to the deception. She had no choice but to do as she did, but none of this was her idea.

In addition, it certainly wasn't Rachel's idea, but, as well, she had no say in the matter either. Her wrong comes in by taking out the situation on Leah, who was not to blame. In fact, the situation had to be very difficult for all three, Jacob, Rachel, and Leah. However, it seems that Leah unjustly suffered the brunt of this scenario. As noted, the Lord didn't take kindly to what was happening.

REUBEN

"And Leah conceived, and gave birth to a son, and she called his name Reuben: for she said, Surely the LORD has looked upon my affliction; now therefore my husband will love me" (Gen. 29:32).

Reuben means, *"See, a son."*

Considering that in those days being barren was a reproach and that having children was a great Blessing, she evidently hoped that her having this child, in effect, giving Jacob his firstborn, would increase his affection for her. To be unloved or even loved less presents a very unsavory situation. It's very hard for anyone to function in such a climate. From the information given in the next Verse, it doesn't seem that the situation was ameliorated.

SIMEON

"And she conceived again, and brought forth a son; and said, Because the LORD has heard I was hated, He has therefore given me this son also: and she called his name Simeon" (Gen. 29:33).

Simeon means, *"Hearing."* She is functioning from the position that the Lord has heard her petition; however, at the moment, it didn't change, but, ultimately, it would.

LEVI

"And she conceived again, and gave birth to a son; and said, Now this time will my husband be joined unto me, because I

have born him three sons: therefore was his name called Levi" (Gen. 29:34).

Levi means, *"Joined."*

She names her son accordingly in the hopes that her husband will be joined to her with greater love. There is evidence that this ultimately did happen (Gen. 31:4, 14; 49:31).

JUDAH

"And she conceived again, and gave birth to a son: and she said, Now will I praise the LORD: therefore she called his name Judah; and left bearing" (Gen. 29:35).

Judah means, *"Praise."* From this Tribe would come both David and, above all, Christ.

Throughout, in the midst of her melancholy, there is a tone of fervent piety and Faith, not merely to God, but to the Covenant Jehovah. Now, slowly, she parts with her hope of human affection and finds comfort in Jehovah Alone.

This time she says, *"I will praise Jehovah."* It was this son of the despised one, whose birth called forth from her this hymn of simple thanksgiving, who was foreordained to be the ancestor of the promised two more sons and a daughter.

In her six sons, we find the Plan of Salvation outlined so dramatically, as well as these men being Types of Christ. In fact, all of the sons of Leah and Rachel were Types of Christ, with each son portraying a particular Ministry of our Lord to Believers. In other words, He was our Substitute in all things. We will look first at the six sons of Leah and how their names draw out the Plan of Salvation.

THE PLAN OF SALVATION

1. Reuben: *"See, a son."* This represents the child that is born into the world, whomever that child may be.

2. Simeon: *"Hearing."* When the child is old enough, it is to hear the Gospel.

3. Levi: *"Joined."* The child is born, it hears the Gospel, and it is joined to Christ.

4. Judah: *"Praise."* The child is born, it hears the Gospel, it is joined to Christ, and it praises the Lord.

5. Issachar: *"Reward."* The son is born, it hears the Gospel, it is joined to Christ, it praises the Lord, and the Lord gives the reward of Eternal Life.

6. Zebulun: *"Dwelling."* The child is born, it hears the Gospel, it is joined to the Lord, it praises the Lord, it has reward, and now it will dwell with the Lord forever and forever.

Thus is the Plan of Salvation wrought out of the six sons of Leah.

The names of all these sons also portray Christ and a particular Work and Ministry which He has carried out for Believers. We will address this in the body of the next Chapter.

All of these children born to Leah, her maid Zilpah, Rachel, and her maid, Bilhah, including the two sons of Joseph, were the heads of the 13 Tribes of Israel, which were recipients of the Word of God and, as well, served as the womb of the Messiah. So, we're seeing here the birth of a people totally unlike any other people on the face of the Earth who has ever been or ever will be. As Christians, we are a part of Israel but only in the spiritual sense.

GIVE ME CHILDREN, OR ELSE I DIE

"And when Rachel saw that she bore Jacob no children, Rachel envied her sister; and said unto Jacob, Give me children, or else I die.

"And Jacob's anger was kindled against Rachel: and he said, Am I in God's Stead, Who has withheld from you the fruit of the womb?" (Gen. 30:1-2)

Concerning this situation, Keil said:

"If not warranted to infer that Rachel's barrenness was due to lack of prayer on her part and Jacob's, we are at least justified in asserting that her conduct in breaking forth into

angry reproaches against her husband was unlike that of Jacob's mother, Rebekah, who, in similar circumstances, sought relief in prayer."[1]

The brief period of some four or five years that had elapsed since Rachel's marriage, in comparison with the 20 years of Rebekah's barrenness, signally discovers Rachel's sinful impatience.

In this thing, she seems to blame Jacob, but she should have known that God Alone could remove sterility. However, jealousy of Leah appears for the moment to have blinded her to this fact.

As we have stated, Rachel here pictures Israel while Leah pictures the Church. In a sense, Paul addressed this very thing even though he actually is writing about Sarah. The Apostle said:

"For it is written, Rejoice, you barren who bears not; break forth and cry, you who travail not: for the desolate has many more children than she who has an husband" (Gal. 4:27).

Leah was not loved very much by her husband, but she had many more children than the one who had the greater love of the husband. The Church, of which Leah is a type, has many more children than Israel, of which Rachel is a type.

Jacob's anger is kindled against Rachel because she should have been taking the matter to the Lord instead of blaming him.

BILHAH

"And she said, Behold my maid Bilhah, go in unto her; and she shall bear upon my knees, that I may also have children by her.

"And she gave him Bilhah her handmaid to wife: and Jacob went in unto her.

"And Bilhah conceived, and bore Jacob a son" (Gen. 30:3-5).

All of this shows little faith in God. Jealousy, envy, and superstition seem to have guided these affairs. To be sure, as sinful as it was, Sarah's resorting to Hagar was much more understandable than Rachel resorting to Bilhah.

Both of these women, Rachel and Leah, seemed to trust

God, but only to a certain degree. It was somewhat a mixture of faith and fancy, not unlike the modern church.

Trust in Christ, at least, to a certain degree, and trust in other things marks the modern church. It leans partly on God and partly on the world!

At this stage, I'm not certain that Leah and Rachel properly understood the significance of all that was going on. They somehow understood that the bearing of a goodly number of children was of great significance. However, there is little indication that they fully understood why.

DAN

"And Rachel said, God has judged me, and has also heard my voice, and has given me a son: therefore called she his name Dan" (Gen. 30:6).

Dan means, *"To judge, or one decreeing justice."*

Calvin said, *"Jacob began with polygamy, and is now drawn into concubinage. Though God overruled this for the development for the seed of Israel, He did not thereby condone the offense of either Jacob or Rachel."*

Calvin went on to say, *"So God often strives to overcome men's wickedness through kindness, and pursues the unworthy with His Grace."*

Exactly what Rachel meant by naming the child Dan, which means, *"Judging,"* is open to question. The indication seems to be that she felt that God had vindicated her, that is, had judged her righteous by giving this son to Bilhah, her maid. Whether God saw it that way is also open to question.

As someone has well said, *"Men rule, while God overrules."* While He in no way ever condones evil or wrongdoing, not even to the slightest degree, at times, He does use such to bring about His Will. There had to be 13 sons born to Jacob in order to found the Nation of Israel. Twelve would be for the regular Tribes while one (Levi) would be for the Priestly Tribe.

To be sure, God had many ways of doing this, but, at the

same time, He has purposely limited Himself to work through human instrumentation. Consequently, He is either limited or expanded according to the faithlessness or Faith of the individual or individuals. Many years later, the Lord would say of Israel:

"Yes, they turned back and tempted God, and limited the Holy One of Israel" (Ps. 78:41).

NAPHTALI

"And Bilhah Rachel's maid conceived again, and bore Jacob a second son.

"And Rachel said, With great wrestlings have I wrestled with my sister, and I have prevailed: and she called his name Naphtali" (Gen. 30:7-8).

Naphtali means, *"Wrestling."*

The contention between Rachel and Leah evidently was great. Rachel likens it as to a *"wrestling match."* Due to the births of both Dan and Naphtali, she considers herself to have prevailed.

Concerning this, Ellicott says:

"Rachel's was a discreditable victory, one by making use of a bad custom, and it consisted in weaning her husband still more completely from the unloved Leah. Now that Bilhah and children were added to the attractiveness of her tent, her sister, she boasts, will be thought of no more."[2]

GAD AND ASHER

"When Leah saw that she had left bearing, she took Zilpah her maid, and gave her Jacob to wife.

"And Zilpah Leah's maid bore Jacob a son.

"And Leah said, A troop comes: and she called his name Gad.

"And Zilpah Leah's maid bore Jacob a second son.

"And Leah said, Happy am I, for the daughters will call me blessed: and she called his name Asher" (Gen. 30:9-13).

Gad means, *"Good fortune,"* while Asher means, *"Happy."* Ellicott says:

"By ceasing to bear, Leah had lost her one hold upon Jacob's affection, and to regain it, she follows Rachel's example."[3]

The struggle of these two women gives us an idea of their Faith, or the lack of such. It seems that neither one of them actually understood, at least, as they should have, what the path of Faith actually was. In other words, their faith was riddled with self-will. They had a great tendency to *"help God!"* Of course, when they helped Him, it was always from the vantage point of jealousy, envy, malice, or some other passion gone awry. As previously stated, this picture drawn out here before us is not totally unlike our modern actions. Despite the Lord appearing to Jacob and giving him great Promises, we find that the Patriarch still has a long way to go.

And yet, placed in his same position, I wonder, *"Would we have done any better, or even as well?"* From our sanctimonious perches, far too often, we ask with a sneer, *"Would you buy a used car from Jacob?"*

We must never make the mistake of judging the work before it is finished; and that, we far too often do! We must not forget that one of the greatest appellatives in history belongs in part to Jacob, *"The God of Abraham, of Isaac, and of Jacob."*

MANDRAKES

"And Reuben went in the days of wheat harvest, and found mandrakes in the field, and brought them unto his mother Leah. Then Rachel said to Leah, Give me, I pray you, of your son's mandrakes.

"And she said unto her, Is it a small matter that you should have taken my husband? and would you take away my son's mandrakes also? And Rachel said, Therefore he shall lie with you tonight for your son's mandrakes.

"And Jacob came out of the field in the evening, and Leah went out to meet him, and said, You must come in unto me; for

surely I have hired you with my son's mandrakes. And he lay with her that night" (Gen. 30:14-16).

At this time, Reuben was probably four or five years old. According to oriental superstition, the mandrake possessed the virtue of promoting fruitfulness and fertility. It was an apple-like fruit.

Somehow, Rachel found out about the situation and asked for some of the mandrakes.

The request, seemingly, didn't sit well with Leah. So Rachel, who held the dominant hand, made a bargain with Leah. For some of the mandrakes, she would not stand in the way of Leah spending the night with Jacob.

ISSACHAR AND ZEBULUN

"And God hearkened unto Leah, and she conceived, and bore Jacob the fifth son.

"And Leah said, God has given me my hire, because I have given my maiden to my husband: and she called his name Issachar.

"And Leah conceived again, and bore Jacob the sixth son.

"And Leah said, God has endued me with a good dowry; now will my husband dwell with me, because I have born him six sons: and she called his name Zebulun" (Gen. 30:17-20).

Issachar means, *"Reward,"* while Zebulun means, *"Dwelling."*

From Verse 17, we know that Leah sought the Lord as it regarded her conceiving another son, which she did. The Lord heard and answered her prayer. This was despite the fact that superstition had been involved regarding the mandrakes. How so much the Lord overlooks in answering prayer for any of us.

THE PROMISES

Even though Rachel and Leah, it seems, were not as knowledgeable of the things of the Lord as they should have been, it would seem that they were influenced by the Promises of God to Abraham. On his posterity were entailed the richest

Blessings, from whom the Messiah, in the fullness of time, was to descend. It was the belief of these Promises that rendered every pious female in those times desirable of being a mother.

Little did Leah realize that, at this time, the child which had been born to her two or three years earlier, Judah, would head up the Tribe from whom the Messiah would come. Near Jacob's dying day, the great Patriarch prophesied:

"The scepter (ruling power) *shall not depart from Judah, nor a Law-Giver from between His Feet, until Shiloh* (another name for the Messiah) *come; and unto Him shall the gathering of the people be"* (Gen. 49:10).

Leah thinks that God has heard her prayer regarding her fifth conception because she has given her maid, Zilpah, to Jacob, who had brought forth two sons for Jacob, Gad and Asher.

Leah conceived again and brought forth a sixth son. She thought this would give her preeminence over Rachel, meaning that Jacob would look at her as the favorite wife, especially considering that Rachel personally had not been able to conceive at all.

DINAH

"And afterwards she bore a daughter, and called her name Dinah" (Gen. 30:21).

Even though Dinah is the only daughter mentioned in the entirety of this family, there is a possibility that Jacob had other daughters, as well, as seems to be evidenced in Genesis 37:35. However, the word, *"Daughters,"* here could, in fact, refer to granddaughters, etc.

At any rate, Dinah is mentioned here because of the incident in her history afterwards related (Gen. 34:1).

JOSEPH

"And God remembered Rachel, and God hearkened to her, and opened her womb.

"And she conceived, and bore a son; and said, God has taken away my reproach:

"And she called his name Joseph; and said, The LORD shall add to me another son" (Gen. 30:22-24).

The Lord demonstrated that the mandrakes could not remove sterility by allowing Rachel's barrenness to continue at least two years longer, though she had made use of this supposed remedy, and by opening Leah's womb without them.

We should learn from all of this how useless superstition is and that the Lord rules in all things. As well, I think it is obvious here that Rachel only exacerbated her situation instead of helping it.

I wonder how much superstition is presently involved in the prayers and Faith of many modern Christians?

RACHEL

Ultimately, God answered Rachel's petition and *"opened her womb."*

She named her son, *"Joseph,"* which means, *"He shall add."* In effect, this was a Prophecy referring to the birth of another son, who, in fact, would be Benjamin.

It seems that Rachel had advanced somewhat in the Spirit and had by now forsaken human devices, such as resorting to mandrakes, etc. She now evidenced a complete dependence on the Sovereign Grace of the Covenant God of Abraham, Isaac, and Jacob.

Concerning this, Horton says of her:

"When God remembers it does not mean He had forgotten. Rather it means that it was God's time and He actively entered the situation to do something about it. This intervention was to answer Rachel's prayers that He had been listening to the entire time of Leah's childbearing years. God, not the mandrakes, made it possible for Rachel to have a son. Barrenness was considered a disgrace. Now that disgrace was removed by the birth of a son. But she was not satisfied, since Leah had six sons.

So she named the boy Joseph, meaning 'He shall add,' and she asked for another son. Unfortunately, the fulfillment of that prayer would cause her death" (Gen. 35:16-19).

The following is how these sons were Types of Christ:

- Reuben: Reuben means, *"A son."* Jesus is the *"Son"* of God.
- Simeon: this means, *"Hearing."* Through Jesus, we *"hear"* God.
- Levi: this means, *"Joined."* Through Jesus, we are *"joined"* to the Father.
- Judah: this means, *"Praise."* Through Jesus, God has accepted our *"praises."*
- Dan: this means, *"Judgment."* Jesus has taken the *"Judgment"* due us.
- Naphtali: this means, *"Wrestling."* Jesus has *"wrestled"* the powers of darkness, all on our behalf, and has defeated the foe.
- Gad: this means, *"Truth."* Jesus has fought on our behalf and has brought us *"good fortune."*
- Asher: this means, *"Happy."* Jesus has made us *"happy."*
- Issachar: this means, *"Reward."* Jesus is our *"reward."*
- Zebulun: this means to *"Dwell."* Jesus has made it possible for Believers to *"dwell"* in the House of the Lord forever.
- Joseph: this means, *"Added."* All Believers are added to the Kingdom due to what Jesus did at the Cross on our behalf.
- Benjamin: this means, *"Strong right hand."* Jesus is the Father's *"Strong Right Hand,"* and sits with Him in Heavenly Places.

FOURTEEN YEARS

"And it came to pass, when Rachel had born Joseph, that Jacob said unto Laban, Send me away, that I may go unto my own place, and to my country.

"Give me my wives and my children, for whom I have served you, and let me go: for you know my service which I have done

you" (Gen. 30:25-26).

Jacob's terminology, *"For whom I have served you, and let me go,"* proves that both Leah and Rachel became his wives immediately, and then he served the 14 years for them.

Some claim that it is highly unlikely that 11 sons and one daughter could have been born to this family in just seven years. However, it wasn't seven years, but rather 14 years.

Having served the 14 years which had been agreed upon, Jacob tells Laban that he now wants to go back to Canaan.

JACOB'S DECISION

"And Jacob sent and called Rachel and Leah to the field unto his flock,

"And said unto them, I see your father's countenance, that it is not toward me as before; but the God of my father has been with me.

"And you know that with all my power I have served your father.

"And your father has deceived me, and changed my wages ten times; but God suffered him not to hurt me.

"If he said thus, The speckled shall be your wages; then all the cattle bore speckled: and if he said thus, The ringstraked shall be your hire; then bore all the cattle ringstraked.

"Thus God has taken away the cattle of your father, and given them to me" (Gen. 31:4-9).

From these Passages, we learn a little more concerning what had taken place between Jacob and Laban. For instance, the Patriarch says that Laban had changed his wages 10 times, which probably refers to *"many times"* instead of the actual number 10. As used in the Old Testament, the number 10 contains the idea of completeness and not necessarily the exact amount, unless accordingly specified.

When he saw that Jacob's flocks were increasing according to the bargain originally made, he then changed the rules. However, as we see, God overruled that particular change and whatever it was that Laban said that Jacob could have, which was reduced from the original agreement, the Lord had them all to turn out in that particular manner.

We should see from this that the Lord doesn't take kindly to His Children being put upon. Sometimes He will step in, even as He did with Jacob; other times, He doesn't. Nevertheless, one can be doubly certain that the Lord knows all things and keeps account of all things.

RACHEL AND LEAH

So that his conversation would not be overheard, the Patriarch asked both Rachel and Leah to come out into the field where he was in order that he might talk to them. His words to them consisted of three parts:

1. He relates to them the change in Laban's manner toward him and his consequent fear of violence.

2. He justifies his own conduct toward their father and accuses him of repeated injustice.

3. Finally, he announces to them that he has received the Divine Command to return to Canaan.

"And Rachel and Leah answered and said unto him, Is there yet any portion or inheritance for us in our father's house?

"Are we not counted of him strangers? for he has sold us, and has quite devoured also our money.

"For all the riches which God has taken from our father, that is ours, and our children's: now then, whatsoever God has said unto you, do" (Gen. 31:14-16).

There is a marked severity toward their father in the answer of Jacob's wives. They are recalling that they received no dowry whatsoever when they married Jacob. So, they are upset with their father, not only as to how he has treated Jacob, but in the manner in which he has treated them as well. So, they tell Jacob, *"Whatsoever God has said unto you, do."*

It's a shame that Laban figures so prominently in the Gospel Message, but yet, never came to know the Lord. His sister and two daughters would be instrumental in bringing into the world those who would be the heads of the great Tribes of Israel, and to whom God would make all the Promises. He was so close, but yet, so far away. He saw the Hand of God move mightily but never came to know the Lord. What a shame!

JACOB DEPARTS

"Then Jacob rose up, and set his sons and his wives upon camels;

"And he carried away all his cattle, and all his goods which he had gotten, the cattle of his getting, which he had gotten in Padan-aram, for to go to Isaac his father in the land of Canaan.

"And Laban went to shear his sheep: and Rachel had stolen the images that were her father's.

"And Jacob stole away unawares to Laban the Syrian, in that he told him not that he fled.

"So he fled with all that he had; and he rose up, and passed over the river, and set his face toward the Mount Gilead" (Gen. 31:17-21).

The Scripture says that Jacob is leaving, *"for to go to Isaac his father in the land of Canaan."* These 20 years that Jacob has been gone are silent regarding Isaac. How so much he must have grieved for his son.

THE GREAT PLAN OF GOD

While Esau, no doubt, provided some comfort for Isaac, there was no spiritual bond whatsoever between Isaac and his oldest son. Esau simply did not know God.

He knew, of course, that God had laid His Hand on Jacob, but these 20 years passed in silence. Did he hear from Jacob during this time? Did Isaac send any news to Jacob from home?

It is believed that Rebekah died while Jacob was away, but no one knows when. The Scriptures are silent regarding her death, only saying that she was buried with Isaac in the tomb of Abraham (Gen. 49:31).

The great Plan of God regarding the formation of Israel as a Nation will now begin. From the time of Abraham, when he arrived in Canaan, to Jacob, when he went into Egypt, was 215 years. When he left Syria, he was about 100 years old. When he went into Egypt, he was 130 (Gen. 47:9). So, he would spend about 30 years in Canaan before going into Egypt, about 20 years of that time grieving for Joseph, whom he thought was dead.

THE IMAGES

From Verse 19, some have concluded that Rachel was an idol-worshipper because she had stolen the images which belonged to her father.

Concerning this, Horton says:

"Rachel had a reason for stealing the teraphim. These were small idols (like figurines) considered the family gods and were kept on a god-shelf, probably in the corner of the main room of the house.

"When there was any question about the inheritance, the person who had the teraphim was considered to have the right to the double portion of the primary heir. When Jacob first came, he was welcomed into the family and adopted as the heir, since Laban had no sons at the time. But Laban had sons born shortly after, and that normally would invalidate Jacob's claim unless he possessed the teraphim. Rachel felt Jacob deserved more than she was getting, so she stole them for his benefit, and for the benefit of Jacob's family. There is no evidence she wanted to worship these images."[5]

This was evidently sheepshearing time, and Laban was busy in this endeavor; consequently, while Laban was busy, Jacob took his vast herds and fled. He passed over the Euphrates River and then set his face toward Mt. Gilead.

THE CHASE

"And it was told Laban on the third day that Jacob was fled.
"Then Laban overtook Jacob. Now Jacob had pitched his

tent in the mount: and Laban with his brethren pitched in the Mount of Gilead.

"And Laban said to Jacob, What have you done, that you have stolen away unawares to me, and carried away my daughters, as captives taken with the sword?

"Wherefore did you flee away secretly, and steal away from me; and did not tell me, that I might have sent you away with mirth, and with songs, with tabret, and with harp?

"And have not suffered me to kiss my sons and my daughters? you have now done foolishly in so doing.

"It is in the power of my hand to do you hurt: but the God of your father spoke unto me yesternight, saying, You take heed that you speak not to Jacob either good or bad.

"And now, though you would need be gone, because you sore longed after your father's house, yet wherefore have you stolen my gods?

"And Jacob answered and said to Laban, Because I was afraid: for I said, Peradventure you would take by force your daughters from me.

"With whomsoever you find your gods, let him not live: before our brethren discern for you what is yours with me, and take it to you. For Jacob did not know that Rachel had stolen them" (Gen. 31:22, 25-32).

THE ACCUSATION

Laban accuses Jacob of carrying away his daughters as captives, but that is totally untrue. Rachel and Leah voluntarily accompanied their husband in his flight.

The idea that Laban would have tendered a great going away party for Jacob is crassly hypocritical. More than likely, the Lord told Jacob to depart as he did because of Laban's hostile intentions.

One thing is certain: there is no way that Laban would have allowed Jacob to take the herds with him, and he probably would not have allowed his daughters or any of the children to go with Jacob. So, his accusations and his claims hold no merit.

He then accuses Jacob of having stolen his gods, which Jacob vehemently denies, and rightly so. Jacob had no idea that Rachel had taken these things. As it would prove out, they were of no consequence anyway as far as the inheritance was concerned. After this meeting, Rachel would never see her father again.

THE IMAGES

"And Laban went into Jacob's tent, and into Leah's tent, and into the two maidservants' tents; but he found them not. Then went he out of Leah's tent, and entered into Rachel's tent.

"Now Rachel had taken the images, and put them in the camel's furniture, and sat upon them. And Laban searched all the tent, but found them not.

"And she said to her father, Let it not displease my Lord that I cannot rise up before you; for the custom of women is upon me. And he searched but found not the images" (Gen. 31:33-35).

To explain the significance of all of this, let us say it again: the idea was, whoever had the small image could, at a given point in time, claim the inheritance. This is, at least, one of, if not the most, important reasons for Laban's diligence in searching for this little idol. As well, it's the reason that Rachel had taken it, but which would do her no good. She would never see her homeland again or her father, for that matter, after he left.

HIDING THE IMAGES

"The camel's furniture," actually was a saddle riding affair made of wickerwork and had the appearance of a basket or cradle. It was usually covered with carpet and protected against wind, rain, and sun by means of a canopy and curtains, while light was admitted by openings in the side. When riding a camel, this was the apparatus which served as a saddle-like affair, at least, for women.

Rachel had hidden the image under the saddle and was sitting on it. She apologized for not standing, claiming that she was having her *"period."* Whether this was correct or not, we have no way of knowing; but there is a good possibility that it was.

She reasoned in her mind that her father surmised that she was having some type of a problem and would not inquire further, which means he would not search under the camel saddle. This proved to be correct. At any rate, Laban did not find them, so Rachel's ruse worked.

THE ANGER OF JACOB

"And Jacob was angry, and did chide with Laban: and Jacob answered and said to Laban, What is my trespass? what is my sin, that you have so hotly pursued after me?

"Whereas you have searched all my stuff, what have you found of all your household stuff? set it here before my brethren and your brethren, that they may judge between us both.

"This twenty years have I been with you; your ewes and your she goats have not cast their young, and the rams of your flock have I not eaten.

"That which was torn of beasts I brought not unto you; I bore the loss of it; of my hand did you require it, whether stolen by day, or stolen by night.

"Thus I was; in the day the drought consumed me, and the frost by night; and my sleep departed from my eyes.

"Thus have I been twenty years in your house; I served you fourteen years for your two daughters, and six years for your cattle: and you have changed my wages ten times.

"Except the God of my father, the God of Abraham, and the fear of Isaac, had been with me, surely you had sent me away now empty. God has seen my affliction and the labor of my hands, and rebuked you yesternight" (Gen. 31:36-42).

CONTENTION

The contention between Jacob and Laban had gone on for

many years. By now, it had reached a fever pitch. No doubt, if the Lord had not spoken to Laban in a dream, he would have taken everything Jacob had, including his wives and children, and possibly would have even killed him. However, he was afraid to lift a hand against him in any manner at this particular time because of what the Lord had told him.

Jacob was now very angry. Instead of the father being sad regarding his two daughters and all of his grandchildren leaving, and knowing that he would possibly never see them again, he was more interested in material things than anything else. It is interesting that Jacob referred to these images as *"stuff"* (Vs. 37).

Jacob then rehearsed his 20 years with Laban and, in effect, was saying that Laban had absolutely no reason to be angry with him. He has treated Laban fairly in every respect, and, in fact, that was correct.

He then reminds Laban that he (Laban) knows that God is with him (with Jacob), and he had best conduct himself toward the Patriarch accordingly.

The loss of Laban's manufactured deities was a ridiculous commentary on the folly of worshipping or trusting in a god that could be stolen. What a spectacle of infinite humor, if it were not so sad—a man seeking for his lost gods! The Gospel presents us with the opposite picture—the ever present God seeking for His Lost Children.

THE PROTECTION OF GOD

"And Laban answered and said unto Jacob, These daughters are my daughters, and these children are my children, and these cattle are my cattle, and all that you see is mine: and what can I do this day unto these my daughters, or unto their children which they have born?" (Gen. 31:43)

Laban wrongly claims everything that Jacob has but recognizes, due to the Power of God, that there is nothing he can do regarding the taking of them. In fact, were he to try anything, he would, no doubt, forfeit his life. He knows this but still doesn't relinquish claim.

How hard is the heart of man; how so difficult to turn, even in the face of the exhibition of the Power of God!

This whole scenario tells us that God is always in charge. Men rule, but God overrules!

Laban had little regard for Jacob, despite the fact that at this particular time, he was a very rich man, all because of the Patriarch. His greed would not allow him to see that, and, as well, he only grudgingly gave God the glory. Instead of allowing Jacob to show him the One True God and service for Him, he, instead, saw only worldly wealth.

THE EMPHASIS

How similar this entire spirit is with many in the modern Charismatic movements, who claim the Word of Faith doctrine, etc. The emphasis is not at all on Righteousness and Holiness, but rather on material things. Let the reader hear and know: if we labor for the meat that perishes, we will perish along with it. That's why Jesus said:

"Labor not for the meat which perishes, but for that meat which endures unto Everlasting Life, which the Son of Man shall give unto you: for Him has God the Father sealed" (Jn. 6:27).

Without a doubt, the situation presented before us regarding Jacob and Laban is, at least, one of the greatest hindrances to the Child of God. Why do we serve God? Is it for worldly accoutrements, or is it for the joy of Christ Himself?

THE GOD OF ISAAC

"And Mizpah; for he said, The LORD watch between me and you, when we are absent one from another.

"If you shall afflict my daughters, or if you shall take other wives beside my daughters, no man is with us; see, God is witness between me and you.

"And Laban said to Jacob, Behold this heap, and behold this pillar, which I have cast between me and you:

"This heap be witness, and this pillar be witness, that I will not pass over this heap to you, and that you shall not pass over this heap and this pillar unto me, for harm.

"The God of Abraham, and the god of Nahor, the god of their father, judge between us. And Jacob swore by the fear of his father Isaac.

"Then Jacob offered sacrifice upon the mount, and called his brethren to eat bread: and they did eat bread, and tarried all night in the mount.

"And early in the morning Laban rose up, and kissed his sons and his daughters, and blessed them: and Laban departed, and returned unto his place" (Gen. 31:49-55).

At this stage, Laban makes a show of piety as it regards his daughters, Leah and Rachel, but his actions have spoken much louder than his words. He is more concerned about material things than anything else.

Laban now adds an oath to the Covenant, calling on the God of Abraham and the gods of Nahor, the gods of their father, to judge between Jacob and Laban. All of this proves that Laban worships many so-called gods. He really doesn't know the God of Abraham but only puts Him into the mix and on the same level as the gods of Nahor, etc. So, Verse 53 should have been translated:

"The God of Abraham, and the gods of Nahor, the gods of their father. . . ."

SACRIFICE

Jacob ignored the gods of Nahor and took his oath only in the name of the One True God, Who was the *"fear"* of, or *"The One Reverenced"* by Isaac.

As well, the Scripture says that *"Jacob offered sacrifice upon the mount, and called his brethren to eat bread"* (Vs. 54).

The sacrifice meant nothing to Laban, even though he was

well acquainted with this practice, but everything to Jacob. In essence, he was saying that he was placing his Faith and confidence in what the sacrifice represented. The very purpose and reason for his grandfather, Abraham, being called out of Ur of the Chaldees, and the actions of his father, Isaac, and his own life, for that matter, were to bring the One into the world Whom the sacrifices represented. As the lamb gave its life, pouring out its blood, with its carcass then being offered on the Altar, likewise, Christ would give His Life, offering up Himself on the Cross as a Sacrifice in order that man might be Saved. The terrible sin debt must be paid, and there was no other way to pay it. God would have to become man, Whom Paul refers to as the *"Last Adam"* and the *"Second Man"* (I Cor. 15:45, 47).

"Laban departed, and returned unto his place" (Gen. 31:55).

Regrettably and sadly, that *"place,"* at least, as far as we know, was eternal darkness, forever without God. In essence, he sold his soul for a few flocks and herds. What a sorry trade!

ESAU

"And Jacob lifted up his eyes, and looked, and, behold, Esau came, and with him four hundred men. And he (Jacob) divided the children unto Leah, and unto Rachel, and unto the two handmaids" (Gen. 33:1).

The time has come that Jacob and Esau will now meet. Jacob sees him coming with his cortege of some 400 men.

At this particular time, Esau must have been a powerful chieftain, at least one of, if not the most, powerful in that part of the world.

While Esau had 400 men, armed, no doubt, Jacob had a host of Angels, unseen, but yet, so powerful!

Some have criticized Jacob as it regards the preparation concerning his family, especially considering that he had just had this great visitation from the Lord, with great Promises further extended to him. I think, however, we do wrong when we always judge Faith according to perfection. No man's

Faith is perfect. Even the best of us, whomever that might be, is always in a growing process. If we demand perfection out of Jacob, why don't we demand perfection of ourselves, especially considering that we are now living under a better Covenant? While never condoning wrongdoing or even a lack of Faith, still, if in his shoes, would we have done any better or even as well? Armchair generals and Monday morning quarterbacks are a dime a dozen. However, until we've been there, it is best to withhold judgment, and rather try to learn the lesson which the Holy Spirit desires to teach us from the Text.

A POINT TO CONSIDER

Many, many years ago, one of the pilgrim fathers preached a Message containing the following points, which we would do well to heed presently. They are:

• When we hear something bad about someone, we should realize that what we are hearing is gossip and treat it accordingly.

• Even if we actually know the facts of the case, the truth is, still, we little know the degree of spiritual warfare involved.

• If we were placed in their shoes, as stated, would we do any better or even as well?

HIS BROTHER

"And he put the handmaids and their children foremost, and Leah and her children after, and Rachel and Joseph hindermost.

"And he passed over before them, and bowed himself to the ground seven times, until he came near to his brother.

"And Esau ran to meet him, and embraced him, and fell on his neck, and kissed him: and they wept" (Gen. 33:2-4).

If it is to be noticed, Jacob put the ones he thought the least important in the forefront, followed by Leah and her children, and then bringing up the very rear were Rachel and Joseph, whom Jacob looked at the most favorably.

As it all proved out, all of this was unnecessary.

As Jacob was approaching Esau, his brother, the Scripture says, *"Esau ran to meet him."* He embraced him and kissed him, with both of them weeping.

It was the Lord Who had mellowed Esau, and I think that is obvious. This should be a lesson to us as well.

The Holy Spirit gave to David the following formula, which he gave to us, and if followed, will lead to spiritual prosperity. It is:

GOD'S WAY

"Trust in the LORD, and do good; so shall you dwell in the land, and verily you shall be fed.

"Delight yourself also in the LORD: and He shall give you the desires of your heart.

"Commit your way unto the LORD; trust also in Him; and He shall bring it to pass.

"Rest in the LORD, and wait patiently for Him . . ." (Ps. 37:3-5, 7).

To abbreviate what is said here, we can reduce it to four words. They are:

1. Trust
2. Delight
3. Commit
4. Rest

A proper adherence to these Passages will solve any problem.

THE MEETING

"And he lifted up his eyes, and saw the women and the children; and said, Who are those with you? And he said, The children which God has graciously given your servant.

"Then the handmaidens came near, they and their children, and they bowed themselves.

"And Leah also with her children came near, and bowed themselves: and afterwards came Joseph near and Rachel, and

they bowed themselves" (Gen. 33:5-7).

All of this proclaims the fact that the entirety of the family of Jacob showed a great respect to Esau, which they should have done. Little did the older brother know (older by a few moments) that this family was the seedbed, so to speak, of the great Nation of Israel, to whom would be given the great Promises of God. Here they stood by the Brook Jabbok, and if the mighty men of the world had taken notice of this retinue, they would have scarcely given it a second glance.

From the time that God had called Abraham out of Ur of the Chaldees to this particular time of Jacob had been a little less than 200 years. The boys upon whom Esau looked would be the beginning of great Tribes. From one of these, Judah, would come the Prince of Glory, of Whom Esau had no knowledge. This, in effect, was the *"birthright"* of which he had no interest. In fact, he never did understand spiritual things because he couldn't understand spiritual things.

SUCCOTH

"So Esau returned that day on his way unto Seir.

"And Jacob journeyed to Succoth, and built him an house, and made booths for his cattle: therefore the name of the place is called Succoth.

"And Jacob came to Shalem, a city of Shechem, which is in the land of Canaan, when he came from Padan-aram; and pitched his tent before the city.

"And he bought a parcel of a field, where he had spread his tent, at the hand of the children of Hamor, Shechem's father, for an hundred pieces of money.

"And he erected there an Altar, and called it El-elohe-Israel" (Gen. 33:16-20).

Several things are wrong as presented in these Passages:

• Jacob was not told by the Lord to go to Succoth.

• This is the first mention of a house being built by a Patriarch. He was to be a pilgrim instead.

• His *"buying a parcel of a field"* only made a bad matter worse.

• He built an Altar, but it was not in the right place.

• He called it, *"God, the God of Israel."* Its name given by him, however, couldn't atone for the Altar being built in the wrong place.

Some, if not all, of these things may seem to be innocent. In fact, they very well may be. However, the idea which we wish to present proclaims the fact that if one is out of the Will of God, everything one does lends toward the wrong direction.

DINAH

"And Dinah the daughter of Leah, which she bore unto Jacob, went out to see the daughters of the land" (Gen. 34:1).

It is believed that Dinah was about 16 or 17 years of age at the time. The thing which took place with her did not happen immediately after Jacob came to Succoth but, more than likely, several years later.

The evidence is, a festive gathering was taking place, and Dinah desired to be a part of the social entertainment.

Her going out to *"see the daughters of the land"* is not meant to imply that she had not done this previously. This particular time is highlighted for the simple reason of what happened to her.

The Believer has to be very, very careful as far as the world is concerned. While we must not become legalistic, at the same time, we must understand that the world and its ways are not our friend. Satan has many temptations and snares in the world, which have tripped up many Believers, Dinah not being the first or the last.

Understanding these things, we are foolish to ignore the allurement of the world and its dangers. While we as Believers are in the world, we must never be of the world. We believe in separation but not isolation. To be factual, separation is very, very important! The moment separation breaks down is the moment the problem begins, even as with Dinah.

SHECHEM

"*And when Shechem the son of Hamor the Hivite, prince of the country, saw her, he took her, and lay with her, and defiled her.*

"*And his soul clave unto Dinah the daughter of Jacob, and he loved the damsel, and spoke kindly unto the damsel*" (Gen. 34:2-3).

Pulpit Commentary says:

"*Dinah paid the full penalty of her carelessness. She suffered the fate which Satan had planned for Sarah and Rebekah in the land of Pharaoh and Abimelech; she was seen and taken by the son of the prince, forcibly it seems, against her will, but yet with the claims of affection by her lover.*"⁶

It does seem that he actually loved her and "*spoke kindly unto her,*" which probably refers to marriage.

Whatever it seemed at the moment, all of this was an attempt by Satan to spoil the godly line with intermarriage, which both Abraham and Isaac sought so diligently to avoid.

The Believer must ever understand that Satan and his demon hosts are forever seeking to hinder and hurt in some way. That's the reason the Scripture plainly tells us to "*watch and pray*" (Mat. 26:41). When we speak of Christians doing certain things or not doing certain things, it's not a matter of legalism, but rather a matter of the possibility of Satan getting the advantage. Because of its great significance, let us say it again:

We as Believers must evaluate every single thing we do, every place we go, and all the things we propose. Can the Evil One use whatever it is we propose to do as an avenue to cause us problems? That's the basic reason that the Scripture also says that we are to "*Abstain from all appearance of evil*" (I Thess. 5:22).

THE PLAN OF SATAN

"*And Shechem spoke unto his father Hamor, saying, Get me this damsel to wife.*

"And Jacob heard that he had defiled Dinah his daughter: now his sons were with his cattle in the field: and Jacob held his peace until they were come.

"And Hamor the father of Shechem went out unto Jacob to commune with him.

"And the sons of Jacob came out of the field when they heard it: and the men were grieved, and they were very angry, because he had wrought folly in Israel in lying with Jacob's daughter: which thing ought not to be done" (Gen. 34:4-7).

The Scripture uses the phrase, *"Jacob's daughter,"* in order to proclaim the fact that this was as bad as it could be. It would have been bad enough if one of Jacob's handmaids had been raped, but his daughter. . . .

Marriages were arranged in those days, so Shechem asked his father, Hamor, to work out the arrangement with Jacob so that Dinah could now be his wife.

The account of all of this tells us that Dinah's brothers were extremely angry when they heard this sordid news about their sister.

In those times, it was thought that a brother was more dishonored by the seduction of his sister than a man could be by the infidelity of his wife. A man may divorce his wife, and then she is no longer his, they reasoned, while a sister and daughter remain always sister and daughter.

ISRAEL

In Verse 7, the word, *"Israel,"* is used for the first time to designate Jacob's descendents, which actually became the great Nation of Israel. The phrase, *"Folly in Israel,"* became a standing expression for acts done against the sacred character which belonged to Israel as a separated and covenanted community as the People of God. This expression was used more so for sins of the flesh than anything else (Deut. 22:21; Judg. 20:10; Jer. 29:23).

Pulpit Commentary says:

"The special wickedness of Shechem consisted in dishonoring a daughter of one who was the head of the theocratic line, and therefore under peculiar obligations to lead a holy life."[7]

Unfortunately, it becomes painfully obvious as to the sordid failure of almost all concerned, even as, shortly, we will read the account of Joseph's brothers seeking to kill him. Despite the fact that the Church is also a holy line in this world, even more so, one might say, than Israel of old, still, the problem is just as acute, if not more so, presently, than then.

DINAH

Dinah was partly to blame, but Jacob and Leah were far more to blame. They should not have allowed their daughter to frequent the festivities of the Canaanites.

It is understandable that young girls and young boys would want companionship of their own age, which, more than likely, Dinah lacked. As well, it is almost certain that the festivities of that particular time were very enticing.

Perhaps Dinah went to this entertainment without the knowledge of her mother and dad; however, that is not likely. Not wanting to say, *"No,"* to their daughter, the thought is probably correct that they allowed her to attend, but to their chagrin. As young girls will do, she, no doubt, pestered them for permission, wanting to go. In such a situation, it is much easier to say, *"Yes,"* than it is to say, *"No."* However, the results of saying, *"Yes,"* can be very painful, as the Holy Spirit here makes very plain.

Without going into detail, the end result of this situation would be catastrophic, to say the least. While Jacob and his family, including Dinah, escaped, of course, the truth is, but for the Lord, their lives were in great danger. They were spared only because of the Grace of God. Actually, we included this short section only because Dinah was the daughter of Leah.

After this, we hear no more of Leah except the location of her burial place at Machpelah in Hebron. This took place presumably before Jacob's descent to Egypt (Gen. 49:11).

Other than that, we are given no details of her death.

As the mother of Reuben, Simeon, Levi, Judah, Issachar, Zebulun, and Dinah, she was acclaimed with Rachel as one of the builders, as previously stated, of the House of Israel (Ruth 4:11).

BENJAMIN

"And they journeyed from Beth-el; and there was but a little way to come to Ephrath: and Rachel travailed, and she had hard labor.

"And it came to pass, when she was in hard labor, that the midwife said unto her, Fear not; you shall have this son also.

"And it came to pass, as her soul was in departing (for she died) that she called his name Ben-oni: but his father called him Benjamin.

"And Rachel died, and was buried in the way to Ephrath, which is Beth-lehem.

"And Jacob set a pillar upon her grave: that is the pillar of Rachel's grave unto this day" (Gen. 35:16-20).

The journey that Jacob was taking was probably to Mamre to visit Isaac. From the last Verses of this Chapter, it seems that Jacob made it there before the great Patriarch died. In the journey to Mamre, they were close to Beth-lehem when Rachel began to go into labor. Twice the Scripture says that she had *"hard labor."*

The baby was born, which occasioned the death of Rachel. However, before she died, *"She called his name Ben-oni,"* which means, *"Son of my sorrow."* She had asked the Lord for another son when Joseph was born, and the Lord had answered her prayer, but it occasioned her death.

In the culture of that day, the mother usually named the child, as here. If the father stepped in, it would be an unusual situation, even as it was here. Jacob felt that the name she had chosen was not appropriate, so the Patriarch countermanded her request and *"called him Benjamin,"* which means, *"Son of my right hand."* Rachel was buried near Beth-lehem.

Great
Women
OF THE
BIBLE
OLD TESTAMENT

Chapter Four

SHIPHRAH AND PUAH
Midwives

SHIPHRAH AND PUAH
Midwives

THE EGYPTIANS

"And the Egyptians made the Children of Israel to serve with rigor:

"And they made their lives bitter with hard bondage, in mortar, and in brick, and in all manner of service in the field: all their service, wherein they made them serve, was with rigor" (Ex. 1:13-14).

According to Pulpit, the word *"rigor"* is a very rare one. It is derived from a root which means, *"To break in pieces, to crush."*[1]

The tide had now turned completely. From the time that the Children of Israel were looked at as favored guests because they were the relatives of Joseph, they now are hated, feared, and are actually made into slaves.

Concerning this, Mackintosh said:

"In reference to the King of Egypt, it may assuredly be said, he did 'greatly err,' not knowing God or His changeless counsels. He knew not that, hundreds of years back, even before he had breathed the breath of mortal life, God's Word and Oath – 'two immutable things' – had infallibly secured the full and glorious deliverance of that very people, in fact a people which at that time, the time of the Oath of God, didn't even exist, whom he was going, in his earthly wisdom, to crush. All this was unknown to him, and therefore all his thoughts and plans were founded upon ignorance of that grand foundation – the truth of all truths, namely, that 'God is.' He vainly imagined that he, by his management, could prevent the increase of those concerning whom God had said, 'they shall be as the stars of Heaven, and as the sand which is upon the seashore.' His wise dealing, therefore, was simply madness and folly."[2]

HARD LABOR

If the *"labor in the field"* included, as Josephus supposed, the cutting of canals, their lives would indeed have been *"made bitter."* There is no such exhausting toil as that of working under the hot Egyptian sun, with the feet in water, in an open cutting, where there can be no shade and scarcely a breath of air from sunrise to sunset, as forced laborers are generally required to do. For instance, in the cutting of the Alexandrian Canal, 20,000 out of 150,000 laborers died as a result of the harsh conditions.

In such a social climate, at this stage, one would not have given the Children of Israel any chance at all. They were servile slaves, and Egypt was the mightiest nation on Earth, so what could they do? However, as we look upon this situation, we must take into account three things:

1. Irrespective of the plans that the evil Pharaoh would make and regardless of what he thought, he would not have the final say, that belonging to God.

2. The Israelites belonged to God and not to Pharaoh. The evil monarch surely thought they belonged to him, but they didn't. As well, it should be remembered that every single Believer in the world presently belongs to the Lord Jesus Christ. Irrespective as to where they might live, how totalitarian their government may be, or how bad the situation looks on the surface, these Believers belong to God, and whatever is done to them is done unto God. That should be remembered!

3. Whatever God wants to do with His People, that He will do, and nothing will stop Him. If men get in the way, even the mightiest on the face of the Earth, as Pharaoh, they will be subdued while the slaves gain supremacy.

Pharaoh would have been 10,000 times better off had he treated these people with dignity and kindness. He would have spared the near destruction of his nation.

Then again, had Pharaoh made the lives of the Children of Israel easy and profitable, the truth is, they would not have wanted to leave Egypt. So, the Lord *"makes even the wrath of man to praise Him"* (Ps. 76:10).

KING OF EGYPT

"And the king of Egypt spoke to the Hebrew midwives, of which the name of the one was Shiphrah, and the name of the other Puah" (Ex. 1:15).

Verses 15 through 22 portray the two leading Hebrew midwives, *"Shiphrah"* and *"Puah."* It is ironic that the names of the mighty Pharaohs of that day are all but lost to history, whereas the names of these two humble women who obeyed God are recognized by multiple millions in every generation.

The Faith of these brave women, for they risked their own lives, is recognized by God, and He dealt well with them. It must not be assumed that they were guilty of falsehood. There is no reason to suppose that what they stated was not perfectly true.

The statement of Verse 21, coupled with the statements of the prior Verses, means that God protected these midwives from being put to death by Pharaoh. As well, because of their Faith, He made them houses; that is, He gave them large families.

The two named here were evidently in charge of many, if not all, of the midwives among the people of Israel.

To portray the eternal consequences of those who served the Lord, the Pharaoh of that particular time cannot be known, as previously stated, as to exactly who he was. And yet, the names of these two women are known to millions in every generation. Even though I've already stated this once, it is so important that I felt it must be repeated.

This tells us that all that is merely human, however solid, however brilliant, or however attractive, must ultimately fall to the cold grasp of death and there molder in the dark, silent tomb. The clod of the valley must cover man's highest excellencies and brightest glories. Mortality is engraved upon his brow, and all his schemes are transitory—and it doesn't matter who he is.

On the contrary, that which is connected with and based upon God and His Word shall endure forever. *"His name shall endure forever, and his memorial to all generations."*

MIDWIVES

"And he said, When you do the office of a midwife to the Hebrew women, and see them upon the stools; if it be a son, then you shall kill him: but if it be a daughter, then she shall live.

"But the midwives feared God, and did not as the king of Egypt commanded them, but saved the men children alive.

"And the king of Egypt called for the midwives, and said unto them, Why have you done this thing, and have saved the men children alive?

"And the midwives said unto Pharaoh, Because the Hebrew women are not as the Egyptian women; for they are lively, and are delivered ere the midwives come in unto them.

"Therefore God dealt well with the midwives: and the people multiplied, and waxed very mighty.

"And it came to pass, because the midwives feared God, that He made them houses.

"And Pharaoh charged all his people, saying, Every son who is born you shall cast into the river, and every daughter you shall save alive" (Ex. 1:16-22).

Evidently, these two women, *"Shiphrah"* and *"Puah,"* who were in charge of all the midwives, which, no doubt, numbered into the thousands, were called before Pharaoh or, at least, one of his emissaries, and given instructions which they were to give to all the midwives. Every boy baby was to be killed as soon as it was born, with only the little girl babies left alive. This murderous scheme hatched up by Pharaoh or someone in his court was supposed to weaken Israel by denying it further growth. As stated, they were multiplying mightily, with Pharaoh becoming more and more fearful of their size and power. Hence, they were reduced to abject slavery, and now this murderous scheme is concocted.

SOWING AND REAPING

In all of this, even though God uses all things, even the

wrath of Pharaoh, still, what we sow, we must reap (Gal. 6:7). Whatever the captions of men in wickedness and in rebellion, they are made subservient to the establishment of the Divine Counsels of Grace and Love ... even the wrath of man is yoked to the chariot wheel of God's Decrees.

Why did God allow the descendants of Abraham to suffer such indignities and trials at the hands of the Egyptians?

To which we have already briefly alluded, had Israel not suffered greatly, they certainly would not have wanted to leave Egypt. As well, Israel was not without blame. Great sin was in their camp as well as in the camp of the Egyptians.

Going some 1,600 years into the future, Israel delivered up Christ into the hands of the Gentiles, and so, into their hands, they also have been delivered. Christ was shamefully treated by the Romans, but yet, the same people were employed by God to punish the Jews. Christ was *"cut off"* out of the land of the living, and from A.D. 70, Israel, too, was *"cut off"* from the land of their fathers, even until 1948. Thus, we see again and again how inexorable is the outworking of the Law of Sowing and Reaping.

As it regards Israel and Egypt, in a sense, Israel was paying for what they had done in the past. Remember the terrible sin against Joseph!

THE REAPING OF JUDGMENT CAN BE STOPPED!

In fact, it can only be stopped in one way. That is by one's acceptance of Christ, which immediately stops all Judgment, and of every description. Christ took all the Judgment at the Cross. For God to continue to visit Judgment upon a person who has truly come to Christ would be a mockery. It would, in essence, say that Christ did not finish His Work, in other words, He did not take all of our Judgment. However, He did take all of our Judgment, and did so in totality.

Terrible things are sowed by all unbelievers, and, to be sure, they will reap the result of what they have sowed as long as they remain in the unsaved state. However, the moment they come to Christ, the reaping of evil stops. While there might be a residue that carries over, even that can be greatly ameliorated.

THE FAMILY CURSE

There is a teaching presently referred to as *"the family curse,"* which has become somewhat prominent and has confused many people. Let's look at that particular teaching:

Is there such a thing as a *"family curse"*?

Most definitely there is such a thing as a family curse, a generational curse, and the curse of the broken Law. In fact, every type of curse that one could possibly think is visited upon the human race because of the Fall.

However, that pertains to the unsaved part of the human race. The moment the believing sinner comes to Christ, making Him Lord and Saviour, all curses are completely stopped. What does the Scripture say?

"Christ has redeemed us from the curse of the Law, being made a curse for us: for it is written, Cursed is everyone who hangs on a tree:

"That the blessing of Abraham might come on the Gentiles through Jesus Christ; that we might receive the Promise of the Spirit through Faith" (Gal. 3:13-14).

Jesus handled every curse at the Cross; none was excluded. This means that no Believer should ever believe the untruth that he is having problems because of a family curse, etc.

Knowing that many Christians do have problems, what then is the cause?

A FAILURE TO UNDERSTAND THE CROSS OF CHRIST

Believers have problems of every nature, unnecessarily so, I might quickly add, because they do not understand the Message of the Cross. They are told by preachers that their problem is a *"family curse,"* and they need hands laid on them by a preacher who understands this problem, and then their difficulties will be solved.

Unfortunately, whatever happens to them when hands are laid on them will not stop their problems, with them finding themselves experiencing the same difficulties as they had previously. Jesus said, *"You shall know the Truth, and the Truth shall make you free"* (Jn. 8:32).

While we definitely believe in the laying on of hands, problems of the nature of which we speak will not respond to such, but only to proper Faith evidenced in Christ and what Christ has done for us at the Cross. This then gives the Holy Spirit, Who is God, the latitude to work within our lives, bringing about whatever it is that is needed. Please understand, the Holy Spirit works exclusively by and through the Cross of Christ, meaning that it is the Cross that gave and gives Him the legal means to do all that He does. When we speak of the Cross, we aren't speaking of a wooden beam, but rather what Jesus there did.

To say it again, every Believer must understand that every single thing that comes to him from God comes exclusively by and through Christ and what Christ has done for us in His Finished Work. Consequently, he is to ever make the Cross the Object of his Faith, not allowing it to be moved to other things.

When he does this faithfully, which, in fact, is the very heart of the Gospel, the Holy Spirit, as stated, will then work mightily on behalf of the Believer, leading him into all Truth and giving him victory over all things (Rom. 6:3-5, 11, 14; 8:1-11; Gal. 6:14; Col. 2:10-15).

THE CROSS OF CHRIST

That and that alone is the answer for the Child of God. This means that the Cross holds the solution to every perplexing problem, the answer to every question, and is the Means by which God gives all good things to His People.

So, how is it that certain preachers proclaim the family curse as the problem?

They are deriving their teaching from an erroneous understanding of Exodus 20:5, and several other similar Passages. That particular Scripture says:

"You shall not bow down yourself to them, nor serve them (idols): for I the LORD your God am a jealous God, visiting the iniquity of the fathers upon the children unto the third and fourth generation of them who hate Me."

The idea is that your great-great-grandfather, etc., did something terrible, and now you are reaping the results of that, hence, the *"family curse."*

However, the Scripture mentions that it only comes upon those *"who hate Me,"* referring to the Lord. In fact, the Sixth Verse of the Twentieth Chapter of Exodus says, *"And showing Mercy unto thousands of them who love Me, and keep My Commandments."*

While there is definitely such a thing as a family curse, and it definitely does come down to the third and fourth generation, it is only against those who hate the Lord. The moment that a person comes to Christ, the *"iniquity of the fathers"* is immediately suspended. The Mercy of God takes over, which is a part of the Born-Again experience. That's the reason that Paul said:

A NEW CREATION

"Therefore if any man be in Christ, he is a new creature: old things are passed away; behold, all things are become new" (II Cor. 5:17).

Now, either the *"old things"* have passed away, or else, the Apostle Paul didn't tell the truth, and those things are still with us. I choose to believe that he told the truth.

Regrettably, and I think I am correct in my assumption, among the Children of Israel at that particular time, most were not saved. They were not abiding by the Covenant. While some certainly were, that number would have been few. I think all of this is proven by the difficulties which Moses experienced with them when the time finally came for them to be delivered. So, in a sense, the Judgment of God was upon the Israelites and, a little later, would greatly come upon the Egyptians. Let us say it again:

All sin must be addressed and punished. It can either be punished by the Judgment of God and the person ultimately dying eternally lost and going to Hell, or else, the believing sinner can accept Christ, Who has taken our punishment and suffered for us. These are the two choices!

THE DESIGN OF SATAN

While Pharaoh desired to weaken the Israelites by demanding that the boy babies be killed at birth, Satan's plan was far more sinister. This is the serpent's enmity against the Seed of the woman. If this could have been carried out concerning the male children being destroyed, there would have been no David, just to name one instance, and if no David, no David's Greater Son.

Even though the midwives possibly feared Pharaoh, they feared God more; consequently, they did not obey this wicked king.

All Believers are to obey government unless such government violates our conscience and the Word of God. Then, we must disobey but, at the same time, be prepared to suffer the consequences. God would protect *"Shiphrah"* and *"Puah,"* and all others who assisted. Not only would the Lord protect them, but He would bless them, as well, by giving them large families, i.e., *"houses."*

Not able to have command obeyed as it regarded the little boy babies being killed at birth, Pharaoh demanded that all boy babies be thrown into the river, with the girl babies alone being saved alive. As we shall see, the Lord greatly and wondrously used this to bring about His Divine Will.

Great
Women
OF THE BIBLE

OLD TESTAMENT

Chapter Five

JOCHEBED
Mother Of Moses

JOCHEBED
Mother Of Moses

THE PARENTS OF MOSES

"And there went a man of the house of Levi, and he took to wife a daughter of Levi" (Ex. 2:1).

Moses was a member of the Tribe of Levi. He was the seventh from Abraham. Abraham was the seventh from Heber and Enoch the seventh from Adam. Miriam and Aaron were already born when Moses was born. Jochebed was his mother, with Amran being his father.

Concerning the birth of Moses, Ellicott said:

"Note the extreme simplicity of this announcement, and compare it with the elaborate legends wherewith Oriental religions commonly surround the birth of those who were considered their founders, as Thoth, Zoroaster, Orpheus. Even the name of the father is here omitted as unimportant. It is difficult to conceive anyone but Moses making such an omission."[1]

The phrase, *"Daughter of Levi,"* doesn't mean that Jochebed was actually the daughter of Levi, who, in fact, had been dead many years, but rather that she was of the Tribe of Levi.

MOSES

Concerning Moses, Pink said:

"From Adam to Christ there is none greater than Moses. He is one of the few characters of Scripture whose chorus is sketched from his infancy to his death. The fierce light of criticism has been turned upon him for generations, but he is still the most commanding figure of the ancient world.

"In character, in Faith, in the unique position assigned him as the mediator of the Old Covenant, and in achievements, he stands first among the heroes of the Old Testament.

"All of God's early dealings with Israel were transacted through Moses. He was a Prophet, Priest, and King in one person,

and so united all the great and important functions which later were distributed among a plurality of persons. The history of such an one is worthy of the strictest attention, and his remarkable life deserves the closest study."[2]

ANOTHER VIEW

Haldeman said of this man:

"The life of Moses presents a series of striking antithesis. For instance, he was the child of a slave, and the son of a Queen. He was born in a hut, and lived in a palace. He inherited poverty, and enjoyed unlimited wealth. He was the leader of armies, and the keeper of flocks. He was the mightiest of warriors, and the meekest of men. He was educated in the court of Egypt, and yet dwelt in the desert. He had the wisdom of Egypt, and the faith of a child. He was fitted for the city, and yet wandered in the wilderness. He was tempted with the pleasures of sin, and endured the hardships of virtue. He was backward in speech, and yet talked with God. He had the rod of a shepherd, and the power of the Infinite. He was a fugitive from Pharaoh, and an Ambassador from Heaven. He was the giver of the Law, and the forerunner of Grace.

"He died alone on Mt. Moab, and appeared with Christ in Judea. No man assisted at his funeral, yet God buried him."[3]

THE FAITH OF JOCHEBED

"And the woman conceived, and bore a son: and when she saw him that he was a goodly child, she hid him three months.

"And when she could no longer hide him, she took for him an ark of bulrushes, and daubed it with slime and with pitch, and put the child therein; and she laid it in the flags by the river's brink.

"And his sister stood afar off, to witness what would be done to him" (Ex. 2:2-4).

That which stands out so vividly in this account is the Faith of Jochebed, the mother of Moses.

I have no doubt that the Lord moved upon Jochebed from the time of the conception of Moses in her womb, in that she sensed there was more here than meets the eye. I also believe that feeling not only persisted but grew in intensity unto the time of her delivery. When the child was born, she knew beyond the shadow of a doubt that there was something extensively unique about this baby; hence, she would go to any length to save its life.

SATAN

Not being successful in attempting to force the midwives to kill the boy babies when they were born, Pharaoh issued another edict, which demanded that all boy babies be drowned in the Nile River at the time of their birth.

As we follow the narrative throughout the Scriptures, we see that Satan does everything within his power to kill those who are truly Called of God. Concerning Christ and Satan, the Scripture says:

"Forasmuch then as the children are partakers of flesh and blood, He (Christ) *also Himself likewise took part of the same* (became flesh and blood); *that through death* (the Crucifixion) *He might destroy him who had the power of death, that is, the Devil"* (Heb. 2:14).

The death which Pharaoh demanded was typical of the eternal death which Satan brought upon the human race as a result of the Fall.

THE POWER OF DEATH

What did Paul mean by the term, *"The power of death,"* and that the Devil had this power?

Satan's power lies in the realm of sin. The Scripture says, *"The wages of sin is death . . ."* (Rom. 6:23). Sin gives Satan the legal right to hold men in captivity, which leads to spiritual death and ultimately means eternal separation from God. In fact, the power of sin and death is so strong that before the Cross, every Saint of God who died, which included all the Old Testament Saints, did not go to Heaven. Rather, they were taken down into Paradise, in the heart of the Earth, and actually held captive there by Satan. While they were not over in the burning side of Hell, with a great gulf separating the Paradise side from the burning side (Lk. 16:26), still, they were held captive by the Evil One. In other words, the sin debt still hung over them simply because the blood of bulls and goats could not take away sins. However, that was all that existed before the Cross, and I speak of the Sacrificial system, which was a stopgap measure until Christ would come (Heb. 10:4).

HE LED CAPTIVITY CAPTIVE

All of the Old Testament Saints were waiting for Christ, Who had been promised, to become a partaker of flesh and blood, and we refer to the Incarnation. It would be the Perfect Human Body that He would offer up in Sacrifice on the Cross, which would atone for all sin. When that happened, and it most definitely did happen, Jesus Christ then went down into Paradise, and the Scripture says, *". . . He led captivity captive, and gave Gifts unto men"* (Eph. 4:8).

The term, *"He led captivity captive,"* is a strange term, but yet, it holds a wealth of meaning. The word, *"Captivity,"* refers to all the Old Testament Saints held in captivity by Satan, even though he could not put them into the burning side of Hell. However, when Jesus died on the Cross, He then went down into Paradise and liberated every single one of these individuals, thereby, making them His Captives, and took them with Him to Heaven. This was all because of the Cross, the price there paid, and, thereby, all sin being atoned. Now, when a Believer dies, and we speak of all time since the Cross, the Saint immediately goes to Heaven to be with Christ because there is no more sin debt hanging over the head of any Child of God (Phil. 1:23).

"Through death," which refers to the Crucifixion, Jesus

destroyed Satan's power of death because all sin was atoned. While the wages of sin still is death, because of what Jesus did at the Cross, any person who comes to Christ, expressing Faith in Him, can have every single sin washed away, which thereby destroys *"the power of death."*

THROUGH DEATH

If it is to be noticed, it was *"through death"* that Jesus accomplished this. It was not the Resurrection or going down into the burning side of Hell and suffering there as a sinner, as some teach such foolishness! It was *"through death"* that Christ accomplished this great thing, which refers to the Cross, and the Cross alone.

So, the death that Pharaoh proposed was actually Satan's motif. However, through this proposed death, the Lord would turn Pharaoh's edict into victory.

Jochebed hid baby Moses for three months, and, incidentally, his name at the time was not Moses. We have no idea as to the name that Jochebed gave him, if any, because the name, *"Moses,"* was actually given to him by the Egyptian princess who adopted him.

Led by the Holy Spirit and evidencing Faith in God, and great Faith at that, Jochebed made a little ark for baby Moses, laid him in the ark, and pushed it out into the Nile. She told his sister, Miriam, to watch from a distance to see what would happen. I think that Jochebed had at least an inkling of knowledge as to what the Lord was going to do. I doubt that she understood it completely, but I believe the Lord told her exactly where to put the ark into the water, which was where the daughter of Pharaoh came to wash herself daily.

THE DAUGHTER OF PHARAOH

"And the daughter of Pharaoh came down to wash herself at the river; and her maidens walked along by the river's side; and

when she saw the ark among the flags, she sent her maid to fetch it" (Ex. 2:5).

The Holy Spirit worked all of this out, even down to the minute details. He told Jochebed exactly what to do and had something in mind that Jochebed could not have possibly dreamed.

As we said in one of the headings, God works in little things as well as He does in the great things. In fact, He takes little things, such as this before us, and turns it into great things; however, all that God does is by and large done according to the Faith of an individual. God seldom works beyond or without our Faith. Jochebed had Faith. She heard the Voice of the Lord, and she obeyed the Voice of the Lord. All of this requires Faith.

The Holy Spirit had everything timed just right—the place, the person, and the progress. The little ark was floating among the flags where the princess would bathe, and her eyes fell upon this which would prove to be such a major part in the great Kingdom of God—Moses.

TEARS

"And when she had opened it, she saw the child: and, behold, the babe wept. And she had compassion on him, and said, This is one of the Hebrews' children" (Ex. 2:6).

The great Power of God that particular day, at least, in this instance, was brought down to the tears on a baby's cheeks.

Concerning this moment, George Williams writes:

"Great events have hung upon a tear, but never greater than those which were brought to pass by the tears of this baby! The defeat of Satan, the Salvation of Israel and of the Nations, the trustworthiness of God's Word, and the Salvation of the world through an Incarnate Savior – all these lay hidden in the tears that wetted that infant cheek upon that day."[4]

FAITH

Let's once again look at Faith as it regards the entirety

of these actions, and especially that of Jochebed and her husband, Amran.

Though Faith vanquished fear as it regards this couple, yet lawful means were used to overcome danger: the mother *"hid"* the child and later had recourse to the Ark. It is not Faith but fanaticism which deliberately courts danger. Faith never tempts God. Even Christ, though He knew full well of the Father's Will to preserve Him, yet withdrew from those who sought His Life (Lk. 4:30; Jn. 8:59). It is not lack of Faith to avoid danger by legitimate precautions. It is no want of trust to employ means, even when assured by God of the event (Acts 27:31). Christ never supplied by a Miracle when ordinary means were at hand (Mk. 5:43).

CIVIL AUTHORITIES

Another important truth which here receives illustration and exemplification is that civil authorities are to be defied when their decrees are contrary to the expressed Word of God. The Word of God requires us to obey the laws of the land in which we live and exhorts us to be *"subject unto the powers that be"* (Rom., Chpt. 13), and this, no matter how wise and just or how foolish and unjust those laws appear to us.

Yet, our obedience and submission to human authorities is plainly qualified. If a human government enacts a law and compliance with it by a Saint would compel him to disobey some Command or Precept of God, then the human must be rejected for the Divine. The cases of Moses' parents, of Daniel (Dan. 6:7-11), and of the Apostles (Acts 5:29), establishes this unequivocally. However, if such rejection of human authority be necessitated, let it be performed not in the spirit of carnal defiance but in the fear of God, and then the issue may safely be left with Him. It was *"by Faith"* that the parents of Moses *"were not afraid of the king's commandment."* May Divine Grace work in us *"like precious Faith,"* which overcomes all fear of man.

(The author is indebted to Arthur W. Pink for the statement on *"Faith"* and *"Civil Authorities."*)[5]

A NURSE

"Then said his sister to Pharaoh's daughter, Shall I go and call to you a nurse of the Hebrew women, that she may nurse the child for you?

"And Pharaoh's daughter said to her, Go. And the maid went and called the child's mother.

"And Pharaoh's daughter said unto her, Take this child away, and nurse it for me, and I will give you your wages. And the woman took the child, and nursed it" (Ex. 2:7-9).

Evidently the baby was beautiful because, immediately, the daughter of Pharaoh fell in love with the little fellow. Of course, we know the Lord had something to do with this as well.

At about the time that Pharaoh's daughter picked up the child, for she, no doubt, did so, Moses' sister Miriam, who had been standing nearby, asked those there if she could get one of the Hebrew women to nurse the child. Miriam, as well, was led by the Lord in this.

PHARAOH'S DAUGHTER

Pharaoh's daughter instantly agreed that this would be the thing to do and told Miriam, with whom she was not acquainted, to go find a nurse. Guess what? Miriam went straight to her mother, who, as well, was the mother of the child. She immediately came to the riverbank.

Pharaoh's daughter told her to take the child and care for it, and she would pay her wages to do so. Of course, she never dreamed that the lady to whom she gave the child was actually the child's mother.

So Jochebed would take care of baby Moses and be paid by the state for doing so. I wonder what Satan thought of this! His plans to defeat the great Plan of God were foiled, with the

Lord even playing a little trick on the Evil One. Getting the court of Pharaoh, which had given instructions for the boy babies to be killed, to rather pay Jochebed to care for the child presents itself not only as a defeat for Satan but, also, an insult to the Evil One. I think from this we have to come to the conclusion that God also has a sense of humor.

Can you imagine what Satan said to the demon spirits who were supposed to have been attending the funeral of little Moses?!

THE ARK

Though Moses was brought to the place of death, he was made secure in the ark. This speaks to us of Christ, Who went down into death for us. The Righteousness of God made imperative the payment of sin's awful wages, and so His Spotless Son *". . . died the just for the unjust, that He might bring us to God . . ."* (I Pet. 3:18).

It was *"Faith"* which placed baby Moses in the ark, and it is *"Faith"* which identifies us with Christ. Again, just as Moses was brought out of the place of death, when Christ rose again, so we rose with Him (Rom. 6:3-5; Eph. 2:5-6).

As well, as the Heavenly Father arranged for the tender care of the baby, He also arranges the same care for us.

All of the events that took place that day were in no way chance happenings. All were designed by the Holy Spirit, as all are always designed by the Holy Spirit, at least, as it regards those who follow the Lord. From this, we can take a lesson as to how minutely the Lord leads and guides, how He plans every detail, and under Grace, we can be certain that His Protection and Care are certainly no less.

Great Women OF THE BIBLE

OLD TESTAMENT

Chapter Six

MAHLAH, NOAH, HOGLAH, MILCAH, TIRZAH

MAHLAH, NOAH, HOGLAH, MILCAH, TIRZAH

THE WOMEN WHO CHANGED THE LAW

"Then came the daughters of Zelophehad, the son of Hepher, the son of Gilead, the son of Machir, the son of Manasseh, of the families of Manasseh the son of Joseph: and these are the names of his daughters; Mahlah, Noah, and Hoglah, and Milcah, and Tirzah.

"And they stood before Moses, and before Eleazar the Priest, and before the Princes and all the congregation, by the door of the Tabernacle of the congregation, saying,

"Our father died in the wilderness, and he was not in the company of them who gathered themselves together against the LORD in the company of Korah; but died in his own sin, and had no sons.

"Why should the name of our father be done away from among his family, because he has no son? Give unto us therefore a possession among the brethren of our father.

"And Moses brought their cause before the LORD" (Num. 27:1-5).

THE DAUGHTERS OF ZELOPHEHAD

Verses 1 through 11 give us one of the most beautiful stories of Faith found in the entirety of the Word of God. Although the illustration is short, still, its impact is notable, to say the least. It is the story of five sisters. So often in the Book of Numbers, we read of the unbelief of Israel; however, Numbers, Chapter 27, presents a striking contrast.

The Second Verse says that the daughters of Zelophehad *"stood before Moses . . . by the door of the Tabernacle."* They had come to make petition. The astounding thing about this was that there was no provision for their petition in the Law.

The Fourth Verse says that their petition was, *"Give to us therefore a possession among the brethren of our father."*

In fact, the Law stated that the possession was to go only to the sons. Actually, this is the first example in Scripture of women pleading for their rights before the judges and leaders of the Nation. Their case concerned inheritances. As stated, no provision had been made for daughters. There were five daughters of Zelophehad of the Tribe of Manasseh in this family, and no sons. As the Law then read, there was no provision made for women, so they were there to plead their cause. I want the reader to notice the example of their Faith.

THE HIGHEST TRIBUNAL

They brought their case before the highest tribunal in the land, Moses himself. Eleazar, the High Priest, and the princes of the congregation were also included.

Under the Law of God, Moses was their intercessor. The modern church should understand the Faith of the daughters of Zelophehad. Today, under the New Covenant, every Believer can go directly to the Father in the Name of Jesus Christ.

Why go to the Virgin Mary when there is no answer from her? Why go to mere men, such as psychologists, when there is no answer from that source either? Why not go directly to God the Father in the Name of Jesus?

Our Lord said:

"And in that day *(after the Day of Pentecost)* you shall ask Me nothing *(will not ask Me Personally, as you now do)*. Verily, verily, I say unto you, Whatsoever you shall ask the Father in My Name *(according to what He did at the Cross and our Faith in that Finished Work)*, He will give *it* you *(He places us in direct relationship with the Father, enjoying the same access as He Himself enjoys)*.

"Hitherto have you asked nothing in My Name *(while He was with them, the Work on the Cross had not been accomplished; so His Name could not be used then as it can be now)*: **ask, and you shall receive** *(ask the Father in His Name, which refers to the fact that we understand that all things are given to us through and by what Christ did at the Cross)*, **that your joy may be full** *(it can only be full when we properly understand the Cross)*" **(Jn. 16:23-24).**

NO SELF-JUSTIFICATION

The daughters of Zelophehad did not justify the sin of their father. They said, *"But* (he) *died in his own sin."* They were pleading Grace, not justice.

The moment we as Christians begin to plead justice before God, in other words, that we deserve something, we have just lost the case. Whenever we plead Grace, as the daughters of Zelophehad did, the answer will be forthcoming. God will operate on no other premise.

NO PROVISION IN THE LAW

Even though there was no provision for them in the Law, they petitioned anyway.

In fact, *"law"* cannot inherit the land. It is impossible! Only Grace can inherit the Promises.

The idea is, if one tries to live for God by means of *"law,"* which is a way that the Lord will not accept, the end result will always be wreckage.

Why?

The Holy Spirit, Whom we must have in our living for God, works entirely within the framework and parameters of the Finished Work of Christ. Those parameters are the Grace of God. Paul plainly told us, *". . . you are not under the Law, but under Grace"* (Rom. 6:14).

While the Law was wonderful and good, still, for the Righteousness of the Law to be had, the Law had to be perfectly kept and kept perfectly, which man, due to the Fall, was and is incapable of doing. In fact, no one, other than the Lord

Jesus Christ, had ever perfectly kept the Law, and He did it all on our behalf. His doing for us what we could not do for ourselves makes it possible for us to place our Faith in Christ, which God intends. This then grants us His Perfection. God cannot tolerate anything but perfection, and, of course, man is so far from perfection that the matter's not even open for discussion. However, Jesus Christ is Perfect, and our Faith in Him, in what He did for us in His Life and Living, and, above all, what He did in His Death on the Cross of Calvary, makes it possible for us to simply extend Faith in what He has done. At that moment, we will be granted the perfect, spotless, Righteousness of God.

Inasmuch as our Lord kept the Law perfectly, and all on our behalf, our Faith in Him transfers us from the position of lawbreakers to the position of Law-keepers. Isn't that wonderful! In fact, when we evidence Faith in Christ and what He has done for us at the Cross, then the entirety of moral Law and all of its demands is kept. However, we must never forget, it's all in Christ. That's the reason that the Lord is not happy at all with Believers trying to obtain Righteousness in any manner or in any way other than by simple Faith in Christ and what He did for us at the Cross.

So, the daughters of Zelophehad led the way as it regards Grace. As stated, there was no provision for them in the Law, but Grace made a way, even as Grace makes a way now, and all in Christ.

A DIRECT PETITION

These daughters of Zelophehad pointedly asked, *"Give to us therefore a possession among the brethren of our father."* They stated exactly what they wanted. Faith always does! Jesus said, *"Ask and you shall receive."* James said, *"We have not because we ask not."* They asked, and exactly as the Bible said, they were given.

However, let us state the fact again: they did not receive it through Law, even as they could not receive it through Law. It could only be asked in Grace and, thereby, given in Grace.

It is the same presently! If we try to function in law, we will fail because the Holy Spirit will not help us in this respect. He knows that we cannot accomplish anything by law. As stated, we are incapable of doing so.

Jesus Christ has already done it all for us, and our trying to resort to law is an insult to Him, which, in effect, is also an insult to the Holy Spirit. So, if we insist upon going by law, the Holy Spirit simply will not help us, and for all of the obvious reasons.

Jesus has done it all, and we are required only to evidence Faith in Him, and in Him exclusively, and what He has done for us at the Cross. Then, the petition will be granted, and only then! As stated, it is called, *"Grace!"*

THE REASON

"And the LORD spoke unto Moses, saying,

"The daughters of Zelophehad speak right: you shall surely give them a possession of an inheritance among their father's brethren; and you shall cause the inheritance of their father to pass unto them.

"And you shall speak unto the Children of Israel, saying, If a man die, and have no son, then you shall cause his inheritance to pass unto his daughter.

"And if he have no daughter, then you shall give his inheritance unto his brethren (brother).

"And if he have no brethren, then you shall give his inheritance unto his father's brethren.

"And if his father have no brethren, then you shall give his inheritance unto his kinsman who is next to him of his family, and he shall possess it: and it shall be unto the Children of Israel a statute of Judgment, as the LORD commanded Moses" (Num. 27:6-11).

All of this was not an oversight by the Lord, but rather an

intended position. He desired for the daughters of Zelophehad to do what they did, thereby, evidencing their Faith.

The Lord wanted this to be an example to all who are downtrodden, dispossessed, and counted as less than others, even as were women of that particular time.

Their Faith obtained for them a promise and, as well, a Blessing for all, even unto this hour.

Actually, some four times the Holy Spirit recorded the Faith of the five daughters of Zelophehad (Num. 26:33; 27:1; 36:11; Josh. 17:4).

Even though they were women and, as stated, no provision had been made for them in the Law as it regarded inheritance, their Faith claimed such just the same as their male counterparts. As well, through Faith, they forged a path, not only for themselves, but for all other families in Israel where all the offspring were females.

Faith spreads and, regrettably, unbelief spreads as well. That's the reason that you as Believers ought to associate yourself with people who believe God, people who look to God, and people who expect great things from God.

Incidentally, the daughters of Zelophehad had their inheritance on the west side of the Jordan River (Josh. 17:6).

Great Women of the Bible

OLD TESTAMENT

Chapter Seven

RAHAB

The Gentile

RAHAB
The Gentile

JERICHO AND THE TWO SPIES

"And Joshua the son of Nun sent out of Shittim two men to spy secretly, saying, Go view the land, even Jericho. And they went, and came into an harlot's house, named Rahab, and lodged there" (Josh. 2:1).

The *"house"* spoken of in Verse 1 was an inn of sorts. The two spies did not know that Rahab was a harlot. As well, some have attempted to claim that Rahab had been forced into temple prostitution; however, the Greek Text of Hebrews 11:31 proves that she was a common harlot.

The *"two spies"* served no military purpose whatsoever. So, why did Joshua send them?

The Lord told him to do so because of Rahab, and because of Rahab alone—even though Joshua did not know or understand such at the time. It is one more comforting thought to realize that the Lord would do all of this for the Salvation of one woman, and a harlot at that. However, the Lord knew that Faith was lodged in the heart of this woman, and He will go to any lengths to honor Faith (Heb., Chpt. 11).

Jericho was and is one of the oldest cities in the world, actually, already a city of antiquity by the time of Joshua. It probably derived its name from the moon god *"Yarih."*

Located at the northern extremity of the Dead Sea, it was the entrance of Canaan from the east. In fact, at the time of Joshua, it was a mighty fortress. It was known for commerce as well as for agriculture. The proximity to the Dead Sea made the citizens dealers in salt, bitumen, and sulfur. However, irrespective of the city itself in the natural, the spiritual implications involved presents a tremendous lesson for us.

This was the entrance to the Promised Land, and it barred Israel's progress. Its conquest, at least, in the natural, was impossible to Israel, for its walls were great and high. But yet, it had to be subdued.

It is a type of Satan's fortresses, which he places in our path in order to keep us from the Great Things of God. In fact, we receive nothing from the Lord without us defeating the satanic forces of darkness in some way. So, in order to take the Promised Land, to have what God had promised them, and to enjoy this land of milk and honey, Jericho had to be first subdued. Is there a Jericho hindering your progress? Is there a Jericho keeping you from having that which the Lord has promised you? Is there a Jericho which stands in your way? As we go forward with our study, we will see God's Way, and we will find out that this is the only way that victory can be brought about. Unfortunately, all too often, Christians attempt to gain victories in the flesh, which can never happen. It can only be done by the Power of the Holy Spirit, Who works entirely within the parameters, so to speak, of the Finished Work of Christ, i.e., *"the Cross."*

THE TWO SPIES

There was absolutely no military reason for Joshua to send these two spies to Jericho in order to spy out the land. This battle would not be fought by natural means anyway, so whatever information they brought back, at least, as it regarded military information, would be useless. So, it must be that the Lord impressed upon Joshua to send in these two men even though Joshua, at the time, didn't understand why.

I think it can be concluded that Rahab was the reason for their being sent. Even though this woman was a vile sinner, which we will deal with momentarily, still, evidence is that a cry of Faith was in her soul. It may have taken many directions, and no doubt did, but it was there. That cry of Faith would be answered by the Lord, as every cry of Faith is always answered by the Lord.

I do not think it would be a stretch of the imagination to portray what happened at Jericho to be a portent of that which is soon to happen in this world. We speak of the coming Great Tribulation and, above all, the Rapture of the Church.

RAHAB

Considering the entirety of the population of the city, whatever it may have been, Rahab and her family were the only ones who were spared. As well, considering the entirety of the population of the world, which presently stands at approximately seven plus billion (in 2012), the number of people comparatively who are truly Born-Again at this time and who will make the Rapture is truly small. So, Rahab definitely could be a type of the Church, which will be delivered out of the coming Judgment.

These *"two spies"* could well represent *"the Word of God"* and *"the Holy Spirit"* sent into this world.

The only way that Rahab and her family could be spared was by adhering totally to what they were told by the two spies. They were not to question it and not to add to it or take from it. Their lives, their souls, and everything they had depended totally and completely upon what the two spies related to them. It is the same presently with the Word of God, on which the Holy Spirit works exclusively.

If Rahab had changed the instructions in any way, she would never have been spared. I'm afraid that much of the modern church presently is most definitely attempting to change the instructions. The Word of God is being replaced presently with religious books that refer to themselves as *"Bibles,"* and I speak of those such as the *"Message Bible,"* etc., but which, in reality, are no Bibles at all. They are merely religious books. How do I know?

These are *"thought for thought"* translations, even if that, which can never pass spiritual and Scriptural muster. If you as a Believer do not have a *"word for word"* translation, such as the King James, which is, as well, THE EXPOSITOR'S STUDY BIBLE, then you really don't have a Bible. To be frank, there are only two or three word for word translations available.

UNDERSTANDING

Some counter that by stating, *"I can't understand the King James,"* etc.

If you have something that you can understand, and it's not really the Word of God, you have not done yourself any good whatsoever. In fact, you have done yourself irreparable harm. A road map that is wrong will never lead one to the right destination. Blueprints that are faulty will never build a house that will stand. Jesus said so!

The Holy Spirit functions entirely on, within, and by the Word of God. In fact, He is the Author of the Word. Peter said:

"For the Prophecy *(the word 'Prophecy' is used here in a general sense, covering the entirety of the Word of God, which means it's not limited merely to predictions regarding the future)* came not in old time by the will of man *(did not originate with man)*: but Holy Men of God spoke *as they were* moved by the Holy Spirit. *(This proclaims the manner in which the Word of God was written and, thereby, given unto us)*" (II Pet. 1:21).

Remember this, we aren't speaking here from the position of personal preference, but rather that which pertains to eternal consequences. If the Word of God is misinterpreted, the person will die eternally lost. So, considering the implications and considering the eternal consequences, I think it would certainly be wise for every Believer to *"make his Calling and Election sure"* (II Pet. 1:10).

THE EXPOSITOR'S STUDY BIBLE

The idea is, if it's not the pure Word of God, meaning that which has not been compromised, then the Holy Spirit, without

Whom we receive nothing, will not and, in fact, cannot function. He functions alone and entirely on the Word of God. So, if we want the Moving and Operation of the Holy Spirit within our hearts and lives, we had better make certain that we truly have the Word of God in our possession and not some hybrid. In view of that, I would strongly recommend that the reader secure for yourself THE EXPOSITOR'S STUDY BIBLE. It is King James but totally different than any type of Study Bible, to our knowledge, that has ever been produced. The explanation of each Scripture is given right with the Scripture. In other words, the explanation is not at the bottom of the page, at the side of the page, or at the back of the Book. It is embedded with the actual Scripture itself, making it extremely user-friendly. So, the idea that the King James cannot be understood has, in a sense, been laid to rest.

RAHAB—THE MEMBER OF A DOOMED RACE

The following is derived from the work of George Williams. He said:

"Rahab was a debauched member of a doomed race. Yet Grace saved her. She based her plea for Salvation upon the fact that she was justly ordained by God to destruction. Many people refuse to bestir themselves in the matter of personal Salvation because of the belief that if they are ordained to be saved, they will be saved, and if ordained to be lost, they will be lost, which constitutes an erroneous interpretation of predestination.

"All sinners are justly ordained to be lost (Rom. 5:12) and therefore, all sinners may be saved. Rahab prefaced her plea for Salvation by declaring that she knew all were doomed to destruction, and because of this Divine Judgment she asked for a true token that would assure her of her safety in the Day of Wrath that was coming."[1]

THE GERM OF FAITH

"And it was told the king of Jericho, saying, Behold, there came men in hither tonight of the Children of Israel to search

out the country.

"And the king of Jericho sent unto Rahab, saying, Bring forth the men who are come to you, which are entered into your house: for they be come to search out all the country.

"And the woman took the two men, and hid them, and said thus, There came men unto me, but I did not know from where they came:

"And it came to pass about the time of shutting of the gate, when it was dark, that the men went out: where the men went I do not know: pursue after them quickly; for you shall overtake them.

"But she had brought them up to the roof of the house, and hid them with the stalks of flax, which she had laid in order upon the roof.

"And the men pursued after them the way to Jordan unto the fords: and as soon as they which pursued after them were gone out, they shut the gate" (Josh. 2:2-7).

As it regards the two spies, we know from the Scriptural narrative that Rahab lied to the two men sent to her by the king. The sacred historian simply narrates the fact and makes no comment whatever upon it.

The roofs of houses then, as now, were flat in those regions. She hid the men on the roof under stalks of flax. The germ of Faith was already stirring in her heart, and it was Faith that would be amply rewarded. We must not judge Rahab, for all of this was shortly before her Conversion. To be sure, we must not judge Rahab at all.

Despite her past, this woman would go down in Biblical history as one of the greatest women of God ever. In fact, she would be in the genealogy of Christ, and nothing could be greater than that (Mat. 1:5).

FAITH

Faith begins in the heart of the sinner and is placed there by the Holy Spirit, even before Conversion. In fact, it has to begin before Conversion, or there can be no Conversion.

What was it that stirred this woman's heart to begin with, especially considering the lifestyle that she was leading as a harlot?

At this time, with over two million Israelites camped on the other side of Jordan, the entirety of the city was abuzz with these proceedings. It seems from what Rahab will say momentarily that all the victories of the recent past regarding Israel were well known in Jericho. As well, Israel's Deliverance from Egypt and the opening of the waters of the Red Sea, even though some 40 years in the past, were all well known. It would seem that from this, in some way, Faith began to build in the heart of this dear lady. To be sure, it was a very simple Faith, very weak, and very much lacking in knowledge; nevertheless, it was there.

IDOL-WORSHIP

In those days, everything was attributed to the god of the particular people or country involved. Consequently, it was known that the God of Israel must be stronger than the many gods of Egypt because Egypt had been left a wreck upon the Deliverance of these people. As well, it would have been deduced that Jehovah was greater than the gods of the Amorites, etc. Therefore, whatever was said, and whatever was deduced from all of this, Faith, on which the Holy Spirit worked, began to build in the heart of Rahab.

While the entirety of the city, as stated, was rife with all of this information, still, it was only Rahab and her family who chose to believe in the God of Israel. Quite possibly, this dear lady was sick of her supposed god, *"Chemosh,"* which she had been worshipping. It was common for little children to be offered up to this god as a burnt offering, which was carried on quite often. This, no doubt, sickened Rahab, with what little she knew about Jehovah striking a positive cord in her heart. At any rate, it would lead to her Salvation and a place in Biblical history all out of proportion to mere human thoughts.

The story of Rahab cannot be said to be anything but a story of Faith. It is Faith which believed God, and such Faith is always honored and recognized.

GIVE ME A TRUE TOKEN

"And before they were laid down, she came up unto them upon the roof;

"And she said unto the men, I know that the LORD has given you the land, and that your terror is fallen upon us, and that all the inhabitants of the land faint because of you.

"For we have heard how the LORD dried up the water of the Red Sea for you, when you came out of Egypt; and what you did unto the two kings of the Amorites, who were on the other side Jordan, Sihon and Og, whom you utterly destroyed.

"And as soon as we had heard these things, our hearts did melt, neither did there remain any more courage in any man, because of you: for the LORD your God, He is God in Heaven above, and in Earth beneath.

"Now therefore, I pray you, swear unto me by the LORD, since I have showed you kindness, that you will also show kindness unto my father's house, and give me a true token.

"And that you will save alive my father, and my mother, and my brethren, and my sisters, and all that they have, and deliver our lives from death.

"And the men answered her, Our life for yours, if you utter not this our business. And it shall be, when the LORD has given us the land, that we will deal kindly and truly with you.

"Then she let them down by a cord through the window: for her house was upon the town wall, and she dwelt upon the wall.

"And she said unto them, Get you to the mountain, lest the pursuers meet you; and hide yourselves there three days, until the pursuers be returned: and afterward may you go your way" (Josh. 2:8-16).

THE PLEA FOR SALVATION

From the conversation of Rahab, it is evident that all the surrounding nations knew of the tremendous Miracles performed by Jehovah in Egypt, and especially the waters of the Red Sea drying up for passage by the Israelites. Also, she was very well acquainted with recent victories pertaining to Sihon and Og. In hearing these accounts and by them being discussed over and over, which they, no doubt, were, in some way, the story of these great victories ignited a spark of Faith in the heart of this poor woman. She knew little of Jehovah; however, she knew enough to know that Jehovah was greater and stronger than all the gods of Egypt, etc. Upon that fact, she was in the process of making some decisions in her heart.

Knowing and seeing the heart of this dear lady, the Holy Spirit would move favorably upon her Faith, which He had tendered her way in the first place. He would do this in spite of her debauched occupation, the terrible vice which gripped her, or what had transpired in the past.

WHY RAHAB AND NOT OTHERS IN JERICHO?

It has ever been in that fashion. Many hear the Gospel, but only a minute few accept the Gospel. As to exactly what causes most to say, *"No,"* and some few to say, *"Yes,"* is known only to God. This we do know:

God does not tamper with the free moral agency of mankind. He will move upon people, deal with people, speak to people, and bring events to pass to impress people, but He will never force the issue. The decision must be, whether *"yes"* or *"no,"* that of the individual.

But yet, as we see the Word of God, we know it is imperative that all be given an opportunity, whatever their decision. The Holy Spirit is insistent upon that. Jesus Himself said:

> "... Go you into all the world *(the Gospel of Christ is not merely a western Gospel, as some claim, but is for the entirety of the world)*, and preach the Gospel to every creature *('preaching' is God's Method, as is here plainly obvious; as well, it is imperative that every single person have the opportunity to hear; this is the responsibility of every Believer)*.

"He who believes *(believes in Christ and what He did for us at the Cross)* and is baptized *(baptized into Christ, which is done by Faith [Rom. 6:3-5], not water baptism)* shall be Saved; but he who believes not shall be damned *(Jn. 3:16)*" (Mk. 16:15-16).

TO BELIEVE

If Jesus had been speaking in this Verse in Mark of *"Water Baptism,"* He then would have also said, *"But he who believes not, and is not baptized in water, shall be damned."* However, He didn't say that, but rather, *"He who believes."*

The words of the Great Commission given in Matthew are a little different because the emphasis is different. Jesus said:

"Go you therefore *(applies to any and all who follow Christ, and in all ages)*, and teach all nations *(should have been translated, 'and preach to all nations,' for the word 'teach' here refers to a 'proclamation of truth')*, baptizing them in the Name of the Father, and of the Son, and of the Holy Spirit *(presents the only formula for Water Baptism given in the Word of God)*:

"Teaching them *(means to give instruction)* to observe all things *(the whole Gospel for the whole man)* whatsoever I have commanded you *(not a suggestion)*: and, lo, I am with you always *(It is I, Myself, God, and Man, Who am – not 'will be' – hence, forever present among you, and with you as Companion, Friend, Guide, Saviour, God)*, even unto the end of the world *(should have been translated 'age')*. Amen *(it is the guarantee of My Promise)*" (Mat. 28:19-20).

THE WAY OF SALVATION

Upon the request of Rahab, the Way of Salvation was immediately made clear and plain to her. It was a very simple way. All she had to do was to hang a piece of scarlet cloth in the window. A child could do that. As well, Salvation presently from the Wrath to come is equally simple; trusting in the Lord Jesus Christ and in His Precious Blood, of which the scarlet cord was a type, secures eternal Salvation.

The assurance of Salvation in Rahab was not built upon an inward experience, but rather upon an outward evidence—that is, the scarlet line. In it was perfection, so to speak; in herself, imperfection. Looking upon that *"true token"* and believing the Testimony respecting it, she was assured of Deliverance in the day of doom that was coming. Thus, the outward token gave an inward peace.

PERSONAL WORTHINESS

The Believer in Jesus enjoys a similar peace. The preciousness of Christ's Blood and the Testimony of the Holy Scriptures concerning it are the outward token which brings assurance of Salvation to the heart that trusts Christ.

It was vain for Rahab to seek for Salvation upon the grounds of personal worthiness, for she was vile indeed. It is equally vain for the most moral to claim Salvation today, for all have sinned, none are righteous, and all are under sentence of death (Rom. 5:12).

The condition was that the red cord would hang from the window and that all must stay in the house where the window was. To leave the house would leave its protection. Safety was guaranteed for all who remained in the house, destruction for all who left the house. It is the same with the Blood of Christ, which the scarlet cord represented.

As long as we remain in the house of safety provided by the Blood, we are safe. To leave this house of safety, which is Faith in Christ and Him Crucified, guarantees destruction.

RAHAB AND THE LORD JESUS CHRIST

A Faith that is born of God always evidences itself by seeking the Salvation of others. Rahab pleads for her father, her mother, her brothers, her sisters, and all belonging to them;

and they were all saved.

The moral effect of a Divine Faith is further seen in Rahab. She became a good woman and joined the People of God, married one of its princes, and her name shines in the genealogy of Jesus Christ. If that is not the most beautiful and perfect example of the Grace of God, then I don't know what else could ever be (Mat. 1:5).

THE SCARLET CORD

Scarlet, or rather, crimson, is the color of blood. Like the blood on the doorposts in Egypt, it was to be the sign which the destroying messengers of God's Vengeance were to respect and pass by. That scarlet cord alone could ensure safety. It would ensure the safety only of those who trusted in it alone. It must be taken, therefore, as the type of Salvation through the Blood of Christ Alone.

Let the reader understand, the only means of Salvation is Faith and Trust in Christ and what He did for us at the Cross, where He there shed His Life's Blood in order that we might be Saved. The Scripture says:

> "But now in Christ Jesus *(proclaims the basis of all Salvation)* you who sometimes *(times past)* were far off *(far from Salvation)* are made near by the Blood of Christ. *(The Sacrificial Atoning Death of Jesus Christ transformed the relations of God with mankind. In Christ, God reconciled not a nation, but 'a world' to Himself [II Cor. 5:19])*" **(Eph. 2:13).**

WHY IS THE BLOOD, OF WHICH THE SCARLET CORD WAS A TYPE, SO IMPORTANT?

The Scripture tells us, *"For the life of the flesh is in the blood . . . "* (Lev. 17:11).

As it regards payment for sin, God demanded life in payment, but it had to be a perfect life, which would necessitate perfect blood. No human being could do that simply because the Fall had poisoned the entirety of the human race for all time.

So, in order to circumvent this terrible problem, the problem of the Fall, God would become Man, have a body, a special Body prepared for Him, and then He would be born of the Virgin Mary, which would bypass, so to speak, the results of the Fall. His Body was Perfect and due to being Virgin Born, His Blood was Perfect. In fact, Simon Peter referred to it as *"Precious Blood"* (I Pet. 1:19).

When Christ hung on the Cross, shedding His Life's Blood, it was Perfect Blood, which came from a Perfect Body, which came from a Perfect Life. God accepted this poured out Life as payment, total payment, for all sin, past, present, and future (Jn. 3:16), at least, for those who will believe.

THE CROSS

In fact, every animal offered in sacrifice, at least, according to the Direction of the Lord, was to be a substitute for the One Who was to come, namely, the Lord Jesus Christ (Gen., Chpt. 4).

So, the blood is important but only as it is the Blood of our Lord and Saviour Jesus Christ. It is important, supremely important, only as it was shed, and shed for you and me.

When He poured out His Life, this atoned for all sin, as stated, past, present, and future, at least, for all who will believe (Rom. 3:22).

Regrettably and sadly, the modern church is dispensing with the Cross. This means they are dispensing with the Blood, which means they are dispensing with Salvation. As stated, the Cross of Christ is the only thing that stands between man and eternal Hell. As well, the Cross of Christ is the only thing that stands between the Church and total apostasy.

RAHAB

"And she said, According unto your words, so be it. And she sent them away, and they departed: and she bound the scarlet line in the window.

"And they went, and came unto the mountain, and abode there three days, until the pursuers were returned: and the pursuers sought them throughout all the way, but found them not.

"So the two men returned, and descended from the mountain, and passed over, and came to Joshua the Son of Nun, and told him all things that befell them:

"And they said unto Joshua, Truly the LORD has delivered into our hands all the land; for even all the inhabitants of the country do faint because of us" (Josh. 2:21-24).

Rahab lost not a moment in making her Calling and Election sure. She bound the scarlet line in the window, and as directly she did so, she was Saved—that is, she was in safety and assured of safety.

Prior to binding the scarlet line in the window, she was ordained to destruction. However, from the moment she trusted that *"true token,"* she was ordained to Salvation, as well as all of her family, provided they stayed in the house. This means that they placed their trust in the scarlet line as well.

The report of the two spies, as it was given to Joshua, was one of Faith, which was totally unlike the report that had been given some 38 years earlier, which doomed a generation to die in the wilderness (Num., Chpt. 13).

THE FALL OF JERICHO

Now, according to directions, the mighty fortress of Jericho will fall to the People of God. Instructions were given to Joshua as to exactly how the battle was to commence. The Holy Spirit said:

"And the city shall be accursed, even it, and all who are therein, to the LORD: only Rahab the harlot shall live, she and all who are with her in the house, because she hid the messengers that we sent" (Josh. 6:17).

THE SAVING OF RAHAB AND HER FAMILY

"But Joshua had said unto the two men who had spied out

the country, Go into the harlot's house, and bring out thence the woman, and all that she has, as you swore unto her.

"And the young men who were spies went in, and brought out Rahab, and her father, and her mother, and her brethren, and all that she had; and they brought out all her kindred, and left them without the camp of Israel.

"And they burnt the city with fire, and all who were therein: only the silver, and the gold, and the vessels of brass and of iron, they put into the treasury of the House of the LORD.

"And Joshua saved Rahab the harlot alive, and her father's household, and all that she had; and she dwells in Israel even unto this day; because she hid the messengers, which Joshua sent to spy out Jericho" (Josh. 6:22-25).

Salvation by the scarlet cord was not only simple, it was also sure. When the day of Wrath came, it gave the safety it promised. Thus will it be in the day of the Wrath to come, and come it shall! That day will prove how sure is the Salvation which follows upon simply trusting Jesus.

Of all those slated for destruction, the Faith of Rahab saved her. Rahab married Salmon, one of the princes of Israel. She is included in our Lord's Genealogy (Mat. 1:5).

To what heights of glory her Faith took her, and so may it be for all who will dare to believe God. The Lord took her harlotry and turned it into Holiness. He took the curse that was upon her and turned it into a Blessing. What He did for her, He will, as well, do for you and me.

The entirety of the family of Rahab was saved because the entirety of her family placed themselves under the protection of the shed Blood of the Lamb, typified by the red cord.

RAHAB

The story of this dear lady is one of the grandest in all of Biblical history. A poor lost daughter of Adam's fallen race, even having given over her life to total licentiousness, she was made an example of Grace simply because of her Faith in Christ. She and her family were the only ones in the entirety of the city of Jericho who took advantage of the Grace of God.

If the leaders of Jericho had come to Joshua and stated that they wished to accept Israel's God, namely, Jehovah, thereby, rejecting their heathenistic idols, they would have been spared to a person exactly as were Rahab and her family. They did not do that and were totally lost!

Rahab is a type of the entirety of the human race, lost, heathenistic, without God, and without hope, but Faith brought her out of this morass of sin and shame, exactly as Faith has brought out untold millions.

"Love Divine, so great and wondrous,
"Deep and mighty, pure, sublime!
"Coming from the Heart of Jesus,
"Just the same through tests of time."

"Love Divine, so great and wondrous,
"All my sins He then forgave!
"I will sing His Praise forever,
"For His Blood, His Power to save."

"In life's eventide, at twilight,
"At His Door I'll knock and wait;
"By the precious Love of Jesus,
"I shall enter Heaven's Gate."

Great Women of the Bible

OLD TESTAMENT

Chapter Eight

DEBORAH AND JAEL

The Deliverers Of Israel

DEBORAH AND JAEL
The Deliverers Of Israel

THE FAILURE OF ISRAEL

"And the Children of Israel again did evil in the Sight of the LORD, when Ehud was dead.

"And the LORD sold them into the hand of Jabin king of Canaan, who reigned in Hazor; the captain of whose host was Sisera, which dwelt in Harosheth of the Gentiles.

"And the Children of Israel cried unto the LORD: for he (Jabin) had nine hundred chariots of iron; and twenty years he mightily oppressed the Children of Israel" (Judg. 4:1-3).

Without proper spiritual leadership, the Church is like a ship without a rudder. Regrettably, there isn't much leadership in the modern church, at least, that which is truly spiritual. What little there is has been rejected by institutionalized religion.

Having 900 chariots of iron tells us that Sisera, evidently the head general under Jabin, was a mighty warlord. Satan always comes against the Child of God with his most powerful weapons.

The words, *"Mightily oppressed,"* proclaim the fact that Israel had virtually become slaves in their own land—slaves to Jabin and Sisera. Sin will take a person further than he wants to go, at a price higher than he can afford to pay.

OPPRESSION

The Holy Spirit is very quick to relate that Ehud, who had been the spiritual leader of Israel at this time, was now dead. Regrettably, there was no one to take his place, and Israel once again drifted into spiritual declension, actually, gross idolatry! Let us state it again:

Without proper spiritual leadership, the Church cannot advance and cannot grow, at least, in a spiritual sense, and, thereby, goes into apostasy.

On his first visit to the United States and the Churches

in this country, one Chinese Believer was asked the question, *"How do you see the Church in America?"*

His answer was most revealing, *"It's amazing,"* he said, *"as to the advancement the Church in America can make without God."*

Quite a statement but, oh, so true!

Due to the gross sinfulness of Israel, the Scripture again emphatically states, *"The LORD sold them* (sold Israel) *into the hand of Jabin king of Canaan."*

The word, *"Sold,"* in the Hebrew is *"maker"* and means, *"To sell as a slave."*

Why would the Lord do this, especially considering that it was being done to His Chosen People?

CHASTISEMENT

As we have previously stated, the Lord by no means desires to do such a thing, as should be obvious. He desires to bless His Children, and desires to do so greatly. However, the Lord loves His People enough that He will take drastic measures, if He has to, in order to bring them back into line. The chastisement will be according to the degree of spiritual drift.

The people to whom He delivered them were mighty and powerful, even with their chief captain, Sisera, heading up a powerful chariot army, actually consisting of *"nine hundred chariots of iron."* In the natural, they were invincible; consequently, they terrorized Israel for 20 years.

As it regards oppression, all of these particular periods of time given in these accounts throughout the Book of Judges were unnecessary. How much unnecessary trouble do we go through simply because we get out of the Will of God, and do so because of self-will?

Israel was a Nation, so the Lord dealt with them accordingly. Today He deals with Believers on a different basis because His Church is not a nation, at least, as we think of such, but is made up of individual members all over the world. So, whatever the Lord does with us individually is still, in some way, a microcosm of what He did with Israel.

This doesn't mean that every bad thing that happens to a Believer is caused by the Believer's sinfulness, etc. While that certainly is the case at times, it's not the case all the time.

Irrespective, whatever it is that happens to a Believer, the Lord either causes it or allows it. Therefore, we must look at whatever it is that's taking place and, by using the situation at hand, whatever it might be, try to learn the lesson which the Holy Spirit desires to teach us.

DEBORAH THE PROPHETESS

"And Deborah, a Prophetess, the wife of Lapidoth, she judged Israel at that time.

"And she dwelt under the palm tree of Deborah between Ramah and Beth-el in Mount Ephraim: and the Children of Israel came up to her for judgment.

"And she sent and called Barak the son of Abinoam out of Kedesh-naphtali, and said unto him, Has not the LORD God of Israel commanded, saying, Go and draw toward Mount Tabor, and take with you ten thousand men of the children of Naphtali and of the children of Zebulun?

"And I will draw unto you to the river Kishon Sisera, the captain of Jabin's army, with his chariots and his multitude; and I will deliver him into your hand.

"And Barak said unto her, If you will go with me, then I will go: but if you will not go with me, then I will not go.

"And she said, I will surely go with you: notwithstanding the journey that you take shall not be for your honor; for the LORD shall sell Sisera into the hand of a woman. And Deborah arose, and went with Barak to Kedesh" (Judg. 4:4-9).

This Chapter and the following could be cited as the women's Chapters. We find that Deborah's Faith brought about a great victory, and Jael's fidelity destroyed a great tyrant. As well, and as will quickly become obvious, we have included both of these women, Deborah and Jael, into one Chapter. Both of these women were raised up by God for their respective Ministries. So, this puts to rest the idea that God does not call women to preach, etc. Paul said that in Christ, *". . . there is neither male nor female: for you are all one in Christ Jesus"* (Gal. 3:28).

Williams says of Deborah, *"There was one heart that did not tremble before Sisera and his 900 chariots of iron. She 'sat as judge' under a palm tree near Bethel. Her namesake, Rebecca's nurse was buried there, about 400 years back."*[1]

Deborah speaks now as a Prophetess, announcing God's Commands, not her own opinion; declaring God's Promises, not merely her own hopes or wishes.

We have little history on Barak. We do know that his Faith seemed to be weak. He wanted someone near and visible upon whom he could lean. To such a feeble Faith, the arm, even of a woman, gives more confidence than the Arm of God. Consequently, God did not honor him because he did not honor God. God is best honored by being trusted.

DEBORAH, THE FOURTH JUDGE

All of Israel at this time trembled before Sisera because he had 900 chariots of iron, but Deborah did not tremble. This woman's Faith would bring about a tremendous victory, and another woman's fidelity (Jael) would destroy a great tyrant. Working together, the Lord through them brought about a tremendous victory for Israel.

It is foolishness to think that God, as stated, does not call women to preach. There are *"Prophets,"* and there are *"Prophetesses."* Actually, the very first one to herald the great Gospel Message of the Resurrection of Jesus Christ was a woman, namely, *"Mary Magdalene."* We find here that God would use two women, Deborah and Jael, to deliver the entire Nation of Israel. In fact, one of the greatest victories in the Bible is recorded as having been brought about by these women, especially

Deborah. The Bible said that she was a *"Prophetess"* (Vs. 4).

Evidently the Lord told her what to do as it regarded the coming battle with Jabin and the king of Canaan, whose military commander was Sisera.

BARAK

Deborah called on Barak to enlist the men, with the intention that he would lead the fight. As stated, the Lord had already spoken to her that victory could be won even though Sisera had 900 chariots of iron. It seems that Barak believed her, at least, somewhat, but not enough to lead the attack. He wanted her to go with him and then flatly stated that if she did not go with him, he would not lead the attack. She did go with him.

And yet, before we criticize Barak too harshly, we must remember that it was to Deborah that the Revelation was given, and not Barak. He was taking her word for all the things that were to happen; therefore, in the back of his mind, he must have reasoned that if Deborah was wrong, he was a dead man. Of that, he was correct, but Deborah wasn't wrong.

I personally think that Deborah had such a reputation that Barak should have believed her without question. He didn't, to his eternal dismay! While the Lord used him, and did so greatly, still, he would find that the honor of the victory would go to a woman, exactly as Deborah had said. That woman would be Jael.

DELIVERANCE BY THE POWER OF GOD

"And Barak called Zebulun and Naphtali to Kedesh; and he went up with ten thousand men at his feet: and Deborah went up with him.

"Now Heber the Kenite, which was of the children of Hobab the father-in-law of Moses, had severed himself from the Kenites, and pitched his tent unto the plain of Zaanaim, which is by Kedesh.

262 Great Women Of The Bible, Old Testament

"And they showed Sisera that Barak the son of Abinoam was gone up to Mount Tabor.

"And Sisera gathered together all his chariots, even nine hundred chariots of iron, and all the people who were with him, from Harosheth of the Gentiles unto the river of Kishon.

"And Deborah said unto Barak, Up; for this is the day in which the LORD has delivered Sisera into your hand: is not the LORD gone out before you? So Barak went down from Mount Tabor, and ten thousand men after him.

"And the LORD discomfited Sisera, and all his chariots, and all his host, with the edge of the sword before Barak; so that Sisera lighted down off his chariot, and fled away on his feet.

"But Barak pursued after the chariots, and after the host, unto Harosheth of the Gentiles: and all the host of Sisera fell upon the edge of the sword; and there was not a man left" (Judg. 4:10-16).

In the natural, what could Israel do against all of these iron chariots? However, they were not functioning in the natural, but rather by the Power of God.

Incidentally, the Hebrew word for *"discomfited"* implies supernatural discomfiture.

It was a defeat that was total, and there is no indication that the army of Israel lost even a single man. Without the Lord, some minor victories may be won, but at a fearful price. With Him, it is total victory, at no loss whatsoever.

VICTORY

Sometime back on one of our trips to Israel, we happened to be in this particular valley through which the river Kishon ran; however, it is now no more than a trickling stream, if that.

And yet, the valley is a perfect setting for chariots, which, no doubt, Sisera reasoned as it regards this conflict. In fact, considering that this valley spread out for quite a ways and that he had 900 chariots of iron, he couldn't see how that he could lose.

I remember walking beside the little stream, knowing the Biblical history of the place, and realizing that a tremendous victory had been here won for the Glory of God. It made me realize several things.

If we are in the Will of God, great and mighty things take place. Also, the Lord strongly desires, insists, that every single foe within our lives be rooted out and destroyed. Among other things, this is what this great example teaches us.

As the Lord that day fought for Israel, He used the elements because He is the Creator of those elements. In whatever manner they were used, Sisera didn't have a chance! As stated, there is no record that Israel lost even a single man.

JAEL

"Howbeit Sisera fled away on his feet to the tent of Jael the wife of Heber the Kenite: for there was peace between Jabin the king of Hazor and the house of Heber the Kenite.

"And Jael went out to meet Sisera, and said unto him, Turn in, my lord, turn in to me; fear not. And when he had turned in unto her into the tent, she covered him with a mantle.

"And he said unto her, Give me, I pray you, a little water to drink; for I am thirsty. And she opened a bottle of milk, and gave him drink, and covered him.

"Again he said unto her, Stand in the door of the tent, and it shall be, when any man does come and inquire of you, and say, Is there any man here? that you shall say, No.

"Then Jael Heber's wife took a nail of the tent, and took a hammer in her hand, and went softly unto him, and smote the nail into his temples, and fastened it into the ground: for he was fast asleep and weary. So he died.

"And, behold, as Barak pursued Sisera, Jael came out to meet him, and said unto him, Come, and I will show you the man whom you seek. And when he came into her tent, behold, Sisera lay dead, and the nail was in his temples" (Judg. 4:17-22).

BLESSED AMONG WOMEN

The mighty military commander of the Canaanites is reduced here to depending on a woman. Such are the Ways of the Lord concerning those who oppose Him.

Williams says, *"God, Who energized Shamgar to destroy the Philistine with an ox goad, strengthened Jael to kill the Syrian with a tent-peg."*[2]

The Holy Spirit labels only two women as preeminently *"blessed among women"*; this one was Jael (Judg. 5:24), and the other, the Virgin Mary (Lk. 1:28). Mary, of course, is associated with the Advent of Israel's and the world's Redeemer; Jael, with the judgment of the oppressor of Israel.

GOD USES ANOTHER WOMAN

If it is to be noticed, most of the time, the Scripture will point out that it is the Lord Who performs the task, yet, individuals of Faith will also be brought into it. They may perform the task, but, at the same time, it is the Lord Who gives them the supernatural Power to do so. As well, at other times, the Lord, distinctly and apart from men and women of Faith, will add to what is already being done. In this case, it would say, *"They fought from Heaven; the stars in their courses fought against Sisera"* (Judg. 5:20). God is looking for Faith. Talent, ability, expertise, knowledge, and wisdom may play some small part in the things which are done, but, by and large, it is the Faith on which God focuses. We never honor God more than when we trust Him.

AN UNPRECEDENTED VICTORY

"So God subdued on that day Jabin the king of Canaan before the Children of Israel.

"And the hand of the Children of Israel prospered, and prevailed against Jabin the king of Canaan, until they had destroyed

Jabin king of Canaan" (Judg. 4:23-24).

As I think should be obvious, this great victory over *"Jabin the king of Canaan"* was one of the greatest recorded in Biblical history.

The beautiful thing about this victory was that which the Lord used in order to bring it about. He used two women.

This tells us that God is able to use anyone and anything.

Even though these women and others were used, still, it was God Who performed the task.

THE SONG OF DEBORAH AND BARAK

"Then sang Deborah and Barak the son of Abinoam on that day, saying,

"Praise you the LORD for the avenging of Israel, when the people willingly offered themselves.

"Hear, O you kings; give ear, O you princes; I, even I, will sing unto the LORD; I will sing praise to the LORD God of Israel.

"LORD, when You went out of Seir, when You marched out of the field of Edom, the Earth trembled, and the heavens dropped, the clouds also dropped water.

"The mountains melted from before the LORD, even that Sinai from before the LORD God of Israel.

"In the days of Shamgar the son of Anath, in the days of Jael, the highways were unoccupied, and the travelers walked through byways.

"The inhabitants of the villages ceased, they ceased in Israel, until that I Deborah arose, that I arose a mother in Israel.

"They chose new gods; then was war in the gates: was there a shield or spear seen among forty thousand in Israel?

"My heart is toward the governors of Israel, who offered themselves willingly among the people. Bless ye the LORD.

"Speak, you who ride on white asses, you who sit in judgment, and walk by the way.

"They who are delivered from the noise of archers in the places of drawing water, there shall they rehearse the righteous

Acts of the LORD, even the righteous acts toward the inhabitants of His Villages in Israel: then shall the people of the LORD go down to the gates" (Judg. 5:1-11).

THE RIGHTEOUS ACTS OF THE LORD

Someone has well said, *"Victory precedes singing, while defeat precedes weeping."*

The people willingly offered themselves to be used of the Lord, and the Lord willingly avenged Israel.

The *"kings"* and *"princes"* of Verse 3 were those of the enemy. They found out as to Who exactly was the God of Israel.

Verse 6 records the fact that Israel was so beaten down by the enemy that they were afraid even to walk on the road. Because of sin, the People of God had been reduced to this low state.

Israel was guilty of idolatry, as Verse 8 proclaims, which had reduced the people to being defenseless. The only defense against Satan is the Cross of Christ; anything else leaves the Believer defenseless (I Cor. 1:17-18). Verse 9 proclaims the fact that the leaders in Israel were to *"Bless the LORD"* because of the great victory that had been won. Verse 10 proclaims the fact that Israel was not only to bless the Lord, they were also to speak the Blessings. What they were to speak is set out in Verse 11.

The idea of Verse 11 is this: the water wells were where gossip was exchanged and news proclaimed. Instead of the Syrians talking at these wells about their great victory over Israel, which would have been the case had they won, instead, Israel would boast. However, they were to boast about the *"RIGHTEOUS ACTS OF THE LORD,"* and not the achievements of individuals.

THE SONG OF VICTORY

Judges, Chapter 5, is the proclamation of revival. Verse 1 says, *"Then sang Deborah and Barak."*

This is a praise to God for victory. Actually, other than

the Psalms, there are some eight songs of praise recorded in Scripture.

They are as follows:

1. Song of Moses (Ex. 15:1-19);
2. Song of Israel (Num. 21:17-18);
3. Song of Moses (Deut. 32:1-43);
4. Song of Deborah—Barak (Judg. 5:1-31);
5. Song of Hannah (I Sam. 2:1-10);
6. Song of David (II Sam. 22:1-51);
7. Song of the Redeemed (Rev. 5:8-10);
8. Song of Tribulation Saints (Rev. 15:3-4).

Verse 6 shows the terrible condition to which Israel had sunk because of her spiritual declension. The land was full of anarchy and confusion, everywhere being infested with bandits. No public road was safe, and the people of the villages were forced to live in fortified places or in great numbers together to protect themselves from roving bands of wicked men.

As all of this relates to us personally, the enemy of our soul so desires to destroy our inheritance that we can take little advantage of the great Blessings that God has afforded us. Of how many Christians can it be said that the highways of Blessings are unoccupied and the roads of victory untraveled?

IDOLATRY

The Eighth Verse of this Fifth Chapter tells us why these problems had come upon Israel:

"They chose new gods."

Regrettably, Israel chose gods that could not save them. They were overcome by their enemies, *"Then was war in the gates."*

The Eighth Verse says, *"Was there a shield or spear seen among forty thousand in Israel?"* So, to face Sisera's 900 chariots of iron and his mighty army, God sent a ragtag army of 10,000 without weapons. We might add, as well, that a woman was leading them. Once again, Israel had been reduced to this state because, *"They chose new gods."*

NEW GODS

Could it be said today that the church, as well, has chosen *"new gods"*?

The god of modern day Christianity is, for the most part, the god of humanistic psychoanalysis—psychology. Psychology is the religion of secularism and humanism. It is atheistic at its core. Its apostles are Freud, Skinner, Maslow, Rogers, and a host of other similar ilk. The church, sadly, has bought it hook, line, and sinker.

The individuals mentioned, who are mostly atheistic or, at least, humanistic, have replaced Matthew, Mark, Luke, John, and Paul. As Israel desperately needed a *"Deborah"* and a Miracle from God, likewise, the church needs the same.

THE MESSAGE OF DEBORAH

"Awake, awake, Deborah: awake, awake, utter a song: arise, Barak, and lead your captivity captive, you son of Abinoam.

"Then He made him who remains have dominion over the nobles among the people: the LORD made me have dominion over the mighty.

"Out of Ephraim was there a root of them against Amalek; after you, Benjamin, among your people; out of Machir came down governors, and out of Zebulun they who handle the pen of the writer.

"And the princes of Issachar were with Deborah; even Issachar, and also Barak: he was sent on foot into the valley. For the divisions of Reuben there were great thoughts of heart.

"Why abode you among the sheepfolds, to hear the bleatings of the flocks? For the divisions of Reuben there were great searchings of heart.

"Gilead abode beyond Jordan: and why did Dan remain in ships? Asher continued on the seashore, and abode in his breaches.

"Zebulun and Naphtali were a people who jeoparded their lives unto the death in the high places of the field" (Judg. 5:12-18).

VISION, PROVISION, AND DIVISION

Verse 12 proclaims Deborah's going back to the time the Lord moved upon her with the Divine Call. The Holy Spirit through Deborah delineates those who helped in the battle and those who didn't. The Tribes of Ephraim, Benjamin, Zebulun, and Issachar helped bring about the victory.

Verse 16 proclaims the fact that God gives the *"Vision"* and brings about *"provision"*; however, Satan then comes in, attempting to bring about *"division."* This is what happened to Reuben, and this, the Holy Spirit is quick to say.

The Seventeenth Verse probably pertains to the Tribe of Gad, whose portion was on the east side of Jordan. They seemed to think that the conflict did not include them simply because of their location. The celebrated harbor of Joppa was in the Tribe of Dan. They did not want to interrupt their business, so the Tribe of Dan neglected to help.

The Holy Spirit speaks very highly of the two Tribes of Zebulun and Naphtali as it regards this conflict. What does the Holy Spirit say about us?

AWAKE

It was time for Israel to be delivered from the terrible bondage of the Canaanites headed up by Jabin and Sisera. As the Holy Spirit looked at the situation in Israel, He found only a woman who would evidence the Faith required in order for this task to be carried out.

God uses people. While, of course, the Lord can use anything, even as we shall see in this Chapter, still, the greater thrust of His Work is always through individuals. However, these must be individuals, whether man or woman, who evidence Faith in the Lord and, due to that Faith, will believe God and carry out the Will of God.

How many grand and glorious things does the Lord have ready, but they cannot be brought to fruition because He cannot find a man or a woman who will believe Him. As we say over and over again, the ingredient is Faith; however, the Faith registered must be in Christ and the Cross. God will honor no other kind (Rom. 6:1-14; Eph. 2:13-18; Col. 2:10-15).

While, of course, Christ and the Cross were only in shadow in Old Testament times, still, the Sacrificial system was designed by the Lord to portray Christ and what He would do at the Cross. While it is true that most of the time Israel did not understand the meaning of the Sacrificial system, that in no way took away from its veracity. Regrettably, despite all the Revelation, most modern Christians still do not understand the meaning of Christ and the Cross.

ONE OF THE GREATEST MIRACLES OF ALL TIME

The word, *"Awake,"* repeated four times by the Holy Spirit, is done so for emphasis. The number of times the word is used proclaims the tremendous significance of the mission at hand. As previously stated, this mission would result in one of the greatest Miracles performed by God in the entirety of Israel's history. In some way, it might even rank close to the Miracle of the tumbling of the walls of Jericho, as well as other tremendous victories won by Joshua, etc.

This can be said for Deborah, she immediately set out to carry out that which the Lord told her to do.

The manner in which the Lord gave this Revelation to Deborah, and by using the word *"awake,"* it seems to proclaim the fact that Israel, at that time, was mired down in a spirit of lethargy. In other words, they saw no way out of this dilemma. How in the world could Israel, who, in essence, had few weapons, come up against Sisera with his 900 chariots of iron?

For 20 years the Lord had allowed this bondage. During this time, even as the bondage deepened, with all of its attendant misery, the people seemingly forgot that God was a God of Miracles. If He was, they may have reasoned, why would He allow them to be in this condition?

Of course, Israel discounted the fact, and we do so, as well, that their negative situation was not the fault of the Lord, but rather their own fault. They had gone into deep sin, even idol-worship, hence, the reason for their present predicament. At any rate, they could see no way out of their dilemma.

At the same time, who would have thought that God would use a woman to bring about one of the greatest Deliverances of all? One thing is certain, had the wisest men in Israel of that time been given the choice of choosing the one who would lead them in battle, it certainly would not have been Deborah. However, while men look on the outward, God looks on the heart. He found in Deborah a woman of Faith whom He could trust, and who would do what He told her to do.

DOMINION

The Thirteenth Verse proclaims the fact that the Lord told Deborah that He would give her dominion over the king of the Canaanites and their mighty military leader, Sisera. I wonder what Deborah thought when the Lord related this to her. How in the world could she as a woman have dominion over these individuals, especially considering that Sisera had 900 chariots of iron?

The truth is, God intended for Israel to have dominion over every single nation on the face of the Earth. Had they obeyed the Lord, that dominion would have been theirs. There will come a day in the coming Kingdom Age when Israel will finally realize this dominion because she finally realizes that it is all in Christ—the very One she crucified!

It is the Will of God presently for every Believer to have dominion over the powers of darkness, over every sin that would so easily beset us, and that we walk in perpetual victory. Paul said:

THE VICTORY OF THE CHILD OF GOD

"For sin shall not have dominion over you *(the sin*

nature will not have dominion over us if we as Believers continue to exercise Faith in Christ and the Cross; otherwise, the sin nature most definitely will have dominion over the Believer): **for you are not under the Law** *(means that if we try to live this life by any type of law, no matter how good that law might be in its own right, we will conclude by the sin nature having dominion over us)*, **but under Grace** *(the Grace of God flows to the Believer on an unending basis only as long as the Believer exercises Faith in Christ and what He did at the Cross; Grace is merely the Goodness of God exercised by and through the Holy Spirit and given to undeserving Saints)*" **(Rom. 6:14).**

OUR METHOD OF VICTORY

It is the same now as it was with Deborah. Salvation and its means are the same, and for all time. It is, *"Jesus Christ and Him Crucified"* (I Cor. 1:23).

The Sacrificial system was instituted by the Lord at the very dawn of time, immediately after the fall of Adam and Eve in the Garden of Eden. Through this system, God proclaimed to the First Family how, despite the Fall, they could have communion and fellowship with Him, and forgiveness of sins. It would be through the slain lamb, which would be a Type of Christ, Who would ultimately come to this world and die on a Cross in order that man might be Saved. A perfect description is given to us in the Fourth Chapter of Genesis. So, Salvation and its method have never changed and, in fact, will never change because there is only one Saviour, as there has ever been only one Saviour, the Lord Jesus Christ.

THE HOLY SPIRIT AND THE TRIBES OF ISRAEL

Several of the Tribes joined in the great battle, but some did not. Of the 10,000 men who fought against Sisera, most came from the Tribes of Ephraim, Manasseh, Benjamin, Zebulun,

Issachar, and Naphtali. Admittedly, some of these Tribes sent only a few men, but the rest of the Tribes did not help at all. The Holy Spirit, even as we shall see, records some of the excuses. We would do well to fasten our attention on what the Holy Spirit here says.

It is interesting that the Holy Spirit in this Fourteenth Verse refers to *"Amalek."*

Amalek pictures the old carnal nature. He was the grandson of Esau, who tried to murder Jacob before and after his birth, and who preferred the mess of pottage to the birthright. This carnal nature wars against the Spirit; *". . . it is not subject to the Law of God, neither indeed can be"* (Rom. 8:7).

THE HOSTILITY OF THE NATURAL MAN

Actually, the first mention of the Bible in the Word of God is in connection with the hostility of the natural man to the spiritual man, with Amalek as the example (Ex. 17:14). *"The LORD swore that He would have war with Amalek from generation to generation"* (Ex. 17:16). Amalek is a type of the flesh, hence, the very first battle enjoined after Israel was delivered from Egypt (Ex. 17:8-16).

The Holy Spirit had Deborah to mention *"Amalek"* in this Fourteenth Verse in order that we may understand the root of this struggle. As stated, Amalek is a type of the flesh, referring to man's personal power, prowess, intellectualism, education, motivation, ability, talent, etc. While these things within themselves aren't necessarily wrong, the wrong comes in when we depend on them to help us live for God. The Holy Spirit through Paul referred to such as the *"flesh."* Amalek is a type of the flesh (Rom. 8:1-2, 8).

DIVISIONS

The Holy Spirit records that the Tribe of Issachar *"was with Deborah."* When He came to the Tribe of Reuben, the

Scripture states that they had *"great thoughts of heart"* as it regarded the coming conflict, but because of *"divisions,"* the record is clear that they sent no men.

"Division," without a doubt, is one of the greatest problems in the Work of God, and even in the modern church. Satan, as should be obvious, is the author of division. As we have previously stated, God gives the *"Vision"* and then makes *"provision"* for the *"Vision"* to be carried out. However, in order to stop this Vision from being carried out, the Devil oftentimes succeeds in bringing about *"division."* The very word, *"Division,"* dissected says, *"Di-vision,"* meaning that the Vision dies.

What caused these divisions in the Tribe of Reuben?

MONEY

Of course, we know that the root cause is always the Devil, but when it came to the individuals themselves, more than likely, some wanted to send soldiers and some didn't.

Quite possibly the question posed by the Holy Spirit, *"Why do you abode among the sheepfolds, to hear the bleatings of the flocks?"* proclaimed the fact that their herds meant more to them than freedom. In other words, they were making money, and they didn't want that disturbed. How often is money put before the Work of God?

If Believers only understood that if we seek first the Kingdom of God and His Righteousness, we'll come out on top to a much greater degree than otherwise. So, if we tend first of all to God's business, He will attend to ours. Reuben would here be sanctioned by the Holy Spirit for time and eternity, and all because they did not obey the Lord. How many of us fall into the same category?

The Scripture says that Gilead, which probably applies to the Tribe of Gad, *"abode beyond Jordan."* They simply reasoned, *"This is not my fight,"* when, in reality, it was their fight as much as the fight of anyone else.

How many Believers do as did Gad, thinking that *"this*

does not apply to me."

Many times we will attempt to raise funds over the SonLife Broadcasting Network in order to cover more territory with the Gospel. When asked to give for this cause, we are always faced with a number of Christians who will contemplate in their minds that this particular part of the world is not in their area, so it doesn't pertain to them. They conveniently forget that someone paid for the Gospel to come to their cities, their towns, and even their homes. It was someone who did not know them but helped to bring the Gospel to their area and, eventually, to their hearts and lives. Tragically, far too many consider that simply because they are *"beyond Jordan,"* whatever that would mean to them personally, whatever the need is, it does not apply to them. The Holy Spirit is quick here to say otherwise!

BUSINESS AS USUAL

The Scripture says that *"Dan remained in ships."* In other words, it was business as usual for the Tribe of Dan. They didn't want to interrupt what they were doing, in their making of money, to send soldiers to help against Jabin and Sisera, so they *"remained in their ships."*

The Tribe of Asher fell into the same category. They were busy unloading the goods brought on by the ships from the Tribe of Dan, so they, as well, did not send any soldiers, even though the call came to them. Again, the Holy Spirit is quick to point all of this out.

FAITHFULNESS

The Holy Spirit, as well, is quick to point out that the Tribes of *"Zebulun and Naphtali"* did everything they could do as it regards the winning of this battle. The Scripture says, *"They jeoparded their lives unto the death in the high places of the field."* As the Spirit of God had pointed out the deficiencies of the other

Tribes, He points out the efficiency of these two Tribes.

They heard the clarion call of Deborah exactly as did the other Tribes, but they did something these other Tribes did not do. They responded to that call!

Actually, these two Tribes furnished the majority of the 10,000 men who fought the Canaanites. The other Tribes provided token numbers, with Reuben, Gad, Dan, and Asher providing no one. How so like the church regarding the great Work of God in taking the Gospel of Jesus to a lost world. Many do absolutely nothing toward the most important part of all, which is telling the greatest Story the world has ever known, the Story of the Lord Jesus Christ and His Power to save. Many, as the Tribes mentioned, give only a token amount to help further this cause, with a few doing most of the giving and most of the work.

It shouldn't be that way!

A DEBTOR

For every single individual who is Saved as a result of the Precious Shed Blood of the Lord Jesus Christ, to say the least, he is a debtor. It is incumbent upon all of us to do the very best we can, whatever that might be, to help take this Gospel to others. We must make doubly certain that what we are supporting is truly of God. Unfortunately, most of the giving as it regards the Work of God, in fact, does not go to the Work of God but something else altogether. That is tragic but true! In this work for the Lord, it doesn't matter how poor the person may be or how rich the person may be. The Lord expects us to be faithful with what we have, as little or as much as that might be.

Remember this:

The Lord has not called us to be successful, but He has called us to be faithful (Mat. 25:21).

THEY CAME NOT TO THE HELP OF THE LORD

"The kings came and fought, then fought the kings of Canaan in Taanach by the waters of Megiddo; they took no gain

of money.

"They fought from Heaven; the stars in their courses fought against Sisera.

"The river of Kishon swept them away, that ancient river, the river Kishon. O my soul, you have trodden down strength.

"Then were the horsehoofs broken by the means of the pransings, the pransings of their mighty ones.

"Curse you Meroz, said the Angel of the LORD, curse you bitterly the inhabitants thereof; because they came not to the help of the LORD, to the help of the LORD against the mighty" (Judg. 5:19-23).

THE ANGEL OF THE LORD

The heathen kings of Verse 19 thought to plunder Israel. Instead, they would be plundered themselves. According to Josephus, a great storm arose in the face of the Canaanites, which led to their utter defeat in this battle.

Regarding Verse 21, the *"river of Kishon"* is normally a very narrow stream; however, the storm evidently caused the river to flood, which played havoc with the chariots, etc.

The inhabitants of the city of Meroz could easily have been of great help and great service in this battle but evidently refused to do so. The Holy Spirit tells us here that a curse was placed on them by the *"Angel of the LORD,"* in other words, the Lord Almighty!

When the Holy Spirit begins to do a certain thing, and Believers take a neutral position, they lose the manifestation and the experience of the Power of God. However, if they are so placed that they can help but refuse to do so, then they bring death upon their souls like these people of Meroz did.

THE WAYS OF THE LORD

In this valley where the river of Kishon ran, which is normally little more than a stream, Israel's 10,000 men without any weapons of war, we might quickly add, would be meat, or so it seemed, for Sisera's chariots.

Incidentally, for these 10,000 men to face Sisera's 900 chariots of iron along with what was, no doubt, tens of thousands of his army, required tremendous Faith, especially when we consider that the People of God were almost defenseless, at least, as it regarded natural weaponry.

In fact, this valley, for I've been there, is perfect for the operation of chariots. Sisera could not lose, or so he thought; however, the Twentieth Verse says, *"The stars in their courses fought against Sisera."*

The Fourth Verse says, *"And the heavens dropped, the clouds also dropped water,"* which means that this small river, normally only a few feet across, became a raging torrent. With a great rain, this can happen in a few minutes' time. It must have thrown his chariots around like fallen leaves.

The Twenty-second Verse uses the phrase, *"The pransings of their mighty ones."* This signifies the arrogancy of Sisera and his military chieftains; however, their pransings were *"broken"* by the Power of Almighty God.

THE CURSE

The Twenty-third Verse records an indictment that should make the Church tremble. It says, *"Curse you Meroz."*

It must be remembered that these words were given to Deborah by the Holy Spirit, *"Said the Angel of the LORD."* This would have been the One we now know as the Lord Jesus Christ. He then says, *"Curse you bitterly."*

And then, *"Because they came not to the help of the LORD, to the help of the LORD against the mighty."*

The Holy Spirit was careful to speak to the two Tribes who provided most of the soldiers. He was also careful to specify those who provided none and then *"curse you Meroz."*

Who these individuals were, we do not know, but this we do know: they had the opportunity to come *"to the help of the LORD,"* and they did not do so.

THE MODERN CHURCH?

How many in the modern church fall into the position of the Tribes who did not help because of difficulties in their own ranks and are actually *"cursed by the Angel of the LORD"*?

Whatever happened to these people of the town of Meroz, we aren't told. However, one can be certain that if a curse is leveled against a place by none other than the Lord Himself, the situation will not turn out positive.

Whenever the Lord carries out a mission, He expects all of His People to get behind that mission. None are excluded!

We can only go here by the Scriptural Text. It says that the Lord cursed this village of Meroz, meaning that He stopped the flow of Blessings to them. This means that they did not enjoy the freedom that Israel now had, but something else altogether. As stated, what actually happened to them, we aren't told. However, we must ask, *"How many modern Believers fall into the same category? How many could have but will not do so? Is it true that a curse is upon such who fall into that category presently?"* Only the Lord can answer those questions; however, I think every Believer should take heed as to exactly how we respond to the Work of the Lord. A curse, especially that leveled by the Lord Himself, is not something to be trifled with.

SHE PUT HER HAND TO THE NAIL

"Blessed above women shall Jael the wife of Heber the Kenite be, blessed shall she be above women in the tent.

"He asked water, and she gave him milk; she brought forth butter in a lordly dish.

"She put her hand to the nail, and her right hand to the workmen's hammer; and with the hammer she smote Sisera, she smote off his head, when she had pierced and stricken through his temples.

"At her feet he bowed, he fell, he lay down: at her feet he

bowed, he fell: where he bowed, there he fell down dead.

"The mother of Sisera looked out at a window, and cried through the lattice, Why is his chariot so long in coming? why tarry the wheels of his chariots?

"Her wise ladies answered her, yes, she returned answer to herself,

"Have they not sped? have they not divided the prey; to every man a damsel or two; to Sisera a prey of divers colors, a prey of divers colors of needlework, of divers colors of needlework on both sides, meet for the necks of them who take the spoil?

"So let all your enemies perish, O LORD: but let them who love Him be as the sun when he goes forth in his might. And the land had rest forty years" (Judg. 5:24-31).

BLESSED!

As stated, the only other woman spoken of in this fashion by the Holy Spirit, as described in Verse 24, was Mary, the Mother of our Lord. To be killed in battle by a woman presented, at that time, the height of disgrace. Verse 31 proclaims a victory that was a foretaste of the final Victory over sin and death, which took place at the Cross and is the Glory of the Redeemed Church.

When we consider that the Holy Spirit sanctioned the Blessing of Jael in the same sense as the Virgin Mary, we tend to see how signally important this great victory actually was.

Incidentally, the name, *"Jael,"* means, *"Profitable for the Lord."* This dear lady most assuredly lived up to her name. She was most profitable for the Work of God.

As is obvious here, the Holy Spirit goes into detail as it regards how Jael put an end to the military career of Sisera who had terrorized Israel for some 20 years.

CALVARY'S CROSS

Inasmuch as Jael drove a nail through the head of Sisera, with the Scripture intimating that she then also cut off his head, this becomes a type of the defeat of Satan at Calvary's Cross. This is the reason that the Holy Spirit gave her such a lordly Blessing, thereby, placing her, in a sense, in the same category as Mary, the Mother of our Lord.

As stricken as Sisera was, as stricken was Satan at the Cross.

When Jesus died on the Cross, He atoned for all sin, past, present, and future, at least, for all who will believe (Jn. 3:16).

"Sin" is the means, and we might quickly add, the legal means by which Satan holds man in bondage. Sin gives him that right; however, with all sin removed, which it was at the Cross, actually taken away and taken away forever, Satan lost that legal right.

So, that being the case, how is it that Satan can hold anyone presently as a captive?

VICTORY IN THE CROSS

We realize that most of the world is in central captivity and is actually a captive of Satan. How can this be if he was defeated at Calvary's Cross?

One might say that Satan places individuals into captivity simply because they give him consent.

How is this done?

For that which Christ did to be effective, one must believe and accept Him as Lord and Saviour. Regrettably, most of the world doesn't want to do that, so they remain in captivity.

How does that explain the millions of Christians who are also in some way a captive of Satan?

In one sense, it is the same as the unconverted. It is because they do not place their faith in Christ and the Cross, but rather something else.

The Believer must understand that it was at the Cross where all Victory was won (Col. 2:10-15; I Cor. 1:17, 18, 23; 2:2; Rom. 6:1-14; 8:1-11). Consequently, for that Victory to be ours in totality, our Faith must be placed where the Victory was won, and that is the Cross. Unfortunately, most Christians, as stated, have their faith in something else. Once the Believer has his Faith anchored solidly in Christ and the Cross, the Holy Spirit, Who Alone can make us what we ought to be, will then work mightily on our behalf. He always works entirely within the framework of the Finished Work of Christ. In doing so, He demands that our Faith be according to that great Truth (Rom. 8:1-11).

Deborah closes out her song by saying, *"So let all Your enemies perish, O LORD."* Then she said, *"But let them who love Him be as the Sun when he goes forth in his might."*

All *"enemies"* were defeated at Calvary's Cross. We will realize the full and complete glory of that in the coming Kingdom Age, which is soon to begin.

"When the trumpet of the Lord shall sound,
"And time shall be no more,
"And the morning breaks eternal bright and fair,
"When the Saved of Earth shall gather,
"Over on the other shore,
"And the roll is called up yonder, I'll be there."

"On that bright and cloudless morning,
"When the dead in Christ shall rise,
"And the Glory of His Resurrection share;
"When His Chosen Ones shall gather,
"To that home beyond the skies,
"And the roll is called up yonder, I'll be there."

"Let us labor for the Master,
"From the dawn till the setting sun,
"Let us talk of all His Wondrous Love and Care;
"Then when all of life is over,
"And our work on Earth is done,
"And the roll is called up yonder, I'll be there."

Great Women of the Bible

OLD TESTAMENT

Chapter Nine

RUTH AND NAOMI

RUTH AND NAOMI

THE REASON FOR THE ACCOUNT OF RUTH
THE MOABITESS IN THE WORD OF GOD

The following is a beautiful statement given in the Pulpit Commentary concerning Ruth. I quote:

"Many have supposed that the true reason of the Book is a matter of genealogy. The ground on which this opinion is maintained is the fact that there is a little bit of genealogy in the five Verses with which the Book concludes. This bit of genealogy connects Pharez the son of Judah with David the son of Jesse. The line passed through Boaz, the husband of Ruth. It is an important historical relationship, more especially to us Christians; for as Christ was 'the Son of David,' He was also the son of Boaz, and consequently the son of Ruth the Moabitess – the Gentile link.

"The fact is all the more significant and suggestive as, in ascending the genealogical ladder upward to Abraham, the father of the Messianic people, we discover that there were other Gentile links which connected the favored descendants of the Patriarch with the outlying 'families of the earth,' and which likewise show, in consequence of the moral peculiarity attaching to them, how wondrous was the boon conferred upon men, when the Lord of Glory humbled Himself to become the 'Kinsman' and the 'Friend' of those whose name is 'sinners.'"[1]

MOAB

"Now it came to pass in the days when the judges ruled, that there was a famine in the land. And a certain man of Beth-lehem-judah went to sojourn in the country of Moab, he, and his wife, and his two sons.

"And the name of the man was Elimelech, and the name of his wife Naomi, and the name of his two sons Mahlon and Chilion, Ephrathites of Beth-lehem-judah. And they came into

the country of Moab, and continued there" (Ruth 1:1-2).

In Old Testament times, famines were sent by the Lord upon Israel as a Judgment because of spiritual declension. Unfortunately, during those times and these times, the righteous suffer along with the unrighteous.

Going to a country outside of Israel to live was forbidden by the Lord; and yet, we will see how the Lord would take this wrong and turn it into right, but with great loss, as accompanies all failure.

In the two Verses quoted, much is stated. Let's look at the geographical location stated here—Beth-lehem-judah. It is given to us in this manner because there was another Beth-lehem in Israel, namely in the area of the Tribe of Zebulun (Josh. 19:15). Therefore, the writer, whomever he might have been, specifies that the Beth-lehem mentioned here is the portion of the Tribe of Judah and not Zebulun.

It was the home of Boaz, the area of Ruth's gleaning and of her marriage to Boaz. In these pastures, in the household of Jesse and among his stalwart sons, was trained the youthful David, who became the hero and the darling, in fact, the king of Israel.

In New Testament history, between the pastures of Beth-lehem where the sheep grazed and the stars of Heaven was sung the Angel's song of goodwill and peace. Here was born the Son of David, Who was the Son of God. So, in a sense, very few places on the Earth, if any, could even begin to rival the significance, and I speak of the spiritual significance, of this beautiful area. So, this is the setting of Ruth the Moabitess.

Even though the very name Beth-lehem means *"house of bread,"* signifying that it is a very fertile area, at the commencing of our story, a famine grips the land.

THE WORD OF GOD

While the information is given regarding Elimelech and Naomi going to Moab, and of the negative circumstances which transpired there, it is noteworthy that there is no hint in the Text itself that the step taken was blamable or blamed. As someone has said and probably should be repeated, *"No man ought to be condemned, whether dead or alive, without proof of guilt; and no certain proof of guilt appears in this present case."*

So, how can we reconcile Elimelech and Naomi leaving Bethlehem and going to a heathen country such as Moab, which was a land of idol-worshippers, with the tremendous Blessing that accrued from this, namely Ruth?

That's a good question!

To understand the why of all of this, we have to first understand that God uses all things to His Glory, whatever those things might be. As well, the Lord is able to take our wrong, put it in His Right, and, thereby, make everything right.

Our immediate reaction to all of this is, if Elimelech and Naomi had not gone to Moab, Ruth could not have been Saved, and her name would have been missing in the genealogy of Christ. However, the Lord, Who knows all things, past, present, and future, knew that Elimelech and Naomi would do this thing; therefore, He accordingly worked out His Plan.

"But, what if they had not gone?" the question may be asked.

That is an incorrect question for the following reason:

Through foreknowledge, God knows everything. So, He knew, as stated, Elimelech and Naomi would do this thing; therefore, He would work His Plan regarding Ruth.

NAOMI: A TYPE OF ISRAEL

"And Elimelech Naomi's husband died; and she was left, and her two sons.

"And they took them wives of the women of Moab; the name of the one was Orpah, and the name of the other Ruth: and they dwelt there about ten years.

"And Mahlon and Chilion died also both of them; and the woman was left of her two sons and her husband" (Ruth 1:3-5).

Verse 3 proclaims the fact that to be out of the Will of God always brings suffering.

It was not forbidden in the Law for a Hebrew to marry a Moabite woman, but a Moabite, because of being cursed by God, was forbidden to enter the congregation of the Lord (Deut. 23:3). However, Faith could overcome that, which it did with Ruth.

Two Books in the Bible are named after women—Ruth and Esther. In the one, a Gentile woman (Ruth) marries a Hebrew, and in the other, a Hebrew woman (Esther) marries a Gentile. Both marriages predict, as foretold, that the Gentiles, as such, are to be brought into the Kingdom of God in connection with Israel (Gen. 12:3; 18:18; 22:18; 26:4; Ps. 72:17; Acts 3:25).

The Fourth Verse says that this family dwelled in Moab for about 10 years. It's very easy, spiritually speaking, to go into wrong direction, however, very hard to leave that wrong direction in order to come back to the right way.

Naomi is a picture of Israel in the last days under the *"famine of the Antichrist,"* when they will flee to *"Moab,"* which will take place at the midpoint of the Great Tribulation. In the coming Great Tribulation, Israel will lose much. In fact, were it not for the Second Coming of the Lord, Israel would be totally destroyed by the Antichrist in that coming terrible time. In fact, Jesus said it would be worse than anything the world has ever seen before and will never see such again. That's bad! (Mat. 24:21). In fact, the great Prophet Jeremiah spoke of this coming time as *"the time of Jacob's trouble";* however, he then said, *". . . but he shall be saved out of it"* (Jer. 30:7).

The Great Tribulation, which is right ahead, and we speak of this present time (2012), will conclude with the Battle of Armageddon portrayed to us in Ezekiel, Chapters 38 and 39. The Battle of Armageddon will conclude with the Second Coming of the Lord (Rev., Chpt. 19). Then Israel will come to Christ, typified by Boaz in our story, who is a Type of Christ. Then Naomi (Israel) and her daughter-in-law Ruth, who is a Gentile and typifies the Church, will come into the riches of our Heavenly Boaz, the Lord Jesus Christ. This will begin the thousand-year Kingdom Age when Jesus will rule Personally in Jerusalem and, in fact, will rule the entirety of the world at that time.

So, the story of Ruth is far more than meets the eye. That which happened, which could have been during the early years of the Prophet Samuel, carries not only the illustration of the Salvation of a soul, which is so very, very important, but, as well, has prophetic overtones that reach out even to us presently.

GENTILES

The Fourth Verse brings into view the two Moabite girls, Orpah and Ruth, who had married the two sons of Elimelech and Naomi, Mahlon and Chilion.

Theological critics have here again raised the question, *"Was it sinful for these Hebrew young men, who were in the Covenant of God, to take in marriage the daughters of Moab?"*

The Jewish Targums did not hesitate regarding their decision. They said, *"And they transgressed the edict of the Word of the Lord, and took to themselves alien wives of the daughters of Moab."* It is noteworthy, however, that in the Text itself, and I mean that which you read in your Bible, even to which we have already alluded, and throughout the entire Book of Ruth, there is nothing of the nature of condemnation, not even the least hint of blame. In fact, it was not forbidden in the Law for a Hebrew to marry a Moabite woman; a Canaanite, yes, a Moabite, no (Deut. 7:3).

Some say that the name *"Ruth"* means *"beauty"* and others say it means *"friend."* Some have even proposed that Ruth was looked at as *"the Rose of Moab."* Orpah, regrettably, will soon fade from view. Ruth, by contrast, will set an example of Righteousness that defies all description.

Although a Gentile, due to her marriage with Boaz, she will be placed in the genealogy of the Lord Jesus Christ, and nothing could be greater than that (Mat. 1:5). As well, and as also stated, she was the great-grandmother of David, the great king of Israel, and the one who would be the namesake of the Lord Jesus Christ.

IS RUTH A TYPE OF THE CHURCH?

I think so, but only in a limited way. I speak of coming into the riches of Christ, which both Israel and the Church will do at the beginning of the Kingdom Age. At that time, Israel will accept Jesus Christ as Saviour, King, Lord, and Messiah.

Williams, the British theologian, has some thoughts on this, which I think are very important. He said:

"Naomi typifies Israel in the latter day – in exile from Canaan, a widow, impoverished, and having no heir. She returns to the Land of Promise bringing Ruth, that is, the Gentile with her. They and their property are redeemed by Boaz, i.e., Christ; the nearer kinsman, i.e., the Law being unable to do so, and unwilling, because it necessitated union with a Gentile, i.e., Ruth.

"Israel having departed from God, and the Gentile being far off from God and outside of the Promises, the Law had no power to establish either of them in blessing.

"In this Book is recorded the operations of Grace in blessing those who merited no Grace; and of the prosecution of God's purposes despite the sin and disorder which marked that time; for God never fails to act even in the midst of evil; and having decreed that Ruth the Gentile should be an ancestress of the Messiah, He bent every circumstance to the accomplishment of that purpose."[2]

DEATH

Abruptly and bluntly we are told that Elimelech died, and then a little later, Mahlon and Chilion died, leaving Naomi with her two daughters-in-law, Orpah and Ruth.

It has been said, *"Many men have had affliction, but none like Job; many women have had affliction, but none like Naomi."[3]*

Why did the Lord allow this to happen?

To be sure, the deaths of these three were definitely the Work of the Lord. The reasons are given to us in this Book of Ruth.

Were these three men, Elimelech, Mahlon, and Chilion, men of Faith? The Scripture is silent; however, the blunt way in which the occasion of their deaths is given probably indicates that they were not individuals of Faith.

Were they Saved?

Only the Lord could give answer to that.

BACK TO ISRAEL

"Then she arose with her daughters-in-law, that she might return from the country of Moab: for she had heard in the country of Moab how that the LORD had visited His People in giving them bread.

"Wherefore she went forth out of the place where she was, and her two daughters-in-law with her; and they went on the way to return unto the land of Judah.

"And Naomi said unto her two daughters-in-law, Go, return each to her mother's house: the LORD deal kindly with you, as you have dealt with the dead, and with me.

"The LORD grant you that you may find rest, each of you in the house of her husband. Then she kissed them; and they lifted up their voice, and wept.

"And they said unto her, Surely we will return with you unto your people.

"And Naomi said, Turn again, my daughters: why will you go with me? are there yet any more sons in my womb, that they may be your husbands?

"Turn again, my daughters, go your way; for I am too old to have a husband. If I should say, I have hope, if I should have a husband also tonight, and should also bear sons;

"Would you tarry for them until they were grown? would you stay for them from having husbands? no, my daughters; for it grieves me much for your sakes that the Hand of the LORD is

gone out against me" (Ruth 1:6-13).

AN ANGEL?

Concerning Verse 6, the Jewish Targums, which were a record of happenings of sorts and were kept for hundreds of years, say that an Angel spoke to her and gave this information. In other words, the famine was over. It evidently lasted a number of years.

It seems that Naomi, at least, at this stage, had so little Faith in the Promises of God and such a poor experience as the result of her own disobedience that she discouraged her daughters-in-law from returning with her. This she should not have done; however, the same faithlessness that caused her and her family to leave Israel plagues her still. However, as we shall see, when she does return to Israel, her Faith will begin to come back. Moab was not the place of Faith, as the world's system is never the place of Faith. Israel was the place of Faith, and so it is presently, spiritually speaking.

Regarding verse 9, Naomi knew that there was no *"rest"* in the land of Moab because it was a place of idolatry, which was hateful in the Eyes of God, and grossly so!

Naomi felt that she had suffered the tragic loss of her husband and two sons because of being out of the Will of God by leaving Israel to come to Moab in the first place. There was, no doubt, some truth in that. However, we must always remember, God doesn't work from what might have been, should have been, or could have been, but rather from *"what is."*

JEWISH LAW

"Are there yet any more sons in my womb, that they may be your husbands?"

Jewish Law stated that if the husband died, then the wife was to marry his brother, that is, if he had a brother and if the brother was not already married. If that was impossible, as it was in this case, she was to marry the next of kin who was not already married. This is the reason for Naomi's words, *"No more sons in my womb"* (Deut. 25:5-9).

Quite possibly, these customs were strange to these two Moabite girls, but yet, they were probably well acquainted with Jewish Law by now because of living side by side with Naomi, etc.

The reason for this had to do with all the families of Israel. Each family was important, very important! Through one certain family in Israel at this time, the Messiah would come. Actually, it would be in the Tribe of Judah (Gen. 49:10). Later, the Lord told David, who would be Ruth's great-grandson, that in this Tribe, the Messiah would come, and it would be through his family (II Sam., Chpt. 7). And yet, every family was important because the Lord would choose from various families in Israel certain individuals to stand in the Office of the Prophet, with some of these Prophets giving us the Word of God as the Lord used them. So, every family was very special in Israel, hence, the reason for every effort being made to maintain each family name.

THE GREAT CONSECRATION

"And they lifted up their voice, and wept again: and Orpah kissed her mother-in-law; but Ruth clave unto her.

"And she said, Behold, your sister-in-law is gone back unto her people, and unto her gods: return thou after your sister-in-law.

"And Ruth said, Entreat me not to leave you, or to return from following after you: for where you go, I will go; and where you lodge, I will lodge: your people shall be my people, and your God my God:

"Where you die, will I die, and there will I be buried: the LORD do so to me, and more also, if ought but death part you and me.

"When Naomi saw that Ruth was steadfastly minded to go with her, then she left speaking unto her.

"So they two went until they came to Beth-lehem. And it came to pass, when they were come to Beth-lehem, that all the city was moved about them, and they said, Is this Naomi?

"And she said unto them, Call me not Naomi, call me Mara: for the Almighty has dealt very bitterly with me.

"I went out full, and the LORD has brought me home again empty: why then call you me Naomi, seeing the LORD has testified against me, and the Almighty has afflicted me?

"So Naomi returned, and Ruth the Moabitess, her daughter-in-law, with her, which returned out of the country of Moab: and they came to Beth-lehem in the beginning of barley harvest" (Ruth 1:14-22).

THE GREAT AFFIRMATION

Orpah left, and we never hear from her again; how sad!

From the statement in Verse 15, *"Unto her gods,"* it is obvious that the great contending factor here was the gods of Moab versus the God of Israel. Orpah chose *"her gods"* and missed the greatest thing that could ever happen to anyone— Eternal Life.

In essence, Naomi asked Ruth if that was what she was going to do as well! Exactly as to what Naomi had in mind, we can only guess. It seems that she didn't want to promise them things that she could not fulfill. This seems to have been her intention. But yet, in all of this, her Faith, it seems, was very, very low.

Verses 16 and 17 record what has to be one of the greatest statements and one of the greatest affirmations of Salvation found in the entirety of the Word of God. In essence, it is that which must characterize all who come to Christ. It is the statement of Faith given by Ruth.

In this consecration, there is no looking back. The die is cast. Ruth will forever turn her back on the world of idolatry and rebellion against God. She will forever throw in her lot with those who worship the Lord of Glory. Even when she dies, she does not want to be sent back to Moab, but rather buried in the land of Israel, which she was. She cut off all ties with the past, even her family and everything else. This is exactly the consecration that is demanded by God of all who come to Him. Anything less constitutes no salvation at all.

NAOMI

The words, *"They said,"* in Verse 19, proclaim a wealth of information. They carry the idea that the poverty which envelops Naomi was obvious to all. Besides that, her husband and two sons were absent, meaning they were dead. As well, and above all, she is accompanied by a Moabitess, which was a reproach within itself, at least, according to their thinking at that time. Little did the people at Beth-lehem realize that this Moabitess would be the ancestress of the Messiah.

In the thinking of Naomi, *"empty,"* as given in Verse 21, described her situation; however, she was far fuller than she could ever begin to think. Ruth would prove to be the greatest blessing of all. Unbelief sees *"empty,"* while Faith sees *"full."*

Verse 22 proclaims the Holy Spirit desiring us to know who Ruth is that we might know what Ruth becomes. He is, at the same time, telling us, as He changed Ruth's life, He can change our lives as well.

The time in question here described was April, Passover time. In effect, the Holy Spirit is saying, *"When I see the Blood, I will pass over you."* There is no sin the Blood cannot cover and cleanse. There is no life the cleansing of the Blood cannot change. It changed Ruth, and it can change us!

THE GREAT ACCLAMATION

The consecration that Ruth makes is recorded in Verses 16 and 17 and is, in fact, the consecration that every person must make in coming to the Lord Jesus Christ. She said:

"For where you go, I will go; and where you lodge, I will

lodge: your people shall be my people, and your God my God: where you die, will I die, and there will I be buried: the LORD do so to me, and more also, if ought but death part you and me."

In this consecration, there is no looking back. The die is cast. She will forever turn her back upon the world of idolatry. The same could be said for her family. In fact, the evidence is, she would never see them again.

She had learned about the God of Israel from Naomi. She had accepted the Christ as her Saviour, her Lord, and her Master. This means, as well, that she turned her back forever upon the gods of Moab. She had now found the peace that passes all understanding, the joy unspeakable and full of glory. Moab now holds nothing for her. Her eyes are cast upon God's Land and God's People, of which she is now a part.

One should study this acclamation as given by Ruth very carefully.

• *"Where you go, I will go"*: by this statement, she means that she is casting her lot with the People of God and doing so forever. This meant, as well, that she would turn her back upon her own family and her Moabite friends, forever making the people of Israel now her kindred.

This phrase also means that whatever the hardship and whatever the difficulties, no matter what she is called upon to do, this she will do.

• *"Where you lodge, I will lodge"*: it doesn't matter where the lodging place will be, how spartan it is, or how palatial it is. In fact, the riches, or lack thereof, of the lodgings present themselves as unimportant.

• *"Your people shall be my people, and your God my God"*: Jehovah is now her God and will be her God forever! She has turned her back totally and completely on the idols of Moab. She is now with the People of God forever, and Jehovah is her God forever. Her own immediate family, although she loves them, are not considered here. She has a new family. In other words, she is cutting all ties with the past.

• *"Where you die, will I die, and there will I be buried"*:

she has made her choice for life. There is no turning back. As stated, she will never see her family again, will never see Moab again, and will never see again the places where she was born and raised. She has forever cast her lot with the People of God, and, in essence, she tells Naomi, *"Wherever it is that you will die, that is the place that I will die, for I am not leaving your side. From your lips I have found the Lord of Glory. You have pointed to me the way. There is nothing else for me in any other place. My past, my present, and my future are with you and, in reality, with your God and my Lord!"*

There could be no more beautiful affirmation and acclamation of this as given by Ruth. It forever rains down through the span of time that which it means as it regards a full consecration to the Lord. How so certain is the sound that comes from her lips! How so sure her consecration!

The Eighteenth Verse says, *"She was steadfastly minded."* Those who are, make it. Those who are not, don't!

THE PASSOVER

The journey from Moab to Beth-lehem was only about 70 or 80 miles. That is not much now but a journey of some length then. It probably took them about a week to make the trip. The miles were insignificant, but the journey for both, Naomi and Ruth, was a journey of unprecedented proportions.

For Ruth, it was a journey from one life to another, a journey, in some measure, which would never end, meaning it has not ended even yet. So it is as it regards any and every person who makes Jesus Christ their Saviour and their Lord. They have just embarked upon a journey that is eternal, a journey with such rewards that literally stagger the imagination.

It is Passover time, the time of the *"barley harvest."* In the time of the Judges, the Passover was little celebrated. So, how much that Ruth knew about this greatest feast of all, celebrating the Deliverance of the Children of Israel from Egyptian bondage, we aren't told. Nevertheless, by inserting the statement,

"In the beginning of barley harvest," the Holy Spirit wants us to know that it was Passover time.

Why is this so important?

It's important simply because Ruth would be the ancestress of the One Who would shed His Immortal Glory and take upon Himself the habiliments of human flesh. This was all for the purpose of going to the Cross where He would there shed His Life's Blood in order that the fallen sons of Adam's lost race might be Saved.

"... when I see the Blood, I will pass over you" (Ex. 12:12-13).

THE ALMIGHTY

When Naomi and Ruth came into Beth-lehem, Naomi was instantly recognized. Scores of people gathered around them, asking the question, *"Is this Naomi?"* She has been gone some 10 years, and now she returns home; however, she returns without her husband or two sons. Above that, she has a Moabitess girl with her, which, to say the least, was very unusual!

Naomi doesn't try to put a face on the situation, even as the questions fly at her thick and fast. Where is Elimelech? Where is Mahlon and Chilion? Who is this Moabite girl, beautiful, but yet, a Moabite?

The Holy Spirit strongly desired that all would know who Ruth was. He referred to her as *"Ruth the Moabitess."*

Why?

The reasons, no doubt, are many! However, the Lord wanted all to know that Faith, which, incidentally, characterized Ruth, evident in her acclamation, can rise above any dilemma. Despite the fact that she had been an idol-worshipping Moabite, in fact, a people cursed by God, still, she would rise above all of that, actually rise to such a height as to defy all description. Her Faith in God would take her there. Her consecration portrays that.

Her Faith would take her to the land of Israel to be a part of the People of God and above all, to serve Jehovah, the only

True God. As well, she would be the great-grandmother of David, the mighty king of Israel. Above all of that, far above all of that, she would be the ancestress of the Son of David, the Lord Jesus Christ, the Saviour of mankind, the Baptizer with the Holy Spirit, the King of kings and Lord of lords, the First and the Last, and the Alpha and the Omega.

"Who is she?" the Holy Spirit asks!

Quickly, the retort is given. *"She is a Moabitess, cursed by God. But yet, rising above all of that and showing every human being who has ever lived, no matter their circumstances, that through Faith in God, they can rise above these problems and see great things, even as did Ruth!"*

BOAZ

"And Naomi had a kinsman of her husband's, a mighty man of wealth, of the family of Elimelech; and his name was Boaz.

"And Ruth the Moabitess said unto Naomi, Let me now go to the field, and glean ears of corn after him in whose sight I shall find grace. And she said unto her, Go, my daughter.

"And she went, and came, and gleaned in the field after the reapers: and her hap was to light on a part of the field belonging unto Boaz, who was of the kindred of Elimelech" (Ruth 2:1-3).

In a sense, Boaz is a Type of Christ, and Ruth, a Gentile, is a type of the Church. The terrible losses in the land of Moab, as addressed by Naomi, portray the dispersion and, thereby, Judgment of Israel.

Boaz will prove to be the kinsman redeemer of Ruth. There is one Hebrew word for *"kinsman"* and *"redeemer,"* for he only had *"the right to redeem"* who was a kinsman. Hence, it was necessary that the Lord Jesus Christ should become Man in order to redeem man. Ruth's marriage into the wealthy home into which she was brought pictured the satisfying joy and fullness of Blessing which the union with Christ secures for the heart that trusts Him.

Verse 2 portrays the fact that Naomi was poverty stricken. The welfare system of Israel in that day, which was given by God in the Law of Moses, stated that during the harvest, the poor could go into the fields and glean the leavings. In this Law, the reapers were instructed to not glean the corners of the field and to leave a little something along the way for the poor and unfortunate (Lev. 19:9; 23:22; Deut. 24:19).

We find that Ruth, although a beautiful young lady, was not adverse to hard work; those who are, are seldom, if ever, used by the Lord.

The Third Verse says, *"Her hap was to light on a part of the field belonging to Boaz."*

As far as Ruth was concerned, she just happened to come on the field of Boaz, not really knowing where she was. Of course, the Holy Spirit was guiding her all the way. She did not know Boaz, but the Lord did. When the Lord plans for us, beautiful things result; when we plan for ourselves, there are no positive results!

THE LEADING OF THE HOLY SPIRIT

The Second Verse says, as exclaimed by Ruth, *"Let me now go to the field, and glean ears of corn"*

As we have already stated, the welfare system of Israel in that day was given by God in the Law of Moses, stating that during the harvest, the poor could go into the fields and glean the leavings. Considering that Naomi was desperately poor, Ruth volunteered to go into the fields in order that they might have food. This shows that Ruth, even though a very lovely young lady, did not feel that she was too good to stoop to the lowest social level in order that she and her mother-in-law might have food to eat.

God could use no other kind. What a lesson we can learn from this. In this, we learn at least two things about Ruth:

1. Her willingness to work, even at the lowest task.
2. Her humility.

THE WAY THE HOLY SPIRIT LEADS

Verse 3 says, *"And her hap was to light on a part of the field belonging unto Boaz."* The way the Holy Spirit has these words constructed tells us that He was guiding Ruth constantly, even though, at the time, she was not aware of such. She may have thought that she chose a field by chance; however, it was no chance at all. The Lord was involved in her going into the field to glean, in the direction she took to get to these fields, and especially that she went to the field of Boaz, not knowing at all who Boaz was, etc.

That memorable day when Ruth set out, probably early in the morning, she little knew where she was going. She just knew they had to have food, and there was no other way for it to be obtained because they had no money. She little understood, at least, at this time, the Leading and Guidance of the Holy Spirit, but, to be sure, He was guiding every step of the way.

Possibly she passed several fields, and then, finally, she saw one that somehow attracted her. This was the Holy Spirit pushing her in that direction. It belonged to Boaz, one of the wealthiest men in that part of the country. She knew none of this, only that she hoped to get a little grain so that some bread could be made that night.

She had made the great consecration to the Lord, and now He was leading and guiding her.

In the Lord's Rewarding of Ruth, He would demand some things of her. Had she been lazy, thinking she was too good to do such back-breaking work, the Lord could not have blessed her; however, He knew what kind of woman she was.

So, as she sets out to try to find a little grain that could be used to bake bread for Naomi and herself, the Holy Spirit has a grand and glorious Plan, and He is guiding her all the way.

Do we understand here what is really happening? Do we realize that the Lord desires to lead and guide us in exactly the same way? She had made the bold consecration, and she meant to stand by what she had said.

Does one think that she might have grown discouraged at her decision to throw in her lot totally and completely with Naomi, as it regards the God of Israel?

I don't think so!

There is no hint in the Text that she ever even remotely was sorry for the choice she had made. Whatever it was that she did, even to this back-breaking work of stooping to find a little grain, she did it, it seems, with relish, thankful to the Lord for the privilege of doing so.

BOAZ NOW TAKES OVER

"And, behold, Boaz came from Beth-lehem, and said unto the reapers, The LORD be with you. And they answered him, The LORD bless you.

"Then said Boaz unto his servant who was set over the reapers, Whose damsel is this?

"And the servant who was set over the reapers answered and said, It is the Moabitish damsel who came back with Naomi out of the country of Moab:

"And she said, I pray you, let me glean and gather after the reapers among the sheaves: so she came, and has continued even from the morning until now, that she tarried a little in the house.

"Then said Boaz unto Ruth, Hear me, my daughter. Go not to glean in another field, neither go from hence, but abide here fast by my maidens:

"Let your eyes be on the field that they do reap, and you go after them: have I not charged the young men that they shall not touch you? and when you are athirst, go unto the vessels, and drink of that which the young men have drawn.

"Then she fell on her face, and bowed herself to the ground, and said unto him, Why have I found grace in your eyes, that you should take knowledge of me, seeing I am a stranger?

"And Boaz answered and said unto her, It has fully been shown me, all that you have done unto your mother-in-law since the death of your husband: and how you have left your father

and your mother, and the land of your nativity, and are come unto a people which you knew not heretofore.

"The LORD recompense your work, and a full reward be given you of the LORD God of Israel, under Whose Wings you are come to trust.

"Then she said, Let me find favor in your sight, my lord; for that you have comforted me, and for that you have spoken friendly unto your handmaid, though I be not like unto one of your handmaidens.

"And Boaz said unto her, At mealtime you come here, and eat of the bread, and dip your morsel in the vinegar. And she sat beside the reapers: and he reached her parched corn, and she did eat and was sufficed, and left.

"And when she was risen up to glean, Boaz commanded his young men, saying, Let her glean even among the sheaves, and reproach her not:

"And let fall also some of the handfuls of purpose for her, and leave them, that she may glean them, and rebuke her not.

"So she gleaned in the field until evening, and beat out that she had gleaned: and it was about an ephah of barley.

"And she took it up, and went into the city: and her mother-in-law saw what she had gleaned: and she brought forth, and gave to her that she had reserved after she was sufficed" (Ruth 2:4-18).

HANDFULS OF PURPOSE

Boaz was extremely wealthy. He was of the Tribe of Judah and in the direct line of the Messiah.

The question of Verse 5, even though asked casually by Boaz, would be answered by the Holy Spirit. Ruth would be the great-grandmother of David and, thereby, of the Son of David.

To those around her, Ruth was reduced to the level of gleaning as she was poverty stricken; also, she was a Moabitess, with all its resultant connotations. However, Heaven would answer the question in a much different way.

Boaz had done far more than merely take notice of her.

Her action towards him denotes humility, a trait, incidentally, enjoyed by precious few.

Boaz made it clear that he had already been informed of her consecration as a proselyte to the Hebrew Faith, and of her decision to leave her own people, her native land and its gods, to live with the people who were strangers to her. He then pronounced a Blessing from the God of Israel upon her. The Hebrew Targums add to this answer of Boaz:

"It has been certainly told me by the word of the wise, that what the Lord has decreed (Deut. 23:3). And it has surely said to me by Prophecy, that Kings and Prophets shall proceed from you because of the good which you have done."

In his instructions to the reapers, Boaz directed them to give Ruth greater liberty than that commanded by the Law. The *"handfuls of purpose,"* in effect, state that handfuls of grain were to be dropped just for her. As stated, she was truly favored.

WHO IS THIS DAMSEL?

Boaz is mentioned 19 times in the Book of Ruth. His greeting to the reapers was, *"The LORD be with you,"* and they answered him, *"The LORD bless you."* This was the daily greeting of godly men and their servants in Israel.

This was the same as the owner of the field asking for the Presence of God to be with the workers and for Divine protection and preservation as they labored. It was the same when the servants expressed a desire for the owner to be blessed of God that he might enjoy the increase of the field and have wisdom regarding how to use it for God's Glory.

If such mutual love and respect were shared alike by employer and employees in all lands at this present time, it would be as near the days of Heaven on Earth as possible.

Boaz comes to this particular field to check with the reapers to see how things are going. He notices the Moabitess and asks, *"Whose damsel is this?"*

THE LINEAGE OF THE MESSIAH

The question, *"Whose damsel is this?"* as asked causally by Boaz, would be answered by the Holy Spirit. Ruth would be the great-grandmother of David and, thereby, of the Son of David. Of course, none of this was known at the time and, in fact, would not be known throughout the lifetimes of both Ruth and Boaz. However, Faith would bring it to pass, and, most certainly, they now both know, and know it very well.

This young lady and this man who characterized this Book of Ruth, and of whom we write, we will all one day meet, that is, if we make Heaven our Eternal Home.

These people, Boaz and Ruth, are so very prominent in the Scriptures simply because they are both in the lineage of the Messiah. Boaz is by direct lineage, and Ruth is by marriage, therefore, uniting the Jew and the Gentile.

In order to redeem the fallen sons of Adam's lost race, God would have to become man and go to a Cross, which was ever His Destination. Angels couldn't do this thing because they were of another Creation. God as God couldn't do this thing because God, as stated, cannot die. So, God would have to become man, the Man, Christ Jesus, in which many things would be done. However, the ever present goal, that which had been decided from before the foundation of the world, was the Cross. There His Life's Blood would be poured out. There Mercy was great, and Grace was free. There all sin would be atoned, past, present, and future, at least, for all who will believe (Jn. 3:16). If man was to be Saved, snatched back from the very jaws of Hell, then this is the price that had to be paid, and only God could pay it. Ruth and Boaz figure so prominently in all of this, thereby, giving us insight into the lives of some of these who would be in this great lineage.

HUMILITY

When Boaz spoke to Ruth, the Scripture says, *"Then she*

fell on her face, and bowed herself to the ground." This denotes her humility.

The great compliment of humility is enjoyed by so few of the majority of Christendom, and yet, it is possibly the greatest Grace that God could ever bestow upon anyone. The only personal thing that Jesus ever said about Himself was, *"I am meek and lowly in heart."*

Ruth would say, *"I am a stranger."* She was, in fact, a stranger to the commonwealth of Israel, an alien to the Promises of God; however, Grace would change her from a stranger to a joint heir (Rom. 8:17).

It is impossible, I think, for any Believer to truly know and understand humility unless such a person understands the Cross of Christ. This is simply because without a proper understanding of the Cross, the emphasis is always, in some way, on self, which is the opposite of humility.

When one properly understands the Cross, then one properly understands oneself. We know that whatever it is that needs to be done, we cannot do such. We have to depend totally and completely on what Jesus did for us at the Cross. Then the Holy Spirit can develop humility within us. Otherwise, not at all!

HANDFULS OF PURPOSE

The Eleventh Verse says, *"And Boaz answered and said unto her, It has fully been shown me."*

The news, evidently, had gotten around all over the little village of Beth-lehem concerning this beautiful Moabitess. Everyone knew of her consecration and how she had converted to the God of Israel, thereby, forever forsaking the idols of Moab. They knew of her consecration, and they knew of her Faith. In fact, it seems that she was the talk of Beth-lehem. When Boaz asked as to who she was, I greatly suspect that he had already suspicioned who she was.

He continued his answer to her by saying, *"The LORD*

recompense your work, and a full reward be given you of the LORD God of Israel, under Whose Wings you are come to trust."

What a beautiful way of proclaiming the Salvation of Ruth.

He then tells the reapers to *"let fall also some of the 'handfuls of purpose' for her."*

Why did Boaz do for her what he did? Also, why did he say the things to her which he did?

He did it for many reasons. Quite possibly, the greatest reason of all, whether he realized it at the moment or not, he was already falling in love with her.

How so much like the Lord on our part. Even though we were strangers, aliens from the commonwealth of Israel and strangers to the Promise, still, despite our lowly, poverty stricken, Gentile position, yet, He loved us. He came to where we were gleaning in the field, trying to get a little sustenance, and gave instructions that there should be *"handfuls of purpose"* left on our behalf.

Oh, dear reader, do you not see that? Do you not feel that? Do you not sense that?

He loves you, and he wants to leave *"handfuls of purpose,"* all on your behalf, and He, as stated, will most definitely do so if we will only believe Him.

Please note the following:

All of this was preceded by Ruth's humility. When he spoke to her, she fell to the ground in prostrated form and asked him, *"Why have I found grace in your eyes, that you should take knowledge of me, seeing I am a stranger?"*

Yes, the correct question and the correct answer was and is *"grace."*

No wonder John Newton wrote so long ago:

"Amazing Grace how sweet the sound,
"That Saved a wretch like me.
"I once was lost, but now I'm found,
"I was blind, but now I see."

NAOMI

"And her mother-in-law said unto her, Where have you gleaned today? and where have you worked? blessed be he who did take knowledge of you. And she showed her mother-in-law with whom she had worked, and said, The man's name with whom I worked today is Boaz.

"And Naomi said unto her daughter-in-law, Blessed be he of the LORD, Who has not left off His Kindness to the living and to the dead. And Naomi said unto her, The man is near of kin unto us, one of our next kinsmen.

"And Ruth the Moabitess said, He said unto me also, You shall keep fast by my young men, until they have ended all my harvest.

"And Naomi said unto Ruth her daughter-in-law, It is good, my daughter, that you go out with his maidens, that they meet you not in any other field.

"So she kept fast by the maidens of Boaz to glean unto the end of barley harvest and of wheat harvest; and dwelt with her mother-in-law" (Ruth 2:19-23).

THE LAW OF THE KINSMAN REDEEMER

The way that Ruth answered the question of Naomi as asked in Verse 19 proclaims more than a mere identification. Naomi sensed something more but would have to fill in the blanks, which she instantly did.

Regarding Verse 20, Naomi was speaking of the Law of the *"kinsman redeemer."* It referred to buying back a relative's property and marrying his widow.

When a Hebrew was forced to sell his inheritance because of poverty, the nearest relative was to redeem it for him (Lev. 25:25). If one acted as a *"kinsman redeemer"* for one who had died without a son, he was obliged to marry the widow. Should he refuse to take possession of the property, he was not under obligation to marry the widow. Boaz had no right to redeem the property until the nearest kinsman refused, which he did.

During the time of barley harvest, which was in April, three Feasts were to be kept: Passover, Unleavened Bread, and Firstfruits. During the time of the wheat harvest, which came in the latter part of May or early June, was to be the Feast of Pentecost. It was 50 days after Passover.

WHERE HAVE YOU GLEANED TODAY?

When Ruth came home the first day of gleaning, bringing the grain with her, she was asked by her mother-in-law, *"Where have you gleaned today?"*

What a simple question, and yet, it is freighted with a glimpse of the ages. Of course, Naomi had no idea at all as to the portend of her question, but it would have significance far beyond her thinking.

Where Ruth gleaned that day was that which had been designed by the Holy Spirit. It had a meaning that reached into eternity, including David as the great king of Israel, which would come about in approximately 100 years. Above all of that, it included the coming of the Messiah, which is actually the answer to the question asked that day by Naomi.

When a person gives his heart to Christ, everything changes. Not only is he changed personally, but direction is changed, and, above all, eternal destiny is changed. Then there is no limit to the worth of such a life, all because it is now linked with the Lord.

Could this young Moabite girl ever even think of dreaming that she would be in the lineage of the Messiah? I think not! But yet, she was, and all because of her Faith. I am persuaded that if every Believer, whomever that Believer might be, will make the consecration that Ruth made, the consequences, extremely positive consequences, will be enormous! Ruth had stated, *"Where you go, I will go; and where you lodge, I will lodge: your people shall be my people, and your God my God: where you die, will I die, and there will I be buried."* The Lord is not so much interested in what we were as to what He can make of us if only we will yield to Him.

THE BARLEY HARVEST AND
THE WHEAT HARVEST

The harvests were the most important times of the year in Israel. Events were reckoned from harvest times.

The three great yearly gatherings of Israel took place at the time of the three harvest seasons (Ex. 23:16; 34:21-22). They are as follows:

1. The Feasts of Passover, Unleavened Bread, and First-fruits were to be held every April in connection with the barley harvest.

2. The Feast of Pentecost was held seven weeks later at the time of the wheat harvest. It was during June. These two harvests, barley and wheat, characterized the time-frame of our story concerning Ruth.

3. The Feast of Tabernacles was held at the end of the year at the time of the fruit harvest. It was October. The Feast of Trumpets and the Great Day of Atonement preceded that of Tabernacles and, in a sense, was joined to Tabernacles.

Pulpit said:

"Ruth's gleaning labors extended to the close of the wheat-harvest, during which time, no doubt, there would be frequent opportunities for a growing intimacy between the beautiful gleaner and the worthy proprietor. Often too, we may rest assured, would Boaz be a visitor in the humble home of Naomi."[4]

How beautiful it is to observe the Leading and Guidance of the Holy Spirit. How so wondrously He works! How so perfectly He leads!

May the Lord give us guidance and strength to follow His Leading.

HE WILL TELL YOU WHAT YOU SHALL DO

"Then Naomi her mother-in-law said unto her, My daughter,

shall I not seek rest for you, that it may be well with you?

"And now is not Boaz of our kindred, with whose maidens you were? Behold, he winnows barley tonight in the threshingfloor.

"Wash yourself therefore, and anoint you, and put your raiment upon you, and get thee down to the floor: but make not yourself known unto the man, until he shall have done eating and drinking.

"And it shall be, when he lies down, that you shall mark the place where he shall lie, and you shall go in, and uncover his feet, and lay you down; and he will tell you what you shall do" (Ruth 3:1-4).

NAOMI, A TYPE OF THE HOLY SPIRIT

In this instance, Naomi may be labeled as a Type of the Holy Spirit, who seeks our good. His Business is to ever lead us closer and closer to Christ.

The *"threshingfloor"* is a type of what the Holy Spirit does in our lives. On the threshingfloor, the husks were separated from the grain. This is a type of what the Holy Spirit does for us by separating us from the *"flesh,"* i.e., *"the frail strength of man"* (Mat. 3:11).

Verse 3 presents types of several things. They are:

• *"Wash yourself therefore"*: this is a type of Redemption (I Cor. 6:11).

• *"Anoint yourself"*: this speaks of the Baptism with the Holy Spirit, hence, the anointing which follows the Salvation experience.

• *"Put your raiment upon you"*: this is the garment of praise. It is not only an inward change, but it is an outward change as well. It is the change effected by the Power of the Holy Spirit working within our hearts and lives. It speaks of an inward change that produces itself outwardly (Isa. 61:3).

• *"Get you down to the floor"*: this speaks of humility. The literal meaning of the word *"humility"* is *"a river that runs low"* (I Pet. 5:5).

There was nothing unseemly concerning what Ruth did as told by Naomi, as outlined in Verse 4. It was a part of Hebrew Law.

She was making a move, as instructed her by Naomi, which would bring Boaz to a place of decision. It is the same as the believing sinner coming to the Feet of Christ, after which, he will inherit everything that belongs to Christ, exactly as did Ruth regarding Boaz.

Concerning this, Williams says, *"Ruth for a time was satisfied with the gifts that flowed from the hand of Boaz, but the sweeter and deeper joy of union with Boaz himself was suggested to her by Naomi.*

"This marks an important stage in Christian experience, and underlies St. John 1:29 as contrasted with St. John 1:36. At first the forgiveness that Christ gives, together with His other Gifts, satisfies the heart; but, later, a deeper desire is awakened to be occupied with the Giver rather than with His Gifts, and the soul hungers for the closest intimacy with our Lord."[5]

FOLLOWING THE INSTRUCTIONS

"And she said unto her, All that you say unto me I will do.

"And she went down unto the floor, and did according to all that her mother-in-law bade her.

"And when Boaz had eaten and drunk, and his heart was merry, he went to lie down at the end of the heap of corn: and she came softly, and uncovered his feet, and laid her down" (Ruth 3:5-7).

Naomi, being a Type of the Holy Spirit, at least, in this instance, gives instructions, and Ruth promptly obeys.

All of this had to do with the Law of the Kinsman Redeemer, which we will momentarily study to a greater depth. Incidentally, Ruth probably little understood this but, nevertheless, obeyed.

We, as well, do not understand everything the Holy Spirit tells us to do, but the explanation will become clearer later on.

It is our business to obey.

ALL THAT YOU SAY UNTO ME I WILL DO

This is the answer that Ruth gives to Naomi, *"All that you say unto me I will do."*

As a Believer, we should read these words several times and do so very slowly. If every Believer would say such to the Holy Spirit, Who seeks to lead and guide us into all Truth, our lives would be far different than they presently are (Jn. 16:13).

As we observe Ruth with Naomi leading and guiding her, we see relationship with Boaz deepening almost by the day. This is what the Holy Spirit seeks to do within our hearts and lives. It is His Business to draw us ever closer to the Lord Jesus Christ. The Spirit doesn't glorify Himself, but rather Christ. He ever seeks to lift up and to build up Christ in our eyes so that we may see Who the Lord Jesus really is. As we have repeatedly stated, this can only be done by the Believer ever making the Cross of Christ the Object of His Faith (Rom. 6:1-14; 8:1-11; Col. 2:10-15).

The Holy Spirit probably speaks to us as little as He does simply because we have little heeded Him in the past. If we will ardently tell the Lord that we desire His Leading and Guidance, ask Him to forgive us of our spiritual blunders of the flesh, and tell Him that we seriously and sincerely want to be led by the Spirit, God will always answer this prayer. The key is in the words of Ruth, *"All that you say unto me I will do."*

AT MIDNIGHT

"And it came to pass at midnight, that the man was afraid, and turned himself: and, behold, a woman lay at his feet.

"And he said, Who are you? And she answered, I am Ruth your handmaid: spread therefore your skirt over your handmaid; for you are a near kinsman.

"And he said, Blessed be you of the LORD, my daughter:

for you have showed more kindness in the latter end than at the beginning, inasmuch as you followed not young men, whether poor or rich.

"And now, my daughter, fear not; I will do to you all that you require: for all the city of my people does know that you are a virtuous woman.

"And now it is true that I am your near kinsman: howbeit there is a kinsman nearer than I" (Ruth 3:8-12).

A KINSMAN NEARER THAN I?

Let the reader understand that there was nothing unseemly or untoward going on here. This was a custom in those days regarding a kinsman redeemer who had not stepped up to carry out the Law.

In effect, what Boaz was saying, as it regards Verse 10, is, *"The kindness which you are showing to your husband now that he is gone is still greater than what you did show him when he lived,"* hence, the words, *"more kindness in the latter end than at the beginning."*

For months, the small town had observed Ruth, and the conclusion was one of virtue, as it regarded her.

The kinsman nearer to Ruth is the one referred to in Ruth 4:1 as *"Ho, such a one."* We might say that this individual represented the Law. In effect, he had first claim; however, he refused the right of Redemption. He refused because the Law can never save. Only Boaz, our Heavenly Redeemer, can save.

A NEAR KINSMAN

In the Old Testament, which we are now studying, Redemption had several meanings.

According to the theocratic arrangement in Israel, the land belonged to God, and the Israelite families only possessed the right to use the fruit of the land. If a family forfeited their use because a parcel of land had to be sold or because there was no heir, the parcel was returned to the initial family at the Year of Jubilee, which came every 50 years (Lev. 25:8-17). Prior to this year, the nearest kinsman had the right and the responsibility to redeem the property, i.e., to liquidate the debt so that the property might be restored to its original owner, that is, if he was able to do so (Lev. 25:23-28).

Closely related to this custom was that of marriage. The brother-in-law or other near kinsman of someone who had died without leaving a male heir was obliged to marry the widow of the deceased in order to preserve the family name and property rights. In the marriage of Boaz and Ruth, both of the above customs were involved. Land had been lost because of the poverty of Elimelech and Naomi. As well, when the husband of Ruth died, they had no children, i.e., no *"male heir."* Therefore, Naomi called the son born to Boaz and Ruth a redeemer because he delivered her from the reproach she had incurred because her family had no surviving male heir (Ruth 4:14).

The birth of an heir now delivered her owner, as it were, from an alien dominion of the property and restored it to her. In a sense, in Jewish thinking, Ruth was not fully a proselyte Jew until this baby boy was born, although she was totally right with God from the moment she made her confession of Faith as recorded in Ruth 1:16-17.

ONE OF OUR REDEEMERS

Naomi referred to Boaz as *"one of our redeemers"* because his position in the family gave him the right to effect the restoration of the family property. She called the son born of Boaz and Ruth, as stated, *"a redeemer,"* because he delivered both Naomi and Ruth from their reproach.

As it regards *"kinsman redemption"* pertaining to Ruth, two things, as also stated, had to be redeemed. The land had to be redeemed, which it was, and Ruth had to be redeemed, which she was, and done so by her marriage to Boaz.

The child that was born as a result of the union of Boaz and Ruth would be the heir of the property just as if he had been Mahlon's son, even though Boaz should have other and older sons by another wife who had died. Of course, this was not the case with Boaz as he had not been married before marrying Ruth.

Boaz was a *"near kinsman,"* but he was not the nearest kinsman, even as we shall see.

BLESSED OF THE LORD

Boaz said to Ruth that night, *"Blessed be you of the LORD, my daughter."*

There is great evidence in the Text that Boaz had fallen in love with Ruth but was reluctant to venture his feelings simply because of his age. He was evidently old enough to be her father.

When she made her move, instead of being in the least degree offended by the steps she had taken, he was relieved and felt full of gratification on the one hand and of gratitude on the other.

Please understand that there was nothing untoward about her coming and lying at his feet that night. When she did, he realized that she was doing all she knew to do to carry out the Law of the Kinsman Redeemer. That's why he said to her, *"You have made your latter kindness better than the former,"* meaning that she was continuing to be faithful to her dead husband.

Her employment of the word, *"Kinsman,"* was evidence to Boaz that she was thinking of the respect which she owed to her husband's memory. Her concern in discharging that duty of *"piety"* struck the heart of Boaz.

His answer to her was straight and to the point, *"And now, my daughter, fear not; I will do to you all that you require."* However, there was one obstacle in the way, and that was *"a kinsman nearer than I."*

In other words, there was an individual who was a nearer kinsman to the family and had the first right of redemption, that is, if he so desired. That problem had to be addressed first.

We will find that it holds a deep spiritual meaning.

UNTIL YOU KNOW HOW
THE MATTER WILL FALL

"Tarry this night, and it shall be in the morning, that if he will perform unto you the part of a kinsman, well; let him do the kinsman's part: but if he will not do the part of a kinsman to you, then will I do the part of a kinsman to you, as the LORD lives: lie down until the morning.

"And she lay at his feet until the morning: and she rose up before one could know another. And he said, Let it not be known that a woman came into the floor.

"Also he said, Bring the veil that you had upon you, and hold it. And when she held it, he measured six measures of barley, and laid it on her: and she went into the city.

"And when she came to her mother-in-law, she said, Who are you, my daughter? And she told her all that the man had done to her.

"And she said, These six measures of barley gave he me; for he said to me, Go not empty unto your mother-in-law.

"Then said she, Sit still, my daughter, until you know how the matter will fall: for the man will not be in rest, until he has finished the thing this day" (Ruth 3:13-18).

SIT STILL

Ruth knew very little about the procedures of the kinsman redeemer, but Boaz knew them minutely.

Concerning Verse 13, Boaz tells Ruth that the one who is a nearer kinsman than he will have the opportunity to *"do the kinsman's part."* Then he went on to say, *"If he will not do the part of a kinsman to you, then will I do the part of a kinsman to you."* The one that we will know as *"Ho, such a one"* is the nearer kinsman. So, we will see how it plays out.

Relating to Verse 14, Boaz spoke to Ruth, telling her that she should not relate to anyone what happened that night. There was no impropriety in Ruth's action. It was the Law and custom of the time.

To draw a portion of a kinsman's mantle over one was the legal way of claiming protection and redemption. Ruth effected this with great delicacy and skill. She chose a public place, such as the threshingfloor, where many persons were present, not to embarrass Boaz, but to give him liberty to act as he wished. She made her claim under the cover of darkness. Boaz, whose character demanded admiration, immediately responded to her Faith and love.

Concerning Verse 17, Christ, symbolized by Boaz, will give us all that we need, and even more, according to what the Holy Spirit, symbolized by Naomi, has told us to do. When we follow the Leading of the Spirit, we will not return empty.

Verse 18 symbolizes the principle of Salvation by Faith. The Second Chapter of Galatians contrasts two principles for the obtaining of life and Righteousness:

The first is *"works of law,"* which pertains to religious ceremonies, personal moral efforts, and works of the flesh. They can never save.

The second is *"Salvation by Faith,"* which depends on no works but totally upon Christ and what He has done for us at the Cross. The Holy Spirit teaches us that nothing can be had upon the first principle, but everything can be had upon the second. So, Ruth would *"sit still,"* wholly trusting Boaz, and as a result, obtain her heart's desire.

HO, SUCH A ONE

"Then went Boaz up to the gate, and sat him down there: and, behold, the kinsman of whom Boaz spoke came by; unto whom he said, Ho, such a one! turn aside, sit down here. And he turned aside, and sat down.

"And Boaz took ten men of the Elders of the city, and said, You sit down here. And they sat down.

"And he said unto the kinsman, Naomi, who is come again out of the country of Moab, sells a parcel of land, which was our brother Elimelech's:

"And I thought to advertise you, saying, Buy it before the inhabitants, and before the Elders of my people. If you will redeem it, redeem it: but if you will not redeem it, then tell me, that I may know: for there is none to redeem it beside you; and I am after you. And he said, I will redeem it.

"Then said Boaz, What day you buy the field of the hand of Naomi, you must buy it also of Ruth the Moabitess, the wife of the dead, to raise up the name of the dead upon his inheritance.

"And the kinsman (Ho, such a one) *said, I cannot redeem it for myself, lest I mar my own inheritance: you redeem my right to yourself; for I cannot redeem it.*

"Now this was the manner in former time in Israel concerning redeeming and concerning changing, for to confirm all things; a man plucked off his shoe, and gave it to his neighbor: and this was a testimony in Israel.

"Therefore the kinsman said unto Boaz, Buy it for you. So he drew off his shoe.

"And Boaz said unto the Elders, and unto all the people, You are witnesses this day, that I have bought all that was Elimelech's, and all that was Chilion's and Mahlon's, of the hand of Naomi.

"Moreover Ruth the Moabitess, the wife of Mahlon, have I purchased to be my wife, to raise up the name of the dead upon his inheritance, that the name of the dead be not cut off from among his brethren, and from the gate of his place: you are witnesses this day" (Ruth 4:1-10).

THE LAW

In Old Testament times, business was conducted at the gate of the city.

The kinsman referred to as *"Ho, such a one"* was nearer kin to Naomi, whoever he was, than was Boaz.

The explanation to the man, as given by Boaz, meant that

he must marry Ruth as well as redeem the land. If a child was born to such a union, that child would inherit the land when the parents died even though the father may even have other children who were older. In this manner, the inheritance would not be lost, which was the intention.

Boaz had to purchase Ruth, at least, to effect the transaction, from a kinsman who had a prior claim but who declared that he could not redeem her.

The Law (typified by Ho such a one) has a prior claim on sinners, but it cannot redeem them. Christ, the Divine Kinsman, became Man in order to redeem. It cost Boaz nothing to redeem Ruth, beyond the setting aside of himself and his own interests, but it cost Christ everything to redeem sinners.

In regard to all of this, Ruth, a *"wild olive tree,"* so to speak, was grafted into, and became a partaker of, *"the root and fatness of the olive tree,"* i.e., Israel. However, she could not boast that this was due to any commanding personal claim. All she could say was, *"Why have I found grace in your eyes, seeing I am a Gentile?"* (Ruth 2:10)

When land was sold, the one previously owning the land would give his shoe to the one who had bought it, signifying that he freely gave up his right to walk upon the soil in favor of the person who had acquired the possession.

By all the names mentioned in Verse 9, even though there was only one estate, there was a succession in the proprietorship.

THE KINSMAN REDEEMER

Boaz had determined this day to settle the matter. He probably knew that everyday the nearer kinsman frequented the business section of the city, which was at the gate; therefore, Boaz went to the gate of the city, *"and sat there."*

As he went that day to complete this transaction, there was no way that he could have had any idea at all, one way or the other, as to how important it actually was.

We look back now on the situation and know the full story

and what it all meant, realizing that Ruth would be the great-grandmother of David. Above all, far above all, she would be the ancestress of the Messiah.

THE LAW

The Second Verse says, *"And lo, the kinsman of whom Boaz had spoken was passing; and he said, Ho, such a one! Turn hither and sit here, and he turned and sat down."*

There is evidence in the original Hebrew Text that Boaz called his kinsman by his name, but the writer does not tell us what that name is. I think the reason is according to the following:

"Ho, such a one," represents the Law. It had a nearer claim on humanity than did Christ, even as *"Ho, such a one,"* had a nearer claim on Naomi and her possessions than did Boaz.

As witnesses, Boaz selected 10 men who could hear this conversation and attest to the decisions here made.

REDEMPTION

The Fourth Verse proclaims Boaz saying to *"Ho, such a one," "If you will redeem it."*

The answer was quick in coming back, *"I cannot redeem it for myself."*

In fact, the Law, which *"Ho, such a one"* typified, could never redeem. The Law was not actually created by God to redeem anything. It was ordained by God that sin would appear to be sin, in other words, to define what sin was and is, and to show the horror of sin. As well, it was the Standard which God demanded of man, but which man could not do because of the Fall. There was no redeeming virtue nor is there any in the Law, even though it is the Law of God.

In fact, in the latter part of the Fourth Verse, *"Ho, such a one"* actually says, *"I will redeem it."* However, after Boaz explained to him what he had to do, which was not only to purchase the land but, as well, to marry Ruth, he could not do such because he was already married.

When it is properly understood what has to be done in order for man to be redeemed, then it is also properly understood that the Law can never function in this capacity. As Paul said, "... *if Righteousness come by the Law, then Christ is dead in vain*" (Gal. 2:21).

The trouble is, man actually thinks that his own works, his own merit, and his personal efforts can actually redeem him. It fails, as fail it must! But yet, Christian man keeps on trying.

TRANSFER OF THE PROPERTY

In Old Testament times, to which we have already briefly alluded, whenever a property transaction was handled, the one who owned the property and had sold it to another individual, pulled off his shoe and gave it to the person who had purchased the land. In essence, he was saying that he did not have the right anymore to walk upon this property and call it his own. Now, with his shoe being given to the purchaser, the man could walk on it and know that it was his. It was attested to by witnesses, hence, the 10 men of Verse 2.

This is what Boaz did. He purchased the land in order that it be kept in the original family name. The man who was nearer kin, even though he had not owned the land and received no money in this transaction, still pulled off his shoe and gave it to Boaz, signifying before witnesses that he had renounced his purchasing rights in favor of Boaz.

BOAZ AND RUTH

"And all the people who were in the gate, and the Elders, said, We are witnesses. The LORD make the woman who has come into your house like Rachel and like Leah, which two did build the house of Israel: and do you worthily in Ephratah, and be famous in Beth-lehem:

"And let your house be like the house of Pharez, whom Tamar bore unto Judah, of the seed which the LORD shall give you of this young woman.

"So Boaz took Ruth, and she was his wife: and when he went in unto her, the LORD gave her conception, and she bore a son.

"And the women said unto Naomi, Blessed be the LORD, which has not left you this day without a kinsman, that his name may be famous in Israel.

"And he shall be unto you a restorer of your life, and a nourisher of your old age: for your daughter-in-law, which loves you, which is better to you than seven sons, has born him.

"And Naomi took the child, and laid it in her bosom, and became nurse unto it.

"And the women her neighbors gave it a name, saying, There is a son born to Naomi; and they called his name Obed: he is the father of Jesse, the father of David" (Ruth 4:11-17).

FAMOUS

The latter phrase of Verse 11, *"And be famous in Bethlehem,"* is more a Prophecy than a statement. Beth-lehem will ever be famous. The reason is that the Son of David, the Great Descendant of Ruth, would be born in Beth-lehem some 1,200 years later. How beautifully and wondrously this Prophecy has come to pass.

To be sure, this *"house"* of Verse 12 was blessed far more than the house of Pharez could ever be blessed and, in fact, every other house, for it would be the House of the Lord Jesus Christ.

When Ruth looked at her newborn baby, I wonder what the thoughts were in her mind. Little did she realize the consequences of it all, and neither do we!

It is Ruth's little son who is the kinsman referred to, the nearest kinsman, still nearer than Boaz. To be sure, the child, who would be the grandparent of David and, ultimately, the Son of David, is linked to fame in a greater way than even these women could begin to think.

Verse 17 means that the baby was born to Naomi through Boaz and Ruth, who were fulfilling the Law by raising up seed for her dead husband and keeping his name alive. Their seed was reckoned, or counted, to carry on his place in Israel (Deut. 25:5-10). This *"Son,"* Who would be born of Israel (Naomi), will one day rule the world. His Name ultimately would be *"the Lord Jesus Christ,"* the Son of David, the Son of Abraham (Mat. 1:1).

THE PROPHECY

Everything that is linked to Christ in any positive way is of significance far beyond our comprehension. Consequently, whoever made the statement in verse 11, whatever they meant to say, and whatever they meant it to be, was actually a Prophecy of gargantuan proportions.

The statement, *"The LORD make the woman who is come into your house like Rachel and like Leah,"* refers to Ruth. To be sure, that request has not only come true, but true in a greater way than ever. In fact, what the Lord did through Ruth was to bring forth the true Israel, even as He was the True Church and the True Man. Of course, we speak of the Lord Jesus Christ.

Regrettably, the *"House of Israel"* was almost destroyed because this *"House"* rejected the One Who was brought forth by this union. Still, this *"House"* will be restored and rebuilt but not until it accepts the One in question. Again, we speak of the Lord Jesus Christ. Their reception and acceptance of Him will be at the Second Coming.

BETH-LEHEM

To be sure, the statement, *"And be famous in Beth-lehem,"* has been fulfilled far beyond the comprehension of anyone. David would be born in Beth-lehem, who would be the crowning king of Israel, but, above all, the King of kings would be born in Beth-lehem, the Lord Jesus Christ.

Every year hundreds of thousands of Christians visit this little town, which is a suburb of Jerusalem, all because of the Lord Jesus Christ Who was born there.

What Beth-lehem will be in the coming Kingdom Age, we aren't told. However, understanding that it was the Holy Spirit Who framed the words, *"Famous in Beth-lehem,"* we must ascertain that this *"fame"* will last forever.

Why the Holy Spirit through the speaker of this Prophecy mentions *"Pharez,"* we aren't exactly told. It could be because Pharez's descendants, the Pharezites of the Tribe of Judah, were particularly numerous and, hence, the good wishes of Boaz's fellow townsmen (Num. 26:20-21).

In fact, Judah became the most powerful Tribe, with the southern kingdom, after the split, being referred to as *"Judah."*

THE RESTORER AND THE NOURISHER

The child's name would be called *"Obed,"* who would be the father of Jesse, who would be the father of David. After the child was born, another great Prophecy was given. Once again, we are not told who the speaker was, but yet, we know the inspiration was from the Holy Spirit.

Even though the speaker was referring to the child that was born to Boaz and Ruth, still, the Holy Spirit was referring to far more than that. He was referring to the Lord Jesus Christ, Who would be the Restorer and the Nourisher. This Christ is to all who will accept Him as Saviour and Lord, irrespective as to whom they might be, whether Jew or Gentile.

THE GENERATIONS

"Now these are the generations of Pharez: Pharez begat Hezron,

"And Hezron begat Ram, and Ram begat Amminadab,

"And Amminadab begat Nahshon, and Nahshon begat Salmon,

"And Salmon begat Boaz, and Boaz begat Obed,
"And Obed begat Jesse, and Jesse begat David" (Ruth 4:18-22).

THE GENEALOGY

Most of the time, the genealogies given in the Bible, exactly as here, are not complete, and neither are they meant to be complete. They are merely meant to link certain individuals with others in the lineage although, at times, several times removed.

We know that Jesse was the father of David; however, we don't know for certain if Obed was the immediate father of Jesse or several times removed. In the Hebrew, there is no word for grandfather, great-grandfather, etc. They are all looked at as the *"father."*

We know that Rahab married Salmon (Mat. 1:5). We also know that Salmon was not the immediate father of Boaz simply because Rahab and Salmon lived several hundreds of years before Boaz. However, we do know that Salmon was the father of Boaz several times removed. So, when these genealogies are observed, they must be observed with the idea in mind that the genealogy is not complete, and neither are they meant to be complete. As already stated, they are merely meant to link certain individuals with others although, at times, several times removed.

All of this is very important because it is an integral part of the genealogy of king David's great descendant, his *"Lord"* and ours. In other words, it pertains to the Incarnation of Christ, God becoming Man, in order to redeem humanity by dying on a Cross. Nothing could be more important than that!

So, from all of this, we see how that Ruth and even Naomi played such an important part in that which would ultimately be known as the *"Plan of Redemption."*

"Break Thou the bread of life,
"Dear Lord, to me,

"As You did break the loaves beside the sea;
"Beyond the Sacred Page,
"I seek You, Lord;
"My spirit pants for You, O Living Word!"

"Bless Thou the Truth, dear Lord,
"To me, to me,
"As You did bless the bread by Galilee;
"Then shall all bondage cease,
"All fetters fall, and I shall find my peace,
"My all in all."

"Teach me to live, dear Lord,
"Only for Thee,
"As Your Disciples lived in Galilee;
"Then, all my struggles are over,
"Then, victory won, I shall behold Thee,
"Lord, The Living One."

Great Women OF THE BIBLE

OLD TESTAMENT

Chapter Ten

HANNAH

The Mother Of Samuel The Prophet

HANNAH,
The Mother Of Samuel The Prophet

HANNAH

"Now there was a certain man of Rama-thaim-zophim, of Mount Ephraim, and his name was Elkanah, the son of Jeroham, the son of Elihu, the son of Tohu, the son of Zuph, an Ephrathite:

"And he had two wives; the name of the one was Hannah, and the name of the other Peninnah: and Peninnah had children, but Hannah had no children.

"And this man went up out of his city yearly to worship and to sacrifice unto the LORD of Hosts in Shiloh. And the two sons of Eli, Hophni and Phinehas, the Priests of the LORD, were there.

"And when the time was that Elkanah offered, he gave to Peninnah his wife, and to all her sons and her daughters, portions:

"But unto Hannah he gave a worthy portion; for he loved Hannah: but the LORD had shut up her womb.

"And her adversary (Peninnah) *also provoked her sore, for to make her fret, because the LORD had shut up her womb.*

"And as he (Elkanah) *did so year by year, when she went up to the House of the LORD, so she* (Peninnah) *provoked her; therefore she* (Hannah) *wept, and did not eat.*

"Then said Elkanah her husband to her, Hannah, why do you weep? and why do you not eat? and why is your heart grieved? am I not better to you than ten sons?" (I Sam. 1:1-8)

A TEST OF HANNAH'S FAITH

Elkanah, the father of Samuel, was a Levite and of the order of the Kohathites, who were responsible for the Vessels of the Sanctuary (Num. 3:27-31).

We find that Elkanah was not untouched by the corruption of his day, for he had two wives. Domestic misery was the result. Hannah had no children and, in those days, to be barren

332 Great Women Of The Bible, Old Testament

was a disgrace.

Hophni and Phinehas of Verse 3 were sons of Eli, the High Priest, and were Priests themselves. They were evil men, and yet, occupied officially a certain relationship to God. Under the Covenant of Law and its divinely appointed Priesthood, such a position was possible. However, under the Covenant of Grace, where there is no earthly priesthood, it is impossible. But yet, despite the fact of occupying these holy positions, still, these men were unsaved and, in fact, died eternally lost.

Coming up to the present time, and I speak now of the Church Age, men, not recognizing the distinction between the two Covenants, have invented an order of priests and clothed them with the sacramental powers of the sons of Aaron, which is an abomination in the Eyes of God!

Concerning Verse 5 and the Lord shutting up the womb of Hannah, this was done for a particular purpose, as the Lord does everything for a particular purpose. It was a test of Hannah's Faith, as everything is a test of our Faith, all meant to do us good.

Evidently Peninnah, the other wife of Elkanah, was provoking Hannah by telling her that she was cursed by God, hence, the failure to bear children. This hurt Hannah very much, as would be obvious, but yet, the Lord allowed it to happen. So, this test was not only for Hannah but Peninnah, as well, with the latter failing miserably!

A DEPARTURE FROM THE WORD OF GOD

Elkanah would be the father of the great Prophet Samuel. His personal consecration to the Lord seemed to be not as strong as that of his wife. In fact, it was the Faith of Hannah that moved the Heart of God.

The Second Verse says, *"He had two wives."* Polygamy was a failure that seemed to be tolerated by God, at least, in the Old Testament, but I think one could say without fear of contradiction that it definitely was not His Perfect Will. One might say that this problem could have been included in the *"hardness of heart"* situation, as discussed by Christ (Mat. 19:8). Although Jesus was speaking of divorce, still, more than likely, His Statement would include the polygamous lifestyle.

In the Garden of Eden, the Lord gave Adam one wife, Eve. It would seem that if He desired or intended that man have more, provision would have been made at that time. It wasn't made. Therefore, one wife for one husband is the Plan of God. This we do know, multiple wives generally cause dissension and difficulty.

The Scripture says, *"The name of the one was Hannah."* In fact, this great lady of Faith is the subject of this Chapter. Few equal her in history. Not only would she bring into the world one of the greatest Prophets ever but, as well, would have the honor and the pleasure of introducing the coming Messiah under a Name that He had not heretofore been known as, *"His Anointed."* She would not only be the first to do this, but, being a woman, this spoke volumes as it regards her Faith and how God honored her.

WORSHIP OF THE LORD

The Third Verse says, *"And this man* (Elkanah) *went up out of his city yearly to worship and to sacrifice unto the LORD of Hosts in Shiloh."*

We see from this one word, *"Yearly,"* how that Israel had departed from the Commandments of the Lord. The original command had required three gatherings a year instead of one. So, it seems that most of Israel, at this particular time, had abandoned all worship of the Lord. For the few who maintained any semblance of worship, it was not according to the stipulations laid down by the Lord.

Men have forever been attempting to change the Word of God for that of their own making. They always do so at their peril. It was the problem then, and it is the problem now.

SACRIFICE

The Holy Spirit used the term *"to sacrifice unto the LORD of Hosts."*

Of course, the *"Sacrifice"* spoke of Calvary, which would yet be about 1,100 years into the future. In those days, the sacrifice of clean animals, such as the lamb, typified the Lamb of God Who was to come (Jn. 1:29). All of this tells us that the Old Testament is filled with types and shadows as it regards the Redemption price. That price was the Death of the Son of the Living God, the pouring out of His Life's Blood on Calvary's Cross.

It is impossible to study the Bible with any degree of honesty without coming to the conclusion that it presents the solution for man's dilemma, and that solution is the Lord Jesus Christ and what He did for the world at the Cross (Jn. 1:1, 14, 29).

Above all, by using the title *"LORD of Hosts,"* we are made to see how Infinite, how Glorious, and how Eternal is the God of Creation, Who is now God our Saviour.

THE LORD AND HANNAH

Hannah was not able to have children, which was a disgrace in those times, because the Scripture says, *"The LORD had shut up her womb."*

Why did He do that?

That's a good question!

Perhaps the following will shed a little light on the subject:

• The Lord is Omniscient (All-Knowing), Omnipotent (All-Powerful), and Omnipresent (everywhere), meaning that He is in total control of everything. The Lord controls this Planet and all its inhabitants; however, He has purposely limited Himself to the free moral agency of man. Of course, the Lord can do anything He desires to do, but He will not infringe upon the freedom of the individual. In fact, the Lord controls this Planet and all of its inhabitants. He controls all of the spirit world and its inhabitants, both good and evil. Satan can only do to a Follower of the Lord what the Lord allows him to do. In other words, Satan is on a tether, so to speak. So, in effect, everything that happens to a Believer is either caused by the Lord or allowed by the Lord.

No, the Lord most definitely does not cause one to sin, but He does allow one to sin if one desires to do so. One will have to suffer the consequences, but God will allow him free will.

• Whenever a great work is to be accomplished, the Lord, at times, allows or causes various severe things to happen to the individual involved to test one's Faith. Great Faith must be tested greatly, hence, Abraham and Sarah, Isaac and Rebekah, Hannah, etc.

• God allows or causes such in order that the individual may learn total dependence on Jehovah. In other words, all hope of the flesh must die.

• As well, there must be no effort of the flesh that succeeds. Therefore, God makes it impossible (whatever the test) in order that the Holy Spirit may be Author of the Victory. To be sure, if there is Victory, He most definitely is the Author, and the Cross of Christ is the Means.

• That which comes to every Child of God, especially to those who are greatly Called of God, comes in the manner of tests. God tests, but Satan tempts. The difference is the temptation by Satan is to get us to do wrong. The test by God is to get us to do right.

So, whatever the Lord allowed, as it regarded Hannah, was in the form of a test. Thank the Lord, she passed that test with flying colors!

HER ADVERSARY

I wonder if Peninnah, the other wife of Elkanah, had any idea that her hateful actions toward Hannah would be recorded by the Lord and would be read by untold millions down through the centuries. Because of her actions, her attitude, her hatefulness, and especially considering that it was against a great Woman of God, she would be disliked, to say the least, by untold millions, which continues unto this very hour.

To be sure, even though the Bible is no longer being written, the Lord chronicles every single thing that every person does, which is kept in the Books of Heaven (Rev. 20:11-15).

It's bad enough to be unkind to anyone, but to be hateful and spiteful to someone who is truly of God, as was Hannah, compounds the problem. To be sure, even as here proclaimed, the Lord took and takes a very dim view of such actions.

BITTERNESS OF SOUL

"So Hannah rose up after they had eaten in Shiloh, and after they had drunk. Now Eli the Priest sat upon a seat by a post of the Temple of the LORD.

"And she (Hannah) *was in bitterness of soul, and prayed unto the LORD, and wept sore.*

"And she vowed a vow, and said, O LORD of Hosts, if You will indeed look on the affliction of Your Handmaid, and remember me, and not forget Your Handmaid, but will give unto Your Handmaid a man child, then I will give him unto the LORD all the days of his life, and there shall no razor come upon his head.

"And it came to pass, as she continued praying before the LORD, that Eli marked her mouth.

"Now Hannah, she spoke in her heart; only her lips moved, but her voice was not heard: therefore Eli thought she had been drunk.

"And Eli said unto her, How long will you be drunk? put away your wine from you.

"And Hannah answered and said, No, my lord, I am a woman of a sorrowful spirit: I have drunk neither wine nor strong drink, but have poured out my soul before the LORD.

"Count not your handmaid for a daughter of Belial: for out of the abundance of my complaint and grief have I spoken hitherto.

"Then Eli answered and said, Go in peace: and the God of

Israel grant you your petition that you have asked of Him.

"And she said, Let your handmaid find grace in your sight. So the woman went her way, and did eat, and her countenance was no more sad.

"And they rose up in the morning early, and worshipped before the LORD, and returned, and came to their house to Ramah: and Elkanah knew Hannah his wife; and the LORD remembered her" (I Sam. 1:9-19).

THE INTERCESSION OF HANNAH

There hasn't been any more earnestness in prayer than what is recorded here. This should encourage every person who has sought the Lord for a long time for a particular thing and still has not received it. The Lord allowed all the hindrances and, as well, placed within her heart an overwhelming desire for that which was impossible in the flesh to conceive, namely a son.

The type of intercession and travail that is recorded here is seldom known or heard of in the modern day church. Hannah would not quit. She would not give up and intended to stay the course until she received what God desired for her to receive.

This test of Faith went on for at least several years. Hannah's womb was barren, and yet, she wanted a child so much, and a son at that. Her adversary would provoke her because she had no children. The implication was that she told Hannah, *"The LORD has shut up your womb"* because of sin, disobedience, or the Curse of God that is upon you. The only thing that would sustain Hannah was her Faith.

It is not too difficult for Faith to be sustained over a short period of time, but under these circumstances, and for testing year after year, most would fail. Therefore, Hannah's great Faith is a tremendous source of encouragement for all.

THE VOW

The Eleventh Verse says, *"And she vowed a vow."*

The vow was that she would give the child to the Lord and that he would be a Nazarite from her womb, *"No razor come upon his head."*

Why it took several years for this prayer to be answered is not known. Perhaps the consecration she makes, as recorded in the Eleventh Verse, throws some light on the subject. Possibly, she did not want to give this child unto the Lord, at least, to this degree and in this fashion. But now, she finally agrees to do so, that is, if it had ever been a question. Evidently, this is what the Lord wanted her to do.

We note the humility of this woman by her referring to herself thrice as *"Jehovah's Handmaid,"* and her kneeling down in the Inner Court.

When she offered her son as a Nazarite, it was not for a protracted period of time but for life.

THE NAZARITE

• The Nazarite was not to partake of any produce of the vine, not even grapes, much less alcoholic beverage, thereby, signifying abstinence from self-indulgence and carnal pleasure.

• He was to take no part in mourning for the dead, even though they were his nearest relatives, because his holier duties raised him above the ordinary joys and sorrows, which included the cares and occupations of everyday life.

• No razor might come upon his head. The free growing hair was at once the distinctive mark by which all men would recognize his sacred Calling, and was also a sign that he was not bound by the usual customs of life.

As well, long hair on a man signified weakness, which, in essence, meant that such an individual must trust the Lord implicitly.

PRAYER

The Thirteenth Verse says, *"Now Hannah, she spoke in her*

heart; only her lips moved, but her voice was not heard."

This type of prayer was spoken before the Tabernacle at Shiloh. It shows us that true prayer comes from the heart. It has little, if anything, to do with the volume of our profession. It is the heart that counts.

The Fourteenth Verse is a sad indictment of that which was evidently taking place before the Tabernacle constantly. Eli says unto her, *"Put away your wine from you."* Due to her weeping and sore travail, he thought that she was drunk. Evidently, he had seen this type of behavior around the Tabernacle.

When we look and compare it with the incident in question, and I speak of possible ungodliness in the Tabernacle, how similar is this to what is presently taking place in the modern church?

There was at least one person in Israel at that time, namely Hannah, who knew that the Tabernacle was where God dwelt and where she should make her petition. Regrettably, there didn't seem to be many others who felt that way. Rather, they paid little respect to the Abode of the Lord and even, at times, appeared drunk, hence, Eli mistaking the contrition, at least, at first, of Hannah.

GOD GRANT YOU YOUR PETITION

The Seventeenth Verse says in the words of Eli, the High Priest, *"And the God of Israel grant you your petition."*

Whether this was wishful thinking on the part of Eli or whether it was a Prophecy is not actually certain; however, there is great indication that it was, in fact, a Prophecy.

Whenever Eli said this to her, the Scripture says, *"So the woman went her way, and did eat, and her countenance was no more sad. After they rose up in the morning early, and worshipped before the LORD, and returned, and came to their house to Ramah: and Elkanah knew Hannah his wife; and the LORD remembered her"* (I Sam. 1:18-19).

This being a Prophecy on the part of Eli, Hannah evidently

felt the witness of the Spirit in her heart and, thereby, felt assured that the Lord had heard their prayer and, in turn, would answer her prayer. In that, she was totally correct. God had spoken to her soul. It would be done.

SAMUEL

"Wherefore it came to pass, when the time was come about after Hannah had conceived, that she bore a son, and called his name Samuel, saying, Because I have asked him of the LORD.

"And the man Elkanah, and all his house, went up to offer unto the LORD the yearly sacrifice, and his vow.

"But Hannah went not up; for she said unto her husband, I will not go up until the child be weaned, and then I will bring him, that he may appear before the LORD, and there abide forever.

"And Elkanah her husband said unto her, Do what seems you good; tarry until you have weaned him; only the LORD establish His Word, So the woman abode, and gave her son suck until she weaned him" (I Sam. 1:20-23).

Samuel would be the last Judge of Israel and, as well, the first man to stand in the Office of the Prophet (Acts 3:24). In fact, he was one of the greatest men of God who ever lived. He would anoint David to be king, through whose family the Messiah would ultimately come, although he would not live to see David ultimately crowned king (I Sam. 16:1, 11-13; II Sam. 7:11-13).

The vow of Elkanah showed that he had ratified Hannah's words by adding thereto a Thank Offering from himself.

As well, Samuel had the distinction of having two Books in the Bible named after him. There could be little honor paid to anyone greater than that.

ANSWERED PRAYER

The Twentieth Verse says, *"She bore a son, and called his name Samuel."* The name means, *"Asked and heard of God."* In Hebrew society, it was the mother's right to give names to her children (Lk. 1:60), and Hannah saw in Samuel, whom she had asked of God, a living proof that she had been heard by Him. The name, therefore, is of fuller significance than the reason given for it.

She had sought the Lord many years for this child, and now the Lord had heard and answered her prayer. For that, she was eternally thankful, more so than we will ever know.

I think that she little realized just how great her little boy would be. He would be used of God in ways that few people have ever been used. Perhaps the greatest thing of all would be that he would anoint David, as stated, to be the king of Israel. Through David, i.e., his family, would come the Messiah (II Sam., Chpt. 7). Nothing could be greater than that!

To be sure, what the Lord ultimately gave her would be well worth the years of waiting, the years of seeking, and the years of asking! Thank God, she didn't quit. No doubt, many times, she grew discouraged, and, no doubt, many times, Satan told her that there was no use. No doubt, the other wife of her husband, who constantly provoked her, and did so severely, caused her much consternation, and yet, the Lord allowed all of this to happen for good reason.

While those reasons may have been many and varied, one of the greatest Blessings of all is, when we as Believers, some 3,000 years after the fact, read her story, read of her Faith, and read of her perseverance, we are greatly encouraged. Therefore, many Believers have Hannah to thank, who served as such a great example; that they didn't quit, that we didn't quit, but that we kept believing, and, as Hannah ultimately received, so have we received, and so shall we receive!

THE LORD HAS GIVEN ME MY PETITION
WHICH I ASKED OF HIM

"And when she had weaned him, she took him up with her, with three bullocks, and one ephah of flour, and a bottle of wine, and brought him unto the House of the LORD in Shiloh: and

the child was young.

"And they killed a bullock, and brought the child to Eli.

"And she said, Oh my Lord, as your soul lives, my lord, I am the woman who stood by you here, praying unto the LORD.

"For this child I prayed; and the LORD has given me my petition which I asked of Him:

"Therefore also I have lent him to the LORD; as long as he lives he shall be lent to the LORD. And he worshipped the LORD there" (I Sam. 1:24-28).

When Elkanah and Hannah took Samuel to the Tabernacle, they offered up three sacrifices, a Whole Burnt Offering, a Thanksgiving Offering, and a Drink Offering.

The word, *"Lent,"* as it is used in Verse 28, is not the best translation. Actually, Hannah is saying, *"I have given him to the LORD."*

The word, *"He,"* in the last sentence of the Twentieth-eighth Verse should have been translated, *"They,"* in that *"they worshipped the LORD there."*

THE SACRIFICE

The sacrifice offered by Elkanah was probably a Whole Burnt Offering. It was the only one of the sacrifices under the old Levitical Law which was burnt wholly on the Altar. The animal was skinned with the carcass, along with the fat, then placed on the Altar and totally consumed. It typified the Lord giving His All and that Israel, in turn, should give Him their all.

The *"ephah of flour"* presented a Thanksgiving Offering, which was the only Offering, at least, of the fivefold Offerings, which did not contain flesh.

The *"bottle of wine"* was a Drink Offering, which specified, as it was poured out, that the coming Messiah, the Lord, would pour Himself out in the giving of Himself on the Cross of Calvary.

So, all of this stipulated that Samuel being given to the Lord was predicated on the Cross, of which, all of this was a type.

The entirety of the Sacrificial system presented itself as a Type of Christ in His Atoning Work, which, of course, would take place at the Cross. In fact, the entirety of the Law was built upon its principle system of sacrifice.

Therefore, we can say, I think, without fear of exaggeration or contradiction that the Ministry of Samuel, one of the greatest Prophets who ever lived, was built on the Foundation of the Cross. To be sure, there is no other foundation!

Even though the Sacrificial system is no more because our Lord has fulfilled it all at Calvary, still, the Sacrifice, i.e., the Sacrifice of Christ, is the Foundation of all that we are, the Foundation of all that we will ever be, and anything built on any other foundation is unacceptable to God. It is ever the Cross! The Cross! The Cross! (I Pet. 1:18-20)

THE SONG OF HANNAH

"And Hannah prayed, and said, My heart rejoices in the LORD, my horn is exalted in the LORD: my mouth is enlarged over my enemies; because I rejoice in Your Salvation.

"There is none holy as the LORD: for there is none beside You: neither is there any rock like our God.

"Talk no more so exceeding proudly; let not arrogancy come out of your mouth: for the LORD is a God of knowledge, and by Him actions are weighed.

"The bows of the mighty men are broken, and they who stumbled are girded with strength.

"They who were full have hired out themselves for bread; and they who were hungry ceased: so that the barren has born seven; and she who has many children is waxed feeble.

"The LORD kills, and makes alive: He brings down to the grave, and brings up.

"The LORD makes poor, and makes rich: He brings low, and lifts up.

"He raises up the poor out of the dust, and lifts up the beggar from the dunghill, to set them among princes, and to make them

*inherit the Throne of Glory: for the pillars of the Earth are the
LORD's, and He has set the world upon them.*

*"He will keep the feet of His Saints, and the wicked shall be
silent in darkness; for by strength shall no man prevail.*

*"The adversaries of the LORD shall be broken to pieces; out
of Heaven shall He thunder upon them: the LORD shall judge
the ends of the Earth; and He shall give strength unto His King,
and exalt the horn of His Anointed.*

*"And Elkanah went to Ramah to his house. And the child did
minister unto the LORD before Eli the Priest"* (I Sam. 2:1-11).

HANNAH PRAYED IN THE SPIRIT OF PROPHECY

• The First Verse says, *"And Hannah prayed."* The Chaldee
reads, *"And Hannah prayed in the Spirit of Prophecy,"* which is
probably the correct translation.

• Verse 2 proclaims the fact that the reason for Hannah's
Holy joy is, first of all, God's Absolute Holiness. The second
reason is His Absolute Existence, in which she finds the proof
of His Holiness.

• Verse 2 also refers to the Lord as a *"Rock."* Hannah as-
signs to Him Strength, Calm, Immovable, and Enduring, but
a Strength which avails for the safety of His People.

• We find in Verse 3 that God judges all things in the Light
of His Omniscience, which signifies every type of knowledge,
past, present, and future. Knowing this, man had best be careful as to what he says and does.

• The Fourth Verse actually says that the working of this
Attribute of Deity tells us human events are not the result of
chance but of God's Direction.

• Verse 5 typifies the Gentile Church, which is now abundant, and is contrasted with Israel, who is now barren, even
though Hannah would not have understood this (Gal. 4:27).

• Oftentimes, even as the Sixth Verse proclaims, the Lord
brings a man to the very brink of the grave and then, when all
hope seems past, raises him up again.

• Verse 7 loudly proclaims that *"promotion comes from the LORD"* (Ps. 75:6-7).

• Verse 8 speaks of Salvation, when man is raised out of dust to the Glory of God. The *"pillars"* refer to everything hanging upon God and God Alone. This is a fact of Divine Government, which is distasteful to man.

• The Lord keeps the feet of His Saints, as recorded in Verse 9, by the Believer placing his Faith and trust exclusively in Christ and the Cross, which then gives the Holy Spirit latitude to work in one's life, Who Alone can bring about the needed change and strength (Rom. 6:3-14; 8:1-11; Col. 2:10-15).

• The phrase of Verse 9, *"For by strength shall no man prevail,"* proclaims the fact that *"the flesh,"* which portrays one's own personal strength and ability, cannot succeed (Rom. 8:1, 8). It is the Holy Spirit Alone Who can make us what we ought to be. Therefore, the modern message of self-improvement cannot bring about any desired results simply because there is no such thing as moral evolution.

• The phrase, *"His Anointed,"* as recorded in Verse 10, presents the first time this term is used. It refers to the Messiah. It is even more special in that Hannah used it. From this point on, others take up the theme of God's Anointed One—the Messiah (Ps. 2:2; 45:7; Isa. 61:1; Dan. 9:25-26), but Hannah was the first. And so, the song of Hannah ends here but actually continues on in the hearts and lives of untold millions.

THE SONG OF THE SPIRIT

This particular song of this great lady expresses the true nature of the song of prayer. It is poetic and, above all, prophetic, and takes its place along with the songs of Moses, Miriam, Deborah, David, Elisabeth, Mary, and others—Psalmists and Prophets whose inspired utterances have been recorded in the Bible.

The particular characteristics of all these songs are that they spring forth from the individual with reference to things of a personal nature. Then, they widen to include the Nature and Acts of God, the Glories of the coming Kingdom of the Messiah, and of God among men in all eternity, making reference to things of the future.

THE BARREN HAS BORN SEVEN

"The barren has born seven," refers to Hannah who was ultimately given seven children. She had three sons and two daughters after Samuel. Therefore, the barren did bring forth. The seventh is not mentioned, so it could be that she had a seventh child who did not live (Vs. 21). However, even though this Passage definitely applies to Hannah personally, still, it has even a deeper meaning, a great spiritual meaning.

"Seven" is God's Number of Perfection, Totality, Completeness, and Universality.

The spiritual and Scriptural meaning of this statement refers to every Believer, at least, those who will truly trust the Lord. It means that no matter how *"barren"* the situation may be, no matter how lacking it might be, no matter how difficult it may seem, and, in fact, no matter how impossible, God can turn the thing around. *"The barren can bring forth seven."*

The problem with Believers, actually, all of us, is that we try to bring forth that which is needed by our own capacity and by our own strength. We can't do it.

There was absolutely nothing that Hannah could do to conceive and have children. In fact, *"The LORD had shut up her womb"* (I Sam. 1:5). Inasmuch as it was the Lord Who shut up her womb, it was the Lord Alone Who could open up her womb, which He most miraculously did.

THE MESSIAH

When Hannah used the word *"King,"* in the Tenth Verse, this was the second Prophecy of God's King, the Messiah. Balaam was the first Prophet, that is, if Balaam could be referred to as a Prophet, to call our Lord, *"King"* (Num. 24:7). This was some 40 to 60 years before Israel had kings.

Then Hannah said, *"And exalt the horn of His Anointed."*

This is the first reference to the Messiah where this term, *"His Anointed,"* is used. So, Hannah was the first one to use this term, making it even more special because she was a woman. From this point on, as we've already stated, others take up the theme of God's Anointed One—the Messiah (Ps. 2:2; 45:7; Isa. 61:1; Dan. 9:25-26).

THE MINISTRY OF SAMUEL

"But Samuel ministered before the LORD, being a child, girded with a linen ephod.

"Moreover his mother made him a little coat, and brought it to him from year to year, when she came up with her husband to offer the yearly sacrifice" (I Sam. 2:18-19).

Regarding Verse 18, Samuel is probably now in his early teens.

The linen ephod was actually a linen robe.

There seems to have been many irregularities in the Tabernacle program at that time. No child was supposed to minister to the Lord in the Tabernacle. The Lord would not hold this against Samuel, but He would hold it against Eli, who was the High Priest, and, therefore, responsible.

The *"little coat"* of Verse 19 was the garment worn under the ephod. In other words, Hannah was dressing Samuel as a Priest. The truth is, a man was not to become a Priest, at least, at that time, until he was 30 years of age (Num. 4:23, 30, 35, 43, 47).

SAMUEL

If it is to be noticed, two things are noted by the Holy Spirit as it regards Samuel, elementary, but so important. They are:

1. He was born.

2. He was named Samuel, meaning, *"Heard or asked of the LORD"* (I Sam. 1:20).

• The Scripture says that Hannah weaned little Samuel,

which means he was probably about three to five years of age (I Sam. 1:24). Then, the Holy Spirit says that he was brought to the House of the Lord in Shiloh. And then, when Hannah brought the child to Eli, a bullock was offered up in sacrifice (I Sam. 1:25). The Scripture then says that she *"lent him to the LORD,"* but probably should have been translated, *"Gave him to the LORD."* Before he was born, she promised him to the Lord as a Nazarite, which he would be all the days of his life. And now, it says that *"Samuel ministered before the LORD, being a child, girded with a linen ephod"* (I Sam. 2:18).

We will see that the Lord would *"call Samuel"* and give him a Revelation that would pertain to the entirety of Israel, and to Eli and his sons in particular (I Sam. 3:1-14).

So, we see the Hand of the Lord upon Samuel even from before his birth. As previously stated, he would be one of the greatest Prophets who ever lived, actually, the first man to stand in the Office of the Prophet.

The *"yearly sacrifice"* mentioned in Verse 19 proclaims the fact that Israel was not adhering to the Word of the Lord as it regarded the yearly sacrifices. There were supposed to be three gatherings a year, which a male of each household was to attend.

The first gathering was to be in April, which was the Passover. The second gathering was to be 50 days after the Passover, which was Pentecost and would be conducted in June. The third Feast was to be in October and would include the Feast of Tabernacles.

There were seven Feasts in all, three conducted in April, one in June, and three in October. However, it seems that the Word of the Lord was falling by the wayside in Israel at this time. In fact, it had been this way for approximately 400 years. However, things are about to change!

AND THE CHILD SAMUEL GREW BEFORE THE LORD

"And Eli blessed Elkanah and his wife, and said, The LORD give you seed of this woman for the loan which is lent to the

LORD. And they went unto their own home.

"And the LORD visited Hannah, so that she conceived, and bore three sons and two daughters. And the child Samuel grew before the LORD" (I Sam. 2:20-21).

The word, *"Loan,"* should have been translated, *"Gift,"* and the word, *"Lent,"* should have been translated, *"Given."*

Hannah had not asked simply for a son, but for a son whom she might dedicate to God. Now, Eli prays that Jehovah will also give her children to be her own. His prayer was answered.

BLESSINGS

It is obvious that both Elkanah and Hannah greatly loved the Lord even though Hannah's Faith stands out the greater. They were faithful to do for the Lord, as it regards the sacrifices, at least, that which they knew to do. As the several years have passed and their faithfulness has been maintained, Eli sees something in these people that is far beyond the norm, especially, for that day and time. Their regular attendance regarding worship and their attendance at appointed seasons, along with their reverent spirits, were in striking contrast with the degenerate habits with which Eli was all too familiar. Their quiet, unassuming conduct, which never varied, proclaimed the deep spirituality of their lives. To be sure, they would make a powerful impression on the Kingdom of God, especially Hannah.

As a result, Eli would pronounce Blessings upon them, which the Lord evidently honored, in giving her three more sons and two daughters. And the Scripture also says, *"And the child Samuel grew before the LORD."*

Even though it took a number of years, Hannah didn't quit until the Lord answered her prayer regarding the giving to her of a son. Now, he is coming into young manhood. I wonder how much that Hannah knew as it regards how significant all of this actually was?

I wonder how much any of us actually know as it regards

the significance of our living for God?

> *"Your Word is a Lamp to my feet,*
> *"A Light to my path always;*
> *"To guide and to save me from sin,*
> *"And show me the Heavenly Way."*

> *"Forever, O Lord, is Your Word,*
> *"Established and fixed on high;*
> *"Your Faithfulness unto all men,*
> *"Abides forever nigh."*

> *"At morning, at noon, and at night,*
> *"I ever will give You praise;*
> *"For You are My Portion, O Lord,*
> *"And shall be through all my days!"*

> *"Through Him Whom Your Word has foretold,*
> *"The Saviour and Morning Star,*
> *"Salvation and peace have been brought,*
> *"To those who have strayed afar."*

Great Women OF THE BIBLE
OLD TESTAMENT

Chapter Eleven

BATH-SHEBA
Wife Of David

BATH-SHEBA
Wife Of David

PROLOGUE

Some may wonder at the wisdom of including Bath-sheba in the *"Great Women of the Bible."* However, we must remember, it is not the beginning so much as it is the ending. To be sure, Bath-sheba ended well, very well.

What happened to her at the beginning was not her fault. Yes, she could have refused David, and that she should have done. Had she done so, I definitely believe that David would have immediately seen his terrible error and would have repented for what he was thinking. However, she didn't do that, and we'll have to leave that between her and the Lord.

As it regards her contribution to the Work of God, to be sure, that contribution was great. Had it not been for her insistence and her place and position, Satan may very well have succeeded in placing someone on the throne of Israel who would have literally destroyed the Nation. To be sure, the Evil One did not fail for lack of trying, but it was Bath-sheba mostly who swung the pendulum, so to speak, in the right direction in that her son Solomon would be named by David as the king.

Some might say that all of this could be contributed to a mother's desire for the betterment of her son. I'm sure that had some part to play; however, the Lord was working in all of this, and I definitely believe that the Lord spoke to Bath-sheba as to the right thing to do. It is for sure that He spoke to Nathan the Prophet, and I have no doubt that our Lord spoke to Bath-sheba, as well, as to what she should do at this most trying time in Israel's history.

We will begin with the near time of death for king David. Despite the problems just mentioned, still, he was one of the greatest Men of God who ever lived. Through his family would come the King of kings and Lord of lords, Israel's Messiah, and the Saviour of the world. Of course, I speak of the Lord

Jesus Christ. In fact, he would be referred to as *"the Son of David,"* and I might quickly state, *"the Greater Son of David."*

KING DAVID

"Now king David was old and stricken in years; and they covered him with clothes, but he got no heat.

"Wherefore his servants said unto him, Let there be sought for my lord the king a young virgin: and let her stand before the king, and let her cherish him, and let her lie in your bosom, that my lord the king may get heat.

"So they sought for a fair damsel throughout all the coasts of Israel, and found Abishag a Shunammite, and brought her to the king.

"And the damsel was very fair, and cherished the king, and ministered to him: but the king knew her not" (I Ki. 1:1-4).

At this time, David was either 69 or 70 years old.

Saul, the first king of Israel, is not once mentioned in I Kings or II Kings; it is as if he never existed. Saul was the people's choice while David was God's Choice. He was actually intended by the Lord to be the first king of Israel.

David's early hardships and later sorrows and anxieties appear to have aged him prematurely. As well, what was suggested was somewhat common in those days; nothing sexual is intimated.

The Fourth Verse declares that David had no intimate relations with Abishag the Shunammite.

DAVID'S LIFE

During the time of David, 70 years of age was considered to be old. Normally, life expectancy did not reach that high unless the Lord, for reasons of His Own, prolonged the lives of certain ones, which He at times did.

As the record shows, however, David's life had not been easy. The glory days began with him killing Goliath, the mortal enemy of Israel; however, those glory days under Saul didn't last very long. Soon he became a hunted man and stayed that way, with times of hardship, we might quickly add, for several years. He was probably about 17 or 18 when he killed Goliath. It seems that he enjoyed the favor of Saul for approximately two years, but certainly not much longer than that. If those numbers are correct, the next 10 years would have been years of acute hardship. He became king of the southern kingdom of Judah when he was 30 years old. He became king of the combined Tribes some seven and one-half years later.

From that time, he was in almost constant war, subduing the enemies which had sworn the destruction of Israel. Then, when he was about 50 years old, the terrible sin with Bath-sheba was committed, with the murder of her husband, Uriah. The balance of his days, some 20 or more years, saw very little but heartache.

It is believed that the firstfruit of his union with Bath-sheba, a little boy, died in infancy. This was followed by the death of Amnon, another son, who was killed by his brother Absalom because Amnon had raped Absalom's sister. Then, when David was about 60 years old, the insurrection of Absalom took place, which was the cause of much heartache, to say the least. Absalom died by being thrust through his heart with a dart by Joab. The truth is, very little peace was accorded David the last 20 years of his life. And yet, despite his failures, for which he paid dearly, he was one of the greatest Men of God who ever lived.

DAVID'S OLD AGE

Despite the verbiage given to us concerning David's physical condition during the time in question, we still have very little knowledge as to the things done.

In those days, it was believed that a close embrace of youth was an obvious way of imparting animal heat to age. So, what was suggested was quite often prescribed during those times.

As stated, David had no sexual relations with the young lady. As well, there is no proof that she was married to him at this time but that she was actually simply an attendant.

ADONIJAH

"Then Adonijah the son of Haggith exalted himself, saying, I will be king: and he prepared him chariots and horsemen, and fifty men to run before him.

"And his father had not displeased him at any time in saying, Why have you done so? and he also was a very goodly man; and his mother bore him after Absalom.

"And he conferred with Joab the son of Zeruiah, and with Abiathar the Priest: and they following Adonijah helped him.

"But Zadok the Priest, and Benaiah the son of Jehoiada, and Nathan the Prophet, and Shimei, and Rei, and the mighty men which belonged to David, were not with Adonijah.

"And Adonijah slew sheep and oxen and fat cattle by the stone of Zoheleth, which is by En-rogel, and called all his brethren the king's sons, and all the men of Judah the king's servants" (I Ki. 1:5-9).

Adonijah is the fourth son of David, and now, apparently the oldest survivor. Adonijah, Joab the military leader, and Abiathar the High Priest would set up their kingdom in opposition to God's Elect King. God had no place in their hearts, so Solomon did not suit them either. In fact, God's Choice never does suit man. This unholy triumvirate is a type of that which controls so much of the church world presently.

Adonijah not only emulated his brother Absalom, but, as well, he had the Absalom spirit.

ABIATHAR

Abiathar had once been very close to David, so he must have chaffed at sharing the Priesthood with Zadok. Now he makes his move to gain the number one spot all to himself.

Such an attitude has no regard for the Will of God or the Call of God. Unfortunately, the modern church is full of such *"religious leaders."*

According to Verse 8, the Holy Spirit is quick to point out these individuals who placed no stock in Adonijah, even though he was the eldest son, but rather waited on the Lord.

Even though sacrifices were offered, which gave it a religious leaning, still, for Adonijah to be king was not the Will of God. In fact, had he gained the throne, it would have destroyed Israel, as all such usurpation *"steals, kills, and destroys"* because it is of Satan (Jn. 10:10).

THE PLOT TO OVERTHROW THE WILL OF GOD

This unholy trio of Adonijah, Joab, and Abiathar present a type of that which controls so much of the modern church world.

• Adonijah: this man represents the world of religion that has no regard for the Call of God or the Will of God, but by religious politics will seek to gain fortune and position in the church. In fact, most of the so-called *"spiritual leadership"* in the modern church is made up of such.

• Joab: he, as well, cares nothing for the Will of God or the Call of God, but will constantly test the way the religious wind is blowing in order that he may throw in his lot with it and, thereby, feather his own nest. The church world is full of these opportunists also!

• Abiathar: this man occupied the High Priesthood of Israel jointly with Zadok. He, as well, is an opportunist. He will see the crowning of Adonijah as an opportunity to secure the Priesthood for himself alone. Also, he will have no regard for the Will of God or the Call of God. Unfortunately, as stated, the modern church is full of these *"religious leaders."*

The Bible student would do himself well to study carefully the ungodly intentions of this trio, for it pictures the modern-day church world. In this Chapter, we will see this effort of

Satan derailed with God's Man being placed on the throne. However, the far greater majority of times in the Bible and throughout Church history, there has been no David to carry out the Will of God. Instead, *"Adonijah, Joab, and Abiathar,"* have gained the ascendancy.

I WILL BE KING

Adonijah was the fourth son of David and now, apparently, the eldest surviving one. At this time, he was probably about 35 years old. The Scripture says, *"He exalted himself, saying, 'I will be king.'"* In reality, even though He was David's son, Adonijah did not know the Lord. In fact, Joab didn't either. Abiathar had once known the Lord in a great way but somehow had lost his way. So, the military leader of Israel, along with the High Priest, seemed to be the strength that Adonijah needed.

So, did Joab know that Adonijah was not David's choice? He had always been faithful to David, whatever his other problems. The truth is, he, no doubt, realized that under any other king than Adonijah his place and position would be extremely precarious. He resolved, therefore, to secure himself by helping Adonijah take the throne.

One can somewhat understand Joab, but Abiathar's defection comes as a surprise. There had been close ties between him and David. He had stayed with David through the hard times and through the good times. However, the idea seems to have been, as with Joab, that David will soon be gone, so he must plan and scheme for himself. And, so he does!

THE WORLD OF RELIGION

It is sad, but what we are seeing here is so indicative of the world of religion, even from the beginning of time. It is no less prevalent today! The truth is, Satan works far better from inside the church than he does outside. He tries to maneuver his man into place and position, and he usually succeeds. For the Lord to get His Man into position has never been an easy task, even as it wasn't easy to get David on the throne to begin with. The world is not only opposed to such a choice, but the church as well. In fact, the church, sad to say, is the greatest enemy of the Will of God and the Call of God. Of course, we are speaking of the apostate church, which makes up the majority of that which refers to itself as *"Believers."*

The short phrase, *"Exalted himself,"* means that God did not exalt him. In fact, had he become the king of Israel, the Plan of God would have been stopped dead in its tracks. More than likely, the split between the tribes would have taken place, as it ultimately did, when the son of Solomon took the throne, which would be some 45 years later. However, as we shall see, the Lord would overrule this effort, which has all the earmarks of Satan.

NATHAN AND BATH-SHEBA

"But Nathan the Prophet, and Benaiah, and the mighty men, and Solomon his brother he (Adonijah) *called not.*

"Wherefore Nathan spoke unto Bath-sheba the mother of Solomon, saying, Have you not heard that Adonijah the son of Haggith does reign, and David our lord knows it not?

"Now therefore come, let me, I pray you, give you counsel, that you may save your own life and the life of your son Solomon.

"You go in unto king David, and say unto him, Did not you, my lord, O king, swear unto your handmaid, saying, Assuredly Solomon your son shall reign after me, and he shall sit upon my throne? why then does Adonijah reign?

"Behold, while you yet talked there with the king, I (Nathan the Prophet) *also will come in after you, and confirm your words"* (I Ki. 1:10-14).

It is clear from Verse 10 that Adonijah perfectly understood that he had in Solomon a rival. The word had, no doubt, gotten around that it was the Will of God that Solomon succeed David.

Verse 11 proclaims the fact that David had nothing to do

with the aspirations of Adonijah, proving that they were not of the Lord.

The Twelfth Verse proclaims the fact that the men in question would go to any lengths to secure their positions, even to killing Bath-sheba, Solomon, and anyone else, for that matter, who would seem to stand in their way. Such is the way and world of religion.

The oath of David to Bath-sheba in Verse 15 is not elsewhere recorded, but it was evidently well known to Nathan and, no doubt, to others as well.

NATHAN THE PROPHET

We see from the above Passages that Nathan the Prophet was highly recognized at this time in the administration of David. We also see that David relied on him extensively.

It was Nathan the Prophet who brought word to David that through his family the Messiah would come, which was the greatest honor that God could ever pay any human being (II Sam. 7:4-17).

And then, it was Nathan's duty to take to David one of the most ominous messages that any man has ever had to deliver. It concerned David's sin with Bath-sheba and the murder of her husband, Uriah. The Lord would speak to Nathan the Prophet, telling him what David had done, and then pronouncing judgment (II Sam. 12:1-14).

Now, the Lord will use Nathan, as well as Bath-sheba, to save the kingdom. What Nathan now did was, no doubt, far more than his own personal sagacity. He was undoubtedly led by the Lord in his actions as it regarded advice to Bath-sheba, and then, of course, to David as well. Thankfully, his advice and counsel would be followed.

SATAN'S PLANS

When Adonijah proceeded to make himself king, the

Eighth Verse of this Chapter proclaims the fact that he did not call Zadok the Priest, Benaiah, one of the military leaders of Israel, Nathan the Prophet, or certain others to be with them at this time. Evidently, the word had gotten out that David's choice was Solomon, who was probably about 20 years old at this time.

Had Adonijah succeeded in his devilish plans, no doubt, Bath-sheba, along with Solomon, and quite possibly, Nathan the Prophet would have been immediately executed.

All of this was a diabolical plan of Satan to thwart the Plan of God. He would use those inside the church, so to speak. They knew God, at least, as far as intellectualism could know Him, but they were not of God. I speak of Adonijah, Abiathar, and Joab, plus, no doubt, scores of others who were with them.

Unfortunately, this type of thing is quite common in the modern church. Very precious few truly seek the Lord as to what His Will actually is, and, to be sure, He most definitely does have a Perfect Will for all things. All too often, religious men have their own desires with little concern as to what the Lord actually wants. This type of thing has hindered and hurt the true Work of God perhaps more than anything else.

Seeing what is happening and, no doubt, led by the Lord, Nathan the Prophet addresses Bath-sheba, informing her as to what she ought to do and the urgency of it.

Apparently, at this time, David was bedridden. Pulpit says that it was more from feebleness rather than age.[1]

DAVID AND BATH-SHEBA

"And Bath-sheba went in unto the king into the chamber: and the king was very old; and Abishag the Shunammite minis-tered unto the king.

"And Bath-sheba bowed, and did obeisance unto the king. And the king said, What would you?

"And she said unto him, My lord, you swore by the LORD your God unto your handmaid, saying, Assuredly Solomon your

son shall reign after me, and he shall sit upon my throne.

"And now, behold, Adonijah reigns; and now, my lord the king, you know it not:

"And he has killed oxen and fat cattle and sheep in abundance, and has called all the sons of the king, and Abiathar the Priest, and Joab the captain of the host: but Solomon your servant has he not called.

"And you, my lord, O king, the eyes of all Israel are upon you, that you should tell them who shall sit on the throne of my lord the king after him.

"Otherwise it shall come to pass, when my lord the king shall sleep with his fathers, that I and my son Solomon shall be counted offenders" (I Ki. 1:15-21).

In essence, Bath-sheba proclaims to David that she knew that he didn't have anything to do with Adonijah attempting to become king. Bath-sheba couched her words as she did in order to prove there was a plot. Pulpit says, *"It showed the cloven foot."*[2] Obviously, the entirety of Israel was waiting for an answer as it regards who would succeed David.

BATH-SHEBA

Bath-sheba was a victim, at least, partially so, of a very evil situation, which resulted in the murder of her husband, Uriah. This brought much sorrow and heartache to the perpetrator, namely David. In spite of this, this woman was of great wisdom and, as well, was greatly close to God. The last Chapter of Proverbs proclaims this.

While her name may, at times, be sullied by religious practitioners who have not thought the subject through, or else, function from the position of self-righteousness, still, God used her. To be sure, despite the involvement in which she found herself, nothing could be higher than to be favorably used of God.

Sometimes preachers have the idea that the Christian experience is one of perfection, or near so, and if there are adverse situations, then the person must be labeled as a weak sister, etc. The truth is, only self-righteousness would come up with such a conclusion. The sadness is, the ones saying such and doing such are oftentimes in worse condition spiritually than the ones they are criticizing.

The clinging vines of the Fall, unfortunately, still attach themselves to each and every Believer. To be sure, Satan takes full advantage of such.

One of the great Divines of the past was asked the question, *"Does Satan oppose every Christian to the same degree?"* His answer was most revealing. *"Satan,"* he said, *"doesn't even know that most Christians are alive."* He went on to say, *"They are doing him no harm, so he, by and large, just leaves them alone."*

If, in fact, that is the case, and it definitely is, this means that those who are greatly used of God must be aware at all times of their precarious position, and must take the necessary defensive steps, which always is the Cross of Christ.

LIVING FOR GOD

Scripturally, there is no reason that any Believer has to fail the Lord. If we do so, or perhaps one should say, *"When we do so,"* we must admit, because it's true, that the fault is entirely ours. If our Faith is properly placed in the right Object on a continuous basis, the Holy Spirit will then grandly help us, which means that we don't have to fail. Of course, I'm speaking of the Cross of Christ as being the Object of our Faith. Unfortunately, getting from point A to point B is not always simple or easy. The moment the believing sinner comes to Christ, he is somewhat like a little baby. He has to be trained and instructed as to what to do and how to live. Unfortunately, most of the training and instruction that he receives is not Scriptural; consequently, such a Believer is going to find the ride very difficult.

NATHAN THE PROPHET

"And, lo, while she (Bath-sheba) *yet talked with the king,*

Nathan the Prophet also came in.

"And they told the king, saying, Behold Nathan the Prophet. And when he was come in before the king, he bowed himself before the king with his face to the ground.

"And Nathan said, My lord, O king, have you said, Adonijah shall reign after me, and he shall sit upon my throne?

"For he is gone down this day, and has slain oxen and fat cattle and sheep in abundance, and has called all the king's sons, and the captains of the host, and Abiathar the Priest; and, behold, they eat and drink before him, and say, God save king Adonijah.

"But me, even me your servant, and Zadok the Priest, and Benaiah the son of Jehoiada, and your servant Solomon, has he not called.

"Is this thing done by my lord the king, and you have not showed it unto your servant, who should sit on the throne of my lord the king after him?" (I Ki. 1:22-27).

NATHAN'S MANNER OF APPROACH

Nathan the Prophet puts forth his statement forcibly in order to draw from the king a disclaimer. The question is asked and the statement made in this manner in order to force David to take action one way or the other.

The fact that Zadok the Priest, Benaiah the son of Jehoiada, Nathan the Prophet, and even Solomon weren't called to that crowning of Adonijah spoke volumes. This tells us that Adonijah knew that David's choice was Solomon. All of this shows that he was determined to take the throne. Nathan's statement is well calculated to impress upon the king the importance of nominating a successor at once in order to foil the plan of Satan.

NATHAN, THE PROPHET OF THE LORD

The fact that Nathan was now able to go before David as he did, and speak to him in the manner in which he did, greatly shows the character of David. This is especially true considering that some years before he had had to denounce David strongly to his face. I speak of the matter concerning Bath-sheba and her husband, Uriah. Even though that had happened years before, it should be understood that David's place and position were not diminished at all in Israel, which speaks volumes as it regards the Righteousness of David. True Prophets before most kings would not have survived the day, much less their place and position maintained.

However, David knew that Nathan was right and that he was wrong. He didn't blame Nathan at all for the situation, even as he should not have, but only himself. In fact, if the truth be known, regardless of how much it hurt and as great as would be the pain and suffering, he was very pleased that the thing had finally now come to a head.

Yet, precious few men would have taken the place and position that David took. The idea is, at least, most of the time, if you don't like the message, kill the messenger.

THE AUDIENCE

The audience before David at this time was important beyond the comprehension of mere mortals. Due to David's age and his obvious feebleness, he was presently not taking the authority that he should have taken. Consequently, he had to be jarred into doing so. Above all, the impression had to be made upon him of the urgency of the matter and that the situation must be addressed immediately. Satan's plan is to put someone on the throne, in this case Adonijah, who was not God's Choice. As a result, he was pushing forth the issue, and doing so severely. To again repeat Pulpit, *"It's easy to see the cloven hoof in all of this."*[3]

DAVID'S ANSWER

"Then king David answered and said, Call me Bath-sheba.

And she came into the king's presence, and stood before the king.

"And the king swore, and said, As the LORD lives, Who has redeemed my soul out of all distress,

"Even as I swore unto you by the LORD God of Israel, saying, Assuredly Solomon your son shall reign after me, and he shall sit upon my throne in my stead; even so will I certainly do this day.

"Then Bath-sheba bowed with her face to the earth, and did reverence to the king, and said, Let my lord king David live forever" (I Ki. 1:28-31).

Bath-sheba had evidently left the chamber when Nathan came in. She now joins him before David. In essence, David uses the term, *"By the life of Jehovah,"* which gives great force to his statement about to be uttered.

The king seems now to realize the urgency and immediately sets about to take steps to right the situation.

THE OATH

In David's answer to Bath-sheba concerning the situation, he uses the phrase, *"As the LORD lives, Who has redeemed my soul out of all distress."*

This is an expression that he has used in one way or the other any number of times through the years.

In II Samuel 4:9, he said, *"As the LORD lives, Who has redeemed my soul out of all adversity."*

Similar expressions are used, *"Out of the hand of all my enemies, and out of the hand of Saul,"* etc.

Pulpit says, *"And it is no wonder that he repeatedly commemorates it, converting every adjuration into an act of thanksgiving."*[4]

In fact, so much is said in that statement!

By these statements, David knew that he did not deserve to have been delivered. He realized that it was not because of his merit that such was brought about but strictly because of the Mercy of God. He never forgot it; it was also, seemingly, always on his mind. As a result, this paean of praise and thanksgiving goes up before the Lord with every given opportunity.

THE LORD GOD OF ISRAEL

As it regards the statement, *"Even as I swore unto you by the LORD God of Israel,"* David had promised Bath-sheba that Solomon, their son, would be the heir to the throne even though he was quite a bit younger than Adonijah. There is more here than meets the eye.

By him using the term, *"The LORD God of Israel,"* this tells us that the Lord had spoken to David's heart as it regarded Solomon. Quite possibly, even though the Scripture is silent, the Lord may have used Nathan the Prophet to do so. This is the reason that it is so urgent that David now take steps. He knows it is the Will of God for Solomon to follow him. He also knows that Adonijah would be a disaster. In fact, anything that's not the Will of God will never turn out right. So, the verbiage given here proclaims the very opposite of an unsettled mind. David knew the Will of God, and now it would be carried out. However, we must give credit to both Bath-sheba and Nathan the Prophet for forcing the issue. The Lord used them, as is obvious!

DAVID'S INSTRUCTIONS ACCORDING TO THE HOLY SPIRIT

Once David sees the Will of God, at least, as it regards the time, he now functions with prompt and vigorous action. His instructions are to the point. It speaks of the David of many years before, not one who is now old and feeble.

There is something about the Will of God and, thereby, walking in His Precepts that renews the soul, lifts the spirit, encourages the heart, and, in a sense, makes an old man young again.

In fact, after this, again, because he was operating solely in the Will of God, David seemed to regain strength and, thereby, delegated the ministry of the Temple, which, of course, his son, Solomon, would build. In fact, had Adonijah gained the throne, the Temple would never have been built.

Every function of Temple doings and worship was given to the Sweet Psalmist of Israel, even in the closing days of his life. All of the Temple functions pointed to the coming Redeemer, the Son of David, and one might say, *"The Greater Son of David."* Nothing was left to chance or happenstance as it regarded the Temple, with everything laid out in perfection, all given by the Holy Spirit. David added nothing. He only carried out in the drawings what the Lord told him to do.

The Lord even gave David the strength to address the entirety of Israel and to give a charge to Solomon. So, we see, and rightly so, how that David closed out his days, and more perfectly, how the Holy Spirit closed out his days, even in the grand style it was meant to be. Satan had tried every way to hinder and hurt, and had succeeded at times, but his evil success did not stop David from finishing the race.

SOLOMON

"So Zadok the Priest, and Nathan the Prophet, and Benaiah the son of Jehoiada, and the Cherethites, and the Pelethites, went down, and caused Solomon to ride upon king David's mule, and brought him to Gihon.

"And Zadok the Priest took an horn of oil out of the Tabernacle, and anointed Solomon. And they blew the trumpet; and all the people said, God save king Solomon.

"And all the people came up after him, and the people piped with pipes, and rejoiced with great joy, so that the Earth rent with the sound of them" (I Ki. 1:38-40).

Zadok was the High Priest.

The Cherethites and the Pelethites had the military might to back up whatever was done. They were David's royal bodyguard, consisting of sizeable forces.

Considering this crack special guard accompanying

Solomon, this must have been quite a procession.

The *"horn of oil"* mentioned in Verse 39 was the *"Holy Anointing Oil"* (Ex. 30:25, 31). They fulfilled exactly what David had told them to do. As well, Solomon was confirmed in his office by the approval of the people. There was great joy in Jerusalem, and rightly so. Despite all of Satan's efforts, he did not take best. The day went to the Lord!

THE ANOINTING OF SOLOMON AS KING

Despite the efforts of the enemy, as we've already stated, God's Choice, who is Solomon, will now grace the throne of David, in fact, the most important throne at that time on the face of the Earth. All of this is so very, very important, actually having to do with the Salvation and Redemption of the entire human race, and for all time. Yes, it is that important!

Through David's family, the Messiah, the Redeemer of all mankind, the Saviour of men's souls, the Baptizer with the Holy Spirit, King of kings and Lord of lords, and God manifest in the flesh will ultimately come. While it would be approximately one thousand years, still, that day would finally arrive and, in fact, did.

Let us all take a lesson from this. Every single Believer who has ever lived is of extreme significance in the great Plan of God. In other words, God has a place and a position for every one of us in this great Kingdom. It behooves us to find what that place and position is, and then to put all of our soul and might into our efforts, whatever it might be.

Never think that any task is too small as it regards the Work of God. As the Psalmist said, *". . . I'd rather be a doorkeeper in the House of my God, than to dwell in the tents of wickedness"* (Ps. 84:10).

Sincere Believers should earnestly seek the Lord as it regards the ministry or church in which they are involved. Tragically and sadly, most efforts are wasted, be it money or labor, simply because what is being preached is not the Gospel of

Jesus Christ, but rather another Jesus (II Cor. 11:4). Unfortunately, that characterizes the greater percentage that goes under the guise of the Work of God.

THE GREAT DAY

This which David organized was quite impressive, to say the least. As stated, the Cherethites and the Pelethites were a royal bodyguard of David, numbering approximately 600 men. These would have been drawn up in organized order, even as befitted the solemn occasion.

The office of the king of Israel was, in effect, at that time, the greatest office on the face of the Earth. The king, a son of David, through whose family the Messiah would come, actually functioned as the Emissary of God on Earth.

In fact, that's the reason that Satan made such an effort to thwart God's Will in this matter.

If the anointing of Solomon as king followed custom, which it, no doubt, did, it was in the following manner: *"Zadok the High Priest"* took the *"horn of oil,"* which was a substantial amount, and stood before Solomon. He then poured the oil on his head, with it running down over his shoulders and soaking his garment, even down to his feet. In fact, a ram's horn, for that was what was used, was a fair size, possibly holding at least a half-quart, if not more.

All of this typified the Holy Spirit, Who was to cover and help the king govern God's People. Unfortunately, during the next approximate 500 years, there were only a few kings who occupied this office who were really godly.

When the Holy Anointing Oil was poured over Solomon's head, *"they blew the trumpet; and all the people said, 'God save king Solomon.'"* In fact, the rejoicing was so great that the Scripture says, *"So that the Earth rent with the sound of them."* And so was the inaugural of Solomon as the next king of Israel. However, we must say again, *"The two most important players in this most important event, all under the Holy Spirit, were*

Bath-sheba and Nathan the Prophet."

BATH-SHEBA

The following account taken from the last Chapter of Proverbs, which was written by Solomon, will come as a surprise to most Believers. Many do not know and realize that this is Bath-sheba, the mother of Solomon, to whom this last Chapter of Proverbs is dedicated. It says:

"The words of king Lemuel, the Prophecy that his mother taught him.

"What, my son? and what, the son of my womb? and what, the son of my vows?

"Give not your strength unto women, nor your ways to that which destroys kings.

"It is not for kings, O Lemuel, it is not for kings to drink wine; nor for princes strong drink:

"Lest they drink, and forget the Law, and pervert the judgment of any of the afflicted.

"Give strong drink unto him who is ready to perish, and wine unto those who be of heavy hearts.

"Let him drink, and forget his poverty, and remember his misery no more.

"Open your mouth for the dumb in the cause of all such as are appointed to destruction.

"Open your mouth, judge righteously, and plead the cause of the poor and needy" (Prov. 31:1-9).

ANOTHER NAME FOR SOLOMON

"Lemuel" was another name for Solomon. His mother was Bath-sheba. The sense of this Proverb is that his mother kept teaching him continually the Things of the Lord. From Verse 2, we know that Bath-sheba dedicated Solomon to God before his birth. He was a child of Repentance and Faith.

The obviousness of immorality is apparent in Verse 3.

However, its deeper meaning pertains to the false woman, idolatry, as is contrasted with the True Woman, the Gospel.

The admonition of the Holy Spirit through Bath-sheba to her son Solomon in verse 4 is clear and plain, *"Leave strong drink alone!"* The pain of *"strong drink,"* even moderately consumed, causes one to *"forget the Law,"* which means to forget the Word of God. Consequently, *"judgment"* is perverted in such a case and in whatever capacity.

Verse 7 pertains possibly to one ready to be executed or another in extreme difficulties. The same is done in modern times with certain drugs prescribed by doctors. Concerning Verse 8, Bath-sheba seems to have a premonition that God will graciously open the heavens regarding wisdom that would be given to her son Solomon. She seemed to know and understand that the helpless, afflicted, and defenseless would come to him in order for him to champion their *"cause."* Solomon was a Type of Christ and, as such, he was instructed through his mother Bath-sheba by the Holy Spirit to *"judge righteously."*

THE PROPHECY

"The words of king Lemuel, the Prophecy that his mother taught him."

As we have stated, Lemuel was another name for Solomon. The idea of this statement is, from the time that Solomon was old enough to comprehend things, Bath-sheba taught him the Word of God and did so continually.

There is sufficient evidence in the Scriptures, I think, to suggest that Bath-sheba became a woman of Faith and character prior to the birth of Solomon (II Sam. 12:24). Self-righteousness can little grasp or understand the truth of this; however, this does characterize all who profess Christ. Grace takes abominable sin and changes it into something of beauty. Only God can do such a thing.

Grace does not hide the sin but neither does it refuse pardon and future Blessing.

Whatever place and position that the minds of the people of Israel gave Bath-sheba at that time is anyone's guess; however, it is very obvious that the Holy Spirit gave her a tremendous place and position in the great Plan of God.

DAVID

The situation with David, as to the terrible sins that he committed regarding the adultery with Bath-sheba and the cold-blooded murder of her husband, Uriah, was not her fault. Some may claim that she should have repulsed him when he made advances toward her, even upon the pain of death. That is true; however, we presently have little knowledge of what actually took place on that terrible day of some 3,000 years ago. We know that David suffered terribly because of the sins he committed, and, no doubt, Bath-sheba suffered as well. However, the fault belonged to David and not Bath-sheba. So, whatever individuals may think about this woman, we find here that the Holy Spirit lauds her as a woman of great Faith and great character. And, what is good enough for the Holy Spirit ought to be good enough for us. We should never forget, reputation is what people think we are while character is what God knows we are.

THE DEDICATION OF SOLOMON TO GOD

The Scripture says, *"What, my son? and what, the son of my womb? and what, the son of my vows?"*

From this Passage, we know that Bath-sheba dedicated Solomon to God before his birth. He was, as stated, a child of Repentance and of Faith.

Self-righteousness would have condemned him to obscurity if not to death. Grace, however, placed him on the throne.

It is generally impossible to rectify mistakes. Neither David nor Bath-sheba could bring back her murdered husband, Uriah. However, they could accept the just Judgment of God with dignity, which they did, and they learned from their terrible wrongdoing to trust God for the future.

The majority of the Christian world does not seem to realize that all of us fall into the same category. While it is true that the sin of most does not equal the adultery and murder committed by David, still, our sin is still sin. Regardless of the gravity, the principle is the same, and, likewise, the Blood of Jesus remains the same. Whatever you do, never underestimate the shed Blood of the Lord Jesus Christ and its ability to cleanse from all sin.

It appears that Bath-sheba knew that her son was promised the throne of Israel. It seems that she did her best to instruct him according to the Touch of God in her life. She vowed to God that she would not fail in the giving of her instruction. This Chapter is evidence that she did not fail.

FORGIVENESS AND MERCY

Were this scene regarding David and Bath-sheba to be played out presently, I cannot even remotely see the modern church allowing Solomon to gain the throne. He was the son of David who committed these most terrible sins. Yet, God placed him on the throne, and there is evidence that the Lord loved him supremely. The Scripture says, *"And the LORD magnified Solomon exceedingly in the sight of all Israel, and bestowed upon him such royal majesty as had not been on any king before him in Israel"* (I Chron. 29:25).

In fact, when Solomon failed the Lord, the Scripture says:

"And the LORD was angry with Solomon, because his heart was turned from the LORD God of Israel, Who had appeared unto him twice *(there is a special Hebrew verb used in the Bible for 'to be angry'; it is only used of Divine anger; it occurs fourteen times; here, and in five other Passages, a form of the verb is used regarding the forcing of oneself to be angry with a person who is loved; in other words, the Lord, because of His Nature, and despite Solomon's spiritual declension, had to force Himself to be angry with Solomon; He loved him that much!)*" **(I Ki. 11:9).**

All of this plainly tells us that David was truly forgiven of these terrible sins, and when God forgives, it is as though the sin was never committed. In fact, there is no such thing as a partial Justification; it is either a total Justification or no justification at all.

Bath-sheba knew that her son would be king of Israel, and, as well, she knew that God had laid His Hand upon him. Consequently, she was determined to do all that she could to teach him the Right Ways of the Lord, which she most definitely did.

BATH-SHEBA'S PRAYER

- She warned her son about the ways that would destroy kings.
- She warned him about the evils of strong drink.
- She warned him that he not fail to *"plead the cause of the poor and needy."* Regrettably, he did not heed her advice regarding the first two, but there are some who think that he did heed what she said regarding the *"poor and needy."*

If Solomon wrote these words toward the close of his life, and there is evidence that he did, how it must have grieved him to have recalled what his mother had admonished him to do and how he had so miserably failed.

A VIRTUOUS WOMAN

"Who can find a virtuous woman? for her price is far above rubies.

"The heart of her husband does safely trust in her, so that he shall have no need of spoil.

"She will do him good and not evil all the days of her life.

"She seeks wool, and flax, and works willingly with her hands.

"She is like the merchants' ships; she brings her food from afar.

"She rises also while it is yet night, and gives meat to her household, and a portion to her maidens.

"She considers a field, and buys it: with the fruit of her hands she plants a vineyard.

"She girds her loins with strength, and strengthens her arms.

"She perceives that her merchandise is good: her candle goes not out by night.

"She lays her hands to the spindle, and her hands hold the distaff.

"She stretches out her hand to the poor; yes, she reaches forth her hands to the needy" (Prov. 31:10-20).

THE EXPLANATION

The word *"virtuous"* is not limited in its meaning in Hebrew as it is in English. It is a covering term suggesting character and ability. Spiritually, the dialogue concerning the *"virtuous woman"* can also apply to the Church and what it ought to be.

Her husband has absolute confidence in her faithfulness.

He is blessed by her tireless and unfailing industry, which will last all the days of her life.

She goes to every length to save money, even *"working willingly with her hands."* There is no hint of laziness about her.

If she buys something, she does so with the idea in mind of using some of it and selling the other to pay for that which she has used. Again, this shows industry.

She takes the lead in guiding the house and expects all who are in the household to follow her example, which they do.

According to Verse 16, she is constantly planning as to how to provide for her growing family.

She keeps herself and her family in good health with proper food and clothing.

Even though she works hard for her money, according to Verse 20, she does not fail to help the *"poor"* and the *"needy."* She does so because she knows that God honors such.

FAR ABOVE RUBIES

"Who can find a virtuous woman? for her price is far above rubies."

While this Thirty-first Chapter describes Bath-sheba, Solomon's mother, and, as well, what womanhood should be in general and can be only in Christ, its spiritual meaning pertains to the Church. In other words, this Thirty-first Chapter is what the Church ought to be.

- Verse 11 says that she is trustworthy.
- Verse 12 says that she is faithful.
- Verse 13 says that she works hard.
- Verse 14 says that she is industrious and resourceful.
- Verse 15 says that she takes the lead in guiding the house.
- Verse 16 says that she's always planning for the betterment of the family.
- She keeps herself and her family in good health with proper food and clothing.
- She is impeccably honest.
- She is constantly laboring, showing her industriousness and ability.
- She is generous with the poor and the needy.

RESOURCEFUL

"She is not afraid of the snow for her household: for all her household are clothed with scarlet.

"She makes herself coverings of tapestry; her clothing is silk and purple.

"Her husband is known in the gates, when he sits among the elders of the land.

"She makes fine linen, and sells it; and delivers girdles unto

the merchant.

"Strength and honour are her clothing; and she shall rejoice in time to come.

"She opens her mouth with wisdom; and in her tongue is the law of kindness.

"She looks well to the ways of her household, and eats not the bread of idleness.

"Her children arise up, and call her blessed; her husband also, and he praises her.

"Many daughters have done virtuously, but you excel them all.

"Favour is deceitful, and beauty is vain: but a woman who fears the LORD, she shall be praised.

"Give her of the fruit of her hands; and let her own works praise her in the gates" (Prov. 31:21-31).

THAT WHICH THE HOLY SPIRIT SAYS ABOUT BATH-SHEBA AND ALL LIKE HER

She has prepared for the coming winter with suitable clothing for all of her household. She thinks ahead. Coming difficulties do not catch her shortsighted. Even though she is very conservative, still, money is not her god; therefore, she does not skimp in providing the furniture for her home or for her own personal clothing. It is such that befits her station in life as one who is blessed by God and is a Child of God.

As her husband was guided in his choice of her, likewise, she was guided by the Holy Spirit in her choice of him. He is a leader in the community. According to Verse 24, once again her business ability places her on a par with her husband. The Holy Spirit gives her no lesser position. She is capable of being a captain of industry and a maker of excellent decisions.

All that she manufactures is done with quality. Her goods are sought the world over. Even though this virtuous woman, whose price is far above rubies, is said by the Holy Spirit to be a captain of industry with striking and startling abilities, still, her *"mouth"* is a mouth of *"wisdom."* Despite all her qualities and riches, still, her *"tongue"* is not harsh but always *"kind."*

Even though she is now greatly blessed, according to Verse 27, still, there is no place for *"idleness"* in her thinking or doing. In essence, industry never stops. According to Verse 28, such women could not be praised too highly.

Bath-sheba was truly led by the Holy Spirit and inspired greatly to write the instructions that she did for her son Solomon. She was quite a lady!

It seems that the husband of this *"virtuous woman,"* namely David, speaks in this Verse. He claims that many have done *"virtuously,"* but this one whom God has given him, his lovely wife, *"excels them all."*

If this is to be carried to its conclusion, as stated, David spoke these words about Bath-sheba, and the Holy Spirit allowed it. Such is God; such is Grace.

The two closing Verses of this Chapter are the Holy Spirit's Conclusion, not only to the Chapter itself, but to the Message of the entirety of the Book of Proverbs. That Message is:

The fear of the Lord secures abiding favor, moral beauty, public approbation, and eternal recompense.

BATH-SHEBA

To proclaim again, this Chapter is speaking of Bath-sheba. As well, it gives us information as to what any woman can be if guided by the Bible with the Holy Spirit as her Helper. Spiritually speaking, it can also refer to the Church. It says:

• She has no fear.

• Her clothing is silk and purple, i.e., *"the Righteousness of God."*

• Her Husband is the Lord Jesus Christ, and she has helped make Him known *"among the Elders of the land."*

• She takes the Gospel to the world, *"delivers girdles unto the merchant."*

• *"Strength and honour"* characterize her.

- She speaks with wisdom.
- She *"eats not the bread of idleness"* but serves as a laborer in the harvest.
- She is praised by the Lord.
- Down through history and all those who have served the Lord, *"she excels them all."*
- She fears the Lord.
- *"Her own works praise her in the gates."*

So ends this great Book of Proverbs. It is remarkable that the Holy Spirit would have Solomon close out this tremendous work with a description of his mother, Bath-sheba. The way the Holy Spirit closes any Book of the Bible is very significant, so this tells us how that wisdom is to be used. To understand that the Lord used a woman to do this, and above all, Bath-sheba, speaks of the Grace of God.

"Sing them over again to me,
"Wonderful words of life;
"Let me more of their beauty see,
"Wonderful words of life;
"Words of life and beauty,
"Teach me Faith and duty:
"Beautiful words, wonderful words,
"Wonderful words of life."

"Christ, the Blessed One, gives to all,
"Wonderful words of life,
"Sinner, list to the loving Call,
"Wonderful words of life,
"All so freely given,
"Wooing us to Heaven;
"Beautiful words, wonderful words,
"Wonderful words of life."

"Sweetly echo the Gospel Call,
"Wonderful words of life;

"Offer pardon and peace to all,
"Wonderful words of life,
"Jesus, only Saviour,
"Sanctify forever,
"Beautiful words, wonderful words,
"Wonderful words of life."

Great Women OF THE BIBLE

OLD TESTAMENT

Chapter Twelve

THE WIDOW WOMAN OF ZAREPHATH

A Gentile

THE WIDOW WOMAN OF ZAREPHATH
A Gentile

THE WONDERS OF THE LORD

Now we come to a dear lady, whom the Holy Spirit did not give us her name. She was just referred to as a *"widow woman."* We know that her financial resources were almost nothing, in fact, were nothing. But yet, this is the one the Lord chose to take care of the greatest Prophet on the face of the Earth, Elijah.

Why would the Lord use her? What did He see in her?

These are questions that, hopefully, will be answered in the narrative. This one thing we know, the Lord never does anything capriciously. In other words, He has a purpose, a reason, and a design about everything, and I mean everything that He does. It is always for the good of the person involved, whomever that might be, and it's always a lesson for the balance of us, even as we learn many things from the situation regarding this *"widow woman."*

To be sure, her story is exceedingly interesting. When you finish reading the information we are given in the Word of God concerning this dear lady, I think that your Faith will rise to a greater degree. If, in fact, that happens, you will not have wasted your time.

THE WORD OF THE LORD

"And the Word of the LORD came unto him, saying,

"Arise, get you to Zarephath, which belongs to Zidon, and dwell there: behold, I have commanded a widow woman there to sustain you.

"So he arose and went to Zarephath. And when he came to the gate of the city, behold, the widow woman was there gathering up sticks: and he called to her, and said, Fetch me, I pray you, a little water in a vessel, that I may drink.

"And as she was going to fetch it, he called to her, and said,

Bring me, I pray you, a morsel of bread in your hand.

"And she said, As the LORD your God lives, I have not a cake, but an handful of meal in a barrel, and a little oil in a cruse: and, behold, I am gathering two sticks, that I may go in and dress it for me and my son, that we may eat it, and die.

"And Elijah said unto her, Fear not; go and do as you have said: but make me thereof a little cake first, and bring it unto me, and after make for you and for your son.

"For thus says the LORD God of Israel, The barrel of meal shall not waste, neither shall the cruse of oil fail, until the day that the LORD sends rain upon the Earth.

"And she went and did according to the saying of Elijah: and she, and he, and her house, did eat many days.

"And the barrel of meal wasted not, neither did the cruse of oil fail, according to the Word of the LORD, which He spoke by Elijah" (I Ki. 17:8-16).

THE WIDOW OF ZAREPHATH

This woman was a Gentile. As we shall see, she was also poverty stricken, so much so, in fact, that she and her son were prepared to die, actually starve to death. Jesus mentioned this incident in Luke 4:25-26.

Even though this woman was a Gentile and, therefore, not a part of the Covenant of Abraham, it must have been that she had turned her back on the heathen gods, which she had previously worshipped, and had called on Jehovah, the God of Israel. Irrespective as to where it is or from whom it comes, God will always honor Faith.

From the request of Elijah, we learn that the Lord was about to test her just as He tests all of us. Please notice that according to Verse 12, the woman subscribed Jehovah to Elijah and not to herself. She had not been serving Jehovah but had previously been serving heathen idols; however, things are about to change. As is obvious, her condition was desperate.

That which Elijah requested of her was her test. What

would she do? Would she obey the Prophet and give the last morsel of bread to him, or would she refuse? A great lesson is taught here. The Economy of the Lord was about to be introduced to this woman.

THE PROMISE

The world says, *"Give to me first, then maybe I'll give something back to you."* However, the Lord says, *"Give to Me first, whatever it is you have, however meager it might be, at least, if it represents your best, then I will give back to you."* The woman now had the Promise before her. Would she believe it and act upon it, or would she reject it? Thank God, she believed the Promise and acted upon it.

To be sure, that Promise given by the Holy Spirit through Elijah so long, long ago is just as apropos today as it was then. If we *"seek first the Kingdom of God, and His Righteousness; then all of these things shall be added unto us"* (Mat. 6:33).

"Her house" refers to her relatives and, possibly, even her friends. No matter how much meal she took out of the barrel or how much oil was taken from the cruse, as much or more remained. Once again, please allow me to state that this is a Law of God, which applies even now, at least, for those who will dare to believe Him.

Having received a Prophet in the name of a Prophet, she received a Prophet's reward (Mat. 10:41-42).

THUS SAYS THE LORD

The Lord now gives Elijah a new mission. His time at Cherith is over. Incidentally, it is not known as to exactly where Cherith actually was. Some believe it could have been near the Dead Sea or, in other words, approximately where Joshua crossed the Jordan; however, that is speculation at best. The Prophet is now to go to *"Zarephath, which belonged to Zidon, and dwell there."* It is believed that this city was between Tyre and Sidon, actually, on the shore of the Mediterranean. This means that the Prophet was in the very heart of the dominions of the heathen idol Eth-baal. As stated, this was a Gentile city. For sure, Elijah had no desire to go to this Gentile place, but this is where the Lord said to go.

How so very much we as Christians sometimes limit God, and, most of the time, we limit Him because of *"religion."* For instance, Elijah's *"religion"* would not have allowed him to be fed by a *"raven,"* which was an unclean bird. Now, he must go to Zarephath, which is a Gentile city and, as well, forbidden. In all of this, the Lord would attempt to teach Elijah a lesson. It would not be easily learned.

None of this was actually against the Law of Moses, but it could be said, even at that early date, they were *"fence laws."* At any rate, these things were not something that a devout Israelite would be inclined to do. However, the Lord had given command to Elijah, and Elijah would obey.

"Thus says the LORD," is getting harder and harder to come by at this present time. However, even as the Lord did Elijah, He still continues to lead and guide His People, that is, if we are close enough to Him to hear His Voice.

GOD'S METHODS

God's Methods aren't our methods. When we think of being sustained by someone, we certainly don't think of a poor widow woman who is starving and, in fact, prepared to die because of starvation. But yet, this is the one chosen by the Lord who would sustain the Prophet. He said, *"Behold, I have commanded a widow woman there to sustain you."*

The Lord told the Prophet exactly what to do.

After he knew that this was the one chosen by God, he would ask for *"a little water in a vessel, that I may drink."*

There is some evidence in the Text that this widow woman knew that Elijah was a Prophet. Whether she had ever heard of him is not known. At any rate, she knew that this was not just an ordinary man.

However, there is one thing here that she certainly did not know, and that was what was about to happen to her, her son, and, in fact, her future. She could never realize, at least, at this moment, that her whole world was about to change. Her story would be written in the Sacred Writ, which would inspire untold millions down through the ages, all because of her Faith.

In her destitute condition, she could easily have rebuffed the Prophet when he asked for water, but she didn't! She hastened to do what he requested. When she was gone to get the water, the Lord whispered to the Prophet that he was to say to her, *"Bring me, I pray you, a morsel of bread in your hand."* While Elijah did not know of her destitute condition, at least, not at this moment, it is for sure that the Lord did.

WHY DID THE LORD CHOOSE THIS PARTICULAR WOMAN?

Every evidence was that she was a Gentile, which means that she had no part in the great Covenant that God had with Israel. In fact, she was or, at least, had been, an idol-worshipper and lived in the very heart of idol country. There is some evidence, however, that she had heard of Jehovah, but she would have had no way of having further knowledge, at least, not at this time.

The Scripture is silent concerning this, so we can only conjecture; however, this one thing we do know, God, as stated, never works capriciously. He always knows exactly what He is doing and has a reason behind everything He does. This we do know:

The one thing that God always honors, irrespective as to whom the person might be, is *"Faith."* Whether this woman, in her destitute position, had finally determined that her idols could afford her nothing, and she had prayed to Jehovah, we have no way of knowing. Maybe it was only that God knew that she would respond favorably and, therefore, selected her.

Whatever the reason, we do know that Faith played a great part. Despite her being a Gentile and despite her destitute condition, this woman would evidence Faith. Let it ever be understood, Faith is the coin that spends in God's Economy and, in fact, the only coin that spends in His Economy.

THE GREAT STEP OF FAITH

As the great Prophet asked for *"a morsel of bread,"* her answer is somewhat revealing. She said, *"As the LORD your God lives, I have not a cake, but a handful of meal in a barrel, and a little oil in a cruse."* Then she said, *"I am gathering two sticks, that I may go in and dress it for me and my son, that we may eat it, and die."*

If it is to be noticed, she said, *"As the LORD your God lives. . . ."* She didn't say, *"My God,"* but rather, *"Your God."* This further tells us that she was a Gentile and, therefore, an idol-worshipper.

In response to her answer, the Prophet lays out a test of Faith for her exactly as the Lord always does. He said unto her, *"Fear not; go and do as you have said: but make me thereof a little cake first, and bring it unto me, and after make for you and for your son."*

THE BARREL OF MEAL SHALL NOT WASTE, NEITHER SHALL THE CRUSE OF OIL FAIL

Then, attached to the request was a gargantuan Promise. The great Prophet said, *"For thus says the LORD God of Israel. . . ."*

This proclaimed, in no uncertain terms, that her idols, in fact, all the idols worshipped in this Gentile land, could not perform a Miracle and could not do anything. So, by the statement used, the Prophet is saying, *"The LORD God of Israel"* can do anything.

Then he said, *"The barrel of meal shall not waste, neither shall the cruse of oil fail, until the day that the LORD sends rain upon the Earth."*

So, there it was, laid out before her.

Would she believe the Prophet, whom she had never seen before, and do as he requested, or would she rebuke him for asking for her last morsel of bread?

This was truly a step of Faith for her. She did not know Jehovah. She did not know His Word. She knew little, if anything, of His Prophet, and he was asking her to give him the bread that she and her son were to eat.

A TEST OF FAITH

God always tests our Faith. What will we do? What will our reaction be? I'm afraid that all too often, we fail the test.

All this woman had to do was simply believe what the Prophet said. Would she believe him, or would she not believe him?

What would you have done?

The Scripture says, *"And she went and did according to the saying of Elijah."* In other words, she believed what the man said, irrespective as to how preposterous it surely seemed at that hour.

What did he mean, *"The barrel of meal shall not waste, neither shall the cruse of oil fail?"*

She had no way of knowing exactly what it did mean. However, one thing she did know, she couldn't lose by accepting the Prophet's proposal. If she had selfishly kept the bread for her and her son, she only had enough for one tiny meal, and then she would stare death in the face. Let's say the same for all.

No one ever has anything to lose by obeying the Lord. In fact, one simply cannot lose by obeying the Lord. As well, I believe that this great Promise given to this widow woman so long ago is still appropriate for us at this present time. I believe the Holy Spirit is saying to you and me and, in fact, every Believer who has ever lived, *"The barrel of meal shall not waste, neither shall the cruse of oil fail."*

God's Word cannot lie. Unless it is specifically meant for a certain person, a certain time, and a certain place, as sometimes it is, then it is appropriate for us to accept that which He gave so long ago and apply it to our own situation presently. God will honor it now just as much as He honored it then.

OBEDIENCE

When she obeyed, evidently, she also invited the great Prophet to stay with her and her son. This means that her house was apparently large enough to accommodate him.

When it was time for the next meal, she went and looked in the barrel and the cruse, and, lo and behold, even though she had emptied it the day before, there was meal in the barrel and oil in the cruse.

Some have attempted to claim that God supplied the need in various ways, trying to explain away the miraculous appearance and continued supply of the meal and the oil. However, I think the Hebrew Text readily proclaims the fact that it happened exactly as the Prophet said it would happen. When she took meal out of the barrel and oil out of the cruse, more meal and more oil miraculously took the place of that which had been taken. In fact, this is God's Way.

HAMILTON'S LAW

There is a law referred to as *"Hamilton's law,"* which states that for everything that we make, build, or perfect, at the same time, some things are depleted. In other words, when a house is built, trees are depleted in order to secure the lumber, with sand depleted in order that brick can be made, etc. That is true!

However, with God, there is never any depletion. He does not destroy something in order to build something. He miraculously supplies it, whatever it might be, as He here did.

Furthermore, the Scripture says, *"And she, and he* (Elijah), *and her house* (all her relatives and friends), *did eat many days."*

The famine was sore in the land and, no doubt, word

quickly got around that this woman had a supply that was unexplainable. She probably had many guests for breakfast, lunch, and dinner, but it didn't matter how many were there, how many sat around the table, or how many partook. The Scripture says, *"And the barrel of meal wasted not, neither did the cruse of oil fail, according to the Word of the LORD, which He spoke by Elijah."*

THE WORD AND THE HOLY SPIRIT

One might well say, also, that the *"meal"* represents the Word of God while the *"oil"* represents the Holy Spirit.

Our Lord, through His Sacrificial, Atoning Death at Calvary's Cross, has made it possible for us to have His Word and for the Holy Spirit to come in to abide within our lives constantly, even forever (Jn. 14:16-17). Those are the three things we cannot do without:

1. The Lord Jesus Christ, Who made all of this possible through His Death at Calvary.

2. The Word of God, typified by the meal, is the single most important thing on the face of the entire Earth. It is that because it is *"the Word of God."* Nothing else equals it, and nothing else even remotely compares with it. Jesus said, *"Man shall not live by bread alone, but by every Word that proceeds out of the Mouth of God"* (Mat. 4:4).

3. The moment we gave our hearts to Christ, the Holy Spirit, with the Power of Regeneration, came into our hearts and lives, and He came there to stay. Now we were ready to be baptized with the Holy Spirit with the evidence of speaking with other Tongues. He will guide us into all Truth. He will take of that which belongs to the Lord and show it unto us. He will give us Power to overcome the powers of darkness. The Holy Spirit is God!

ANOTHER TEST OF FAITH

"And it came to pass after these things, that the son of the

woman, the mistress of the house, fell sick; and his sickness was so sore, that there was no breath left in him.

"And she said unto Elijah, What have I to do with you, O you Man of God? are you come unto me to call my sin to remembrance, and to kill my son?

"And he said unto her, Give me your son. And he took him out of her bosom, and carried him up into a loft, where he abode, and laid him upon his own bed.

"And he cried unto the LORD, and said, O LORD my God, have You also brought evil upon the widow with whom I sojourn, by killing her son?

"And he stretched himself upon the child three times, and cried unto the LORD, and said, O LORD my God, I pray You, let this child's soul come into him again.

"And the LORD heard the voice of Elijah; and the soul of the child came into him again, and he revived.

"And Elijah took the child, and brought him down out of the chamber into the house, and delivered him unto his mother: and Elijah said, See, your son lives.

"And the woman said to Elijah, Now by this I know that you are a Man of God, and that the Word of the LORD in your mouth is truth" (I Ki. 17:17-24).

A MIRACLE

Whenever the Lord moves mightily, as He did here, Satan will then attack. This means that the second trial of Faith is sometimes harder than the first trial. However, please remember: all of it, irrespective of the course it might take, is a test of our Faith.

Elijah laid the corpse upon his own bed. Why did the Prophet take the boy to his own personal room afforded him by the widow? It was done as a token to show that his presence in her house was definitely a Blessing and not a curse. In his prayer, Elijah proclaims the fact that God controls all things, especially life and death.

The request, *"Let this child's soul come into him again,"* proves that the boy was dead. Why *"three times"*? The Lord evidently told him to do this. It actually had nothing to do with the Miracle which transpired, but was rather to symbolically portray the Triune God—*"God the Father," "God the Son,"* and *"God the Holy Spirit."*

Death had been suspended by and through the barrel of meal and the cruse of oil not failing, and now, again, it had been suspended by being miraculously dismissed (Jn. 10:10). The statement made by the woman, as given in Verse 24, presents a statement of Faith far greater than the present Miracle: this Gentile woman was exclaiming the fact that Israel's God was now her God.

DEATH!

Why did the Lord allow the child to get sick and die? This woman had obeyed the Lord in doing exactly what He wanted, but now her child dies.

Death is a terrible enemy and is prevalent because of the Fall. All must eventually die, but it is so sad to see the young who have to die!

Evidently, this child, who must have been a preteen, was all that the woman had. If she lost him, there was nothing left. One can well imagine how much she loved the little boy.

Now, he was dead!

By her statements, she seems to want to blame God, the same One Who miraculously supplied the meal and the oil, but she seems to be fearful of doing that. So, in a sense, she blames Elijah.

O YOU MAN OF GOD

Her question, *"What have I to do with you?"* in essence, says, *"Why have you done me this way?"* She then adds, *"O you Man of God."* Even though she cannot explain the present situation concerning her son, beyond the shadow of a doubt, she does know that Elijah is *"a Man of God."* This means that as something was done about the barrel of meal and the cruse of oil, likewise, something, she believes, can be done for her son.

There is a great lesson to be learned from all of this. God works through men and women, in this case, Elijah. When the Man of God is accepted, God, at the same time, is accepted. When the Man of God, whomever he might be, is rejected, at the same time, God is rejected. We seem to be slow in learning this great lesson. To be sure, this woman had accepted Elijah in totality! By taking the problem to him, severe as it was, as should be obvious, she, in effect, was taking it to the Lord.

YOUR SON LIVES!

Elijah prayed and God answered! Any dead raised by the Power of God was to show that the Lord is able to suspend death. Each case, as well, was a portent of the coming Resurrection.

"Since my soul is Saved and sanctified,
"Feasting, I'm feasting,
"In this land of Canaan I'll abide,
"Feasting with my Lord."

"Feeding on the honey and the wine,
"Feasting, I'm feasting,
"Gathering the clusters from the vine,
"Feasting with my Lord."

"Day by day we have a new supply,
"Feasting, I'm feasting,
"And the food is never stale nor dry,
"Feasting with my Lord."

"Many times we have an extra spread,
"Feasting, I'm feasting,

"Then to deeper truths I have been led,
"Feasting with my Lord."

"Often there are only just us two,
"Feasting, I'm feasting,
"Then He tells me what He will have me do,
"Feasting with my Lord."

"If perchance the cupboard's scarce of drink,
"Feasting, I'm feasting,
"On the hidden manna I am fed,
"Feasting with my Lord."

Great Women of the Bible

OLD TESTAMENT

Chapter Thirteen

ESTHER
The Wife Of The King

ESTHER
The Wife Of The King

INTRODUCTION

Concerning the Book in the Bible which bears the name of Esther, queen of the Persian Empire, we find Israel under a just Judgment by God, with Gentiles now given the preeminence. Not much short of 60 years before, the scepter of power had fallen from the faltering hands of the kings of Judah and was now in the hands of the Gentiles, referred to by our Lord as *"the times of the Gentiles"* (Lk. 21:24). Beginning with Nebuchadnezzar, monarch of the great Babylonian Empire, that scepter of power has remained in the hands of Gentiles and today is held in the hands of the United States. The responsibility of this power delegated by God is awesome indeed! Of all the many directions it entails, without a doubt, the protection of Israel is foremost. If that is rightly done, the problems facing this nation presently, such as the economic dilemma, etc., will somehow be solved. At the time of Esther becoming queen, that scepter of power rested in the hands of the Babylonians but would soon pass to the Persians. That is ironic considering that Iran, which was the seat of the ancient Persian Empire, is now a bitter enemy of Israel.

THE FEAST

"Now it came to pass in the days of Ahasuerus, (this is Ahasuerus who reigned, from India even unto Ethiopia, over an hundred and seven and twenty provinces:)

"That in those days, when the king Ahasuerus sat on the throne of his kingdom, which was in Shushan the palace,

"In the third year of his reign, he made a feast unto all his princes and his servants; the power of Persia and Media, the nobles and princes of the provinces, being before him:

"When he showed the riches of his glorious kingdom and the

honor of his excellent majesty many days, even an hundred and fourscore days.

"And when these days were expired, the king made a feast unto all the people who were present in Shushan the palace, both unto great and small, seven days, in the court of the garden of the king's palace;

"Where were white, green, and blue, hangings, fastened with cords of fine linen and purple to silver rings and pillars of marble: the beds were of gold and silver, upon a pavement of red, and blue, and white, and black, marble.

"And they gave them drink in vessels of gold, (the vessels being diverse one from another,) and royal wine in abundance, according to the state of the king.

"And the drinking was according to the law; none did compel: for so the king had appointed to all the officers of his house, that they should do according to every man's pleasure.

"Also Vashti the queen made a feast for the women in the royal house which belonged to king Ahasuerus" (Esther 1:1-9).

AHASUERUS

Ahasuerus is a kingly title and could have applied, and no doubt did, to several individuals at given times.

The Book of Esther presents to the reader the captives of Israel scattered among the Gentiles under the just Judgment of Hosea, Chapter 1, Verse 9, and, yet, loved and cared for in secret by God. Being *"Lo-ammi,"* the Lord could not publicly recognize Israel. That recognition could only be given to the Gentiles to whom the Lord had committed supreme power. Without revoking the Judgment pronounced through the Prophet Hosea, the Lord secretly watched over them and without displaying Himself, shaped public affairs in their interests.

They had lost all title to His Protection and, therefore, it is an extremely important and comforting study to observe in the Book of Esther how the Lord's Hidden Hand prepared and directed everything for a people, in themselves unlovely, but beloved for the Father's Sake. Hence, the Holy Spirit, with design, is careful not to let the Name of God appear in the Book, though it lies concealed in the Hebrew Text. As well, the absence, therefore, of that Name is a great encouragement to Faith, for the argument and the lesson which its omission conveys is that behind the visible events of history, there is an Almighty and Faithful Love that cherishes and protects the broken and scattered People of God.

Ahasuerus was soon to be the master of the world of that day. The position would be given to him by God even though he did not recognize such.

Many believe this particular Ahasuerus was Xerxes. This festivity listed in Verse 3 lasted for some six months. It was for men only. Vashti the queen also conducted a particular feast for women only.

THE POWER OF PERSIA AND MEDIA

The time of Esther was a few years before the Medo-Persian Empire overthrew Babylon. It is not known how that Mordecai and Esther got to Shushan and the palace in Persia, considering that they were taken captive by Nebuchadnezzar and that Babylon did not rule the Persian Empire. However, later we will see how all of this worked out according to the Plan of God. Men rule but God overrules. From the time of Esther until the Medes and the Persians would overthrow the Babylonian Empire would be approximately 17 years.

A little over 30 years before, Daniel had prophesied that the Medo-Persian Empire would overthrow Babylon. He said, *"And behold another beast, a second, like to a bear, and it raised up itself on one side, and it had three ribs in the mouth of it between the teeth of it: and they said thus unto it, Arise, devour much flesh"* (Dan. 7:5).

On the statue of Chapter 2 of Daniel, which concerns the dream had by Nebuchadnezzar, the Medo-Persian Empire was represented by a breastplate of silver. The statue, as seen in Nebuchadnezzar's dream, represented these kingdoms as man sees them. The dream given to Daniel represents these kingdoms as God sees them, i.e., *"ferocious."*

The term, *"Raised up itself on one side,"* simply means that the strength of the Persians ultimately was greater than the Medes. The three ribs in the mouth of it between the teeth refer to the bear devouring much flesh. The three ribs symbolized the conquest of Babylon, Lydia, and Egypt.

SOME OF THE LESSONS TAUGHT
IN THE BOOK OF ESTHER

• God's Continued Love and Compassion for a people who had long since forsaken Him.

• Even in the midst of a backslidden people, there are those with the Faith of a Mordecai and Esther.

• Even though in exile and, therefore, in captivity, God still heard and answered prayer for those who would believe in His Great Name.

• Even though the Plan of God for His People was delayed, it was not halted, only interrupted.

• Despite the failure of man, God cannot fail, has never failed, and, in fact, never will fail.

• Behind the visible events of history, there is an Almighty and Faithful God Who is shaping events to suit His Purpose and His Will.

• Even those who are evil are made to do His Will in order that His Great Plan, whatever that is, may be carried out even though, most of the time, they are unaware of His Hand.

• As in the case of Mordecai and Esther, irrespective of circumstances, God can bring victory out of disaster if we show Faith in His Great Name.

• We find that men rule, but, at the same time, God over-rules.

• Mordecai and Esther being taken to the Persian court would ultimately figure prominently in the Jews going back to the Holy Land after some 70 years of dispersion.

• While God is never the cause of wrongdoing, not in any fashion, still, He does use events, whatever they might be, to bring about His Will.

In this instance, a king would get drunk and would make immoral demands of his queen. While the Lord was not the author of any of this, He did use this moment in history to further His Cause, which would ultimately mean the freedom of His People at the exact time so prophesied.

What a Mighty God we serve!

VASHTI THE QUEEN

"On the seventh day, when the heart of the king was merry with wine, he commanded Mehuman, Biztha, Harbona, Bigtha, and Abagtha, Zethar, and Carcas, the seven chamberlains who served in the presence of Ahasuerus the king,

"To bring Vashti the queen before the king with the crown royal, to show the people and the princes her beauty: for she was fair to look on.

"But the queen Vashti refused to come at the king's commandment by his chamberlains: therefore was the king very wroth, and his anger burned in him" (Esther 1:10-12).

Little did the king realize at this time when he sent for Queen Vashti that the events which followed would literally influence the entirety of the world for all time, all orchestrated by God. This doesn't mean that God forced such action but that He took advantage of that which happened. God never overrides man's free moral agency.

As well, the queen's refusal to obey the king would play a great part in all of this, all to further the Plan of God.

Let us say it again because it is so very important. While the Lord does not orchestrate events if they include wrongdoing or evil of any nature, to be sure, He most definitely does orchestrate His Use of these events, whatever the events might be, exactly as He did as it regards Esther. All of these people, both good and bad, become but tools in the Hand of God. We must never forget that!

WHAT SHALL WE DO WITH QUEEN VASHTI?

"Then the king said to the wise men, who knew the times, (for so was the king's manner toward all who knew law and judgment:

"And the next unto him was Carshena, Shethar, Admatha, Tarshish, Meres, Marsena, and Memucan, the seven princes of Persia and Media, who saw the king's face, and who sat the first in the kingdom;)

"What shall we do unto the queen Vashti according to law, because she has not performed the commandment of the king Ahasuerus by the chamberlains?

"And Memucan answered before the king and the princes, Vashti the queen has not done wrong to the king only, but also to all the princes, and to all the people who are in all the provinces of the king Ahasuerus.

"For this deed of the queen shall come abroad unto all women, so that they shall despise their husbands in their eyes, when it shall be reported, The king Ahasuerus commanded Vashti the queen to be brought in before him, but she came not.

"Likewise shall the ladies of Persia and Media say this day unto all the king's princes, who have heard of the deed of the queen. Thus shall there arise too much contempt and wrath.

"If it please the king, let there go a royal commandment from him, and let it be written among the laws of the Persians and the Medes, that it be not altered, That Vashti come no more before king Ahasuerus; and let the king give her royal estate unto another who is better than she.

"And when the king's decree which he shall make shall be published throughout all his empire, (for it is great,) all the wives shall give to their husbands honor, both to great and small.

"And the saying pleased the king and the princes; and the king did according to the word of Memucan:

"For he sent letters into all the king's provinces, into every province according to the writing thereof, and to every people after their language, that every man should bear rule in his own house, and that it should be published according to the language of every people" (Esther 1:13-22).

THE COMMAND OF THE KING

The *"law and judgment"* of Verse 13 was *"the law of the Medes and the Persians."*

These seven princes named in the Text seem to have had access to the monarch at all times. From the reply of Memucan of Verse 16, we realize that there was no Persian law which provided for a penalty for such a case. The idea seems to be that they would now make up a law, which, of course, was unjust.

However, even though the Lord did not cause these events to take place, He most definitely did take advantage of the events, even as we shall see.

EVENTS WHICH FALL INTO
THE HANDS OF THE LORD

The question begs to be asked as to what the Lord would have done had these events not taken place.

That is a valid question as it regards human beings; however, it's not a valid question as it regards the Lord, Who is able to do anything. In other words, there are always events transpiring, of whatever stripe, which the Lord can use to further His Own Purposes and Design. As we have previously stated, He never violates anyone's free moral agency and, in fact, will not do so. Being God, Who is Omnipotent and Omniscient, as well as Omnipresent, He can do anything. Jesus plainly said, *". . . With men this is impossible; but with God all things are possible"* (Mat. 19:26).

The king is going to choose another queen, and this will be the opportunity for the Lord to work.

THE SEARCH FOR A QUEEN

"After these things, when the wrath of king Ahasuerus was appeased, he remembered Vashti, and what she had done, and what was decreed against her.

"Then said the king's servants who ministered unto him, Let there be fair young virgins sought for the king:

"And let the king appoint officers in all the provinces of his kingdom, that they may gather together all the fair young virgins unto Shushan the palace, to the house of the women, unto the custody of Hege the king's chamberlain, keeper of the women; and let their things for purification be given them:

"And let the maiden who pleases the king be queen instead of Vashti. And the thing pleased the king; and he did so" (Esther 2:1-4).

The idea seems to be that the king somewhat regretted what he had done concerning Vashti; however, the die was now cast, and he must follow through.

As stated, they didn't have a law in the kingdom covering this, so they had to devise a law, which they did.

A new queen would now be chosen, with the Lord maneuvering Esther into this position.

This position would be extremely important because the son that would be born to Esther and Ahasuerus, Darius by name, would be raised, many believe, in the fear of God and would be instrumental in helping the Jews go back to the Holy Land. What a Mighty God we serve!

MORDECAI AND ESTHER

"Now in Shushan the palace there was a certain Jew, whose name was Mordecai, the son of Jair, the son of Shimei, the son of Kish, a Benjamite;

"Who had been carried away from Jerusalem with the captivity which had been carried away with Jeconiah king of Judah, whom Nebuchadnezzar the king of Babylon had carried away.

"And he brought up Hadassah, that is, Esther, his uncle's daughter: for she had neither father nor mother, and the maid was fair and beautiful; whom Mordecai, when her father and mother were dead, took for his own daughter.

"So it came to pass, when the king's commandment and his decree was heard, and when many maidens were gathered together unto Shushan the palace, to the custody of Hegai, that Esther was brought also unto the king's house, to the custody of the Hegai, keeper of the women.

"And the maiden pleased him, and she obtained kindness of him; and he speedily gave her her things for purification, with such things as belonged to her, and seven maidens, which were meet to be given her, out of the king's house: and he preferred her and her maids unto the best place of the house of the women.

"Esther had not showed her people nor her kindred: for Mordecai had charged her that she should not show it.

"And Mordecai walked every day before the court of the women's house, to know how Esther did, and what should become of her" (Esther 2:5-11).

THE DEPORTATIONS

Mordecai was with Nehemiah, an exile in Shushan. He held a high position in the palace. At the same time, Daniel was exiled in Babylon, about 200 miles due west of Shushan, with Ezekiel exiled in some other part of Babylonia, of which the exact location is unknown.

• The first deportation of certain individuals from Jerusalem was carried out by Nebuchadnezzar in 605 B.C. Daniel was among this group.

• The second deportation included Mordecai, Esther, and Nehemiah, which took place in 597 B.C.

• The third deportation took place in 586 B.C., and Jerusalem was then burned and the Temple completely destroyed—all under Nebuchadnezzar.

Whether Mordecai formally adopted Esther is not known.

However, it is known that he took her to live with him and treated her as if she had been his own child. From this, we know that the man was kindly and benevolent. Evidently, because of Esther's beauty, she was chosen, among many others, as a possible choice to be the new queen. Esther did not at this time divulge that she was Jewish. This was instruction given to her, as stated, by Mordecai.

MORDECAI

Approximately four years would elapse between the rejection of Vashti and the selection of Esther. Now, Mordecai comes on the scene. He is a Benjamite, meaning from the Tribe of Benjamin.

Haman, who was an Amalekite and who will come on the scene shortly, was a descendant of Agag, the king of the Amalekites. Mordecai, as stated, was a Benjamite, a descendant of Saul, who had been king of the Israelites many years before. In fact, Haman's death ended God's War with Amalek, one which had waged several centuries. So, Mordecai did what Saul failed to do (Ex. 17:16; I Sam., Chpt. 15).

Mordecai held a high position in the government, with some claiming that he was a finance officer. He, as we shall see, will figure prominently in the Plan of God, proving to be a man of great Faith and sagacity. In other words, he proved to be one of God's Champions.

ESTHER

Esther was Mordecai's own first cousin, although probably much younger than he. She had lost her father and mother, by what means, we do not know, with Mordecai taking her *"for his own daughter."*

In her own way, Esther will prove to be one of the greatest Women of God recorded in the Word of God. She will be used mightily by the Lord, never for one moment, it seems from the

Sacred Text, allowing her place and position as the first lady of the mighty Persian Empire to take her away from her real mission.

As Joseph would become the second most powerful man in the world, serving as the prime minister, so to speak, under Pharaoh, likewise, Esther would become the first lady of the might Persian Empire. Only God could do such a thing! Only the Lord could orchestrate events in this fashion! Again, what a Mighty God we serve!

The Scripture says that Esther was *"fair and beautiful."* In any case, she was selected among scores of other young ladies from the Persian Empire. They were all brought to *"Shushan the palace,"* where one of them would be selected. Of course, Esther already lived in the capital city, with her uncle, as stated, holding a high place in government.

At any rate, Esther evidently made an excellent impression upon *"Hegai,"* who was in charge of the women, in other words, of this entire procedure. The Scripture says, *"She obtained kindness of him; and he speedily gave her her things for purification,"* whatever that meant.

THE PURIFICATION OF THE WOMEN

"Now when every maid's turn was come to go in to king Ahasuerus, after that she had been twelve months, according to the manner of the women, (for so were the days of their purifications accomplished, to wit, six months with oil of myrrh, and six months with sweet odors, and with other things for the purifying of the women;)

"Then thus came every maiden unto the king; whatsoever she desired was given her to go with her out of the house of the women unto the king's house.

"In the evening she went, and on the morrow she returned into the second house of the women, to the custody of Shaashgaz, the king's chamberlain, who kept the concubines: she came in unto the king no more, except the king delighted in her, and that she was called by name.

"Now when the turn of Esther, the daughter of Abihail the uncle of Mordecai, who had taken her for his daughter, was come to go in unto the king, she required nothing but what Hegai the king's chamberlain, the keeper of the women, appointed. And Esther obtained favor in the sight of all them who looked upon her.

"So Esther was taken unto king Ahasuerus into his house royal in the tenth month, which is the month Tebeth, in the seventh year of his reign.

"And the king loved Esther above all the women, and she obtained grace and favor in his sight more than all the virgins; so that he set the royal crown upon her head, and made her queen instead of Vashti.

"Then the king made a great feast unto all his princes and his servants, even Esther's feast; and he made a release to the provinces, and gave gifts, according to the state of the king" (Esther 2:12-18).

THE MANNER OF ESTHER

A year's purification was considered necessary before any maiden could approach the king. Any maiden who would be queen was entitled to demand anything that she liked in the way of dress or ornaments, and it had to be given her so that she might look her best, or what she thought was her best.

Esther would not trust to ostentatious dress or ornaments but would leave it up to Hegai as to what she should wear, which, evidently, portrayed her natural beauty. Esther, over all the other women, was chosen to be queen of the mighty Persian Empire. Thus, in the Providence of God and by His Overruling of human folly, she was seated upon the throne. This was at the very time that Satan made a supreme effort to destroy every member of the Tribe of Judah in particular, and the Israelites in general, so as to make impossible the advent of the Promised Redeemer.

Satan was defeated by the hidden Hand of God. The

Judgment threatened in Deuteronomy 31:16-18—*"I will hide My Face"*—came to pass. However, though Israel proved faithless to Him, the Lord abode faithful to her, for He could not deny Himself and, though He hid Himself, yet was the Lord's Care over them as real as ever. Due to the selection of the new queen, the king ordered a relaxation from taxes for a short period of time.

ESTHER CHOSEN TO BE QUEEN

No matter how beautiful she might have been, the chances in that day of a young Jewish girl becoming queen of the mightiest empire on the face of the Earth were astronomically small. In fact, but for God, it would have been absolutely impossible.

As we have said, while the Lord in no way staged these events, meaning that He did not cause the king and his cohorts to get drunk and to demand certain immoral things of the woman who was then his queen, still, He most definitely did take advantage of the situation.

At the same time, the Lord most definitely did put the thought in the minds of those around the king as to how a new queen would be chosen. Young virgins would be chosen from all over the kingdom, no doubt, because of their beauty, and the king would make the choice as to which one would replace Vashti. Esther was in that group.

These women, whomever they might have been, could adorn themselves, as stated, with anything they so desired, which included jewels of every description and anything else. The Scripture says that Esther *"required nothing but what Hegai the king's chamberlain, the keeper of the women, appointed."* This, no doubt, referred to the purification process only, as was outlined in Verse 12.

As Esther stood before the king that day, her natural beauty did shine forth, which made her stand out above and beyond all the other young women who stood before the king. The Scripture says, *"And Esther obtained favor in the sight of all them who looked upon her."*

She was chosen above all the other young maidens of the Medo-Persian Empire to be the queen of that great kingdom.

MORDECAI SAVED THE KING'S LIFE

"And when the virgins were gathered together the second time, then Mordecai sat in the king's gate.

"Esther had not yet shown her kindred nor her people; as Mordecai had charged her: for Esther did the commandment of Mordecai, like as when she was brought up with him.

"In those days, while Mordecai sat in the king's gate, two of the king's chamberlains, Bigthan and Teresh, of those who kept the door, were wroth, and sought to lay hands on the king Ahasuerus.

"And the thing was known to Mordecai, who told it unto Esther the queen; and Esther certified the king thereof in Mordecai's name.

"And when inquisition was made of the matter, it was found out; therefore they were both hanged on a tree: and it was written in the book of the chronicles before the king" (Esther 2:19-23).

Mordecai sitting in the king's gate signified that he had a place of position and authority in the realm of government.

Despite the fact that Esther was now queen, she still heeded the counsel of Mordecai as always, and rightly so! As it regards Mordecai uncovering the plot by two of the king's chamberlains who were going to kill the monarch, Josephus says that a certain man by the name of Pharnabazus, a slave of one of the conspirators, betrayed them to Mordecai.

Esther revealed to the king that Mordecai had relayed to her this information, which would save the king's life.

THE HAND OF GOD

Whatever type of plot it was to kill the king, the Lord orchestrated events so that it was revealed to Mordecai who, in turn, revealed the information to the necessary authorities, which saved the king's life. Strangely enough, it seems that nothing was done at that time to recognize Mordecai for his part in saving the king's life. The Lord worked that as well.

I think we Believers do not fully understand the degree to which the Lord guides events as it respects our life and living. That goes for all the Saints, even the least of us, whomever that might be. Every Believer understands this according to the degree of his or her relationship with the Lord.

To establish proper relationship, every Believer ought to have a proper prayer life. We must take everything to the Lord, and I mean everything, be it little or large. At the same time, we must trust the Lord, believing that He will guide us in all things, and that He is orchestrating events in our favor. We as Believers, even the most enlightened of us, have little understanding as to the future, while the Lord knows everything. We must understand that He desires to bless us and desires to have control of our lives; however, it's control that we must favorably give Him because He will not forcibly take such control. Paul said:

> "And we know that all things work together for good *(but only if certain conditions are met)* to them who love God *(the first condition)*, to them who are the called according to His Purpose *(this means it's 'His Purpose, and not ours,' which is the second condition; otherwise, all things will not work together for our good)*" (Rom. 8:28).

WHAT PART DID MORDECAI AND ESTHER PLAY IN THIS SCENARIO?

Of course, we know that Mordecai and Esther had absolutely nothing to do with the king's drunken revelry, which caused him to reject his queen, Vashti, and which began this entire scenario. As well, we know that Mordecai and Esther had absolutely nothing to do with the manner in which the king would choose a new queen. And yet, whenever the news went out that the most beautiful young virgins in the kingdom were to be brought before the king, there is a possibility that Mordecai maneuvered Esther into this position. Evidence is that he had a high place in government and considering her beauty, he may very well have been impressed by the Holy Spirit to do this thing, although the Scripture is silent, only saying, *". . . and when many maidens were gathered together unto Shushan the palace, to the custody of Hegai, that Esther was brought also unto the king's house, to the custody of the Hegai, keeper of the women."*

At any rate, the Lord was in charge of this process from beginning to end, taking advantage of every situation that developed, even until Esther would be selected as queen. As we shall see, the Lord had much more in mind than just blessing this young lady and giving her one of the highest positions in the world. To be sure, the Lord always has much more in mind than we could ever begin to contemplate or think.

HAMAN

"After these things did king Ahasuerus promote Haman the son of Hammedatha the Agagite, and advanced him, and set his seat above all the princes who were with him.

"And all the king's servants, who were in the king's gate, bowed, and reverenced Haman: for the king had so commanded concerning him. But Mordecai bowed not, nor did him reverence.

"Then the king's servants, who were in the king's gate, said unto Mordecai, Why do you transgress the king's commandment?

"Now it came to pass, when they spoke daily unto him, and he hearkened not unto them, that they told Haman, to see whether Mordecai's matters would stand: for he had told them that he was a Jew.

"And when Haman saw that Mordecai bowed not, nor did him reverence, then was Haman full of wrath" (Esther 3:1-5).

THE AMALEKITE

It is believed that Haman was an Amalekite.

Prostration was, in the mind of Mordecai, an act of worship, and it was not proper to worship anyone except God (Rev. 22:9).

Mordecai explained to the palace officials that his not reverencing Haman was not due to discourtesy to Haman or disobedience to the king, but because he was a Hebrew. That is, he worshipped the One and Only True and Living God.

Refusal to bring this homage brought Daniel into the den of lions and the three princes into the fiery furnace. It may justly, therefore, be assumed from Mordecai's statement that he was a worthy companion of Daniel and the three Hebrew children. In fact, Haman, as stated, was an Amalekite. As such, he was an enemy of God, and Jehovah had sworn to have war with him forever (Ex. 17:16). God's Enemies were Mordecai's enemies, for Mordecai was a Servant of God. This fact representing Haman was an added reason that faithfulness to God demanded this seeming discourtesy to Haman.

HAMAN THE AGAGITE

It is believed that several years separated the events of Esther being chosen queen and this scenario regarding Haman.

We are given no information regarding Haman as it pertains to his rise to supremacy. Somehow, however, he had gained the favor of Ahasuerus and had been thusly given the second place in the kingdom. This means that every government official was placed under Haman. He had, in fact, become *"grand vizier or chief minister."*

In order to place Haman high in the eyes of all of the officials in the empire, it was commanded that all should bow down before him when in his presence, which we find was something that Mordecai could not do.

Why?

Mordecai was a Jew who served Jehovah Only and bowed to no man, at least, in the form of worship, which Haman demanded (Rev. 22:8-9).

The Bible says, *"And when Haman saw that Mordecai bowed not, nor did him reverence, then was Haman full of wrath."*

SATAN'S PLOT

"And he thought scorn to lay hands on Mordecai alone; for they had showed him the people of Mordecai: wherefore Haman sought to destroy all the Jews who were throughout the whole kingdom of Ahasuerus, even the people of Mordecai.

"In the first month, that is, the month Nisan, in the twelfth year of king Ahasuerus, they cast Pur, that is, the lot, before Haman from day to day, and from month to month, to the twelfth month, that is, the month Adar.

"And Haman said unto king Ahasuerus, There is a certain people scattered abroad and dispersed among the people in all the provinces of your kingdom; and their laws are diverse from all people; neither keep they the king's laws: therefore it is not for the king's profit to suffer them.

"If it please the king, let it be written that they may be destroyed: and I will pay ten thousand talents of silver to the hands of those who have the charge of the business, to bring it into the king's treasuries.

"And the king took his ring from his hand, and gave it unto Haman the son of Hammedatha the Agagite, the Jew's enemy.

"And the king said unto Haman, The silver is given to you, the people also, to do with them as it seems good to you" (Esther 3:6-11).

THE BIG LIE

In the mind of this evil man, Mordecai, as a Jew, had insulted him, and the Jews, and that meant all the Jews, would pay the penalty. That penalty was death!

Verse 7 does not mean that 12 months were employed in seeking, by means of the lot, a propitious day for the slaughter of the Jews. It means that the diviners (astrologers) sought for a favorable day, month by month, and, at last, chose the thirteenth day of the twelfth month as promising success, as outlined in Verse 13.

The basic thrust of Haman's claim was, pure and simple, a *"lie."* There might be an occasional royal edict which a Jew could not obey, but that was rare. Anyway, as long as it didn't hurt the kingdom, the Persians allowed all the conquered nations to retain their own laws and usages.

"Ten thousand talents of silver" would presently be worth in 2012 dollars approximately $360,000,000. This money was earmarked to give to those who killed Jews. Evidently, they would get so much for each Jew they killed. Sounds familiar, doesn't it?

The *"ring"* given by the king to Haman was, in essence, the royal seal, which gave Haman liberty to do about whatever he desired. All the property and wealth of the Jews, whatever it might have been, was to be the property of the state.

DESTROY ALL THE JEWS

From the very beginning of the Nation of Israel, as it began from the womb of Sarah and the loins of Abraham, Satan has tried to destroy these people, i.e., *"destroy the Jews."*

The Holocaust, with Hitler slaughtering some six million, was but the latest attempt. The latest threats by the present so-called leader of Iran are but a continuation of that which has ridden the crest of evil for some 4,000 years. The threat of the Iranian leader will not, regrettably, be the last. The greatest effort of all is to take place soon under the Antichrist, who will come very close to succeeding in *"destroying the Jews."* In fact, were it not for the Second Coming of the Lord, which will most assuredly take place, he would succeed. Jesus said this would be a worse time for the Jews than they had ever faced in the past and, thankfully, would never have to face such again (Mat. 24:21-22).

Why?

There are two major reasons for this animosity. They are:

TWO EVIL REASONS

1. The Jews were raised up as a Nation for the express purpose of giving the world the Word of God, of serving as the womb for the Messiah, and to evangelize the world. Despite their own foolishness and every effort of Satan to stop them from carrying out that which was ordained of God, they succeeded in the first two but, in a sense, failed miserably in the third, yet, in a sense, did succeed. Paul, of course, was Jewish and all of the Apostles, and they were the Evangelism, so to speak, of the Early Church. So, in a sense, even though the Nation of Israel was bitterly opposed to these men, they still established the Church and world Evangelism, as well, one might say.

Even though they did bring the Messiah into the world, sadly and regrettably, they crucified Him and have suffered horribly from that day until now.

2. The next reason is the place and position that Israel as a Nation is to occupy in the coming Kingdom Age, in which they will be the leading Nation of the world, but under Christ. In fact, before this can be brought to pass, Israel must recognize the Lord Jesus Christ as their Messiah, their Saviour, and their Lord, which they will do at the Second Coming (Zech., Chpts. 12-14).

While the enemies of Israel have been numerous down through the many centuries, especially during Bible times, her present nemesis is the religion of Islam and those who embrace that Antichrist system. It is the age-old conflict between Isaac and Ishmael and will not be settled until the Second Coming.

THE PLAN OF SATAN TO KILL EVERY JEW

"Then were the king's scribes called on the thirteenth day

of the first month, and there was written according to all that Haman had commanded unto the king's lieutenants, and to the governors who were over every province, and to the rulers of every people of every province according to the writing thereof, and to every people after their language; in the name of king Ahasuerus was it written, and sealed with the king's ring.

"And the letters were sent by posts into all the king's provinces, to destroy, to kill, and to cause to perish, all Jews, both young and old, little children and women, in one day, even upon the thirteenth day of the twelfth month, which is the month Adar, and to take the spoil of them for a prey.

"The copy of the writing for a commandment to be given in every province was published unto all people, that they should be ready against that day.

"The posts went out, being hastened by the king's commandment, and the decree was given in Shushan the palace. And the king and Haman sat down to drink; but the city Shushan was perplexed" (Esther 3:12-15).

TO ASSIGN AN ENTIRE PEOPLE TO DESTRUCTION

All edicts were in the king's name, even when a subject had been allowed to issue them, as Haman. The command was explicit; all Jews were to be killed. As stated, this was Satan's plan to destroy the possibility of the Messiah being born into the world, Who had to come through the Jewish people and more specifically, the Tribe of Judah (Gen. 49:10).

These two, the king and Haman, having assigned an entire people to destruction, proceeded to enjoy themselves at *"a banquet of wine"* (Esther 7:2).

The city of Susa being perplexed had to do with a widespread feeling among many of other nationalities that the precedent now being set was a dangerous one. They couldn't see the justice of this, not at all, and were thereby confused.

As well, almost every time in the Bible that we see alcoholic beverage being used, it is, as here, used in a negative sense.

Back in the Seventh Verse, it spoke of casting lots to see which would be the most favorable time to request the destruction of the Jews. The month chosen by this wicked prognostication (witchcraft) would be April; the day would be the thirteenth.

Satan's plan seemed to be foolproof. The money was appropriated. The letters had the seal of the king. God's People would be destroyed; however, God always writes the final Chapter to any and every book. He will write this final Chapter as well.

MORDECAI

"When Mordecai perceived all that was done, Mordecai rent his clothes, and put on sackcloth with ashes, and went out into the midst of the city, and cried with a loud and a bitter cry;

"And came even before the king's gate: for none might enter into the king's gate clothed with sackcloth.

"And in every province, whithersoever the king's commandment and his decree came, there was great mourning among the Jews, and fasting, and weeping, and wailing; and many lay in sackcloth and ashes" (Esther 4:1-3).

THE STATE OF GOD'S PEOPLE

Due to his manner of dress, Mordecai was not allowed to pass through the gate into the palace. To do what Mordecai had done could be punishable by death. At any rate, God would even use this event, as we will see momentarily.

Mordecai will now do what all godly men do in time of trouble, fast and pray. While the Scripture doesn't exactly say that they prayed, it is obvious they did. Regrettably, the modern church little seeks the Face of God anymore. Rather, it leans on the frail arm of flawed man.

Satan was now swinging his plan into action. The decree by the king had been made. All Jews must die, women and children included. Despite Israel's sin and even their being held in captivity, still, they were God's Chosen People. The Mission that God had outlined for them to bring the Messiah into the world had not changed and would not change, *"For the Gifts and Calling of God are without Repentance"* (Rom. 11:29). Regardless, Satan, with his relentless efforts, would continue to seek their destruction. He is still doing the same thing presently.

This king obviously was not one of the wisest men to have graced that throne. To have allowed himself to be placed in this position, the position of killing an entire nationality of people, was, as would be obvious, senseless! To do this because one of his henchmen, Haman, claimed to be offended was to drive the stake of stupidity even deeper.

It should be obvious that some of the greatest contributors to his kingdom were Jews, and now he proposed to kill them all. However, the evidence seems to be that he was not aware that his queen was Jewish, or Mordecai, one of his most trusted lieutenants. But, Jewish they were, and under the executioners' axe they would fall.

Seemingly without investigation, he was taking the word of one man, which would involve the shedding of a river of blood.

SIN, A FORM OF INSANITY

Sin is the most destructive force in the annals of human history. It has soaked the Earth with blood, actually turning the Planet into a graveyard. It is the cause of all pain, suffering, privation, want, and all of man's inhumanity to man. Sin steadily gets worse and will do so until all is lost. That's the reason it must be eradicated from the Universe. That's the reason that it took the Cross of Christ to address this monster.

The world without God has tried without any success at all to ameliorate this destructive force. It has ever failed, as fail it must! The tragedy is, the Church of Jesus Christ all too often adopts the ways of the world and fares no better.

There is only one answer for sin, only one, and that is the

Cross of Christ (Heb. 7:27; 9:26-28).

ESTHER

"So Esther's maids and her chamberlains came and told it to her. Then was the queen exceedingly grieved; and she sent raiment to clothe Mordecai, and to take away his sackcloth from him: but he received it not.

"Then called Esther for Hatach, one of the king's chamberlains, whom he had appointed to attend upon her, and gave him a commandment to Mordecai, to know what it was, and why it was.

"So Hatach went forth to Mordecai unto the street of the city, which was before the king's gate.

"And Mordecai told him of all that had happened unto him, and of the sum of the money that Haman had promised to pay to the king's treasuries for the Jews, to destroy them.

"Also he gave him the copy of the writing of the decree that was given at Shushan to destroy them, to show it unto Esther, and to declare it unto her, and to charge her that she should go in unto the king, to make supplication unto him, and to make request before him for her people.

"And Hatach came and told Esther the words of Mordecai.

"Again Esther spoke unto Hatach, and gave him commandment unto Mordecai;

"All the king's servants, and the people of the king's provinces, do know, that whosoever, whether man or woman, shall come unto the king into the inner court, who is not called, there is one law of his to put him to death, except such to whom the king should hold out the golden scepter, that he may live: but I have not been called to come in unto the king these thirty days.

"And they told to Mordecai Esther's words" (Esther 4:4-12).

THE REASON

Esther, in the seclusion of the harem, knew nothing of what the king and Haman had determined to carry forth. So, as stated, she didn't know the reason for Mordecai's great consternation.

Esther's marriage took place in the seventh year of the reign of Ahasuerus (Esther 2:16). This murderous decree was issued five years later (Esther 3:7). Esther did not realize that these past 30 days had been spent by Haman in persuading the king to kill all the Jews.

THE PLAN OF SATAN

Esther found out about the decree to destroy all the Jews through her cousin's unlawful act of going before the king's gate in sackcloth and being in bitter mourning. Even the king did not know that Esther was Jewish.

Otherwise, she may have been so sheltered from the outside world that she might have passed the whole time away in ignorance.

Esther's reaction to seeing her cousin Mordecai in such a state at the king's gate was that of grief. She sent raiment to clothe him so that he might not be arrested for appearing thusly, but from Mordecai's viewpoint, desperate action needed to be taken, and soon. He rejected the clothing. Then Esther sent a messenger to find out what the trouble was.

THE ANSWER OF MORDECAI

Mordecai's answer was fourfold:
1. He sent word of all that had happened to him.
2. He told of the sum of money which Haman had promised to pay the king's treasury for the destruction of the Jews.
3. He sent her a copy of the decree to destroy all Jews.
4. He charged that she should go into the king in order to make supplication and request before him for her people.

As stated, up to this time, it was not known to the king that he had married a Jewess and that he had made a decree to destroy all her people.

Mordecai wanted Esther to go before the king, to reveal her identity as a Jewess, and to plead for mercy for her people. To be sure, this was not a light request.

Anyone who appeared before the king without being summoned was to be executed unless the king held out the golden scepter to him. Esther had not been called before the king in the past 30 days, the very time of Haman's plot. She had no idea as to what would happen if she did appear before him, and she conveyed as much to Mordecai.

FOR SUCH A TIME AS THIS

"Then Mordecai commanded to answer Esther, Think not with yourself that you shall escape in the king's house, more than all the Jews.

"For if you altogether hold your peace at this time, then shall there enlargement and Deliverance arise to the Jews from another place; but you and your father's house shall be destroyed: and who knows whether you are come to the kingdom for such a time as this?" (Esther 4:13-14).

YOU ARE JEWISH

"Due to the fact that you are Jewish," Mordecai says, *"you will die as well!"* Mordecai is confident that God will not allow the destruction of His People, but he also knew that even if the Lord spared the Nation, still, many Jews could die, *"And you and I,"* he said, *"will definitely be among them."*

He said to her, *"And who knows whether you are come to the kingdom for such a time as this?"* To be sure, this is exactly why the Lord had raised up Esther in this particular position. The Lord knows all things, past, present, and future; therefore, He functions accordingly. Inasmuch as He is also Almighty, He can basically do whatever He likes without violating the free moral agency of anyone. When the Bible says that the Lord is *"Almighty,"* that means there is absolutely nothing that He cannot do.

THE PLAN OF GOD

I think it is obvious that Mordecai was a man of great Faith and trust in the Lord. Regarding this situation, he believed two things:

● He believed that the Lord would spare the Nation, in other words, that no power on Earth could destroy the Jews as a people and as a Nation. However, at the same time, he knew that still many, many Jews would be killed if something weren't done.

● By asking the question, *"And who knows whether you are come to the kingdom for such a time as this?"* it tells us that he believed that Esther's selection as queen was of far greater consequence than mere place and position, as great as that was.

He was right on both counts.

Both Mordecai and Esther showed tremendous Faith in God. They believed that their lives were more than a sum of years strung together. They believed that they had a purpose and a destiny, and, to be sure, they most definitely did.

The truth is, every single Believer has a purpose in the great Plan of God. I think it can be said without fear of contradiction that the statement uttered by Mordecai, *"That you are come to the kingdom for such a time as this,"* can be applied and, in fact, should be applied to every Believer. The question is, *"Do we understand properly the place and position in which the Lord has positioned us?"* In other words, are we seeking His Face in order that the Holy Spirit may have His Way within our lives?

I wish I could say that most Believers understand their place and position, and I speak of the Call of God on their lives. However, I'm afraid that most do not understand. Thank God for the few who do, but the truth is, most don't!

Mordecai and Esther realized that the Lord had put them in a place of high responsibility. It was not done for the sake of ego, for the Lord had a Plan in all that He did. When the time came, and that time was now, they must rise to the task. Thank God, they did!

THE ANSWER

"Then Esther bade them return Mordecai this answer,

"Go, gather together all the Jews who are present in Shushan, and fast you for me, and neither eat nor drink three days, night or day: I also and my maidens will fast likewise; and so will I go in unto the king, which is not according to the law: and if I perish, I perish.

"So Mordecai went his way, and did according to all that Esther had commanded him" (Esther 4:15-17).

Even though it doesn't specifically say that the Jews prayed, it can be assured that their fasting three days and nights was accompanied by soul-searching prayer. All the Jews were to hold a prayer meeting outside of the palace while Esther was doing the same thing inside the palace. This showed her belief that God hears and answers prayer and that He is a Very Present Help in time of trouble.

This noble woman resolved, if necessary, to sacrifice her life for the sake of her people. Unfortunately, in a time of trouble, far too many modern Believers are taught to turn to anything and everything except the Lord!

ABANDONMENT TO THE WILL OF GOD

In fact, Esther had come to the kingdom for such a time as this. This orphan girl would be used by God to foil Satan's efforts of destruction and to save the Jewish people.

Regarding the danger of appearing before the king without being called, her answer is recorded in the Sixteenth Verse for time and eternity, *"And if I perish, I perish."*

A total abandonment to the Will of God, even to laying one's life on the line, is what is demanded by the Lord. Anything less is not total consecration. Even though Esther was one of the most beautiful women in the world, and even though she had gained the ascendency of being the most powerful woman in the world, still, her allegiance was totally to the Lord. She was not trying to maintain her position; she was trying to carry out the Will of God. What an example for us to follow!

ESTHER

"Now it came to pass on the third day, that Esther put on her royal apparel, and stood in the inner court of the king's house, over against the king's house: and the king sat upon his royal throne in the royal house, over against the gate of the house.

"And it was so, when the king saw Esther the queen standing in the court, that she obtained favor in his sight: and the king held out to Esther the golden scepter that was in his hand. So Esther drew near, and touched the top of the scepter.

"Then said the king unto her, What will you, queen Esther? and what is your request? it shall be even given you to the half of the kingdom.

"And Esther answered, If it seem good unto the king, let the king and Haman come this day unto the banquet that I have prepared for him.

"Then the king said, Cause Haman to make haste, that he may do as Esther has said. So the king and Haman came to the banquet that Esther had prepared.

"And the king said unto Esther at the banquet of wine, What is your petition? and it shall be granted you: and what is your request? even to the half of the kingdom it shall be performed.

"Then answered Esther, and said, My petition and my request is;

"If I have found favor in the sight of the king, and if it please the king to grant my petition, and to perform my request, let the king and Haman come to the banquet that I shall prepare for them, and I will do tomorrow as the king has said" (Esther 5:1-8).

ESTHER'S INTELLIGENCE

The *"third day"* of Verse 1 was the third day of the fast. Concerning these happenings, Williams says, *"Esther's intelligence and tact were admirable. Her life and that of her people hung on a thread. She was playing with edged tools, and the slightest mistake would have been fatal.*

"To invite the King to a banquet was a master-stroke of policy; and to include his favorite minister, Haman, in the invitation was not only an added evidence of skill and of a deep knowledge of human nature, but it was, at the same time, a clever plan for getting Haman into her power."[1]

No doubt, the Lord had told her exactly what to do.

The king sensed that Esther had something more in mind than what was now being done. He knew that she must have a request, a real favor that she wanted him to grant; therefore, he repeated the inquiry and the promise that he had made previously.

Esther said to the king, *"I will make known tomorrow my actual request."*

The repetition of her invitation showed extraordinary wisdom. At the first banquet, the king rightly divined that some important matter lay behind the importation; else, why should Esther risk her life by coming uninvited into his presence? It was surely not merely to invite him and Haman to a dinner.

Esther, by repeating the importation and postponing the secret petition, enhanced its importance while, at the same time, she increased her personal interest in the king's affections and more deeply excited his curiosity. Furthermore, she more effectually threw Haman off his guard and so secured his fall.

THE COURAGE OF ESTHER

Following the third night, Esther put on her royal robes and stood in the inner court of the king's house. He was seated on the throne in the royal house over against the gate. When he saw Esther, she obtained favor in his sight, and he held out the golden scepter to her. When she drew near and touched it, the king inquired of her request and promised that it would be granted even to half of his kingdom. The queen's simple request was that the king and Haman should make haste and attend a banquet prepared by her. Who gave her the wisdom to carry out such a plan is not stated.

It could be that she had a conference with Mordecai, or it may be that Divine inspiration alone guided her. In either case, what she did was the right thing, and God worked out every detail of the Plan for the good of His People.

If it is to be noticed, while Esther and Mordecai sought the Lord earnestly for some three days and nights and, as well, importuned other Jews to do the same thing, with many, no doubt, crying to the Lord, still, they put some legs to their prayers, so to speak.

As stated, as to exactly how Esther came to this particular plan, we aren't told. Whether the Lord moved upon the heart of Mordecai, with him relating such to Esther, or whether the Lord guided Esther alone, irrespective, it was the Lord's Action, and it would come out to a complete and successful fruition.

Her plan of having two banquets only increased the curiosity of the king. He evidently was greatly amused at her actions. Little did he realize what was at stake. However, to be sure, Esther most definitely knew.

HAMAN

"Then went Haman forth that day joyful and with a glad heart: but when Haman saw Mordecai in the king's gate, that he stood not up, nor moved for him, he was full of indignation against Mordecai.

"Nevertheless Haman refrained himself: and when he came home, he sent and called for his friends, and Zeresh his wife.

"And Haman told them of the glory of his riches, and the multitude of his children, and all the things wherein the king had promoted him, and how he had advanced him above the princes and servants of the king.

"Haman said moreover, Yes, Esther the queen did let no man come in with the king unto the banquet that she had prepared but myself; and tomorrow am I invited unto her also with the

king" (Esther 5:9-12).

According to Verse 9, Mordecai showed his utter contempt for Haman by not even acknowledging his presence. Such infuriated Haman!

Because of his anger at Mordecai, Haman now concocted a plot as it regarded what to do with Mordecai. In other words, killing would not be enough. He wanted his death to be a spectacle.

Let us say it again, *"Men rule, but God overrules!"*

HAMAN'S ANGER AT MORDECAI

Even though Mordecai was already condemned to die in the mind of Haman, he wanted, as stated, a spectacle made of his death. So, he would concoct a plan that would make this Jew pay for the slight, which had been shown to the great Haman. He figured, but he figured without God. In fact, he did not even believe in Jehovah, not at all. After all, in his thinking, if the God of these Jews was so powerful, what were they doing dispossessed from their land?

The Lord had most definitely permitted such because of their sin against Him, and we speak of the sin of the Nation as a whole and not the sin of Mordecai and Esther. I think it is obvious that they had remained faithful to the Lord; however, in the type of Judgment that was poured out upon Israel, the innocent suffered with the guilty.

THE GALLOWS

"Yet all of this avails me nothing, so long as I see Mordecai the Jew sitting at the king's gate.

"Then said Zeresh his wife and all his friends unto him, Let a gallows be made of fifty cubits high, and tomorrow you speak unto the king that Mordecai may be hanged thereon: then you go in merrily with the king unto the banquet. And the thing pleased Haman; and he caused the gallows to be made" (Esther 5:13-14).

Haman would find his wife held the solution to his problem as to what to do with Mordecai, or so he thought! The gallows that she and his friends suggested on which Mordecai was to be hanged were some 75 feet high. It would certainly be a spectacle!

It was obvious that Haman was very sure of himself. Pride goes before destruction and a haughty spirit before a fall.

THE PLAN

In the plotting of Haman to make a spectacle out of the death of Mordecai, little did he know and realize that the God of Mordecai, in fact, the One and the Only True God, was, at the same time, planning the destruction of Haman, whose death would be the spectacle that he had planned for Mordecai. The Fourteenth Verse contains the record of *"a world of iniquity,"* and shows us to what lengths sinners may proceed in their evil plans. Thankfully, there is One, the Lord of Glory, Who says to the raging sea of man's iniquity, *"Hitherto shall you go, and no further; and here shall your proud waves be stayed!"*

Concerning this hideous scheme as it regarded the death of Mordecai, the Scripture says of this murderer, *"The thing pleased Haman!"*

Unfortunately, wicked men of such stripe at times gain ascendancy of position, but woe unto the people over whom such rules.

THE CHRONICLES

"On that night could not the king sleep, and he commanded to bring the book of records of the chronicles; and they were read before the king.

"And it was found written, that Mordecai had told of Bigthana and Teresh, two of the king's chamberlains, the keepers of the door, who sought to lay hand on the king Ahasuerus.

"And the king said, What honor and dignity have been done to Mordecai for this? Then said the king's servants that ministered unto him, There is nothing done for him" (Esther 6:1-3).

To be sure, the Lord orchestrated the sleeplessness of the king.

The Holy Spirit, as well, placed it on the king's mind to have the record read, and, more than likely, the king didn't even really know why he was doing such. He was to find out shortly!

Had Mordecai complained of the non-recognition of his services at the time that he saved the king's life (Esther 2:21-23), he would have lost the extraordinary honors recorded in this Chapter. It is always better and more dignified not to seek for human recognition, but to walk in fellowship with God, doing one's duty, and waiting for the honor that comes from above. It will surely come, as this Chapter proves.

When the man began to read the book of records of the chronicles, he found where Mordecai had discovered a plot, which was aimed at taking the life of the king. Uncovering that plot by God's Man saved the life of the king.

THE KING

"And the king said, Who is in the court? Now Haman was come into the outward court of the king's house, to speak unto the king to hang Mordecai on the gallows that he had prepared for him.

"And the king's servants said unto him, Behold, Haman stands in the court. And the king said, Let him come in.

"So Haman came in. And the king said unto him, What shall be done unto the man whom the king delights to honor? Now Haman thought in his heart, To whom would the king delight to do honor more than to myself?

"And Haman answered the king, For the man whom the king delights to honor,

"Let the royal apparel be brought which the king uses to wear, and the horse that the king rides upon, and the crown royal which is set upon his head:

"And let this apparel and horse be delivered to the hand of one of the king's most noble princes, that they may array the

man withal whom the king delights to honor, and bring him on horseback through the street of the city, and proclaim before him, Thus shall it be done to the man whom the king delights to honor.

"Then the king said to Haman, Make haste, and take the apparel and the horse, as you have said, and do even so to Mordecai the Jew, who sits at the king's gate: let nothing fail of all that you have spoken.

"Then took Haman the apparel and the horse, and arrayed Mordecai, and brought him on horseback through the street of the city, and proclaimed before him, Thus shall it be done unto the man whom the king delights to honor" (Esther 6:4-11).

A SENSE OF HUMOR?

What must have been Haman's thoughts when the king said this should be done to Mordecai when, all the time, he thought, surely, it was for himself?

Considering some of the things the Lord does, and He definitely did this, we must come to the conclusion that the Lord has a sense of humor. Only the Lord could work out a situation in this manner.

Haman had backed himself into a corner. There was no ground on which he could decline this task thrust upon him. So, he does exactly what the king has demanded to be done, as galling as it must have been. Also, Mordecai must have been just as pleasantly surprised as Haman had been dismally dejected.

This man Haman should have learned from this event that things were happening beyond which he had control and beyond which he could understand.

THE MAN THE KING DELIGHTS TO HONOR

The words, *"The man the king delights to honor,"* were spoken by Haman, thinking he was speaking of himself. As a result, he laid it on thick, thinking it was all for him.

What a shock it must have been when the king spoke up and said that all of these honors were to go to Mordecai! Haman could not have been more shocked and could not have been more perplexed. How had this happened?

All that he said, thinking it would be lavished upon him, instead, was to go to Mordecai, the man he hated, the man he intended to hang in just a matter of hours.

He must have realized the danger that he was now in. The idea that he was going to hang a man whom the king was honoring greatly could not bode well for him.

The royal command could not be disputed or evaded, so Mordecai was escorted through the city by his enemy, who had expected to be superintending his death about that very time.

Only the Lord could bring about such a happening! Only the Lord could engineer such a direction! Only the Lord could cause such events to come to pass!

There was no way out; Haman must do exactly what the king had said do, and without delay. There was no ground on which he could decline the office thrust upon him. Reluctantly, but without a word, he performed the king's bidding.

MORDECAI

"And Mordecai came again to the king's gate. But Haman hasted to his house mourning, and having his head covered.

"And Haman told Zeresh his wife and all his friends everything that had befallen him. Then said his wise men and Zeresh his wife unto him, If Mordecai be of the seed of the Jews, before whom you have begun to fall, you shall not prevail against him, but shall surely fall before him.

"And while they were yet talking with him, came the king's chamberlains, and hasted to bring Haman unto the banquet that Esther had prepared" (Esther 6:12-14).

Haman *"having his head covered"* was a sign of acute dejection. It meant that he knew he was being boxed into the proverbial corner but knew of no way to stop the situation.

As it regards Verse 13, with the so-called *"wise men"* speaking to Haman, for one time, they were right! Haman would fall before Mordecai!

Haman now went to the banquet that Esther had prepared but not with the jubilant spirit that he had had the day before. Once again, he sensed a trap from whence there was no way out, and the Lord, very carefully, was the One setting the trap.

THE BANQUET

"So the king and Haman came to banquet with Esther the queen.

"And the king said again unto Esther on the second day at the banquet of wine, What is your petition, queen Esther? and it shall be granted you: and what is your request? and it shall be performed, even to the half of the kingdom.

"Then Esther the queen answered and said, If I have found favor in your sight, O king, and if it please the king, let my life be given me at my petition, and my people at my request:

"For we are sold, I and my people, to be destroyed, to be killed, and to perish. But if we had been sold for bondmen and bondwomen, I had held my tongue, although the enemy could not countervail the king's damage.

"Then the king Ahasuerus answered and said unto Esther the queen, Who is he, and where is he, who does presume in his heart to do so?

"And Esther said, The adversary and enemy is this wicked Haman. Then Haman was afraid before the king and the queen" (Esther 7:1-6).

Obviously, the king is very pleasantly curious as to what Esther wants.

If all the Jews had been killed in the Persian Empire as was planned, or even if they were sold as slaves, the king's revenues would have been injured beyond compensation. So, the empire was going to lose in every capacity, at least, if this thing was carried out.

Esther added the word, *"Enemy,"* to the list, with the insinuation that, in actuality, Haman was an enemy of the king also, which he most definitely was. In other words, he was playing the king for all he could get and was being very successful, at least, up until now.

ESTHER'S REQUEST

Having received three definite promises from the king that he would grant her request even to the half of his kingdom, Esther asked for her own life and the lives of her people.

In the question of Verse 5, we find another acrostic in which the Name of Jehovah is hidden in the ancient Hebrew Text. The question is, *"Who is he, and where is he?"* The Hebrew letters *"EHYEH"* are the abbreviation for *"I am that I am."*

When Esther answered the question and said, *"The adversary and enemy is this wicked Haman,"* this was one of the greatest surprises of the king's life. To think that anybody would presume in his heart to kill his queen and her people! This shows that neither the king nor Haman knew that she was a Jewess and, accordingly, that her people were Jews. No doubt, the king would not have made such a decree if he had realized who the people were that Haman wanted to destroy.

Regrettably, the king had agreed to a monstrous plot, which, if carried out, would have been horrible, to say the least, and, as well, would have done great damage to the empire. The most intelligent people in his kingdom were the Jews. Though they had been taken captive by Nebuchadnezzar and were sold as slaves, still, this in no way impacted the contribution that they could make and, no doubt, were making to the empire. In fact, as it regards Jews, that has been the case from the very beginning even unto this present time. Our nation of America has been blessed in part because of our open door for the Jews and because of our protection for the State of Israel. This is, no doubt, very high as it regards priorities on God's List.

THE KING

"And the king arising from the banquet of wine in his wrath went into the palace garden: and Haman stood up to make request for his life to Esther the queen; for he saw that there was evil determined against him by the king.

"Then the king returned out of the palace garden into the place of the banquet of wine; and Haman was fallen upon the bed whereon Esther was. Then said the king, Will he force the queen also before me in the house? As the word went out of the king's mouth, they covered Haman's face.

"And Harbonah, one of the chamberlains, said before the king, Behold also, the gallows fifty cubits high, which Haman had made for Mordecai, who had spoken good for the king, stands in the house of Haman. Then the king said, Hang him thereon."

"So they hanged Haman on the gallows that he had prepared for Mordecai. Then was the king's wrath pacified" (Esther 7:7-10).

THE LORD ORCHESTRATED ALL OF THIS

In his pleading with Esther for his life, more than likely, Haman sought to grasp the feet of Esther or her garments, as was usual with supplicants in the east. At that moment, the king returned. Misunderstanding Haman's action, or pretending to do so, the king accused Haman of attacking the queen. At that moment, at the king's command, guards standing nearby covered Haman's face, which meant that he was doomed.

To be sure, the Lord orchestrated all of this, even for the king to come back at the exact moment he did.

Evidently, Haman had erected the gallows within the compound of his home, which, no doubt, was quite large and included many acres of gardens, etc. Now, he would hang on his own gallows.

The king realized that Haman had made a fool of him, so he determined to settle the score in the worst way of all, which he did.

DIVINE RETRIBUTION

As we are now beginning to see, the Lord most definitely answered the cry of Mordecai and Esther and, no doubt, many thousands of other Jews who wept for Deliverance. Little did the king realize what Esther wanted, and, above all, he did not realize that he was being played for a fool by Haman. However, the Lord would orchestrate the entire scenario to where there would be absolutely no doubt as to what was taking place.

When Esther made her request and then pointed a finger at Haman as the culprit, this must have been quite a shock to the king who, as we have stated, was being played for a fool.

The king was so overcome with consternation that he stepped outside the room for a moment, no doubt, to let all of this sink in. Now was Haman's last chance. Could he excite the pity of the queen? Could he prevail on her to intercede for him and make his peace with the king? In his petition to her, he most likely tripped and fell on the couch, no doubt, across Esther, which the Lord, as well, most assuredly orchestrated. So, when the king reentered the room, which he did at that very moment, and saw Haman in that position, he gave the signal for one of the attendants to *"cover Haman's face,"* which was the death sentence.

Then, one of the men standing nearby, who evidently knew all the circumstances of the case and, more than likely, was not too enamored with Haman, suggested that the gallows prepared for Mordecai would serve well for the execution of Haman. The king readily consented to this suggestion, with the sentence being carried out immediately. Haman was impaled on the gallows, which he had erected for his enemy in the court of his own house.

THE BLESSING THAT CAME TO ESTHER

"On that day did the king Ahasuerus give the house of Haman the Jew's enemy unto Esther the queen. And Mordecai came

before the king; for Esther had told what he was unto her.

"And the king took off his ring, which he had taken from Haman, and gave it unto Mordecai. And Esther set Mordecai over the house of Haman" (Esther 8:1-2).

All the property of Haman being given to Esther, to be sure, had to have been considerable simply because Haman had been one of the richest men in the empire. Now it all belonged to Esther, and Haman was dead, all orchestrated by the Lord. Actually, the king made Mordecai his prime minister. Joseph and Daniel were also prime ministers to heathen princes.

If God, in the pursuit of His Purposes, places one of His Servants in such a high position, He will give him Grace and Wisdom to glorify the Lord in that position. However, an ambitious Christian, who grasps at such a post by his energy and talent in order to gratify himself, cannot count upon God to deliver him from its snares and temptations.

LOOK WHAT THE LORD HAS DONE!

Who would have thought a week earlier that this situation would have turned out as it did? Who would have thought that Haman would now be dead, all of his property given to Esther, and Mordecai made prime minister of the Persian Empire? The Lord Alone could turn around something of this magnitude and do it so quickly.

The truth is, Israel had that type of help throughout their existence, at least, as long as they were attempting to live for God. Of course, when they would turn their backs upon the Lord and begin to adopt the ways of the world, which pertained basically to idol-worship, such activity would close the door to the Blessings of God.

So, the Way of the Lord was set before Israel, and if they obeyed, there was great Blessing; however, if they disobeyed, great trouble was the result. It is the same presently for modern day Believers, with one glaring difference.

The difference is, since the Cross, the Holy Spirit can now

live permanently within our hearts and lives, and He can help us at all times and in all things. Old Testament Saints did not have that privilege.

The situation, as it regarded Mordecai and Esther, proves to us that the Lord can work anytime, anywhere, and anyplace if His People will dare to believe Him.

THE REQUEST OF ESTHER

"And Esther spoke yet again before the king, and fell down at his feet, and besought him with tears to put away the mischief of Haman the Agagite, and his device that he had devised against the Jews.

"Then the king held out the golden scepter toward Esther. So Esther arose, and stood before the king.

"And said, If it please the king, and if I have found favor in his sight, and the thing seem right before the king, and I be pleasing in his eyes, let it be written to reverse the letters devised by Haman the son of Hammedatha the Agagite, which he wrote to destroy the Jews who are in all the king's provinces:

"For how can I endure to see the evil that shall come unto my people? or how can I endure to see the destruction of my kindred?" (Esther 8:3-6).

The golden scepter was held out by the king simply to express a readiness to do as Esther desired.

With the laws of the Medes and Persians being irrevocable, the king could not recall his decree. However, he could issue a fresh one authorizing Esther's people to defend themselves against all who should attack them.

As we shall see, the Lord doesn't work with half measures. When He does something, as here, it is done all the way.

HOW CAN I ENDURE TO SEE THE EVIL. . . ?

As is obvious, Esther had to do all she could do, even to risking her life, in order to counter this plan concocted by Satan.

She had seen the Lord work mightily as it regarded Haman, and now He must work again as it regarded saving her people. These were Jews, incidentally, who were scattered all over the Persian Empire. She would find out that the Lord could easily handle this situation also.

In reality, the Message of the Cross is the Gospel of Jesus Christ and, actually, is the meaning of the New Covenant. I feel that Believers, who truly know the Lord and truly know and understand the Message of the Cross, must have, in a sense, the same urgency, the same feeling, and the same desperation as did Esther as it regards the modern Church of the Living God. I'm afraid that to say the modern church is in a terrible condition would be a gross understatement. It is worse, far worse, than any of us realize, even we who do have a modicum of knowledge as it regards this all-important situation.

Almost the entirety of the church has been given over to humanistic psychology. This means they have no faith or confidence in the Cross of Christ, but rather in the ingenuity of man, which, in reality, holds no help at all, but rather harm. Having taken themselves out from under the Protecting Hand of the Lord and placed themselves in the hand of man means that the majority of modern Believers are in terrible bondage, in one way or the other, to the demon forces of darkness. One might liken the modern church to the Children of Israel who were held as slaves in Egypt. As they were under the jackbooted heel of that despot, so to speak, millions of true Believers are under the heel of Satan.

KING AHASUERUS

"Then the king Ahasuerus said unto Esther the queen and to Mordecai the Jew, Behold, I have given Esther the house of Haman, and him they have hanged upon the gallows, because he laid his hand upon the Jews.

"Write you also for the Jews, as it likes you, in the king's name, and seal it with the king's ring: for the writing which is

written in the king's name, and sealed with the king's ring, may no man reverse.

"Then were the king's scribes called at the time in the third month, that is, the month Sivan, on the three and twentieth day thereof; and it was written according to all that Mordecai commanded unto the Jews, and to the lieutenants, and the deputies and rulers of the provinces which are from India unto Ethiopia, an hundred twenty and seven provinces, unto every province according to the writing thereof, and unto every people after their language, and to the Jews according to their writing, and according to their language.

"And he wrote in the king Ahasuerus' name, and sealed it with the king's ring, and sent letters by posts on horseback, and riders on mules, camels, and young dromedaries:

"Wherein the king granted the Jews who were in every city to gather themselves together, and to stand for their life, to destroy, to kill, and to cause to perish, all the power of the people and province who would assault them, both little ones and women, and to take the spoil of them for a prey.

"Upon one day in all the provinces of king Ahasuerus, namely, upon the thirteenth day of the twelfth month, which is the month Adar.

"The copy of the writing for a commandment to be given in every province was published unto all people, and that the Jews should be ready against that day to avenge themselves on their enemies.

"So the posts who rode upon mules and camels went out, being hastened and pressed on by the king's commandment. And the decree was given at Shushan the palace" (Esther 8:7-14).

THE FASTEST HORSES IN THE KINGDOM

According to Verse 8, the king, in effect, was saying to Mordecai, *"Surely you can devise something which will save your people without calling on me to retract my own words, which would break a great principle of Persian law."*

According to Verse 9, it seems that copies of the former edict of destruction regarding the Jews had not been sent specifically to them. They had been left to learn their danger indirectly from the people among whom they dwelt. However, Mordecai took care that they should be informed directly of their right of defense.

It seems that the older manuscripts do not contain the words mules, camels, etc., but rather thoroughbred horses exclusively, which, no doubt, is correct. That would be the fastest mode of transportation in those days.

The earlier edict had given permission to the Jews' enemies to kill and to take. The new law, while not forbidding the former, as well, gave the Jews the same privilege, and in every respect.

"Adar" is the month of March. This was the time designated by the former edict to be carried out. Now, the Jews had been given the freedom to protect themselves. So, that day, which was determined to be a day of infamy regarding the Jews, would turn out to be the opposite, all because of what the Lord had done.

Verse 14 should have been translated, *"Royal studs,"* in other words, the very fastest horses, as stated, in the kingdom.

THE WORD OF THE LORD

The letter would be sent by the fastest horses in the kingdom, and sent to every town and city in the kingdom, which would give the Jews power to gather together in any and every city and defend themselves against anyone who would seek to carry out Haman's original edict.

Without a doubt, the great Deliverance of the Jews at the time of Esther and Mordecai presented one of the greatest answers to prayer and one of the greatest Miracles recorded in the entirety of the Word of God.

Satan's plan, at least, at the beginning, seemed to be foolproof. He would destroy these people, using wicked Haman to do so. However, there were Jews in the kingdom who knew how to believe God, with Esther and Mordecai taking the lead. How wondrously the Lord can turn everything around. Not only would Satan's plan fall to the ground, but, as well, the Jews in the Medo-Persian Empire would be greatly elevated, even with Mordecai made prime minister of the kingdom.

How many modern Believers are taught to take their burdens, their cares, their difficulties, and their troubles to the Lord?

Not many, I'm afraid!

A BETTER CONTRACT

If the Lord answered prayer as He did for Esther and Mordecai and, in fact, for all the Jews in the kingdom, how much more will He do the same today because we now have a Better Covenant. The Word says:

> "But now *(since the Cross)* has He *(the Lord Jesus)* obtained a more excellent Ministry *(the New Covenant in Jesus' Blood is superior and takes the place of the Old Covenant in animal blood. In fact, Jesus Christ is Personally the New Covenant)*, by how much also He is the Mediator of a Better Covenant *(proclaims the fact that Christ officiates between God and man according to the arrangements of the New Covenant)*, which was established upon Better Promises. *(This presents the New Covenant explicitly based on the cleansing and forgiveness of all sin, which the Old Covenant could not do)*" (Heb. 8:6).

THE BLESSINGS OF THE LORD

"And Mordecai went out from the presence of the king in royal apparel of blue and white, and with a great crown of gold, and with a garment of fine linen and purple: and the city of Shushan rejoiced and was glad.

"The Jews had light, and gladness, and joy, and honor.

"And in every province, and in every city, whithersoever the king's commandment and his decree came, the Jews had joy and gladness, a feast and a good day. And many of the people of the land became Jews; for the fear of the Jews fell upon them" (Esther 8:15-17).

As the capital city had been perplexed at the first concerning the original edict, they now rejoiced at the second.

According to Verse 17, many of the Persians evidently became proselyte Jews, which means they adopted the Mosaic Law, at least, as far as they could, and, thereby, the worship of Jehovah as the One True God.

Many converted from heathenism to Jehovah because the news spread fast as to what had happened to Haman, etc. The fact that Esther, a Jewess, was now the queen, and Mordecai, a Jew, was now the prime minister certainly paved the way for many Conversions.

To be sure, every Persian who sincerely opted for the Covenant of the Lord was definitely Saved. As well, there were, no doubt, many who became proselyte Jews for other reasons. That being the case, they were not saved. Salvation has always been by Grace through Faith, whether under the Old Covenant or the New Covenant (Rom. 5:1-2).

THE DECREE

"Now in the twelfth month, that is, the month Adar, on the thirteenth day of the same, when the king's commandment and his decree drew near to be put in execution, in the day that the enemies of the Jews hoped to have power over them, (though it was turned to the contrary, that the Jews had rule over them who hated them;)

"The Jews gathered themselves together in their cities throughout all the provinces of the king Ahasuerus, to lay hand on such as sought their hurt: and no man could withstand them; for the fear of them fell upon all people.

"And all the rulers of the provinces, and the lieutenants, and the deputies, and officers of the king, helped the Jews; because the fear of Mordecai fell upon them.

"For Mordecai was great in the king's house, and his fame went out throughout all the provinces: for this man Mordecai waxed greater and greater.

"Thus the Jews smote all their enemies with the stroke of the sword, and slaughter, and destruction, and did what they would unto those who hated them.

"And in Shushan the palace the Jews killed and destroyed five hundred men.

"And Parshandatha, and Dalphon, and Aspatha,

"And Poratha, and Adalia, and Aridatha,

"And Parmashta, and Arisai, and Aridai, and Vajezatha,

"The ten sons of Haman the son of Hammedatha, the enemy of the Jews, killed they; but on the spoil laid they not their hand.

"On that day the number of those who were killed in Shushan the palace was brought before the king.

"And the king said unto Esther the queen, The Jews have killed and destroyed five hundred men in Shushan the palace, and the ten sons of Haman; what have they done in the rest of the king's provinces? now what is your petition? and it shall be granted you: or what is your request further? and it shall be done.

"Then said Esther, If it please the king, let it be granted to the Jews who are in Shushan to do tomorrow also according unto this day's decree, and let Haman's ten sons be hanged upon the gallows.

"And the king commanded it to be done: and the decree was given at Shushan; and they hanged Haman's ten sons.

"For the Jews who were in Shushan gathered themselves together on the fourteenth day also of the month Adar, and killed three hundred men at Shushan; but on the prey they laid not their hand.

"But the other Jews who were in the king's provinces gathered themselves together, and stood for their lives, and had rest from their enemies, and killed of their foes seventy and five thousand,

but they laid not their hands on the prey,

"On the thirteenth day of the month Adar; and on the four-teenth day of the same rested they, and made it a day of feasting and gladness.

"But the Jews who were at Shushan assembled together on the thirteenth day thereof, and on the fourteenth thereof; and on the fifteenth day of the same they rested, and made it a day of feasting and gladness.

"Therefore the Jews of the villages, who dwelt in the un-walled towns, made the fourteenth day of the month Adar a day of gladness and feasting, and a good day, and of sending por-tions one to another" (Esther 9:1-19).

THE FEAR OF MORDECAI

The number *"thirteen,"* which is so feared by the supersti-tious children of this world, is a gladsome number to the People of God, for on that day in March, the Amalekite and all his allies were destroyed.

"The fear of Mordecai" pertained to the fact that he was now prime minister, which refers to one who actually runs the government. In effect, there was no man in the Persian Empire who was more powerful than Mordecai, with the exception of the king.

All of this was looked at by the Lord as war. It is the same as when Joshua or David overcame the enemy, killing, at times, thousands of them.

Presently, the United States has the Scriptural right to put down any nation in the world that is seeking to take peace from the world. Such is sanctioned by the Word of God, but only as a matter of last resort (Rom. 13:1-7).

Notwithstanding the clause in the edict, which allowed the Jews *"to take the spoil of their enemies for a prey,"* neither in the capital nor in the provinces did the triumphant Israelites touch the property of those opposed to them. This was an evi-dent wish to show that they were not motivated by greed but simply desirous of securing themselves from future harm.

VICTORY

The Sixteenth Verse says that 75,000 of the enemies of the Lord were killed; however, some of the older manuscripts have the number *"15,000,"* which is probably the correct number. There are no original copies of Biblical Scrolls left, as would be obvious. However, there are tens of thousands of copies of individual Books of the Bible, or parts thereof. When making copies, sometimes an error will be made, mostly in numbers. In both the Hebrew and the Greek languages, there was no such thing as numbers, with letters actually standing for numbers, making it even easier to make a mistake.

The Jews would have lived in daily fear of the vengeance of these men if they had not been destroyed. Esther's wise conduct gave perfect peace to her people and, at the same time, punished with death men worthy of death.

THE SMITING OF THE ENEMIES

It is ironic that, according to the Third Chapter and according to witchcraft, the thirteenth day of the twelfth month would be the day of the Jew's destruction. Instead, God turned the curse into a Blessing. As well, Satan has placed a curse on all of humanity. Only God can lift such a curse and, above all, turn it into a Blessing.

Even though Israel had sinned greatly and was now held in captivity because of their sin, still, because Mordecai and Esther, as well as many other Jews, sought the Lord earnestly with all of their hearts, God would bless them abundantly.

If the reader will only understand that irrespective of the difficulty, circumstances, or situation, God will take the circumstance, whatever it is, and turn it into a Blessing. The only thing required is for the Believer to totally commit his way to the Lord by humbling himself before Him and repenting in contrition and humility of any and all wrongdoing.

Tragically, as previously stated, the church too often does not seek the Lord, but rather man; consequently, nothing is done. Man has no answer. God Alone holds the answer.

THE LORD ALONE

Only the Lord could have turned this ugly situation in the Persia of that day of so long ago into a Blessing. Now, the man who had shortly before been sentenced to death, Mordecai, was second only to the king in power. Look what God has wrought!

Some may take umbrage at Esther's request for the slaughter of these individuals; however, her request was inspired by the Holy Spirit. Just a few hours before, all of these individuals were whetting their swords in the anticipation of killing every single Jew in the Persian Empire and confiscating their property. There was no more Mercy that could be shown to them by the Lord. Haman, his sons, and the thousands mentioned were energized by Satan. If this had not been done, the Jews would have lived in daily fear of these individuals. Esther's wise conduct gave perfect peace to her people and, as stated, at the same time, punished with death men worthy of death.

LETTERS

"And Mordecai wrote these things, and sent letters unto all the Jews who were in all the provinces of the king Ahasuerus, both near and far,

"To stablish this among them, that they should keep the fourteenth day of the month Adar, and the fifteenth day of the same, yearly,

"As the days wherein the Jews rested from their enemies, and the month which was turned unto them from sorrow to joy, and from mourning into a good day: that they should make them days of feasting and joy, and of sending portions one to another, and gifts to the poor.

"And the Jews undertook to do as they had begun, and as Mordecai had written unto them;

"Because Haman the son of Hammedatha, the Agagite, the enemy of all the Jews, had devised against the Jews to destroy them, and had cast Pur, that is, the lot, to consume them, and to destroy them;

"But when Esther came before the king, he commanded by letters that his wicked device, which he devised against the Jews, should return upon his own head, and that he and his sons should be hanged on the gallows.

"Wherefore they called these days Purim after the name of Pur. Therefore for all the words of this letter, and of that which they had seen concerning this matter, and which had come unto them,

"The Jews ordained, and took upon them, and upon their seed, and upon all such as joined themselves unto them, so as it should not fail, that they would keep these two days according to their writing, and according to their appointed time every year;

"And that these days should be remembered and kept throughout every generation, every family, every province, and every city; and that these days of Purim should not fail from among the Jews, nor the memorial of them perish from their seed.

"Then Esther the queen, the daughter of Abihail, and Mordecai the Jew, wrote with all authority, to confirm this second letter of Purim.

"And he sent the letters unto all the Jews, to the hundred twenty and seven provinces of the kingdom of Ahasuerus, with words of peace and truth,

"To confirm these days of Purim in their times appointed, according as Mordecai the Jew and Esther the queen had enjoined them, and as they had decreed for themselves and for their seed, the matters of the fastings and their cry.

"And the decree of Esther confirmed these matters of Purim; and it was written in the book" (Esther 9:20-32).

THE FEAST OF PURIM

The Feast of Purim has continued among the Jews, at least, in some form, even unto this day.

The first letter is the one which is mentioned in Verses 20 and 26. A *"second letter"* of Purim was now issued *"confirming"* and establishing the observance. It went forth, not as an edict or in the king's name, but as a letter in the names of Esther and Mordecai.

Great is the Lord and greatly to be praised.

The Feast of Purim was not actually instituted by the Lord, but rather by Esther and Mordecai. However, the very fact that it is mentioned in Scripture, and especially the way it is mentioned, tells us that the Holy Spirit sanctioned that which was done by Esther and Mordecai.

When hung upon the gallows, Haman's sons were already dead. This public confirmation of the fact exhibited the justice of the king and confirmed the tranquility of the people.

Three times in this Chapter (Vss. 10, 15-16), it is pointed out that on the spoil, they laid not their hand. No doubt, they remembered the lesson of I Samuel, Chapter 15.

"The Church's one Foundation is Jesus Christ our Lord;
"She is His New Creation by water and the Word:
"From Heaven He came and sought her to be His Holy
    Bride;
"With His Own Blood He bought her,
"And for her life He died."

"Elect from every nation, yet one over all the Earth,
"Her charter of Salvation, One Lord, one Faith, one Birth:
"One Holy Name she blesses, partakes one holy food,
"And to one hope she presses,
"With every grace endued."

"Mid toil and tribulation, and tumult of her war,
"She waits the consummation of peace forevermore;
"Till, with the Vision glorious, her longing eyes are blessed,
"And the great Church victorious,
"Shall be the Church at rest."

BIBLIOGRAPHY

INTRODUCTION

Ellicott's Commentary on the Whole Bible, Zondervan Publishing House, Grand Rapids, pg. 22.

Stanley M. Horton, *Genesis: The Promise of Blessing*, World Library Press, Missouri, 1996, pg. 33.

The Preacher's Complete Homiletical Commentary on the Old Testament, Funk & Wagnalls, 1892, pg. 63.

Matthew Henry & Thomas Scott, *A Commentary upon the Holy Bible: Genesis to Deuteronomy*, The Religious Tract Society, pg. 13.

George Williams, *The Student's Commentary on the Holy Scriptures*, Grand Rapids, Kregel Publications, 1949, pg. 10.

H.D.M. Spence, *The Pulpit Commentary: Vol. 1*, Grand Rapids, Eerdmans Publishing Company, 1978, pg. 64.

Matthew Henry & Thomas Scott, *The Comprehensive Commentary on the Holy Bible: Genesis to Judges*, Fessenden and Co., 1835, pg. 37.

Rev. R. Payne Smith, *The First Book of Moses called Genesis*, Cassell & Company, London, pg. 99.

Matthew Henry & Thomas Scott, *A Commentary upon the Holy Bible: Genesis to Deuteronomy*, The Religious Tract Society, pg. 16.

Ellicott's Commentary on the Whole Bible, Zondervan Publishing House, Grand Rapids, pg. 27.

Matthew Henry, *An Exposition of the Old and New Testaments*, *Vol. 1*, Haswell, Barrington & Haswell, Philadelphia, 1838, pg. 48.

H.D.M. Spence, *The Pulpit Commentary: Vol. 1*, Grand Rapids, Eerdmans Publishing Company, 1978, pg. 74.

CHAPTER 1

Charles Henry Mackintosh, *Notes on the Book of Genesis*, Loizeaux Brothers, New York, 1880, pgs. 138-139.

Matthew Henry & Thomas Scott, *A Commentary upon the*

Holy Bible: Genesis to Deuteronomy, The Religious Tract Society, pg. 44.

Ibid.

George Williams, *The Student's Commentary on the Holy Scriptures,* Grand Rapids, Kregel Publications, 1949, pg. 20.

Matthew Henry, *Notes on the Book of Genesis,* George Morrish, London, pg. 159.

George Williams, *The Student's Commentary on the Holy Scriptures,* Grand Rapids, Kregel Publications, 1949, pgs. 20-21.

Ellicott's Commentary on the Whole Bible, Zondervan Publishing House, Grand Rapids, pg. 74.

George Williams, *The Student's Commentary on the Holy Scriptures,* Grand Rapids, Kregel Publications, 1949, pg. 22.

C.H. Mackintosh, *Notes on the Book of Genesis,* Loizeaux Brothers, New York, 1880, pg. 212.

Stanley M. Horton, *Genesis: The Promise of Blessing,* World Library Press, Missouri, 1996, pg. 96.

George Williams, *Williams' Complete Bible Commentary,* Grand Rapids, Kregel Publications, 1994, pg. 25.

C.H. Mackintosh, *Notes on the Book of Genesis,* Loizeaux Brothers, New York, 1880, pg. 200.

CHAPTER 2

C.H. Mackintosh, *Notes on the Book of Genesis,* Loizeaux Brothers, New York, 1880, pg. 246.

Matthew Henry & Thomas Scott, *A Commentary upon the Holy Bible: Genesis to Deuteronomy,* The Religious Tract Society, pg. 77.

George Williams, *The Student's Commentary on the Holy Scriptures,* Grand Rapids, Kregel Publications, 1949, pg. 31.

Matthew Henry & Thomas Scott, *A Commentary upon the Holy Bible: Genesis to Deuteronomy,* The Religious Tract Society, pg. 79.

Ibid.

Ellicott's Commentary on the Whole Bible, Zondervan Publishing

House, Grand Rapids, pg. 106.

CHAPTER 3
H.D.M. Spence, *The Pulpit Commentary: Vol. 1*, Grand Rapids, Eerdmans Publishing Company, 1978, pg. 364.
Ellicott's Commentary on the Whole Bible, Zondervan Publishing House, Grand Rapids, pg. 113.
Ibid.
Stanley M. Horton, *Genesis: The Promise of Blessing*, World Library Press, Missouri, 1996, pg. 132.
Stanley M. Horton, *Genesis: The Promise of Blessing*, World Library Press, Missouri, 1996, pg. 136.
H.D.M. Spence, *The Pulpit Commentary: Vol. 1*, Grand Rapids, Eerdmans Publishing Company, 1978, pg. 404.
Ibid., pg. 405.

CHAPTER 4
H.D.M. Spence, *The Pulpit Commentary: Vol. 1*, Grand Rapids, Eerdmans Publishing Company, 1978, pg. 11.
C.H. Mackintosh, *Notes on the Book of Exodus*, George Morrish, London, pg. 5.

CHAPTER 5
Ellicott's Commentary on the Whole Bible, Zondervan Publishing House, Grand Rapids, pg. 195.
Arthur W. Pink, *Gleanings in Exodus*, 2002, pg. 16.
I.M. Haldeman, *Friday Night Papers*, New York, 1901, pg. 241.
George Williams, *The Student's Commentary on the Holy Scriptures*, Grand Rapids, Kregel Publications, 1949, pg. 44.
Arthur W. Pink, *Gleanings in Exodus*, 2002, pg. 17.

CHAPTER 7
George Williams, *The Student's Commentary on the Holy Scriptures*, Grand Rapids, Kregel Publications, 1949, pg. 109.

CHAPTER 8
George Williams, *The Student's Commentary on the Holy*

Scriptures, Grand Rapids, Kregel Publications, 1949, pg. 123.
Ibid.

CHAPTER 9
H.D.M. Spence, *The Pulpit Commentary: Vol. 1*, Grand Rapids, Eerdmans Publishing Company, 1978, pg. 228.
George Williams, *The Student's Commentary on the Holy Scriptures*, Grand Rapids, Kregel Publications, 1949, pg. 135.
H.D.M. Spence, *The Pulpit Commentary: Vol. 1*, Grand Rapids, Eerdmans Publishing Company, 1978, pg. 4.
H.D.M. Spence, *The Pulpit Commentary: Vol. 1*, Grand Rapids, Eerdmans Publishing Company, 1978, pg. 43.
George Williams, *The Student's Commentary on the Holy Scriptures*, Grand Rapids, Kregel Publications, 1949, pg. 136.

CHAPTER 11
H.D.M. Spence, *The Pulpit Commentary: Vol. 5*, Grand Rapids, Eerdmans Publishing Company, 1978, pg. 5.
Ibid., pg. 6.
Ibid.
Ibid., pg. 7.

CHAPTER 13
George Williams, *The Student's Commentary on the Holy Scriptures*, Grand Rapids, Kregel Publications, 1949, pg. 271.

NOTES

NOTES

NOTES

NOTES